HISTO

OF THE

CHURCH OF ENGLAND

FROM THE ABOLITION

OF

THE ROMAN JURISDICTION.

BY ✓✓

RICHARD WATSON DIXON, M.A.,

VICAR OF WARKWORTH;

HONORARY CANON OF CARLISLE.

Third Edition, Revised.

VOL. I.

HENRY VIII.—A.D. 1529–1537.

LONDON:

GEORGE ROUTLEDGE AND SONS, LIMITED,

BROADWAY, LUDGATE HILL,

MANCHESTER AND NEW YORK.

1895.

𝔒𝔵𝔣𝔬𝔯𝔡:

HORACE HART, PRINTER TO THE UNIVERSITY

ISBN 978-1-331-49913-8
PIBN 10198363

1 MONTH OF
FREE
READING

at
www.ForgottenBooks.com

By purchasing this book you are eligible for one month membership to ForgottenBooks.com, giving you unlimited access to our entire collection of over 1,000,000 titles via our web site and mobile apps.

To claim your free month visit:
www.forgottenbooks.com/free198363

English
Français
Deutsche
Italiano
Español
Português

www.forgottenbooks.com

Mythology Photography **Fiction**
Fishing Christianity **Art** Cooking
Essays Buddhism Freemasonry
Medicine **Biology** Music **Ancient**
Egypt Evolution Carpentry Physics
Dance Geology **Mathematics** Fitness
Shakespeare **Folklore** Yoga Marketing
Confidence Immortality Biographies
Poetry **Psychology** Witchcraft
Electronics Chemistry History **Law**
Accounting **Philosophy** Anthropology
Alchemy Drama Quantum Mechanics
Atheism Sexual Health **Ancient History**
Entrepreneurship Languages Sport
Paleontology Needlework Islam
Metaphysics Investment Archaeology
Parenting Statistics Criminology
Motivational

CONTENTS

OF

THE FIRST VOLUME.

———◆———

CHAPTER I.

HENRY VIII., A.D. 1529, 1530, 1531.

CHAPTER II.

HENRY VIII., A.D. 1532.

CHAPTER III.

HENRY VIII., A.D. 1533, 1534.

CHAPTER IV.

HENRY VIII., A.D. 1535.

CHAPTER V.

HENRY VIII., A. D. 1536.

CHAPTER VI.

HENRY VIII., A. D. 1536.

CHAPTER VII.

HENRY VIII., A. D. 1537.

HISTORY

OF

THE CHURCH OF ENGLAND.

———

CHAPTER I.

HENRY VIII.—1529, 1530, 1531.

IN the year 1529, the twenty-first year of the reign of
King Henry the Eighth, the year of the fall of Wolsey,
after an interval of several years, a new Parliament
was called. It met in the midst of the various feelings
which had been excited by the recent trial of the King
and Queen of England in the court of the Roman
Legates : it has been marked in the annals as having
been summoned chiefly for the purpose of ecclesiastical
legislation.* The Church of England was believed, or
pretended, to be full of abuses which were incurable
from within. By the temporal powers she was now to
be taken in hand in good earnest ; and that which she
was unable to do for herself was to be done for her.
The more ardent, indeed, looked for nothing less than
the subversion of the ancient constitution of the Church

---

* "In the 21 year was holden a Parliament wherein was reformed
divers enormities of the clergy."—*Hardyng* (Grafton continuator), 605.
"A Parliament for enormities of the clergy."—*Fabian*, 699.

and the alienation of her patrimony.* This anticipation was not fulfilled; but the Church of England was so handled by the assembly which now began to sit as she had never been handled before. This was the Parliament which by successive Acts, within a few years, took away most of the ancient liberties of the Church; which caused her to renounce all dependence upon the See of Rome; which backed the King in his contest with the Convocations of the clergy; and which gave a partial sanction to the dissolution of the religious houses, a vast revolution in property, which seems, however, to have been contemplated even in the very first session.†

This was indeed the most memorable Parliament that ever sat. It was the assembly which transformed old England—the England of Chaucer and Lydgate—into modern England. At the time when it met, England herself resembled one of those great edifices, dedicated to religion, with which she abounded then, but which were soon to fall in ruin beneath the axe and hammer of the Reformation. Those marble piles stood in their bewildering vastness, containing many chapels, cells, and shrines beneath a common roof.

---

* The celebrated proposal of the "Unlearned Parliament" of Henry IV., to secularise all Church property, was kept in mind by its successor. In a list of bills of 1529 it was proposed to renew "a bill put up to the king in his Parliament in A. D. 1410 concerning the temporal possessions being in the hands of the Church." Mr. Brewer's Lett. For. and Dom., vol. iv. p. 2692. There has been found also a draft land bill of the same date : "That all entails be annulled, and all possessions held in fee simple : that no use be available unless recorded in the Court of Common Pleas : and registers to be kept in every shire : and deeds of gift to be read in churches of parishes where the land lies." This was not to affect the estates of barons.—Lett. For. and Dom., p. 2693.

† In Darcy's Memoranda for Parliament Matters, for the year 1529, there is this item : "That it be tried whether the pulling down of all the abbies be lawful and good or no, for great things hang thereon."—*Ibid.*, p. 2554.

They stood often in defenceless solitudes, guarded by a feeble garrison of inmates and frequenters, a prey ready to the hand of the spoiler, whenever he should come up against them.   Not otherwise stood England herself, as she had been raised by the counsels of former ages : a vast system of corporations, of guilds and fraternities, both lay and clerical : of societies which had outgrown the population, and were now to fall in the prodigious re-distribution of land and property which was about to ensue. The religious edifices might be empty, but they would have contained and educated the multitudes yet unborn : the corporate bodies were a vast provision for a numerous posterity, but a provision which posterity was never to enjoy. The Parliament whose proceedings we are to consider laid the axe to the tree.   A full generation at least of the fiercest hacking and hewing followed, ere the ancient system was spread upon the ground. The fury of a great revolution, which was designed to have been general, fell first, as in all such cases, upon religion and the Church.

This seems to have been the true nature of the great movement of the sixteenth century in England. As to what are commonly termed the causes of the Reformation, there seem to have been none which have not been exaggerated. Everybody knows what is said of the breaking up of the frost of ages, the corruptions of the old system, the influence of German Protestantism, and the explosive force of new ideas generated by the Revival of Learning : and everybody has grown accustomed to set the old against the new, as if they were totally repugnant forces, which simply strove to destroy one another. Much of this may be dismissed as no more than a graphic contrivance for enabling us to comprehend a memorable epoch, but historically untrue. The old system had already, at the opening of the Reformation, shewn itself expansive enough to contain the new ideas which were transforming literature and art : and need never have become irreconcilable with the religious developments of the age, if discrepancy had not been forced into disruption by design. As to German Protestantism, it undoubtedly had a factitious influence here, but it had made no deep impression upon the nation when the Reformation came on. So far as England is concerned, there seem to have been no causes at work which had not been at work long enough, and with very much the same degree of activity, when accident precipitated the Reformation.

But there was at the moment, besides the usual elements of disquiet which always threaten danger to an established order of things, an extraordinary combination of dangerous circumstances, which can hardly be expected to occur again. The ancient nobility had perished in the civil wars. Their place was being filled by a swarm of political adventurers, many of whom were among the worst men in the kingdom. New creations of nobility continued throughout the sixteenth century. These new men nearly all ranged themselves on the side of the party of innovation. At the head of all was a King who was more completely the man of the times than any person in his realm. A man of force without grandeur : of great ability, but not of lofty intellect : punctilious, and yet unscrupulous : centred in himself : greedy and profuse : cunning rather than sagacious : of fearful passions and intolerable pride, but destitute of ambition in the nobler sense of the word : a character of degraded magnificence. Such a King was no safe guardian of the rights of the realm. The only quality which preserved him from being a mere revolutionist was his cautious love of acting under constitutional

and legal forms. A tremendous revolution in property—a revolution of the rich against the poor—was
carried on in the latter years of Henry the Eighth; and
was continued after his death by men whom he set up;
but it was carried on, almost without exception, under
some form of constitutional or legal procedure.

That such a king was on the throne was the circumstance above all others which brought on the Reformation. The usual elements of disturbance were at
work; but they might have been overruled, as they
had been hitherto, but for Henry and his personal character and history. The laity had always been more or
less opposed to the claims of the clergy: the patrimony
of the Church had always been sapped by the avarice
both of laymen and not less of ecclesiastics and religious
societies: proposals far more revolutionary, as regarded
the endowments of the Church, than any that were
carried at the Reformation had been made to the King
of England in open Parliament a hundred years before:
and the corruption of the clergy and the religious orders
had been the theme of the satire of men who were
themselves under no religious obligations, and owned
no master but their will, for two centuries. But the
King of England had hitherto stood in the gate to protect the one party from the other, and to preserve the
rights of all. Now he lent the sanctity of the crown to
an enormous devastation; and the elements which
might have been controlled became uncontrollable.
They raged: they gathered so much voice and volume,
as to have led to the common notion that they were now
evoked by something rotten in the state of things which
had not been in existence before, or had now at length
overpassed all endurance. Whereas the waters had
always been behind the floodgates; but he who letted
them was not hitherto out of the way. When the King

headed the movement, when he called the assemblies of the realm to abet him, when he surrounded himself with adventurers to whom every hazard could be but gain, when he allowed the privilege of printing to every needy and ribald pen, then indeed the roar grew loud; then he commanded applause; and, to use the repeated phrase, he had the nation at his back. He had with him the needy and the greedy and the rich and the noisy.

The word "revolution" is the most appropriate designation that can be applied to much that was done. But this designation may be said to have acquired a peculiar meaning in English history. No English revolution has ever been such an uprooting and subversion of the institutions of society and of the State as has been witnessed repeatedly in many other countries. Alterations have been made within the general framework, but the framework itself has never been pulled down. The continuity of the State, both Civil and Ecclesiastical, in all the great parts and institutions, has remained unbroken from the earliest English antiquity to the present day. It remained unbroken now, when the nation and the Church were exposed to the great convulsions which were impending. A revolution was effected, first in property, then in religion, but none in polity, none in the ancient constitution of the Church of England. It was effected within the constitution, and not by the subversion of the constitution. It was effected by solemn procedure. Those who openly opposed it were made to take the position of rebels and traitors. In the beginning, in the early acts which are now to be considered, when the Roman jurisdiction was shaken off, and the clergy were reduced, and even in the more questionable instance of the destruction of the religious houses, we find a constant disclaimer of revolutionary violence, and repeated references, more or less justifiable, to some kind of precedent. This formal adherence to antiquity, this continued maintenance of the old constitution in all parts and branches, is the most characteristic and admirable feature of the English Reformation. But at the same time it must be carefully noticed that much of all this was no more than formal: that there was a real transferrence of power made from one part of the old constitution to another : and that many things survived henceforth as shadows which had hitherto been of the force and activity of substance.

I propose to devote time and pains to the examination of this complicated history, many parts of which may still require elucidation. I hope to write in the spirit of candour : the first part of which seems to be to lay before the reader the general proposition which he will find maintained in the work that invites his attention. The study of the English Reformation, not pursued without considerable labour, has led me to the conclusion that at the time of the abolition of the Papal jurisdiction a reformation was needed in many things : but that it was carried out on the whole by bad instruments, and attended by great calamities. The Church was taken out of the hands of the clergy, to be managed by the laity. The King, and the temporal estates overruled the spirituality. If the Church had been left to her proper officers to be reformed, and the needful compulsion given to them which it was always in the power of the King and the temporality to apply, the state of the nation would have been better at this day. I shall endeavour in the course of my work to follow out the difficult question of the relation of the clergy to the reformatory movement : an important question, to which the general answer is, that while

the management of the Church in discipline and the
temporalities may be said to have been taken from the
clergy, and taken far more absolutely than seems
generally thought, the reformation of doctrine was left
to them in great measure; and yet by no means always
left to them in their collective capacity, to their convocations or synods, to the Church Representative, or
assembly of the spirituality, but, in many important instances, assigned to certain of them sitting in commissions. A long chapter in the history of the Church of
England is opened from the time of the abolition of the
Papal authority; and the most comprehensive title of this
would be, of the Church of England under Formularies
of Faith and Acts for the Uniformity of Religion. It
will be a distinct feature of this work to give a sufficient
account of those authoritative formularies, both of doctrine and discipline, and of those acts of ecclesiastical
legislation, which from that time began to be multiplied.
These documents convey the faithful reflection of the
times in which they were severally written, and will
assist to form that delineation of the Church in her
eventful fortunes which it is my hope to convey.

It was on the 3rd of November, in the twenty-first
year of Henry, that the memorable Parliament was
opened which began the Reformation. The King
came by water to his palace of Bridewell, where he
and his nobles put on their robes of Parliament; and
so came to the Church of the Black Friars, where the
Mass of the Holy Ghost was solemnly sung by the
King's Chapel. The session was then prorogued from
the City of London to the next day, and then continued
at Westminster.

The most conspicuous figure on that day was the
new Lord Chancellor, Sir Thomas More. It had been
difficult to find a successor to Wolsey. Warham, the

Archbishop of Canterbury, a man of ability and eloquence, who was suggested, was refused by the King, who would have none of another ecclesiastic. When he chose More the King, indeed, seemed resolved to have a man as different as it was possible from the late Chancellor. And yet what did Henry expect to find in More? Not a judge in a second Divorce Court: for matrimonial causes were yet of spiritual cognisance, and More was a layman. Wolsey, the last of the long line of illustrious Churchmen who had held the high office of Chancellor, had fallen in the midst of stupendous diplomatic efforts to preserve England to the Holy See by inducing the Pope to cancel the Dispensation granted by his predecessor, under which Henry had married Katharine. More, on the other hand, had not concealed his opinion that the divorce ought not to be entertained at all. The wittiest of moralists and the most moral of wits was little fit to take part in the miserable intrigues of which Henry's policy consisted. The frankest of counsellors could ill please the ear of a tyrant. But the author of Utopia was known for tolerant and liberal: he was a humanist and a reformer: the writer of the first great original book that appeared in the Revival of Learning: the most renowned of Englishmen then living: almost the most renowned of living men. The countenance of such a man may have appeared desirable in the changes now beginning to be meditated. The King, who had used him familiarly for twenty years, with whom he had been wont to walk the palace leads at night, in his earlier and happier years, gazing the stars, knew perhaps little of the unshaken firmness that lay beneath the surface of the merriest of companions. That More was the unflinching champion of Catholic doctrine might seem but to increase his usefulness: for who was crying louder for Catholic doctrine than the Defender of the Faith? When Henry entered the lists against Luther, and the great heretic " played the very varlet with the King," had not More stepped to his sovereign's side, and so dressed " Luther in his own sauce malapert," that neither he nor any of his followers ever dared put pen to paper in reply? Certainly expectations were formed of More : and he was destined to disappoint them.* After a brief tenure of office he was compelled to retire from the excesses of a revolution which he could neither control nor sanction. His hold on the royal confidence was still briefer than his tenure of office. Crumwell rose as Wolsey set; and between the ascendency of Wolsey and that of Crumwell the interval of More lasted but a day.

The new Lord Chancellor, when he had assumed the robes of office, was led through Westminster Hall to the Star Chamber, between the great Dukes of Suffolk and Norfolk, who had been associated lately in carrying out the disgrace of Wolsey : and in sight of the high seat of justice, which he was for a time to grace, he pronounced an oration which has been variously reported. According to one account he likened his predecessor to a rotten sheep, and the King to the good shepherd who had judiciously segregated it. According to another his speech was full of humility, and contained an eloquent panegyric on the fallen minister.† The Commons, meantime filled up the

---

* The capital charge laid against More when he was condemned to death was, that he had disappointed the expectations of the King by ingratitude. (See Chapter III.)

† The former report of More's speech, in which he likens Wolsey to "a great scabbed wether" infecting the flock, is generally repeated by historians. It rests on the authority of the chronicler Hall, who was notoriously prejudiced against the clergy. It seems unlike More to have insulted Wolsey so ; but the speech may have been kinder than it seemed, for More added that the gentle punishment which had befallen

place which More had occupied among them by elect-
ing Sir Thomas Audley for their Speaker.   Audley, a
dextrous and unscrupulous man, made his oration also,
beseeching the King in a strain of affected humility to
forbear to lay upon him the burden of an office for
which he felt himself unfit.*

It was a packed Parliament.† The debates (of
which the rumour has been preserved by the bitterness) appear to have manifested a spirit of violent
hostility towards the clergy.   The two arguments
which may be observed in every agitation against
the Church were freely advanced : that the clergy got
too much and that they did too little.   A vast number
of Bills for the reduction of these abuses was brought
in.   The fees exacted in the Spiritual Courts for
probate of testament and other such business were
denounced as excessive.   " To prove a single will,
in which I was executor," cried one member, " I was
compelled to pay a thousand marks to the Lord
Cardinal and the Archbishop of Canterbury."   He
was followed by others with stories of the shameful
exactions of spiritual men.   As to mortuaries, or the
offerings made at burials, it was said that the clergy,
such was their charity, would take the dead man's
only cow from his beggared children rather than
forego their due.   Priests occupied farms, granges, and

the offender had satisfied the King.   The fate of Wolsey was still in the
balance when More said this ; his enemies were thereby warned off him.
On the other hand, according to More's Life of More, More said nothing
of the kind, but extolled Wolsey.   More, the biographer and great
grandson of Sir Thomas, was no admirer of Wolsey, that he should put
a laudation of him into the mouth of his ancestor ; but he may have
wished to exalt the magnanimity of the latter.   He certainly in one
respect puts into his mouth what Sir Thomas never said, for he makes
him speak as if Wolsey had been dead at that time.

* Hall.

† "There had been great industry used in carrying elections."—
Burnet.

grazing; the poor husbandman could get nothing but of them, and dearly had he to pay for what he got. The heads of the religious houses kept tanneries, and bought and sold wool like temporal merchants. Beneficed men, instead of residing, were found lying at the Court in lords' houses; they took all from their parishioners, and did nothing for them; so that the poor lacked refreshing, and all the parish was without preaching and instruction in God's word, to the great peril of their souls. One priest, being little learned, would hold ten or twelve benefices, and reside on none; while there were very well learned scholars in the university, able to teach and preach, who had neither benefice nor exhibition.*

The temper of the Commons was not cooled by the reception which their Bills met with in the Lords. Two of them, on probates and mortuaries, were so warmly contested by the spiritual peers that they came to nothing in the original form. On this occasion a well-known episode occurred, in which Fisher, the aged Bishop of Rochester, figured. Fisher, the ornament of the bench and of the kingdom, was the last survivor of the counsellors of Henry the Seventh. To Margaret, Countess of Richmond, and mother of that monarch, he had been confessor; it was by his advice that the venerable countess determined upon the noble academical foundations which have perpetuated her name; and at the beginning of the century he

---

* The six allegations above given are found in Hall, from whom Fox has taken them, and put them into a paragraph, which he has entitled "Grievances of the Commons against the Clergy of England." Thus arrayed, these "Grievances" look so like a copy of a formal document, that they deceived Wilkins, who inserted them in his work (iii. 739) under the title that Fox bestowed on them. One modern historian, at least, seems to have confounded them with the Supplication of the Commons against the Ordinaries of 1532.

became the first Margaret Professor of Divinity at Cambridge. By Henry the Eighth he had been valued as the guide of his youth; and the King was wont to boast that no prince in Christendom had a bishop worthy to compare with Rochester. But the part which he had recently taken in the divorce had obliterated the memory of his past services, and he was now exposed to a brush which warned him how precarious was the footing of those who stood upon the ancient order of things. When the Bills came up from the Commons, Fisher solemnly protested against them. " My Lords," said he, " you see daily what Bills come hither from the Commons House, and all to the destruction of the Church. For God's sake see what a realm the kingdom of Bohemia was, and when the Church went down, then fell the glory of the kingdom : now with the Commons is nothing but Down with the Church : and all this, me seemeth, is for lack of faith only." When this was reported to the Commons their rage was extreme. " We are slandered," they exclaimed, " as heretics in the presence of the Lords." After a long debate, they sent their Speaker with thirty of their number to the King. Audley set forth with full eloquence the indignity beneath which the Commons were smarting. " Are we infidels, are we Turks, are we Saracens, are we pagans and heathens," said he, " that the laws which we establish should be thought not worthy to be kept by Christian men ? I beseech your Highness to call that bishop before you, and bid him speak more discreetly of such a number as be in the Commons House." The King intervened ; Fisher explained his words,* and, as to the Bills, a compromise

---

* Hall. Fisher's explanation was that he meant that the doings of the Bohemians were for lack of faith, not the doings of the Commons. This the Commons are said to have treated as "a blind excuse ;" by

was effected to the mutual gratification of the King and the Commons. The enormous debts of the insolvent King were cancelled in a Bill which was sent down to the Commons after passing the Lords : and in return for a complaisance which cost them many groans, a number of the Commons were appointed to meet with some of the Lords, both spiritual and temporal, to frame new Bills about probate and mortuaries. When this committee met, the plainness of Fisher was at least equalled by a lawyer among the Commons, who, when the spiritual Lords defended their courts on the ground of prescription and usage, answered that it was the usage of thieves to rob on Shooter's Hill, *ergo*, it was lawful. The same person told the Archbishop that the exaction of probate and mortuaries, as it was then used, was but open robbery and theft. Against these speeches the spiritual men protested in vain: the temporal Lords who were joined with them went over to their enemies : the Bills were prepared, presented to Parliament, and carried.*

A third and more important measure was directed to limit the abuses of plurality and non-residence.

modern historians it is called an equivocation. Certainly in Hall's version the words will not bear the explanation. But the explanation was confirmed by the bishops, who heard the words. According to Bailey (Life of Fisher, 96), Fisher said to the Lords, "You shall see all obedience drawn, first from the clergy, and secondly from yourselves ; and if you search the true causes of all these mischiefs that reign among them (the Commons), you shall find that they all come through want of faith." This was explicit enough ; but the words have the ring of a later age. According to the same author, Fisher made no explanation of his words, nor did the Commons complain of one phrase in particular, but of the whole speech ; and Fisher merely answered that, "being in counsel, he spoke his mind in defence of the Church." I have shortened Hall's version of Audley's remonstrance. The aptness of the Commons to take offence, a character of innovators, was amusingly shown in their rushing from Bohemia to Turkey. The King did not behave badly in the matter.

* Hall or Holinshed.

This, as it originally came from the Commons, seems to have aroused a greater opposition than the former Bills. It was keenly contested in the House of Lords by the spiritual peers : outside the walls of Parliament the priests are said to have railed on the Commons, calling them heretics and schismatics.* At length the King resorted to his former expedient of a conference between a number of both houses; and the same result followed. Eight of the Commons were appointed to meet eight of the Lords in the Star Chamber. The temporal Lords of the number deserted the Bishops, who were then unable to prolong their resistance : the Bill, with some modifications, was adopted, and was carried through Parliament on the following day. This expedient of doing things by committee we shall find continually repeated in the course of the Reformation. It frustrated any opposition which might be offered by the spiritual peers in open Parliament, while the Convocation of the clergy was, in numerous instances, wholly ignored. And yet the ancient constitutional practice was to submit measures touching the Church to the assembly of the clergy ; and at the opening of the Reformation the assembly of the clergy was more representative of the Church than it became as the Reformation proceeded.

Among the numerous propositions touching the Church which in a session of six weeks emanated from the Commons, these three only passed into law. They were succeeded so swiftly by stronger measures that it is less necessary to examine the remedies which they applied than the diseases which they professed to cure. They seem to have been levelled against

---

* Some of them are said to have been punished for this : we are not told who they were, nor how they were punished. The whole rests on no better author than Hall.

real abuses. The state of the ecclesiastical courts, at which the former of them aimed, was bad unquestionably. Swarms of clerical men, of various grades, got their living out of these courts : it was to the interest of these practitioners to make business for them: many causes which now belong to the temporal were then of spiritual cognisance : many offences which are now free from the danger of human laws exposed the suspected to the scrutiny of an ecclesiastical official. The diocesan courts were seldom presided over by the bishops in person. In the great Provincial courts the judges were dependent upon fees and other accidental emoluments. It was an established custom for them to receive money from suitors, not exactly in the way of bribes, for it was often accepted from both parties, but for getting an early hearing. The suit of a poor man might be delayed perhaps for years, if he could not afford an inducement to expedition. And yet, if the spiritual courts could be compared with the temporal administration of justice, it would perhaps be found that in exorbitance, corruption, and delay they were not unsurpassed. It ought to be borne in mind that for ages, throughout the most distressful times of English history, these courts Christian had been the refuge of the people against the enormous injustice and cruelty of the royal courts and the courts baron. If they were in a state of corruption now, when the lawyers of the House of Commons undertook to amend them,* it should be remembered that many of their worst evils remained unaltered by the hands of the reformers. Law courts are less easily reformed by

---

* " The burgesses of the Parliament appointed certain of the Common House, men learned in the law, to draw one bill for probate of testaments, another for mortuaries, and the third for non-residence, pluralities, and taking of farms by spiritual men." *Hall.*

law than any other institutions. It is easy to carry statutes of amendment, but the state of the court still depends upon the character of the officers employed in it; and the character of the ecclesiastical lawyers and officials improved in nowise as the Reformation went on.

Nor must it be supposed that there had been no efforts made to reform the spiritual courts before they were taken in hand by the Parliament. Both Warham and Wolsey had made strenuous efforts to reform the great Provincial Courts, the Court of Arches and the Court of Audience, in which the most important business and the worst exactions were found. At the end of the reign of Henry the Seventh, Archbishop Warham issued a number of ordinances for the better regulation of the Court of Audience, and secured for them the consent of the advocates and proctors. He raised the character and lessened the number of the practitioners; the causes of the poor he ordered to be assigned to certain advocates to be undertaken without fee; scribes, notaries, and judges were to expedite the causes of the poor for charity, accepting no money for examining processes or pronouncing sentence. If an advocate took payment in such causes, or shewed himself more remiss in them than in others, he was to be expelled the court for ever. The regulations were to be read publicly from the tribunal at the beginning of every term. Nor were they wholly inoperative.* But, for a reformer seeks to centralise, the Archbishop,

---

* Wilkins, iii. 650. That these reforms were not inoperative we may gather from the Supplication of the Commons of the year 1532, where it was mentioned that Warham had reduced the proctors to the number of ten, which still subsisted. The same reforms were applied to the Court of Arches, *Godolphin's Abridg.*, 103, and afterwards renewed by Cranmer.—*Strype's Cranmer*, b. i. c. 12.

having put in order his courts, endeavoured to draw into them the business of the other courts of the Church. Probate of wills, the administration of goods, and such like, which were shared with the diocesan courts, he pretended to belong to him by prerogative; and forthwith found himself involved in a serious struggle with his suffragans. The latter demanded in vain to know the extent of the prerogative which he claimed. They received no answer: but, as they complained, they found their jurisdiction usurped by the Archbishop in a manner that none of his predecessors had ever used. Their courts were impoverished, and (it is curious to read so long before the abolition of the Roman authority) appeals made to the Apostolic See were frustrated, and judges specially delegated by the Holy Father were inhibited by the English Primate.*

The bishops who resisted Warham were nevertheless willing to accept the attempted reformation of the ecclesiastical law which followed twenty years later under Wolsey. † When, at the express and urgent solicitation of the King, Wolsey was made by the Pope first a cardinal, then a Legate a latere, and Vicar-General of England, he turned his attention to the spiritual courts, but not so much to reform as to supersede them. By a composition with the English Primate he set up his Legatine Court in Westminster, as a supreme court of appeal, and in his own house a second court for matters testamentary. The result which soon followed was a struggle between the courts of the Church and the legatine faculties of Wolsey,

---

* " Summa Litis motæ in Convocatione de Approbatione Testamentorum." 1512. *Wilkins*, iii. 653.

† "Omnes Prælati, præsertim Episcopi, suos assensus et studia alacres, ni fallor, adhibebunt."—*Fox, Bishop of Winchester, to Wolsey. Strype, Orig. No.* 10.

similar to that which had arisen between the bishops and their metropolitan. The Legate's courts absorbed the business of the courts of the Church : the practitioners of the latter found themselves aggrieved : and the good understanding between Warham and Wolsey was broken. Bickerings arose between them, until the whole thing was involved in the ruin of Wolsey.* The attempt to overrule the courts of the Church of England by the authority of a legate was, indeed, ill-judged and rash. All that Wolsey effected seems to have been to complicate matters that were confused enough before, not to render justice cheaper or more expeditious. When, in the present parliament, Sir Henry Guilford declared that to prove a will he had spent a thousand marks between the Cardinal and the Archbishop, he related a grievance which arose out of the interference of Wolsey : and though that famous anecdote has been handed down to posterity as an instance of the ordinary exactions of the spiritual courts of England, yet in truth it was an extraordinary case, and issued out of the attempt to supersede those courts by legatine authority.

The measure by which the Parliament sought to prevent spiritual persons both from taking farms and from holding pluralities illustrated curiously the spirit of the times, and of the Legislature. In a long preamble, written in that peculiar style which was now invented by the genius of reformation, it was set forth that, " For the more quiet and virtuous increase and maintenance of divine service, the preaching and teaching the word of God, with godly and goodly example giving, the better discharge of curates, the

---

* Hook, in his Life of Warham, pp. 233–260, gives an excellent account of the whole question. Cf. Strype, i. 107.

maintenance of hospitality, the relief of poor people, the increase of devotion, and good opinion of the lay fee towards the spiritual persons," no spiritual person, secular or regular, should take any lands to farm, on pain of forfeiting ten pounds a month, half of which was to go to the King, half to the informer. All leases made to spiritual persons were to be void in a year, and no such person was to buy or sell again for lucre or profit any kind of merchandise, corn, cattle, or other commodity. It was only for the necessary maintenance of their houses, persons, or servants that spiritual persons or societies were to be allowed to sell again what they had bought; it was only for their expenses in their households and hospitalities that they were to take lands in farm, and not for any other lucre, commodity, or advantage. All abbots and masters of religious houses, colleges, and hospitals, holding lands not above the yearly value of seven hundred marks, might occupy lands and farms, for maintenance of hospitality, in as ample a manner as they had occupied for the space of one hundred years. All spiritual persons who had in farm any lands or tenements were ordered to sell or give them forthwith to any lay person or persons whom they chose.*

It is difficult to estimate the effect which these curious enactments might have had: how far it would have been possible to distinguish between maintenance and lucre, between necessity and commodity, and to control all bargains made by spiritual persons. It seems, however, plain from the last clause which has been mentioned that the meaning of all was to facilitate the transferrence of ecclesiastical property to lay-

---

* 21 Hen. VIII. 13.

men. The Act has been cited as the first outburst of
the noble indignation of the English laity against
corruption, rapacity, and fraud. It is indeed memorable as the first attempt made in this age to deal
with the property of the Church.

The wealth of the Church at the opening of the
Reformation was sufficient to make plurality of benefices, always an abuse, less of a necessity than it
afterwards became. It appeared, therefore, to be
moderately enacted that if any spiritual person or
persons, having already a benefice of the yearly
value of eight pounds or above, should accept any
other, the first should be adjudged void; but that
persons already possessed of more than one benefice
might keep those which they had, to the number
of four but not above. In the vast alienation and
spoiling of livings which soon followed it was impossible to pass another such law or to observe this.
" Double beneficed men " and pluralists of every shade
increased and abounded through the progress of the
Reformation : the gross abuse, which had come in
during the Roman usurpation was not diminished, but
increased, since the salutary rigour of a statute which
sought to limit spiritual persons to one benefice apiece
only preceded the calamities which left few benefices
capable of supporting an incumbent if they were held
singly. The lawgivers themselves, however, appeared
to be sheltered from the danger of their own Act by
a number of remarkable exceptions. All ecclesiastics,
who were of the King's Council, might hold three
benefices. The chaplains of the nobility and of the
bishops, the chaplains of the chief officers of the royal
household, might each of them hold two : and the
same privilege was extended to graduates in divinity
and law, and to the brothers and sons of every lord

and knight. But this composite statute was most notable in that it dealt the first blow against the spiritual empire of Rome. The dispensation or license of the Roman pontiff was a weapon which had been wielded in time past far more frequently against the ordinances of English bishops than against the decrees of English parliaments : but it was in the same spirit of independence which had often animated episcopal protestations against the interference of the Pope that the Legislature now ordained that all persons who procured any license from the Court of Rome to hold more benefices than those that were limited in their statute should incur the considerable penalty of twenty pounds.

The Convocation of the Province of Canterbury met according to the custom of the realm at the same time with the Parliament, under the magnificent roof of Old St. Paul's. Small favour has been shewn by the general historians to the attitude and behaviour of the clergy at this crisis of their history. They are usually represented as a crew of decrepit shavelings, wedded to abuses, sunk in corruption, from whom it was in vain to expect a reformation. The degenerate successors of a once noble order, they had lost the sympathy of the nation. Their cowardice, when the long-gathering storm of public indignation at length fell upon them, was only equalled by their arrogance in power and their insolence in impunity. Such are the invectives which are repeated by some of the most popular among modern writers from the hostile chroniclers and ribald balladmongers of the time. And yet the clergy of England, at the beginning of the Reformation, were the purest in the world. They were the furthest removed from Rome and the immeasurable filth in which Rome had been buried in the fifteenth century. Whatever may have been the state of other countries, no proof of deep corruption has been made good against the clergy of England. As to their alleged pusillanimity in misfortune, they were in truth too weak to resist the coalition of the King and the Commons, by which the Reformation was carried; and were treated by both with a scornful insolence which at once laid bare the secret of their weakness. But, if there is any dignity discernible in the assemblies of the English State in those years, it is to be seen in the Convocations of the clergy, not in the slavish Parliaments, composed of "servants of the King," who only met to do his pleasure. The clergy alone ventured upon any remonstrances against the despotic actions of the King, and continued to use some freedom of speech amidst the fines and insults to which they were subjected. So far is it from being true that they were a merely obstructive body, hating to be reformed, that we shall presently find them labouring for the reformation of abuses and the restoration of discipline, at the very time when the power of action was taken from them for ever. To a clerical reformation they were not averse. A clerical reformation, a reformation of discipline without meddling with the Catholic faith, had been attempted already by the best of the clergy throughout Europe. Three great Councils had been held to bring it about, within the last hundred years, and to each of these Councils England had sent representatives. The defeat of this attempted reformation by Councils, which was effected by the intrigues of Rome, and above all by the skill of the last of the great Popes, Martin the Fifth, is the most mournful event of modern history. It caused despair: it gave weight to the clamour that no reformation was to be expected from the Church herself: and thus it opened the way for the invasion of the temporal power, and for the doctrinal revolution which presently overswept Northern Europe. Nevertheless it is probable that, though the clerical reformation fell through in Europe at large, it would have gone on in England, if the clergy had been left to themselves. It was always in the power of the King and the temporal estates to have put such pressure upon them as would have compelled them to move as fast as it was desirable that they should have moved in the path of constitutional reform. They seem to have been willing enough to obey every call of the King and nation, notwithstanding all that is said to the contrary. Consultation might have been held with them, and measures concerted to have increased their use, and conciliated a cordial understanding between them and the other estates of the realm. Instead of which they found themselves set aside from the first. With the unfailing instinct of party they knew where their danger lay. They saw that nothing which they could have offered in the way of reformation would have satisfied their enemies : that behind the grievances alleged by the Commons there lay other designs indefinite indeed as yet, and scarce known to the minds in which they were being formed, but not the less real. What they had to fear above all things was a doctrinal reformation which might give to these designs the power of enthusiasm and the pretence of sanctity. They were the official guardians of "the true Catholic faith," which, with reason, they declared ever to have been maintained in England. To deny what was taught would be the most powerful method of attacking the position of the teachers ; and hence Fisher touched deeply when he spoke of "lack of faith" in connection with the doings of the Commons. The party of alteration were not willing to enter the doctrinal arena as yet. Their head, the King, was Defender of the Faith. It was well for the realm that the doctrinal reformation, which came at last, was not added to the calamities of the end of the reign of Henry.

The clergy, placed in this position, are found acting not without consistency and dignity in the Convocation which is now to be considered. They pursued the clerical reformation—the reformation of abuses, which was the thing really wanted—with some added solemnity apparently, but almost as tranquilly as if their enemies in Westminster had no existence. And while they made laws against simony, or for converting appropriations into vicarages on the one hand, they continued, on the other hand, to condemn the heretical books which were brought into the realm from beyond seas, and tried to stop the mouths of the heretical preachers and lecturers who were infesting the country. Their course was at least consistent.

The leading men among the prelates were Fisher, Warham, Tunstall, West, and Clark; to whom may be added Stokesley and Gardiner, who were soon afterwards raised to the episcopate. Between all the rest and Fisher there is a great difference to be set. There are some men who grow inflexible after yielding up to a certain point. The martyr of the Roman primacy was of that rarer order of men who are inflexible from the first. He absolutely disapproved of the dissolution of the King's marriage; and though he was not forward in putting forth his opinion without reason, yet he had given it unmistakably on the most proper occasion. He could not see that it was better for the Holy See to revoke a sentence and sacrifice a woman than to lose England. He was not one of those Churchmen who ran about the Continent from the Cardinal of York to the Pope, and from the Pope to the French King, in negociating about the secret matter. In the late trial before the Legates, being one of the Queen's advocates, he had not used his office fashionably. It was he who first broke the subservient silence of all public men, and awoke an opposition to the wishes of the King. To the surprise and fury of Henry, he appeared in the court and boldly protested that the marriage with Katharine could not be dissolved by any power, divine or human. "The follower of Christ," said he, "must become the follower of Christ's forerunner, and the example of John the Baptist, who died in a cause of matrimony, may encourage him, since the state of matrimony has been made more holy by the shedding of Christ's blood."* Having thus taken his stand from the first, it was easy for Fisher to be firm and decisive on every question that arose out of the fatal germ of the Divorce. The tall and fleshless figure of this celebrated prelate, his muscular face, well-opened and impetuous eyes, bespoke the vital strength, the fearlessness, and the fineness of his nature. He was now in his seventieth year.

Warham was a man of integrity and ability, celebrated for his eloquence, a sincere reformer of abuses, and an eminent friend of the Humanists. To him the great foreign printers dedicated their choicest editions. Under his hospitable roof Erasmus had met

---

* "As John the Baptist in olden times regarded it as impossible to die more gloriously than in a cause of matrimony—and it was not so holy then as it has since become by the shedding of Christ's blood—he would not encourage himself more ardently, more effectually to face any extreme peril with greater confidence than by taking the Baptist for his own example."—*Brewer*, iv. 2539. It was not known before Mr. Brewer that this was historically true, though Bailie in his Life of Fisher declared that the bishop spoke boldly for his client the Queen. Fisher was seconded by one bishop and the Dean of Arches. Mr. Brewer has discovered that Henry himself wrote an answer to Fisher, in the form of a speech, and reviled him with every term of abuse that rage and indignation could furnish.

with Colet and More; Erasmus had sallied from his
gates on his memorable pilgrimage to the shrine of
St. Thomas of Canterbury. But the day of Warham,
like the day of the earlier Humanists, was nearly
over. Already now in his seventy-ninth year, he was
destined to retire early from the scene; and yet not
before he had witnessed some part of the great revolution which cast down his order from their ancient
dignity. It was not in him to withstand the revolution, like Fisher: he dallied with the elements of
change: and when they grew into a combination that
was intolerable in his eyes, it was his part to hurl
against them the feeble thunderbolt of a dying protestation.

To these survivors of an earlier generation it is
difficult not to add the name of Edward Fox, the
lately deceased Bishop of Winchester. This prelate,
one of the most trusty counsellors of the late reign, a
man famed both for munificence and integrity, had
welcomed the clerical reformation as proposed to be
carried out by Wolsey. From his letters to the great
Cardinal a truer notion of the state of things may be
obtained than from the party challenges of the Commons, or the unmeasured invectives of "desperately
affected" enthusiasts. He acknowledged in those letters that a reformation was needed: he longed for that
happy day, as Simeon in the Gospel for the Messiah's
coming. All that belonged to the ancient integrity of
the clergy, and especially of the monks, was depraved
by license and corruptions, or abolished by the ma-
lignancy and length of time. But this reformation was
to be wrought by ecclesiastical authority—by Wolsey
as Legate from the side of the Father of universal
Christendom, aided by the King of England, and com-
missioned to a work for which the diocesan bishops

had no jurisdiction wide enough. Such a reformation
the bishops would not oppose, but welcome and further; and by means of such a reformation the common
people would be pacified, who were always crying out
against the clergy.* Such had been the hopes entertained of Wolsey's Legation by many of the best of the
clergy. In their eyes it appeared to be a supreme
effort to carry the clerical reformation. The extraordinary power of a legate, exercised by an Englishman, and always limited by the supreme power of the
Crown, was not repulsive to the nation. From Wolsey
much was expected: by Wolsey much might have
been done under another king. But even without the
intervention of a legate of the Holy See it was perfectly
possible for the Church of England to have restored
her ancient discipline by means of her own assemblies
and ordinances put in force by her own officers, if these
officers had been supported by the head of the State.
The power of the King would have been sufficient for
this. But other things were in store.

Cuthbert Tunstall, now Bishop of London, but
soon to be translated to the great Northern diocese of
Durham, with which his name is perpetually associated,
was a younger man, being now of the age of fifty-five.
It was his destiny to live in the reign of every one of
the Tudors: to witness the beginning and almost the
end of the Reformation. The character of Tunstall
was solid and prudent; his countenance, refined though
florid, expressed benevolence and intelligence; his
·learning, which recommended him to the favourable
notice of Erasmus, had gained him a reputation beyond
the shores of England. For some years he was regarded as the leader of the constitutional party among
the Churchmen, a position which he enjoyed so long

---

* Strype, Orig. No. 10, vol. ii. p. 25.

as moderation, dignity, and integrity were sufficient to maintain it. But he failed to shew the energy of a leader as the troubles of the times increased; and the place which he had filled in the public eye was occupied by his younger contemporary, Gardiner. About this time he was engaged in his somewhat simple attempt to suppress Tyndale's version of the New Testament, by buying up the first edition and committing it to the flames.

West and Clark, the Bishops of Ely and of Bath, had been, with Fisher, Warham, and Tunstall, among the advocates of the Queen in the late trial. They were both celebrated canonists and devoted adherents of the old religion. The former of them was removed within a few years by death, but not before he had taken part in several of the memorable scenes of the revolution; the latter, who remained alive for ten years from this time, distinguished himself by the determination with which he upheld the cause of the Queen in the Convocation, so long as resistance was possible.

Stokesley and Gardiner were raised almost at the same moment, within a few months after this date, to the episcopal order and the contiguous dioceses of London and of Winchester. As they were neighbours, so they appear to have been attached friends, and men of the same mind, or at least of the same opinions. Both had been trained in the school of Wolsey, and employed largely in his Italian embassies, in which the diplomatic skill of both, but especially of Gardiner, had been conspicuous. They had learned to look on the Divorce with less repugnance than some of their brethren. Stokesley had collected sentences for it in the foreign universities; Gardiner had haughtily told the Pontiff to his face that unless he yielded he would lose England, and deserve to lose a country of which he respected not the freedom. They were, therefore, prepared to regard without alarm the rejection of the Papal jurisdiction and the assumption of the title of Supreme Head by the King, which were the consequences of the Divorce. England remained still a Catholic country after those great changes. Stokesley, who is said to have been a man of some severity of temper, died while the Catholic settlement, which Henry the Eighth hoped that he had established after all his changes, was still in force. Gardiner, who survived, was destined to rise to his full height, and to become one of the most memorable of English prelates, when that settlement·was overturned in the following reign.

The Convocation was consulted in their third session, November 12, by the Archbishop, on the reformation of abuses. Several articles were submitted to them. Provision was to be made for ordaining clergymen. None were to be admitted into holy orders but those who were of proper age, of good morals; and sufficient learning. The manners of the clergy were to be reformed. They were forbidden to frequent taverns or indecent spectacles, to play at prohibited games, to pass the night in suspicious places. Excess in apparel was to be restrained. Reformation was to be made in the promotion of ecclesiastical persons by simoniacal pravity. For the abuses connected with the churches appropriated to monasteries and other places provision was to be made. A great number of churches had fallen into the hands of the monasteries, having been made over by lay patrons for innumerable reasons : but the patronage of these churches was, in general, ill exercised by the monastic bodies ; the vicars whom they appointed were very badly paid ; at one time they had been removable at the will of those who appointed them. By the Parliamentary Acts of former reigns a remedy had been attempted for these and other abuses; but the appropriated churches still remained in an unsatisfactory state, particularly .with regard to the maintenance of the vicars. It was proposed to pass an ordinance of Convocation for the remedy of these evils.

The reformation of abuses among regular persons, or monastics, also occupied attention; and it seems that the religious houses were already suffering in reputation from the revelations or slanders of those of their number who were weary of their habit, and longing to return to the world. These would be the worst characters among them. An ordinance was made that none should make revelations to any person whatever unless he belonged to the house.* The Archbishop afterwards held a secret communication with his suffragans, all others being excluded; then with the abbots; and lastly with the friars mendicant. At this time the Convocation included the heads and representatives of the religious bodies, who thus met in council with the clergy of the Church of England. Much was deliberated also concerning heretics; partly, it would appear, at the instance of the King.†

In one of these sessions the clergy of the Lower House sent up to the Fathers a spirited remonstrance against the doings of the Commons in Parliament. They demanded that the Church of England should enjoy the rights, liberties, and immunities which had been granted by the former Kings of England in their charters and concessions.‡ They requested that, as it

---

* Wilkins, iii. 717: " Ne aliquis revelet extra domum aliquibus personis cujuscumque status, nisi inter semetipsos."

† One expression is curious: " Regia majestas prosequitur ecclesiam Anglicanam cum sua defensione circa libertates ecclesiasticas et reprimendos hereticos."—*Ibid.*

‡ Particularly in the Magna Charta, in the Charter of the Forest, in

was impossible always to avoid the danger of the law without knowing what the law was, cases which fell under the Statutes of· Præmunire might be accurately defined : and that in future a writ of Præmunire should not issue from a King's court against any ecclesiastical judge or litigant, unless a Prohibition were first issued. They complained that the liberties of the Church and the force of their canons was weakened by the Acts of the present Parliament, to the great grievance of the clergy, and the manifest peril of the souls of those who enacted or executed the same ; that they themselves had never been consulted, either by themselves or their proctors, in making those Acts, nor had consented to them; that the statutes in themselves were heavily penal, and yet so captious, that it was hardly possible not to transgress them, and hard and uncharitable in their terms; and that they tended to diminish hospitality by preventing poor vicars from farming their ˙rectories so as to have the means of hospitable living. They therefore besought the Fathers to provide a remedy both for the present and future inconveniences of these Acts.*

the Charter Super Articulis Cleri of Edward II., and in the Breve, Circumspecte Agatis, of Edward I.

　* Collier, Rec. xxviii., Petitio Cleri, &c. : " Ut Ecclesia Anglicana gaudeat et fruatur omnibus et singulis juribus, libertatibus, consuetudinibus antiquis, et privilegiis et immunitatibus concessis a nobilis memoriæ regiæ majestatis progenitoribus, regibus Angliæ, prout in chartis et concessionibus eorundem, præsertim in Charta Magna, in Charta de Foresta, in Charta Edwardi super articulis cleri, et in brevi Circumspecte agatis, necnon Edwardi quarti (?), aliis item immunitionibus suis quibuscunque.

　" Et quia clerus summopere affectat vitare offensa regiæ sublimitatis, et æquum non est ut aliquis pœnam violatæ legis incurrat quam scire non potuit : ut dignetur sua sublimitas curare ac jubere ut in præsenti parliamento certi ac præscripti limites clare designentur casuum statutorum de Præmunire, quod extra illos casus declaratos aliqua non incurratur pœna : et ne de cætero decernatur a curia regia emittendum contra ullum

Such were the chief of the proceedings of the venerable assembly of the English Church in the Southern Province, as given in the imperfect records which remain. The northern Convocation appears not to have met, perhaps in consequence of the fall of Wolsey. The position taken by the clergy is easily intelligible. They continued the clerical reformation, and protested against the invasion of the ancient rights of the Church. But the temper of the Commons made it dangerous to do more. It is not known that the Prelates ventured on an appeal to the King, in consequence of the petition which they received from the clergy of the Lower House against the doings of the Commons. It is not known that the Parliament condescended to consult the Convocation on any of their measures, according to the ancient custom of the realm.

Throughout the next year the public mind was occupied by the King's " secret matter." The business of the Divorce was destined to defile the character or

---

judicem ecclesiasticum, aut partes litigantes, Breve præfatum de Præmunire, nisi præmissa Prohibitione regia, et in casibus prædictis.

" Præterea, quum clerus multum gravaminis ac damni sustineat, ratione statutorum in præsenti Parliamento editorum, libertatem ecclesiasticam et sanctiones canonicas enervantium, in animarum statuentium et quorumcunque executionem demandantium periculum manifestum, sententiamque excommunicationis notorie et damnabiliter incurrendo : ad quæ facienda nec consenserunt per se nec per procuratores suos, neque super eisdem consulti fuerunt : ipsaque ea statuta tam graves, tam inevitabiles pœnas in se contineant; nonnihil etiam iniquitatis habeant contra caritatem et canonicas sanctiones edita : sintque in se adeo captiosa, ut difficile sit ea non violare ; hospitalitati quoque non parum derogantia, miseris vicariis rectoriarum suarum conductiones, uti videtur, prohibentia ; ut iidem patres (quorum est veritatem canonum annuntiare) remedium opportunum in statutis prædictis provideant tam presenti tam futuris temporibus debite consulentes."

Collier, who has preserved this document, is certainly mistaken in supposing that it was a petition from the clergy to the King. It was from the Lower House of Convocation to the Upper.

touch the safety of every one who had to meddle with
it.   Already it had ruined Wolsey, shaken More, and
prejudiced Fisher ; Stokesley and Gardiner, the envoys
and instruments of Wolsey, had played in it a part
more suitable to courtiers than to churchmen.   In the
late scene of the trial of the King and Queen in the
court of the Legates, the whole nation had suffered
a degradation hardly to be matched out of the annals
of John Lackland.   The King's matter was now come
to the second stage ; namely, the collection of the
sentences of Universities, both at home and abroad.
For this, the delay of the Roman Curia furnished an
ostensible cause : it led at last to the renunciation of
the jurisdiction of Rome.   Corruption and intimidation,
the resources of tyranny, were exhausted to procure
sentences in favour of the King ; and though with the
foreign Universities Henry met with but partial success,
he carried his will in his own.   After a resistance not
dishonourable to their renown, both the Universities
were forced into sentences for the Divorce, by means
which even the advocates of Henry pretend not to
justify.   This second stage of the process was illustrated by the simultaneous rise of two men whose
names bear a formidable import to the Church of
England : Thomas Crumwel and Thomas Cranmer.

The business of the Divorce seems to have suspended the struggle between the Parliament and the
clergy.   Both bodies were summoned and prorogued
several times in this year, without meeting for the
despatch of business.   Meanwhile it behoved the
Defender of the Faith to do his office : and Henry
displayed his orthodoxy by a series of Instruments and
Proclamations against heretics and erroneous books.
A Commission was appointed, consisting of a certain
number of the most learned of the two Universities,

and of other eminent persons; as Warham, More, Tunstall, Gardiner, Sampson, Crome, Leighton, Hugh Latimer, and William Latimer. They met in the Old Chapel, formerly called St. Edward's Chamber, in the palace of Westminster; and, after careful examination, unanimously proceeded to condemn a number of books, enumerating the errors contained in them. The King dignified their final session by his presence, May 24, 1530; and ordered their determinations to be attested, sealed, and promulgated as his own decree.

It was not without reason that they who maintained the Catholic Faith, as it was then understood, endeavoured to stop the effusion of heretical books. The increasing activity of the press was the greatest danger to which they stood exposed. Even in infancy the tremendous power of irresponsible publication made itself felt. Books filled with general charges against the standing system, written with incredible scurrility and ribaldry, poured from the press, and found an eager welcome among that easy class which has always been the feeding ground of dissidence, the class which gets money, and with money the leisure to speculate on the doings of others, and which turns its attention to those who bear office, and particularly to those whose burden it is to maintain the religious system of the country. These publications sometimes also found their way into the hands of the poor, and filled them with discontent, envy, and hatred. Often anonymous, or pseudonymous, often printed beyond the seas, but not unfrequently in England with foreign towns falsely assumed for the place of printing, stealthily circulated, these books were found a pestilent thing alike by humanist, statesman, and prelate. By all who bore public responsibility they were abhorred. As every system suffers the most from those who desert it, the worst of them were written by runagate monks or clergy. Their ferocity was generally matched by their dulness: to the modern reader they are intolerable, and are now remembered but by name; but the power exerted by them was not measured either by their sense or truth: they fed an increasing demand, and evaded every effort to suppress them. A secret society, bearing the name of the Brethren, or the Christian Brethren, composed of printers, booksellers, pedlers, wandering clerks, broken merchants, and other adventurers, successfully braved the much exaggerated perils of the prohibitory mandates, to circulate these dainty sheets. The great scene of their activity was the city of London, and the seaport towns. The authorities had done something against these productions already, but with little effect. In the year 1526, Warham ordered his bishops to require a number of them to be delivered up by those who had them, under pain of excommunication and suspicion of heretical pravity. In 1529, the King by proclamation prohibited more than a hundred of them: and set in motion the whole power of the law, the judges, justices, sheriffs, bailiffs, and constables, against those who possessed or concealed them.*

The books now condemned by the Commission were the same in general that had been condemned on these former occasions: the tracts of Wycliffe, Huss, Luther, and Zwingle, and the various productions of contemporary English heretics, as Fish, Joy, Tyndale. Those which appeared particularly obnoxious were "The parable of the Wicked Mammon," "The Obedience of a Christian Man," "The Revelation of Antichrist," "The Sum of Scripture," "The Supplication

* Wilkins, iii. 7c6, 737; and Fox, who gives the list at full length, which Wilkins does not.

of Beggars," " The Primer in English," and the versions of various parts of the Old or New Testament which had hitherto appeared.* Most of them were the work of William Tyndale, the translator of the Scriptures. To Tyndale the translator it will be necessary to recur; but now he must appear in the character, in which he is familiar to the reader of Sir Thomas More, of chief of the English heretics. He was a runagate friar, living in foreign parts, and seems to have been a man of severe temper and unfortunate life. Even after the doctrinal revolution, which he had no small share in effecting ultimately, much of Tyndale's teaching remained at variance with the English Church. But before the doctrinal revolution it was one mass of heresy. From the " Parable of the Wicked Mammon," or the " Obedience of a Christian Man," the Commissioners easily extracted a long list of blasphemous errors, and opinions deemed dangerous to the Commonwealth. The nature of justification came in everywhere. " Faith only justifies," said Tyndale : " the law makes us hate God, because we are born under the power of the devil. We are damned of nature; and so conceived and born, as a serpent is a serpent, and a toad a toad, and a snake a snake, by nature. As long as we look on the law, we see but sin and damnation : whereas we were damned before we were born, we cannot love God. Labouring in good works to come to heaven thou dost shame Christ's blood." He illustrated these

---

* Wilkins, iii. 727. As the English Primer is a subject to which I shall return, it may be noticed that the Primer here condemned seems from the errors enunciated in it to have been the original of the Primer of 1535, the first of the " Three Primers of Henry VIII," reprinted at Oxford in 1848, and known as Marshall's Primer. This Primer of 1535, it is curious to see, includes several tracts which were among those separately prohibited by the Proclamation of 1529, mentioned in the text. These are— Dialogue between the Father and the Son, Matins and Evensong, and some of the Psalms. *See* Wilkins, iii. 739.

positions with some shocking expressions. " Christ in all His deeds did not deserve heaven. Thou canst not be damned unless Christ be damned, nor Christ be saved unless thou be saved with Him. So far as pleasing God went, it were as good to wash dishes as be an Apostle." Behind this strong doctrine there lay principles which might easily become fatal to the established order of things, when they were put in the way of those who wanted an excuse for their own avarice or insubordination. "Alms deserveth no meed." " Build no more churches nor abbeys, but feed the poor." " Ceremonies of the Church have brought the world from God." " Churches are for preaching only." Beneath all lay communism bad or good. "Among Christian men love maketh all things common." " If the whole world were thine, yet hath every brother his right in thy goods." " Thy neighbour's need hath as good right in thy goods, as hath Christ himself."

With modern historians it is a favourite hypothesis that Lollardy was dead when Lutheranism, or Protestantism, was born. These writers are such vigorous necessitarians : they are so fond of marking evolutions and successions, and making everything the striking and inevitable consequence of something else, that they are to be heard with startled respect when they abandon their usual method, to affirm that one great religious movement had come to an end when another of a similar character began. It is, however, as difficult to agree with them as it is easy to see whence they have drawn this supposition. In so far as Lollardy had gone on to communism, at the end of the fourteenth century, it had arrayed against itself all the conservative forces of the country, and was put down by fire and sword at once. But as an attack on the Church, Lollardy never died out. The same alarmed legislators who passed the Heresy Act against Lollards, which began religious persecution in England, proposed soon afterwards in open parliament to confiscate the whole of Church property. The score of martyrs who graced the Lollard cause were not put to death in Cobham's rebellion, but were spread evenly over the century between the first Heresy Act and the accession of Henry the Eighth. During the same period the complaints of the clergy concerning the inquietation of the times never ceased. The tracts of Wycliffe continued to be read, and passed in manuscript from hand to hand until printing was invented. On the invention of printing they were the first of heretical books to appear in type. The statesmen and prelates of Henry the Eighth saw no difference between the heresies of their own day and the older Lollardy. To them a Lutheran was synonymous with a Lollard.* It is true that printing gave the means of greater activity to the heretics of Henry the Eighth. It is true also that those heretics knew instinctively the destructive disposition of the King, and that they strove to flatter his love of power in their writings. But these were no more than favourable circumstances; and we cannot conclude from them that one great religious movement had become extinct, and then that another began long after. The same thing was always in existence. If Lollardy was crushed in so far as it attacked private property, so in turn was Lutheranism or Protestantism in so far as it attacked private property. The Lollard socialists of the fourteenth and fifteenth centuries were succeeded by the Anabaptist socialists of the sixteenth century; and if the Lollard

---

* For instance, in this Proclamation of 1529 we read that " cognisance of heresies, errors, and Lollardies appertaineth to the judge of Holy Church."—*Wilkins*, iii. 739.

socialists were exterminated by sword and faggot most ruthlessly, the Anabaptist socialists who reached England dropped into a flame that withered them as fast as they arrived. There were more Anabaptists burned by Henry the Eighth than Lollards were burned in the whole of the previous century. But because, when Lutheranism was developed into socialism, it was stamped out, no one would say that Lutheranism died, and was afterwards succeeded by a separate movement in Puritanism. It is just as untenable that because Lollardy was stamped out when it went on to socialism, it died entirely, and was afterwards succeeded by another movement in Lutheranism. The three things were the same under different names, and socialism or communism was the final tendency of them all. Throughout those troubled ages the most serious thing to be contemplated is the ease and merciless-ness with which every attack on private ownership was repelled, in the midst of the most fearless and deliberate spoliation of the property of the Church.

The proper historical designation of those who set themselves against the doctrinal system of the Church at this time is one which they have seldom obtained in general history. If, according to the wont of history, they are to bear the name which their contemporaries gave them, they must be called the Heretics. To call them Lollards would not be wrong, since, as it has been seen, they were so called in contemporary documents ; nor is high modern authority wanting for this designa-tion.* But the name of Lollard is so identified with an earlier period, that it can scarcely be used as a common term in this. To call them Lutherans is to give too much prominence to a foreign element in their composition, as well as to exclude other foreign ele-

* Mr. Brewer uses it in his Introduction.

ments which their mingled nature gratefully received ; and it seems to bind them to terms of doctrine where they only imbibed a spirit. To call them Protestants is open to the same objections in strictness ; and, moreover tends to perpetuate a designation which the Church of England, even after the alteration of doctrine, has never received. To call them the New Learning is convenient, and is sanctioned by the older historians. It expresses their opposition to the Old Learning, to the " Duns men," to the scholastic theology, which to Latimer was " foolery," and to Tyndale, "Antichrist :" and it expresses their opposition to the old laws of the Church, which they unjustly called the Pope's laws. But the term must not be understood so as to confound them with the humanists, or men of culture, the greatest of whom abhorred and despised them. Their proper historical name is that which they have received the least.

The public instrument which the Commissioners published by order of the King is remarkable for containing a " Bill in English," to be set forth by those of the Commission who were preachers : perhaps the earliest example of a prescribed Homily. In executing the office of preacher they were to denounce the books enumerated as erroneous and heretical. and to warn the people to beware of false prophets. In particular it was declared that the versions of the Holy Scripture, now made in English, French, or Dutch, were full of error ; and the King, " for the incomparable zeal which he had to Christ's religion and faith," forbad all such books to be read or promulgated in his realm. He had heard, he added, the reports which were spread that all men were to have the Old and New Testament in the English tongue : and that himself, his nobles, and prelates were bound to suffer them to have the same. But he had consulted the said primates, and other persons well-learned in divinity; and by them all it was thought not necessary that the Scriptures should be in the hands of the common people; but that it should be left to the discretion of the superiors. The translation of the Scriptures would rather be the occasion of the increase of error among the people, than any good to their souls: and it was better for the Scriptures to be reserved to be expounded by the preachers in their sermons, as heretofore. This determination, however, was by no means inexorable; and if it appeared thereafter to the King's Highness that his people did utterly abandon and forsake all perverse, erroneous, and seditious opinions, and that all the corrupt translations were exterminated, "His Highness intended to provide that the Holy Scriptures should be by great, learned, and Catholic persons translated into the English tongue, if it should then seem to His Grace convenient to do." It is important to remark how early the project of an authorised version of the Bible was entertained by the Old Learning.

The Commissioners recorded particularly the freedom and unanimity with which they had acted. "Free liberty and license was granted," they said, "unto every man to say as his conscience and learning served him, without any reproach or blame to be imputed or convicted for anything to be spoken there, whose person soever was touched, of any necessity to agree to the more part, but only to say that his own learning and conscience could maintain and justify." They had come to their determinations "by a whole consent, no man repugning or gainsaying." Six months later, however, one of them saw fit to express his dissent from the conclusions in which he had agreed with the rest:

and Hugh Latimer wrote his celebrated letter to the
King, December 1, 1530, about allowing the Scriptures.
Latimer, now of the age of forty years, was rising fast
in reputation and in the favour of the King. As one of
the Commissioners who were preachers, it went doubtless against the grain with him to have to denounce
the books, and especially the versions of Scripture,
which were his favourite study. Rising therefore at
length, perhaps somewhat unnecessarily, into the style
of an Apostle, he addressed the King, who was about
his own age, with the salutation of "Grace, mercy, and
peace from God the Father by our Lord Jesus Christ."*
Proceeding in a strain of mingled dignity, earnestness,
and flattery, interlarded with puns and jokes such as
the King loved, he pleaded for the freedom of existing
versions of the Scriptures. He said that he would be
a Judas unto Christ no longer, nor a Scribe, nor a
Pharisee: that the people were blinded with customs,
ceremonies, and Banbury glosses, and punished with
cursings, excommunications, and other corruptions,
corrections he would say. He said that between the
King and himself, as concerning majesty and power,
there was as great difference as between God and man:
but in that the King was a mortal man, they were both
members of one body, and needed salvation. He said
that the Saviour was very poor, and His followers and
vicars ought not to regard riches: but it was possible
to have very little and yet have a greedy mind: and
there were those who professed wilful poverty and yet
had lords' lands and kings' riches. Such as these
were, he said, would set debate between king and
king, between realm and realm, between king and subjects, and cause rebellion against the temporal power,

---

* Sir Thomas More somewhere observes that all the Heretics wrote as
if they were Apostles.

rather than lose one jot of what they had. He said
that the King might see that the spiritualty (as they
would be called) were no true followers of Christ, by
the crafty means which they devised to break the laws
made by the last Parliament against their superfluities.
He meant not, however, to say, he said, that all of the
spiritualty were corrupt with this ambition, for there
were some good of them : and he meant not that the
King should take away the goods of the Church, but
take away evil men from the goods, and put better in
their place. He named no persons, all that he said
was, "By their fruits ye shall know them." He then
went on to shew himself well acquainted with the
forbidden books and glosses, by quoting St. Matthew
thus : "Seeing they called me Beelzebub, what marvel
is it if they call you devilish persons and heretics?"
and declaring that those who forbad the Scriptures had
belly-wisdom enough to wish to keep "the Wicked
Mammon." As concerning the Scriptures, he said that
he hoped the King would speedily perform his promise,
and let the people have them ; the late prohibition was
caused by those whose evil living and hypocrisy the
prohibited books exposed. There were three or four
present at the time when they were prohibited who
would have had the Scriptures go forth in English ;
but the most part had overcome the better. He said
that the proclamation was not the King's, nor was it
taken as the King's, but as set forth in the King's name
by false persuaders who would send a thousand men to
hell ere they would send one to God, and who forbad
the English New Testament on pretence of error,
though it was meekly offered to any man that would
amend it. Some had been punished for retaining those
books, he said, and worldly men sought to persuade his
Grace that they would cause insurrections and heresies,
but that was all false : only let the people have curates

that did their duty, and neither those books nor the devil himself could hurt them. His purpose in writing to the King was, he said, love to God, allegiance to his Grace, and not to hide his own talent, but chaffer it forth to others, and to warn the King to avoid mischievous flatterers, and their abominable ways and doings.* Thus Latimer delivered his soul. He was quite safe in so doing. The King was diverting himself in private with the Book of Beggars.

The Proclamations against heresy urged upon the bishops and clergy a course of conduct which was little likely to increase their favour with the people. They were to destroy books and imprison heretics. The relapsed they were to deliver over to the secular jurisdiction. In their inquisitions they were to be assisted by the sheriffs, mayors, bailiffs, and constables ; but they themselves were to pay all the costs incurred by those officers in hunting after heretics.† Under these mandates some of the ordinaries were impelled into an unfortunate activity. Many enquiries were instituted, many abjurations were made, many penances performed, and several noted executions for heresy disfigure this part of the history of the Church. But so far was Henry from designing to increase the authority or dignity of the clergy, that he was even then devising against them a piece of degradation which could not have been safely practised upon any other body of men within the realm, and which would be incredible of any other king.

It seemed somewhat incredible that the King should have ruined Wolsey, under the old statutes of Præmunire, for exercising the office of a Papal legate, when he had himself in the strongest terms urged

---

* Fox or Latimer's Remains.
† Wilkins, iii. 740.

the Pope to make him a Papal legate, when he had granted him a license under the great seal to use the authority of a legate, and had allowed the functions of legate to be discharged by him for fifteen years. It may perhaps seem more incredible that he should now have strained the force of those ancient safeguards of English liberty against the whole clergy, for having submitted to the legate whom he himself had set over them. This, however, was the measure which the head of the State ecclesiastical and civil had now matured. To do him justice, it came not of his own unaided wit. He was now fallen under the influence of the worst enemy that the Church of England ever had.

Thomas Crumwel was the son of a blacksmith, of Putney. An aptness for the times has often stood in the stead of public virtue or of high ability: and the unparalleled rise of Crumwel can only be regarded as the luck of a keen but low-minded political adventurer. In his youth he had been, as he said himself, "a ruffian." Like many of the leaders of the Reformation, he had been fond of rambling about foreign countries, instead of taking to some honest calling at home, and met with some remarkable adventures in his travels.* He had been a trooper, a clerk, and a money-lender. He was a good cook : and he had a traveller's knowledge of the modern languages : to which

---

* The story of the pardons of St. Botolph's of Boston, and the jellies which Crumwel made for the Pope, is to be seen in Fox, where there are other stories of the youth of Crumwel, which are disproved by chronology. In fact, Fox's life of Crumwel is a mere romance. The character which he gives of his favourite hero would need qualifying if it were applied to an Alfred. "Such was the activity and forward ripeness of nature in him, so pregnant in wit, and so ready; he was, in judgment discreet, in tongue eloquent, in service faithful, in stomach courageous, in his pen active ; that, being conversant in the sight of men, he could not be long unespied, nor yet unprovided of favour and help of friends to set him forward in place and office : neither was any place or office put unto him whereunto he was not apt and fit," &c.

he added perhaps a smattering of Latin. His memory was strong, if it be true that he learned by heart on his road back to England the whole of Erasmus's Paraphrase on the New Testament. That celebrated work opened his eyes to the importance of the New Learning. He was "touched and called to a better understanding." He saw all things perfectly.* At the same time he had learned from other studies another lesson. He is said (though this may be doubted) to have read Machiavelli, and from that great writer to have imbibed the principles which a bad mind may easily extract. He held that vice and virtue are but names, fit to amuse the learned, but not to be esteemed by him who would rise in the courts of princes. The great art of the politician was, in his judgment, to penetrate into the secret inclinations of sovereigns, and discover the means of gratifying them without appearing to outrage decency and religion.† He therefore learned to disguise for the present his conversion to the New Learning: his political maxims he was less careful to conceal.

Thus prepared by study and travel, he contrived after his return to get himself received into the household of Wolsey.‡ He was preferred to be Solicitor to the Cardinal; and was entrusted with the work of suppressing the small religious houses which Wolsey

* Fox.

† This Machiavellian story rests on a weak foundation. Pole says that he heard Crumwel holding this language in Wolsey's palace; and that Crumwel told him he got it out of a book which he offered to lend him; he adds that long afterwards he met with the same sentiments in the Prince of Machiavelli, which he therefore supposed to be the book that Crumwel meant. (*Ap. ad Cæs.*) But the Prince was not published till 1532, though it was certainly written in 1513.

‡ Fox, who erroneously says that he was an inmate of Wolsey's house along with More and Gardiner, takes the opportunity of comparing him with those illustrious men. If there was more of human learning in More and Gardiner, there was, it seems, in Crumwel "a more heavenly light of the mind, and more prompt and perfect judgment," together with "a more heroical and princely disposition."

dissolved to found his colleges. In this he showed great industry and forwardness, not forgetting to enrich himself: though at the same time he incurred much enmity and censure from the less enlightened "for his rude manner and homely dealing in defacing the monks' houses, and in handling of their altars."* Such was Crumwel's first essay in the art of suppression.

On the fall of the Cardinal, he found himself in danger. Whatever was blamed in the conduct of Wolsey was, it seems, imputed to him. He was the object of general detestation; and there were not wanting those who spoke unfavourably of him to the King. He immediately took a resolution as bold as it was prudent; to abandon the Cardinal, and seek the King in person. After the lacrymose scene in the great chamber at Asher, which is so graphically described by Cavendish, Crumwel rode to London, resolved, in his own phrase, "to make or mar."† He had

---

* Cavendish. Compare Darcy's Articles against Wolsey: "Item, the abomination, ruin, and seditious and erroneous violations used at the pulling down of the abbies by his commissioners, and servants at his commandments, and the great robberies and spoilings, may be weighed to the worst act, or article of Martin Luther's: as will be proved, if good trials and examination be had thereof, which is over odible and spiteful against the law of Christ to be written in this bill, and never punishment of any person so offending as yet, but rewarded with his high gifts and promotion."—*Brewer, Lett. For. and Dom.* iv. p. 2551.

† Crumwel has obtained the praise of fidelity to his master; but it is impossible to allow that he deserved it greatly. 1. Cavendish, in his Life of Wolsey, describes the "very strange sight," of Crumwel, leaning in the window at Asher, with a Primer in his hand, praying and weeping, because he had got an ill name in his master's cause. Presently, when Wolsey comes in, Crumwel reproaches him for not having enriched his *servants*, though he had promoted his *chaplains* to rich preferments. Wolsey answers that he had only spiritual preferments to give. The enemy of the clergy then proposes that the chaplains disburse to pay the servants; and another scene follows in which this is done, Crumwel himself disbursing five pounds, though he had just been complaining of his poverty. 2. Having thus conciliated the gentleman servants of the cardinal, he rides off to London "to make or mar." 3. The same evening, November 1,

friends at court, and among them Sir John Russell, the founder of one of the great sacrilegious families of England ; and by force of intrigue he immediately contrived, in his own phrase again, " to put his foot into Parliament," by some means not clearly known.* The memorable Parliament of 1529 was on the point of assembling; and Crumwel presently gained a great reputation for magnanimity by defending his fallen master against the articles of treason which were brought into the Commons. But before Crumwel ventured on the defence of Wolsey, the King had already signified his pleasure not to proceed to extremities.

Crumwel's next object was to obtain an interview with the King : and in this he succeeded by the aid

1529, after his departure, comes his friend, Sir John Russell, on horseback from London; makes a lame story about being sent by the King to comfort the Cardinal, and departs before day, declaring that " he would not for anything" that his visit to Asher were known. 4. Crumwel gets into Parliament, as Cavendish believed, perhaps wrongly, by taking the place of the son of Sir Thomas Rush, "a special friend of his;" and having ascertained that the King was inclined to leniency, returns to Asher in a day or two, "with a much pleasanter countenance than he had at his departure." Here he had a secret interview with Wolsey, rode back the same night, and next day won glory by defending his master. 5. Crumwel however, certainly befriended him after his fall, but never to his own danger. He was always willing to do a good turn when it suited him; this was his way with everybody : "he served all their turns, so that they had their purposes, and he their good wills." Cavendish generally insinuates this whenever he speaks of him.

* Crumwel was member for Taunton in 1529; Rush was member for Ipswich. How Crumwel got his seat Mr. Brewer has not been able to ascertain (Lett. and Pap. iv. p. xxxviii.) ; but adds subsequently a letter from Ralph Sadler, who was sent to London to secure him a seat, to say that he had spoken to Vice-Chamberlain Gage to speak to the Duke of Norfolk to get him a "burgesse's room of Parliament," and that the Duke had spoken to the King, who was content to have him elected if he would follow the Duke's instructions. Sadler advises Crumwel to speak to Norfolk "as soon as possible to-morrow to know the King's pleasure how you shall order yourself in Parliament." 1st Nov., 1529 (p. 3178). Mr. Green says that Crumwel had sat in the Parliament before this.— *Hist. of English People*, p. 326.

probably of Norfolk or of Russell. Russell had before this informed the King, with great truth, that there was no man in England so fit for his purposes as Thomas Crumwel. A more momentous interview never took place than that which followed, when these two men first looked on one another. Crumwel had not studied in vain to penetrate the secret mind of princes, when for the first time he knelt before the formidable despot who was to use him, to enrich and ennoble him, to delegate to him his own highest functions, and then to cast him out to infamy and death. His cunning was deep, his resources and ability considerable, his boldness great : but it would have been well for him and for his country if he had never matched those ordinary qualities against that unscrupulous will and that remorseless heart.*

The thing that stood nearest with the King was the Divorce, and the humiliation of the clergy who opposed the Divorce. His passion for Anne Boleyn was goaded to madness by the art which neither yielded nor denied : the delays of the Papal Chamber in giving sentence added to his uncertainty and rage. Pending the sentence of the Pope, the clergy, and especially the regulars, were bold in their denunciation of the project. In the pulpit and in private discourse they hesitated not to declare that for the King to put away his wife for the cause alleged, and to marry

* I place this interview in the few days which elapsed between Crumwel's first journey from Asher and his return thither. He left Asher November 1. Parliament opened November 3. He came back to Asher "within two or three days after his entry into Parliament," says Cavendish, "with a much pleasanter countenance than he had at his departure," and after an interview with Wolsey, rode back the same night to London to defend Wolsey in Parliament next morning. He had no doubt ascertained the King's merciful intentions to the fallen Cardinal, and Pole expressly says that it was the day after the King's intentions were known that Crumwel obtained an audience.—*Pole*, p. 120.

another, was to commit adultery. Crumwel lamented the anxiety of his sovereign. He presumed to think, he said, that the difficulties of the King arose from counsellors who regarded outward appearances, and feared the opinion of the vulgar. But the learned were in his favour. The sentences of the Universities had been given. Why wait for the approbation of the Pope, which might indeed be useful to prevent the interference of the Emperor for his aunt, the Queen, but could not alter the right of the King? Let the King follow the example of the German princes who had thrown off the yoke of the Pope : let him, with the aid of Parliament, declare himself Head of the Church within his own realm. At present England was a monster with two heads. But let the King assert the authority which was now usurped by the Pontiff, and every anomaly, every difficulty would vanish. The clergy, holding their lives and goods at his disposal, would become the obsequious ministers of his will.*

This discourse, delivered, perhaps, in that high flourishing manner, that mixture of deference and "stoutness," by which Crumwel afterwards recommended his company to the King, was heard with pleasure. It flattered three of the worst passions of Henry's nature : his love of Anne, his love of money, and his love of power. Crumwel was forthwith admitted to the favour and intimacy of the King : he was confirmed in the stewardship of the lands of the dissolved monasteries, which he had held under Wolsey : and in no long time began that unexampled accumulation of offices and dignities upon himself, through

* It is not likely that Crumwel said all this. It is Pole who gives the discourse, adding that he was putting together what he had heard Crumwel and others say at different times, but that he had invented nothing : "quæ minime ex meo ingenio excogitavi, ut verisimilia, sed ex illorum ore excepi." *Apol. ad Cæs.*

which for ten terrible years the fortunes of the Church of England were at his mercy. Throughout the year 1530 he was frequently in personal communication with the King; and by giving pensions to laymen out of Wolsey's see of Winchester, out of the revenues of St. Albans, and of the Cardinal's colleges in Oxford and Ipswich, he formed a powerful party at court.*

During the same year (in which, as it has been seen, the sittings both of Parliament and of Convocation were suspended) the mine was deliberately laid against the Church and the clergy, to which the match was applied in the month of December.

In December 1530 the Attorney-General was instructed to file an information in the Court of King's

---

* That Crumwel immediately gained the King's intimacy after his first interview, may be concluded from the fact which Cavendish relates, that in February 1530, four months after that interview, he "made only suit to the King's own person" on behalf of Wolsey (to whose house he had returned), that the Cardinal might be allowed to change his residence (vol. i. p. 226). The persons to whom pensions were granted out of the lands of Winchester appear to have been the Duke of Norfolk, Lord Sandys, and his son Thomas, Sir William Fitzwilliam, Sir Henry Guilford, Sir John Russell, Sir Henry Norris, and George Boleyn, Viscount of Rochford and father of Anne. These grants were confirmed by a special Act, 22 Hen. VIII. 22. How Crumwel climbed into power may be illustratively shewn from what Cavendish says about this : "Then began both noblemen and other, who had any patents of the King, out either of Winchester or St. Albans, to make earnest suit to Master Crumwel for to solicit their causes to my lord (Wolsey), to get of him their confirmations, and for his pains therein sustained they promised every man, not only worthily to reward him, but also to shew him such pleasures as should at all times lie in their several powers, whereof they assured him. Wherein Master Crumwel perceiving an occasion and a time given him to work for himself, and to bring the thing to pass which he long wished for, intended so to work in this matter, to serve their desires, that he might the sooner bring his own enterprise to purpose." "In process of time he served all their turns, so that they had their purposes, and he their good wills. Thus rose his name and friendly acceptance with all men. The fame of his honesty and wisdom sounded so in the King's ears, that, by reason of his access to the King, he perceived to be in him no less wisdom than fame of him had made report," &c.— P. 230.

Bench against the whole body of the Clergy, for having fallen under the Statutes of Præmunire and Provisors, by acknowledging the legatine authority of Cardinal Wolsey. The beauties of this procedure will bear a close inspection. At the beginning of the parliamentary session of the year before, when the usual General Pardon was granted, "all offences and contempts committed and done against the Statute or Statutes of Provisions and Præmunire, or any of them, and all forfeitures and titles that might grow to the King's Highness by reason of any of the same statutes"* had been among the exceptions. This was done at the time in order to exclude Cardinal Wolsey himself from the General Pardon. It was now discovered that it also excluded the whole body of the clergy : and that they stood exposed to the penalties of the violated laws. It would have been in vain to have urged that, if the clergy had incurred a Præmunire, the laity were in the same case ; that the whole kingdom was under a Præmunire ; that every suitor who had brought his case into the court of the late unfortunate legate rather than into the ancient ecclesiastical courts of England was a special offender ; and that the King himself, who had set up the legatine court, was the most guilty of all.† More hazardous, if equally just, would have been the retort that the King had lately broken the same statutes, if they were broken at all, in a far more scandalous manner by bringing his own case into the court of legates, one of whom was a foreigner, even though he held another

---

* 21 Hen. VIII. i. 7.

† If the case came under the statutes at all, then it is true, as Mr. Froude has pointed out, that one of them provided for the contingency of a violation of them by the King himself, and ordered the person at whose instance the King acted to be punished, if an ecclesiastic, by the loss of his temporalities for one year. This did not touch *all* the clergy. The same statute also ordered that, if he were a temporal person, he should pay the value of his lands and possessions not moveable for one year, or be imprisoned one year. (13 Rich. II. 11.)

office in the realm.* It would have availed nothing to
have argued that after all the case was not within the
purview of those statutes, which do not so much as
mention the character of legate. To have argued the
circumstances of the case, granted even that it came
by construction within the statutes, to have alleged
that when the statutes were passed a dispensing power
was given to the sovereign to suspend their operation
at his discretion, and that Henry had exercised this
power by giving to Wolsey a patent under the Great
Seal : this would have been a line of argument possible
to the Commons, possible to the meanest corporation
of laymen in the kingdom, but which the clergy of
England could not venture to pursue. They dared
as little to have insinuated that for them to be
singled out for prosecution, while the King and the
laity left one another alone, was peculiarly hard, since
the only resistance that had been offered to the
legate and his courts had come from them.

These pleas, all of which might have been urged
with the utmost justice by the clergy, were not urged.
They remain merely as illustrations of the monstrous
injustice which any one of them would have been sufficient to prove. The clergy knew their weakness better.
They knew that they had to expect justice as little from
the King's lawyers as from the King; that, after such
a beginning, the process, if it had been carried out,
would have ended in their utter ruin: they would have
been pronounced out of the King's protection, their
goods and lives would have been at the mercy of him
and of all men. In the same way the man whose Legation furnished the pretext for the whole proceeding,

* It may, however, be urged that the King's case was of spiritual
cognisance, being a case of matrimony, and that he was not wrong in
submitting it to the Roman legates.

Wolsey, had felt his weakness when the Præmunire was alleged against him. He had forborne to urge any of the above pleas, which he might as justly have used then as the clergy now, and preferred to throw himself upon the King's mercy. Of the King's mercy he received some poor share during the year that he lingered on earth after his fall; but of the clergy it may be said that though their composition with the King forestalled the full rigours to which they might have been exposed, yet the King probably extorted from them as much as he would have dared to take if the legal process had been carried to an end.*

Wolsey died the month before this attack upon the clergy was opened. The foremost man of his age, the last of the great ecclesiastical ministers of England, in foresight and ability at least the not unworthy successor of the Beckets and the Langtons, he expired with words upon his lips which shewed that he understood the true nature of the impending revolution. It is the fault of an age of progress to believe itself unlike every previous age. The notions and opinions which agitate the leaders of progress are by them believed to be discoveries which have never been made before; whereas in truth the same elements, the elements of conservation and of change, have struggled together in every age, and revolution has always developed itself in the same manner. In listening to the dying words of Wolsey we may perceive the same forces at work, organised in the same manner, in the sixteenth century,

---

* The defence which Mr. Froude sets up for this procedure of the King is very remarkable. The clergy "were to be punished indirectly for their other evil doings, and forced to surrender some portion of the unnumbered exactions which they had extorted from the helplessness of their flock." "Their punishment, if tyrannical in form was equitable in substance, and we can reconcile ourselves without difficulty to an act of judicial confiscation."—Vol. i. pp. 294, 296.

which are seen in all times of revolution, and which
may be seen now. The attack upon the Church first:
the carelessness or amusement with which the temporal
estates regard the struggles of the clergy to maintain
themselves, as if the temporal estates and dignities
would not be the next assaulted, if the Church were
overthrown: and communism lurking at the bottom
of all.*

The struggle now actually commencing between

---

* "Say furthermore that I request his Grace, in God's name, that he
have a vigilant eye to depress this new pernicious sect of Lutherans, that
it do not increase within his dominions through his negligence, in such a
sort that he shall be fain at length to put harness upon his back to subdue
them: as the King of Bohemia did, who had good game to see his rude
commons (then infected with Wickliffe's heresies) to spoil and murder
the spiritual men and religious persons of his realm: the which fled to the
King and his nobles for succour against their frantic rage: of whom they
could get no help of defence or refuge, but they laughed them to scorn,
having good game at their spoil and consumption, not regarding their
duties nor their own defence. And when those erroneous heretics had
subdued all the clergy and spiritual persons, taking the spoil of their
riches, both of churches, monasteries, and all other spiritual things,
having no more to spoil, they caught such a courage of their former
liberty, that then they disdained their prince and sovereign lord with all
other noble personages, and the head governors of the country, and began
to fall in hand with the temporal lords to slay and spoil them, without
mercy or pity, most cruelly. Insomuch that the King and other his
nobles were constrained to put harness upon their backs, to resist the
ungodly powers of these traitorous heretics, and to defend their lives and
liberties, who pitched a field royal against them: in which field those
traitors so stoutly encountered, the party of them was so cruel and
vehement, that in fine they were victors and slew the King, the lords, and
all the gentlemen of the realm, leaving not one person that bare the
name or port of a gentleman alive, or of any person that had any rule
or authority in the commonweal. By means of which slaughter they
have lived ever since in great misery and poverty without a head or
governor, living all in common like wild beasts abhorred of all Christian
nations.... In the history of King Richard the Second, which lived in
that same time of Wickliffe's seditious opinions, did not the Commons,
I pray you, rise against the King and the nobles of the realm of England:
whereof some they apprehended, whom they without mercy or justice put
to death? and did they not fall to spoiling and robbery to the intent they
might bring all things in common?" &c.—*Cavendish*, vol. i. p. 321.

the King and the clergy, which ended in the victory of
the former, consisted of two great parts or actions,
rapidly succeeding one another, in which the spiritual
jurisdiction was destroyed. The first was the Præmunire, which led to the King's new title of the Supreme
Head of the Church. The second was the Supplication of the Commons, of the year following, which
brought about the formal Submission of the clergy.
The history of the conflict has not been preserved
with exact accuracy amid the fame of the victory: and
the glory of the conqueror has been doubled by the
singular process of detracting from the firmness and
skill of his adversaries. But strict inquiry will teach
us in great part to reverse the popular representations,
and will make it apparent that the resistance of the
defeated party was by no means inglorious; that the
triumph of the victor, so far at least as words went,
was not so complete as it is generally supposed; and
that though the fruits of victory passed to the stronger,
the honours of the day remained with the weaker of
the combatants. But before attempting this investigation, it is necessary to ascertain what was the object
of contention, what the position which the King and
the clergy attacked and defended.

Crumwel is reported to have told the King on
one occasion that England was a monster having two
heads. By this he meant, if he ever spoke the words,
that the Pope possessed here a spiritual supremacy
that was co-ordinate with the temporal supremacy of
the King, and that the King possessed a temporal
supremacy only. The illustration would have commended itself to a sovereign who from the beginning
of his reign had shown the strongest inclination to
aggrandise his prerogative at the expense of the
liberties both of his people and his church. And this

view of the case has been repeated in effect by many writers. It has been asserted that before this time the King's supremacy was temporal only, and that it was the object of Henry to acquire to the crown the spiritual supremacy also, which had hitherto belonged to the Pope. But this notion, though now universal, is wholly modern and contrary to the truth. We must not be misled by the term "supremacy," which first began to be applied to the papal power in England after that power had been taken away. It was not applied to the papal power so long as the papal power existed; while on the other hand, it was always applied to the kingly power and properly expressed the nature of the same. What the Pope possessed in England was spiritual jurisdiction: he was the head of the spiritual jurisdiction of the realm, by the King's consent, because he was the spiritual father of Christendom. But this jurisdiction was neither in word nor deed a supremacy rivalling that of the sovereign.* The sovereign was at all times the head of the realm, both of the spiritualty and the temporalty, whether or not he bore a title to express his spiritual supremacy. Sometimes he had borne titles which did express it. In the laws of Edward the Confessor he was termed the Vicar of Christ: a title which seems as expressive as that which was taken by Henry the Eighth. The jurisdiction of the Pope had been limited by one statute after another: and that part of it which had been allowed to remain (the appeal in purely spiritual things, as matrimony, divorce, presentment, and right

---

* I question whether the word "supremacy" is ever applied to the Papal jurisdiction in any of the documents of the age. Power, jurisdiction, or authority are the names applied to it by those who lived under it and by those who abolished it. But to the royal prerogative the word "supremacy" is constantly applied, because supremacy was what the King had.

of tithes), was matter of grant from the temporal power. Hence the Pope might be termed "the Apostle" in English law books; his see might be acknowledged the See Apostolic by the English Church; the primate of all England might be of the number of his legates born; without this jurisdiction making him co-ordinate with the head of the imperial realm.

The Papal jurisdiction, or authority in spirituals, was not the object of Henry's attack, but the liberties of the Church of England. The proof of this is, that the Pope's jurisdiction fell after the fall of those liberties, not before it. The Pope's jurisdiction fell in consequence of the fall of those liberties; and they were not abridged, that it might be abrogated. At the time when Henry was attacking the clergy, he was acknowledging the Pope's jurisdiction in the amplest manner by suing before him. At the time when the clergy were defending their liberties, they professed themselves ready to renounce the obedience of the Pope. By both parties, therefore, the liberties of the Church were considered a different thing from the jurisdiction of Rome :* and the notion that the object of the one was to impugn, and of the other to maintain the Pope in England falls to the ground.

Were, then, the liberties of the Church in themselves of a nature to endanger or enfeeble the supreme authority of the Crown? This cannot be affirmed, for the simple reason that they were matters of grant from the Crown. The clergy of England, as accredited magistrates and ministers of the spiritual body politic,

---

* Perhaps it would be more correct to say that to acknowledge the Pope was one—and only one—of the liberties of the Church; that it was one for which the clergy seem to have cared little; and that it was the one which fell last, after all the others had been swept away.

had been invested with certain privileges and immunities. They made spiritual laws and canons in their own assembly without the royal assent. They had privilege of sanctuary and privilege of clergy. They had considerable executive power. Such liberties as these had been granted and confirmed to them by the greatest English kings, who held it to be for the advantage of the realm that the Church should be free. But every time that they had been granted or confirmed their true nature was declared: that they were concessions from the Crown. Every time that the clergy petitioned the King to respect them, the same thing was acknowledged. They, indeed, claimed some of them by right divine. But the admission of the claim, like the admission of Christianity itself within the realm, lay with the prince. He refused it, indeed, at his proper peril, but he might refuse it: and in the present instance he did refuse it.

Henry, therefore, cannot be said to have introduced a new principle into the English system when he took away the liberties of the Church. He took away what his predecessors had granted, and he did this oppressively and abominably. But he was the supreme head of the realm as much before he did it as he was when he had done it.

As the King could hardly hope to detain all the goods of the clergy in forfeiture under his allegation of a Præmunire, it seems to have been intimated to them that a composition in money would be accepted. They, on the other hand, shrunk from a trial in King's Bench, where, though they might have suffered in purse no greater loss than they were likely to sustain without trial, they would have had every point strained to insure their condemnation. A composition by money, therefore, was the solution which was most acceptable

to both parties : and it was on this understanding that
the clergy mustered to begin that memorable struggle
with the Crown which is now to be recounted.

The Convocation of Canterbury met, January 21,
1531, not in St. Paul's, but in the Chapter House of
Westminster, as being a more convenient place.   On
this occasion the abbot of the exempt monastery of
Westminster put in a protestation that the meeting
was to be without prejudice to the privileges of his
house : which protestation was formally admitted by
the Archbishop.   The King's spiritual subjects then
proceeded to consider the situation in which they stood.
As they had decided to waive every plea and to accept the alternative of a fine, rather than risk certain
condemnation in a Crown court, they wisely resolved
to say nothing whatever about the Præmunire, but to
vote their forfeiture in the usual manner of a subsidy
or grant.   The subsidies of the spiritualty had been
larger in proportion, granted with a better grace, and
paid more regularly than those of the laity, in all times
of English history.   They now resolved to pay, in the
name of a subsidy, a fine which promised to gratify
the royal cupidity, even if the amount were not already
prescribed.   A hundred and forty-four thousand pounds
eight shillings and eight pence, payable in five years,
was the offering which they made to the violated law.
As the clergy of York followed, May 4, with the grant
of eighteen thousand eight hundred and forty pounds
and ten pence, the whole spiritualty was mulcted in a
sum nearly equal to two millions of our money.*

In the " book " or instrument in which they made
this extraordinary concession or grant they exhausted
the language of flattery, while they avoided the least
allusion to the real circumstances of the case.   The

* Wilkins, vol. iii. pp. 724, 744.

cause of their benevolence they declared to be the great and incomparable benefits of the King towards them, which required not only verbal thanks and praise, but also a spontaneous oblation of money. So great were the merits of his Majesty that they could be equalled by no praises, answered by no thanks, repaid by no services, much less recompensed by gifts. In former days he had defended the universal Church by sword and pen so mightily, so victoriously, that he had earned eternal fame, and opened for himself a passage to the heavens. A thousand foes, the Lutherans especially, had conspired against the Church and clergy of England, and by books crammed with lies and bad language sought to bring them to contempt with the people. But his Majesty, as the pious Defender of the Faith and of the Church, had quelled their audacity by his labours, studies, counsels, monitions, edicts, and authority. This was wise in him, since the attack was not only on the Church and the prelates, but against all princes. There was, indeed, a hypocritical pretence of religion and following of the Gospel, but the real design was to pull down the Church and seize her possessions. They were unwilling that his Majesty should deem them ungrateful for all his benefits towards them.*

But the weapons of fear were employed in vain. It soon appeared that money would not satisfy the violated majesty of justice wholly. The clergy had sent off their book or instrument of grant, when, February 7, several judges and members of the Privy Council presented themselves in the Chapter House. They brought back the book, with certain articles or clauses to be added to it before the offered subsidy would be accepted. These emendations were five in

* Wilkins, vol. iii. p. 742.

number : their tenor is famous in history. The first required the King to be styled the only Protector and Supreme Head of the Church and clergy of England. The second was a sort of corollary of this : that the cure of souls was committed to his Majesty. The third limited the duty of the King, as Defender of the Church, to the maintenance of those only of her privileges and liberties which derogated not from his regal power and the laws of his kingdom. The fourth brought in the condition which the clergy had wished to evade, and extended the King's general pardon to them as offenders against the Statutes of Præmunire. The fifth seemed merely to provide that laymen into whose hands the goods of the Church should come pending the payment of the subsidy (as through vacancies of livings or otherwise), should bear their share of the burden.*

The judges and councillors came back again next day, and the debate began. The last article was taken first ; and this was passed without difficulty. But when it came to the fourth, concerning the pardon, the judges and councillors said that they had no commission to

---

* " Reverendissimus, habita secreta communicatione cum quibusdam consiliariis et justitiariis domini regis, tractatum instituit cum prolocutore, decanis, &c., et clero super materia articulorum additorum in proemio libri concessionis subsidii, qui hujus erant tenoris.

" 1. Ecclesiæ et cleri Anglicani, cujus Protector et Supremum Caput is solus est.

" 2. Quem metum atque periculum rex noster invictissimus a nobis depulit, et curavit ut in quiete et secura pace Deo ministrare, et curæ animarum ejus majestati commissæ et populo sibi commisso debite inservire possimus.

" 3. Privilegia et libertates ejusdem (sc. ecclesiæ) quæ regali suæ potestati et legibus regni sui non detrahant, confirmando defendit.

" 4. Generalem veniam et pardonationem de omnibus eorum transgressionibus poenalium legum et statutorum hujus regni tam cæterorum in tam ampla forma concedere dignetur, quam in isto parliamento suis omnibus subditis (statutis de Præmunire nobis adauctis) concessa fuit.

" 5. Ita quod omnes laici sint inde onerati."—*Wilkins*, vol. iii. p. 725.

conclude upon that before the bishops and clergy had
concluded upon the first three, concerning the Supremacy of the King. The clergy who had granted away
their money without difficulty, hesitated to acknowledge the supremacy in the new terms proposed. This
is that mind of the clergy which seems inconceivable
to some of the writers of English history. They
were the official guardians of the Church : they knew
the Church to be passing through a great crisis :
and it seemed to them that if there were any necessity
now to make a formal acknowledgment of the royal
supremacy, it should be made in more moderate terms.
It is owned, however, even by their avowed enemies
that it was to their credit, whether they were right or
wrong, that their resistance began upon points touching
.their position, not their purses.

For three sessions they held debate with the
King's councillors to obtain some modification of the
first article. At length the King sent the father of
his mistress, now Viscount Rochford, to them with
power to add the words "next God" (*post Deum*) to
Supreme Head : and refused further conference on
the matter. The debate was nevertheless renewed
among the clergy : and at last, February 11, the Archbishop proposed the article in these terms : "We
acknowledge his Majesty to be the singular Protector,
only and supreme Lord, and, so far as the law of
Christ allows, Supreme head of the English Church
and clergy."* The amendment was received in silence.
" Whoever is silent seems to consent," said the Archbishop. To which someone replied, " Then, are we
all silent." Thereupon the article was subscribed to
by both houses ; and with this the King was content.

* Ecclesiæ et cleri Anglicani, cujus singularem protectorem, unicum
et supremum Dominum, et, quantum per Christi leges licet, etiam
Supremum Caput, ipsius Majestatem recognoscimus.—*Wilkins, ib.*

The clergy were not less successful in obtaining modifications of the remaining articles. The second of these, in the form in which it was first propounded to them, declared the cure of souls to be committed to the King. This unaccustomed phrase was altered to the cure of the souls of the people committed to the King. The third article, which spoke of the King defending those privileges and liberties of the Church which were not derogatory to the regale and the kingdom, might mean much or nothing; and yet seemed meant to have opened questions which would certainly have been decided against the Church. It was entirely expunged, and an expression of confidence inserted instead that the Defender of the Faith would manifest his wonted zeal against all who attacked the Church. The fourth article, touching the General Pardon, was modified so as to exclude all mention of the previous session of Parliament, in which the General Pardon had been granted. This was important, because when the General Pardon had been granted all offenders whatsoever against the Statutes of Præmunire had been expressly excepted. If, therefore, the clergy were now pardoned, the laity still remained under the exception. But the original draft of the article had been cunningly framed to imply that the General Pardon had been extended already to the lay subjects, the clergy only being reserved under penalty: which was the opposite of the truth. By the amendment, which they carried, the clergy made it clear that the pardon was only now extended to them, and that all other transgressors of the statutes were still under penalty: which was the truth.*

---

* These three articles finally stood thus:—"Et curæ animarum populi ejus majestati commissi dehinc servire possimus. Summe confidimus quod ejus celsitudo ex sua in Deum ingenti pietate, proque clarissimo

The victory which the Southern clergy may be considered to have obtained over the King and his councillors, as it regards the amendments in the terms in which the supremacy was acknowledged, was enhanced by the boldness of their brethren of the North. It seems that even the qualified acknowledgment which had been made was immediately wrested by the ill-affected into a denial of the jurisdiction of bishops. Tunstall, Bishop of Durham, hereupon committed to writing his solemn protestation against the title of Supreme Head, even though limited by the clause, "so far as the law of Christ allows." The title, he said, might have three meanings, referring either to temporals, or to spirituals, or to both; the limiting clause was ambiguous, since it left uncertain what it was that the law of Christ allowed. All worldly and earthly honour was to be given to the King which could be given to a Christian prince by his spiritual and priestly subjects; but words were not to be put forth which might be perverted to a scandalous meaning by the weak or the malignant. He desired his protestation to be entered in the registry of the Convocation of York.*

The example of Tunstall was followed by others of the Northern bishops, and their protestations were deemed of sufficient importance to receive an answer

---

fidei Defensoris nomine, quod præ cæteris regibus longe honoratissimum jam olim promeruit, Christi fidem et ecclesiam solito zelo contra bereticos et alios oppugnatores potenter defendet. Et ut omnibus et singulis prælatis, clericis, et religiosis . . . . generalem gratiam et pardonationem de omnibus eorum transgressionibus pœnalium legum, et statutorum hujus regni, tum ceterorum tum etiam statutorum De Provisionibus et Præmunire, in tam amplo modo et forma, prout suæ Majestati ex solita sua benignitate in subditos suos sæpius ostendere placuit, concedere dignetur, nobis ea condonans, quæ nobis humilibus suis subditis prodesse, et ab angustiis, quibus versamur, liberare poterunt."— *Wilkins,* iii. 743.

* Wilkins, iii. 745.

from the King. He wrote at some length, and in an
argumentative and conciliatory tone. The new title
he explained in an inoffensive sense. He denied,
indeed, the position which (according to him) the
bishops had taken up, that the jurisdiction of princes
and of priests was co-ordinate, the one being over
temporal things and the other over spiritual. The
power and jurisdiction of the prince was over both ;
and ecclesiastical persons were under him on the one
hand, as the civil magistrates were under him on the
other. But he meant no intrusion into the sacerdotal
functions. Only so far as spiritual things included
property and justice, whatever power was necessary to
preserve the peace of society was comprehended in
the commission borne by the supreme ruler.*

It is difficult, in truth, to understand what Henry
meant by assuming the uncustomary style of Supreme
Head of the Church, unless it were to alarm the Pope,
depress the clergy, and imitate the Lutheran Princes
of Germany. If he meant to encroach on the proper
functions of the bishops and clergy, he was defeated :
nor, indeed, is it possible to impute such a design to

---

* Wilkins, iii. 762 ; Collier, ii. 63 (1st ed.). Two letters remain
which the King caused to be written in answer to the Northern bishops.
Neither of these is in answer to Tunstall, whose protestation perhaps
never went southward ; nor are the protestations preserved to which they
were written in answer. If these bishops held their jurisdiction to be
co-ordinate with that of the King, they took a higher view than the clergy
of England have held in general at any time. It may be remarked that
the modern objection to the limiting clause, " quantum per Christi legem
licet," that it amounted to nothing, was alleged by one of these bishops,
who illustrated it by the similitude, " Homo immortalis est, quantum per
naturæ legem licet." "This," answered the King, "is nothing like ; for
'naturæ lex' is not immortality, as is 'lex Christi' to superiority ; for 'lex
naturæ,' nor speaketh nor can mean of any immortality at all, considering
that the law of nature ordaineth mortality to all things ; but Christ's law
speaketh of superiority, admitteth superiority, sheweth also and declareth,
'obediendum esse principibus,' as ye do allege." The King thought there
was some force in the clause.

him without mixing in his arrogance a degree of folly which never belonged to his character. He was pro- bably astonished at the resistance which he aroused ; and on all occasions afterwards he shewed himself particularly careful to avoid all possibility of miscon- struction.* But the title. as he himself explained it, added no new authority to the crown. A year before he took his new title Henry himself had asserted his supremacy in a proclamation in which he declared his resolution of putting in execution the laws of his pre- decessors for the protection of religion, and called upon all who held office. ecclesiastical or civil, to assist him.† There was nothing in the title beyond the strong asser- tion of an ancient right : but the right was questioned by none, and it was a piece of folly to surprise the clergy and the country by strange language. The title, as soon as it was assumed. began to be misinterpreted ; and the King was obliged without delay to explain it.

The avowed enemies of the clergy, who have had of late years a monopoly in writing the history of England, have made themselves merry over an incident which happened in the September of this year. on the occa- sion of the first payment of the subsidy or fine granted or incurred by the clergy. Stokesley, Bishop of Lon- don, had called together the clergy of London, to the Chapter-house of St. Paul's, to make arrangements for the payment of the first instalment. They attended to the number of six hundred, accompanied by many lay- men. The Bishop wished to speak to them in detach-

---

* For instance, in the Commission appointing Crumwel his Vicar- General he said :—" In terris Supremam Ecclesiæ Anglicanæ sub Christo auctoritatem. etsi regiæ nostræ dignitati ut præcellenti jam inde ab adepto primum, Divina disponente gratia, hujus regni nostri sceptro. jam nobis competierit, nunc denuo exercere quodammodo impellimur."— *Wilkins.* iii. 784.

† Wilkins, iii. 737 ; Hook's Lives of Archbishops, vi. 339.

ments; or perhaps to arrange the unpleasant business with a few who might communicate with the rest. But when his officers called in six or eight priests by name, a great number entered. The doors being shut again with difficulty, those who remained without, encouraged by the laymen, made a rush, crying out, "We will not be kept without and our fellows be within : we know not what the Bishop will do with them." The doors were forced, the officers hustled and beaten, and the spokesman of the intruders exclaimed that they had broken no laws, meddled with none of the late Cardinal's faculties, and incurred no Præmunire. Their livings were small enough, cried he, without paying fines : "Twenty nobles a year was but a bare living for a priest : victual and all else was so dear that poverty enforced them to say nay :" the bishops and abbots had offended alone, and had great preferments : they only ought to be punished and pay the fine. The Bishop vainly explained that the payment must be shared by all, which had been granted by both Houses of Convocation in the name of all. The tumult increased : blows were exchanged, the delighted laymen urging on the fray. The Bishop at length, after being brought in bodily peril, appeased them with good words, and dismissed them with his blessing, promising that none should be called in question for the uproar. But five laymen and twenty-five priests were put in prison for it by More, the Lord Chancellor.* Such was the operation of the injustice and avarice of Henry.

This scene may be compared with another, arising

---

* Mr. Froude, i. 340, after Hall and Burnet. I follow Fox, who says that the Bishop had called together all the London clergy, but wanted to speak to them in detachments. The others say that he had only invited six, but that six hundred came.

out of the same business of the Præmunire, in which
the actors were not clergy but laity. When the Bill
for the pardon of the clergy, ready signed by the
King's hand, was sent from the Lords to the
Commons, alarm was instantly excited. The Bill was
drawn in agreement with the amendments proposed in
the clergy-house. It referred to the clergy alone : and
the Commons were not slow to perceive that, if the
clergy alone were pardoned, where all had been guilty,
they themselves remained without a pardon. They
were out of the King's protection : their lives and
property were forfeited to him. It is probable that
the King would have been glad if they had over-
looked this. He, of course, never thought of laying
his hand upon them as he had done upon the clergy.
He would have been willing that they should have
forgotten the whole thing, or concluded that the clergy
only had been concerned from the beginning, or have
implicitly trusted that nothing further was meditated,
now that the clergy had been punished. It has been
seen that the article sent to the clergy concerning
the pardon had been originally worded to express
that the clergy alone were excepted from the General
Pardon granted at the previous session of Parliament,
though the exceptions to that Act of grace involved
in truth the laity not less than the clergy. This ignominious position had been refused by the clergy: and
the Bill now before the House was for the pardon of
the clergy alone, not for the laity. Were the Commons
then to leave themselves unguarded to the clemency
or forgetfulness of the King? Not so was Henry
known. If it were impossible for him to outlaw the
whole body of his subjects : if the whole world would
not have contained the indignation of any corporation
or guild among them that should have been visited

as the clergy had been : yet utter ruin might fall upon particular individuals whenever the revenge or caprice of a tyrant might urge him to revive the memory of the most unavoidable of misdemeanours.

As soon as the Bill was read, some of the Commons exclaimed that all were not pardoned, though all had transgressed and incurred the penalties of the statutes. They therefore refused their assent to the Bill. The King's party replied that his Majesty was not to be compelled to give another pardon ; that to reject the Bill for the pardon of the clergy, who had suffered so heavily, would be uncharitable to them : and that to sue to the King would be unwise. The malcontents, however, appear to have been in the majority, and it was resolved to send the Speaker to the King forthwith.

Sir Thomas Audley, accompanied by a strong deputation, waited upon the King. He represented that "the Commons sore lamented and bewailed their chance, to think and imagine themselves to be out of his gracious favour, because that he had graciously given his pardon of the Præmunire to his spiritual subjects and not to them ; therefore they most humbly besought his Grace of his accustomed goodness and clemency to include them in the same pardon." The irritable temper of Henry was roused by the perspicacity of his lay subjects. He roughly answered that he was their prince and sovereign lord ; with him it lay to use the extremity of his laws, or mitigate them ; he might have pardoned the spiritual subjects of his realm under the Great Seal, without asking for their consent ; as they had brought such a request, he would be well advised before he pardoned them : for he would never be known to have been compelled to it.

The Commons left the presence " very sorrowful

and pensive," and on their return to the House some
of them began to inveigh against Thomas Crumwel,
who was by this time a Privy Councillor. He, they
said, had betrayed the secrets of the Commons. A
serious disturbance seemed imminent; the Commons
were "unquiet," when "of his mere motion, of his
benignity, special grace, pity, and liberality," the King
vouchsafed to send them his pardon in a separate
Bill.* The Commons having escaped both danger
and penalty, were somewhat florid in their gratitude.
They "willingly thanked the King, and much praised
his wit, that he had denied it to them when they
had unworthily demanded it, and had bountifully
granted it when he perceived that they sorrowed and
lamented." † Finding them in this gracious humour,
the King, on the last day of the session, March 30,
caused the Lord Chancellor More to read before them
the sentences in favour of the Divorce which had
been extorted from the Universities of Europe. The
Chancellor bade them report at home in the country
what they had heard; that the King might gain the
good opinion of his subjects in the matter. The
Commons, however, seem to have proceeded to no
formal resolution of approbation.

The session which thus closed was barren of direct ecclesiastical legislation. The temporalty proved,
indeed, their superiority to the clergy in humanity by
boiling a man alive, and by making laws for the
banishment of gipsies, and the whipping of aged and
infirm beggars. But the struggle between the King
and the clergy suspended for the time the interference
of Parliament with the Church. Even an Act which
was passed concerning sanctuaries and sanctuary-

---

* Holinshed: 22 Hen. VIII. 16.   † Holinshed.

persons. made no reference to the clergy.*   The right
or privilege of affording sanctuary to persons endangered by petty treason, murder, or felony, was derived
from the earliest English antiquity, and had been
found both humane and politic in an unsettled state of
society.   A person who took refuge in sanctuary might
be either a clerk or a layman.   If he were a clerk and
wished to clear himself he was tried by his bishop,
like any other clerk, not by the lay courts; benefit of
clergy belonged to him, and his case was of spiritual
cognisance.   If this state of things had grown into
a serious evil, if the sanctuaries had been crowded
with clerical villains who needed only to apply to their
bishops. to obtain an easy composition for any crime,
we might expect to hear something of it when the
Parliament of Henry undertook the better regulation
of those dens of vice.   But we hear nothing.   No
allusion whatever is made to the clergy: and some
negative evidence is thus afforded that their condition
was not so low as it is generally held to have been.
This was the first of the numerous Acts concerning
sanctuary which illustrated the later years of Henry
and the progress of the Reformation.

* 22 Hen. VIII. 14.

CHAPTER II.

A. D. 1532.

THE scandalous business of the Præmunire was not quite ended even yet. In their alternate attacks upon the spiritual estate the King and the Commons relieved one another. It was now the turn of the Commons, who had been looking on while the King was hotly engaged; but, at the opening of the session of 1532, a partial breach for a moment separated the allies. The Commons, indeed, as soon as ever they mustered again in January, prepared a formidable battery of assault in their famous "Supplication against the Ordinaries." They were ready for immediate action: the memorable document which began the second act of the great constitutional struggle of the age was already drawn and under discussion, when an indiscretion on the part of the King and his courtiers instantly turned their devotion into mutiny. A Bill descended on them from the Lords, which proved to them that their interests and those of the King and the greater landowners were not as yet the same.

Of all the claims which arose out of the old system of tenures, the heaviest and the most lucrative were connected with wardship. The rapacity of lords, from the King downwards, was excited and gratified by the accidental opportunities which might be afforded by the infancy or premature marriage of their wards, not less than by the inevitable customs of primer seisin and livery. To prevent the decay of estates in ward by the abuse of the powers of wardship had been a capital part of English legislation from the time of the Magna Charta; while the ingenuity of men was constantly exercised to make such settlements of their estates by their last wills and other deeds as might evade the claims made by the King or nobles. These exactions, to which the oft denounced fees paid to the spiritual courts were light, remained in vigour until the abolition of tenures. Both the rapacity of the lords, and the expedients by which it was frustrated, had been carried to the utmost in the last reign, under the domination of Empson and Dudley: and it seemed that Henry was treading in his father's steps, when now he sent among the Commons a Bill of Wards for regulating the law to secure the advantages which the grea lords found at times to elude their grasp.

The Commons rejected the Bill peremptorily: and shewed themselves unmoved by the frown of the monarch whom they had so lately extolled for his benignity. They, however, pressed forward the accusations which they had framed against the clergy, and laid them at the feet of the King; betraying at the same time the alarm into which they were thrown, by requesting an immediate dissolution. They urged the cost, charge, and pains which they had incurred since their first session, and prayed to be allowed to return home. The answer of the King was stern. Restored to justice by anger, he told them that, if they made complaint of the clergy, it was right for him to hear both parties; that it was inconsistent in them to pray for a dissolution of Parliament at the same time that they complained of things which could not be amended

without Parliament ; that, as they murmured at their
long attendance, he had stayed as long as they, and
yet he still had patience, and so they must have.
Upon their rejection of the Bill of Wards he expostulated severely.   He had lately offered them, he
said, a great mitigation of what he might have done
against them by the rigour of the law ; if they now persisted, he would try the utmost severity which the
law allowed, and would not offer them such a favour
again.   This allusion to the late Præmunire must have
convinced the Commons that they had displayed no
unnecessary caution when they sued for the King's
formal pardon.   But the threat which the King used
had no effect.   The Commons have ever been firm
in defence of the purse : they were not to be moved
to reconsider the Bill of Wards, and the King angrily
prorogued them to Easter.   Henry succeeded indeed,
in after years, in establishing his Court of Wards ; his
exchequer was increased in the end of his reign by the
mulcts of infants, idiots, and impatient widows ; and
of all the judicial novelties projected by him this was
destined to have the longest continuance.   But this
was not to be until, by dividing to them the enormous
booty of the Abbeys and the Church, he had bound
the Commons to him by a more constant sentiment of
gratitude than they were as yet obliged to entertain.

The transient breach was healed by absence ; and
after the prorogation the Commons met with no rebuff
when they again brought forward their Supplication
against the Ordinaries.   This document, together with
the answers which were made to it by the clergy, now
demands the attention of the reader.   This it was
which fully revealed the sweeping measures which
were now meditated against the liberties of the

* Hall and Burnet.

Church, and opened that part of the short but decisive conflict which ended with the formal submission of the clergy.

The Supplication of the Commons against the Ordinaries may be divided into two parts. It began by attacking the right which the clergy had hitherto exercised, of making spiritual laws in Convocation without the assent of the King or any of the laity. After this capital accusation it descended upon the mere abuses which existed in the Church. These were treated at great length, and form the greater part of the Supplication.*

To complain of the right or power which the clergy had hitherto exercised in making canons and constitutions was to allege a theoretical grievance from which no inconvenience had ever arisen. But if no more had been intended than to reduce the statutes of the clergy to the same footing as those of the temporalty, the annexing of the formal " Le Roi le veult " to their ordinances, the point raised might have been more interesting to the canonist curious in the history of cleric right than to the world at large. Through their long and varied history the venerable assemblies of the English clergy have partaken the mingled characters of a parliament and of a synod. In the earliest English antiquity they agreed with the national

---

* Mr. Froude wrongly places the Supplication of the Commons, and the first Answer made to the same by the clergy, in the year 1529. He has printed both (i. 208 *sq.*) from MSS. in the Rolls House ; but I have ascertained that those MSS. bear no date. He has probably confused the Supplication, which was of 1532 beyond question, with the " Grievances charged by the Commons upon the Spiritualty " in 1529, which Hall and Fox talk about. These " Grievances," however, were not a document, but were vamped up by Hall out of the three comparatively moderate Church Acts of 1529. The mistake makes the Reformation open pointblank with the attack on Convocation ; and it runs through a great part of Mr. Froude's first volume. (See above, p. 12.)

Gemotes in time and place of meeting, on the one hand; but, on the other hand, in the national Gemotes, composed both of spiritual and temporal persons, it is known from several instances that the spiritual and temporal parts of the convention consulted together or apart according to the nature of the business.* In the ages after the Conquest the assemblies of the clergy generally answered to the Parliamentary character, as regarded the time of meeting; but in their place of meeting and manner of proceeding they took, or retained, the synodal character. The writs of the King summoned the chief clergy to the great councils of the nation, assigning time and place; but, though the time they could not elude, their tendency was to meet in a separate house, and hold their deliberations in their own manner. The partial independence of the See of York, effected by the countenance of the Pope after the Conquest, remained in this particular complete; the clergy of the Northern Province grew accustomed to attend on the Parliament in Westminster in a convocation held in York, and by their example perpetuated the separation of the Southern clergy also from the lay estates. The well-known efforts of Edward the First (who more than once summoned the Northern clergy to Westminster) to include both clergy and laity in one symmetrical system failed to conquer the tendency to disunion.

But it was questionable whether in any part of English antiquity the King had possessed the power of consent to the canons and ordinances of the Church. . The King had his own proctors occasionally sitting in the Convocation House, these proctors being always clergymen; occasionally he condescended to sit there

* Atterbury's Rights, p. 31.

in person.* As the head of the State he commanded the obedience of the clergy; in his writs of summons he could warn them to enact nothing contrary to the realm; † and by writs of prohibition from the temporal courts he could intromit in their deliberations. In those spiritual things which touched on property or justice the Parliaments could always legislate, and might at any time supersede an ordinance of the Church. These safeguards and remedies had hitherto been found sufficient. They left the Convocations in the position both of a synod and of the assembly of an estate. They neither affirmed that the spiritual jurisdiction was necessarily dependent on the temporal powers, nor that it was necessarily independent of the same. If the existing compromise were overturned, and more were given to the temporal powers than they had possessed hitherto, what security was there that the clerical conventions would remain either a synod or the assembly of an estate? Where was the assurance that the royal supremacy would not pass into a continual supervision and vexation of the clergy: that statutes and ordinances would not be decreed by the King, or by the lay estates, and only submitted to the clergy to be approved: that he would not take the place of the archbishop, and act as a born legate: that spiritual laws, in things pertaining solely to the ministry or the faith, would not be ordained by the Parliament alone, with the royal assent, like the statutes of the realm? These thoughts may have moved some of the clergy when they first heard of the Supplication of the Commons; and such forebodings were justified by events. Whenever, in the strife of parties, a theoretical grievance is alleged, something else is meant.

* Atterbury's Rights, p. 20.
† Nicolson's Hist. Lib., vol. iii. p. 196.

The Commons began, then, by allowing that new, fantastical, and erroneous opinions had increased of late through "frantic seditious books contrary to the very true Catholic and Christian faith;" but they coupled, as a co-ordinate cause of these errors, the extreme and uncharitable behaviour of some of the ordinaries and their commissaries in dealing with them. Seditious factions and deadly hatred they affirmed to be daily bred between the spiritual and temporal subjects of the realm, and to arise from several chief fountains and occasions. The foremost of these was that the prelates and clergy in their Convocations had hitherto made, and still made, laws, constitutions, and ordinances without the royal assent, and without the assent and consent of any of the lay subjects; which the lay subjects were constrained to obey in their bodies, goods, and possessions; while they were daily incurring the censures of the same, against all equity, right, and good conscience. And yet the said lay subjects never had these laws declared to them in the English tongue or otherwise published. Laws so made they said that they supposed to be not only to the diminution of the imperial jurisdiction and prerogative royal of the King, but also to the great prejudice, inquietation, and damage of his subjects.

They then descended to their particular griefs, arising principally out of the state of the ecclesiastical courts, and the processes pursued by the ordinaries in exercising their spiritual jurisdiction. Some of the charges which they brought were made up out of old rejected Bills of their own late sessions: for others a legislative remedy had been found by themselves the very moment before, in their present session, though they spoke as if nothing had been done. For other disorders of which they complained a remedy had been lately attempted by the clergy themselves. Archbishop Warham, amongst his other reforms, had reduced the number of proctors to ten in the Courts of Arches and Audience.* The only acknowledgment which the Commons made of Warham's reforms was to argue that as the proctors were deputed by the Archbishop, and were sworn to promote the jurisdiction of his courts, they might not be indifferent counsel for any laymen who might have a cause against any of the judges in those courts; or they might confederate together to delay suits. They therefore urged that the King should have the nomination of a number of proctors, sworn to prefer his prerogative, and to expedite the causes of laymen.† The lay subjects, they said, were daily convented and summoned before the spiritual ordinaries and their commissaries, *ex officio;* sometimes from malice, sometimes at the promotion of summoners and apparitors, without lawful or credible cause, but merely for the sake of exacting fees, which they had to pay, whether guilty or innocent: an intolerable hardship, which fell specially upon those of the poorest sort within the realm. And yet, when the Commons thus complained, they had just passed a law to redress the injury.‡ They went on to say that they were vexed and grieved with the excessive

* See first chapter.

† This was the substance of a draft Bill about proctors of 1529, which has been published lately by Mr. Brewer, Lett. and Pap., iv. p. 2695.

‡ 23 Hen. VIII. 9: "An Act that no person shall be cited out of the diocese where he or she dwelleth, except in certain cases." That this Act was already passed when the Commons drew up their Supplication appears from the Answer of the Ordinaries. Mr. Froude, who wrongly puts the Supplication in 1529, says of this Act that "*it received the royal assent* two years later" (i. 234), as if it was in existence two years before it got the royal assent, i.e. in 1529. It was *made* two years later, in the beginning of 1532, new style; and got the royal assent when it was made, like other Acts. The Oath *ex officio*, or power of ordinaries to require suspected persons to answer questions on oath, long survived the Tudors.

fees taken in the spiritual courts for citations, inhibitions, proxies, certificates, libels, sentences, judgments, and other processes. The probate duties were enormous, through the number of judges, scribes, apparitors, summoners, appraisers, and other ministers, who were to be satisfied before any testament could be proved. And yet in their first session, as we have seen, they had legislated to reduce these exactions; and they might have legislated again, if they had deemed it necessary, without more words. They now recommended that the judges appointed by the ordinaries over the spiritual courts should have some spiritual stipend for their support, without taking any fees whatever.*

They proceeded to complain that sums of money were allowed by the ordinaries to be exacted by the parsons, vicars, curates, and parish priests even for the sacraments and sacramentals of Holy Church, which were sometimes denied until the payment was made. This accusation, again, was made up out of an old draft Bill.† The fees demanded from spiritual persons on induction into benefices were very large; and the ordinaries frequently took bonds for the first-fruits of benefices before they would present. This was against all laws, right, and good conscience; it was simony, and against the laws of God.

It is easy to see how these general accusations may have grown out of particular instances known to indignant members. The clergy have always suffered,

---

* Mr. Froude labels this, "The Commons require paid judges." The judges were not, however, to be paid out of the Exchequer, but by having some "spiritual promotion, stipend, and salary."

† A Bill about money received for sacraments is enumerated in a list of measures before Parliament, in 1532, in the handwriting of Speaker Audley, which is on the first sheet of the Commons' Supplication in the Record Office.

and will always suffer, above every other class of men from general accusations : but when these general accusations proceeded from an assembly of legislators, it was to be regretted that those legislators (who were fond of old statutes) could not have been reminded that their ancestors had once deemed it necessary to legislate against the impeachment of ordinaries on general charges of extortion and oppression without certainty.*

The Commons further alleged that benefices were daily conferred by the ordinaries "upon certain young folk, whom they called their nephews, or kinsfolk," who were under age, and unfit to serve any cure : the ordinaries retaining the revenues of the benefices, while the souls of the people perished for lack of doctrine. The number of superfluous holidays, especially in time of harvest, was another grievance, of which we shall hear again in the course of this history. "Great, abominable, and execrable vices, idle and wanton sports, were used and exercised" in these holidays; which, it was recommended, should be made fewer in number, and be more religiously observed.

The rest of the Supplication turned upon the processes and examinations used by the ordinaries, especially concerning heresy. Persons found processes made out against them by sinister procurement; and

---

* I allude to the Statute of Clergy, 25 Edward III. 9. As this old statute, in brevity not less than in sense, forms an admirable contrast to the bloated enactments of Henry VIII., I give it all :—"Item. Because that the King's justices do take indictments of ordinaries, and of their ministers, of extortions and oppressions, and impeach them, without putting in certain wherein or whereof, or in what manner, they have done extortion ; the King will that his justices shall not from henceforth impeach the ordinaries, nor their ministers, because of such indictments of general extortions and oppressions, unless they say, and put in certain, in what thing, and of what, and in what manner the said ordinaries, or their ministers, have done extortions or oppressions."

were ordered to appear to answer in secret places, not openly, before the ordinaries, upon articles proposed *ex officio*. When they appeared they were committed to ward, sometimes for a whole year, without knowing the name of their accuser, or the cause of their imprisonment. If nothing could be proved against them, when all was examined, they were set at large again, without amends for their cost and sufferings, and, for the most part, without any remedy against their wanton accusers. In case of heresy, the ordinaries and their ministers used to put "such subtle interrogatories concerning the high mysteries of the faith, as were able quickly to trap a simple, unlearned, or yet a well-witted layman without learning." If through such subtleties heresy were confessed in words, though never committed in thought or deed; then "the silly soul must either make his purgation with loss of honesty and credence for ever, or else be utterly destroyed." If the accused party denied the heresy, and put his adversaries to prove it, then witnesses were brought; and were allowed by the ordinaries, even were they but two in number, and never so sore defamed: a party condemned after abjuration was delivered to secular hands without remedy: if he were condemned, but had never adjured before, he had to make his purgation, and bear a faggot, to his extreme shame and undoing. In conclusion, the Commons returned to their first position, that cn the one side there was outrageous violence, on the other lack of charity, patience, and good will. The remedy lay with the King alone. Let him "make and ordain on both sides such strait laws against transgressors and offenders as shall be too heavy, dangerous, and weighty, for them, or any of them, to bear, suffer, and sustain." If he would provide the means of reconciliation and unity, he would do the most princely feat that ever did sovereign lord upon his subjects.

The Commons, it will be perceived, were not heretics. They were Catholics, remonstrating against the severities exercised in defence of the faith which was still held by the realm. Part of their complaint was that the heretics had gone to a frantic pitch of audacity and violence; and against the ordinaries they alleged, not that they withstood them, but that there was too much severity and too little charity in their opposition. The heretics would have fared no better at the hands of the Commons than they fared with the ordinaries. Indeed, the Commons demanded severer laws against both : their real object was the removal of the spiritual jurisdiction. The readiest way to redress the severities already in practice would have been to have repealed their own heresy laws, in accordance with which the ordinaries, ever spurred on by royal proclamations, had been compelled to proceed. And two years afterwards they certainly did repeal one of those Lancastrian edicts which first brought the blood of heretics upon the realm. But they left the severest of those laws unrepealed; and their present Supplication led to nothing but the depression of the clergy. Not a stake the less was set in ground, when the clergy had bent to the storm, for the dreadful punishment of the few who dared to die for their opinions : not a faggot the more was spared the shoulders of the many who began that warfare without counting the cost.

Nor ought it to escape notice that in the long and elaborate exposure of the ecclesiastical courts, which is contained in this memorial, there is made no mention of the easy compositions which the clergy are often alleged to have obtained there for immorality,

ill discipline, and "unthriftness." Much has been made
by modern writers of this alleged abuse. Examples
of great vice lightly punished have been culled out of
the diocesan registers, and set in array, to induce the
conclusion that the clerical order was generally depraved. But these examples are not numerous in
comparison with the whole number of the clergy; nor,
so far as I have examined, do the punishments appear
so very light. They all involved public disgrace, and
the payment of a sum which may have been heavy on
the offender.* And if a great public scandal had been
caused by these proceedings it would not have escaped notice here. There is nothing in the Supplication which amounts to a general accusation of
immorality against the clergy; and this is a strong
negative proof that they had not fallen into such a state
as to make them abominable in the eyes of the nation.†
This fashionable view is but little sustained by the
trustworthy documents of the time. The real drift of
the swollen grievances of the Commons was in their
first article. They aimed to destroy the spiritual
jurisdiction—to deprive the spiritualty of the power of
making canons or spiritual laws—on the allegation
that the spiritual laws which they made were contrary
to the dignity of the Crown and the statutes of the
realm. But they offered no collection out of the canon

---

* A great number of cases of incontinency are given in the Chapter
Book of Ripon, printed by the Surtees Society. They are both lay and
clerical. Both clergy and laymen usually compounded by a fine. The
fines levied on the clergy were no lighter than those of the laymen.

† There is the allusion to the young folk, whom the ordinaries called
their nephews or kinsfolk. Mr. Froude, in noticing this allusion, says,
"whom the *bishops* called their nephews" (i. 220). An ordinary was not
necessarily a bishop. I have ventured to say that if a general accusation
could have been brought against the clergy, it would have been brought
in this instrument. It may be answered that the Supplication was not
against the clergy, but the ordinaries.

law, nor brought forward a single instance of the contrariety which they alleged.*

The Convocation of the clergy of Canterbury, when the thunderbolt of the Commons fell upon them, were actually engaged in making canons. A body of new laws, chiefly concerning the reformation of abuses, had been slowly growing under their hands during their previous sessions, and had now nearly attained their final form. These laws would have been sufficient, if they had been enforced, to have freed the Church from the worst of her corruptions, while they preserved her ancient jurisdiction. They never became laws upon her authority: the power of making laws was taken from her before they could pass through her assemblies; in this, as in so many other things, the clerical reformation was stopped by violence: but to cast a glance upon the last attempt at independent ecclesiastical legislation in this realm may not be unentertaining to the curious, nor uninstructive to the serious student of history.†

Archbishops and bishops were to show themselves the glory and example of the flock. The frequent absences of many of those great officers, and the management of their dioceses by inferior deputies, was indeed a most serious evil, and lay at the root of many of the irregularities of which the age complained. It excused, while it fostered, remissness in the clergy;

---

* While the English Church still owned herself a daughter of Rome it would have been difficult for them to have made such a collection. Cranmer made one after the abolition of the Roman power, chiefly consisting of canons confessing the Roman superiority. Burnet Coll., book iii. No. 27.

† Wilkins (vol. iii. p. 717) wrongly places these "Statuta et Ordinationes Prælatorum in Concilio Provinciali edita" under the year 1529. They were no doubt agitated then, as they were again in 1530 (*ibid.*, p. 725); but they were brought to the form in which they have been preserved in 1532 (*ibid.*, p. 746).

above all, it filled the diocesan courts with the oppressions and exactions of middle-men.   They we.e exhorted and admonished, by the Convocation, to be
present in their sees on the principal feasts, or at least
at Christmas, Easter, Whitsuntide and Holy Week;
to make visitations through their dioceses, reforming
the monasteries and hospitals, correcting the clergy and
people.   In conferring orders and instituting to benefices they were to be more careful than hitherto; to
restrain liberty of absence, and altogether take away
the leasings of livings for money.   The exactions and
severities of their own officials they were to check;
throughout their dioceses they were to send forth
proper and able teachers; to put down heresies and
errors, and be diligent in seeking out heretical books.
As the monastic schools, not less than the universities,
were the seminaries of the faith, it was their duty to
restore the abbots and the rest of the religious to the
strictness of the monastic conversation.   Clerical delin-
quents were to be more severely brought to order;
proprietaries, rectors, and vicars to be compelled to
make, or cause to be made, frequent sermons in their
churches; and not to neglect the due distributions
among their parochial poor.   The simoniacal deposed,
the carnal castigated, the sumptuous in apparel reduced
to a prescribed vesture, the hunters and hawkers
among the clergy recalled to graver conversation,
might have lessened (if that were ever possible) the
mark of envy in the ministers of the Church.

Of the manners and learning of Churchmen and
the management of the Church some curious particulars may be gathered from these ordinances, which
branch out largely upon more special abuses.   No
person was to be ordained a subdeacon unless he were
sufficiently exercised in the gospels and epistles, or at

least in those contained in the Missal, to be able readily
to give the grammatical sense of them to an examiner.
The practice of appearing by proxy to be instituted
into a living was forbidden : all who sought institution
were to appear personally before the bishop or his
vicar-general ; because, among other reasons, religious
persons were wont to come by proxy, representing
themselves as secular clerics, and thus to intrude
themselves into the benefices of the Church. In this
way, it seems, was the statute of Henry the Fourth
evaded, by which it was ordered, to prevent the
vicarages which the monasteries had acquired from
being filled by monks, that all such benefices should
be served by none but the secular clergy. There were
beneficed men, again, who absented themselves on the
false pretence of study. The ordinaries were to in-
quire strictly after such men ; and a corporal oath was
to be taken of the authorities of the Universities that
they would hunt them out of the colleges, halls, and
hospitals. To avoid idleness, the mother of vices, all
curates, rectors, vicars, chantry and stipendiary priests,
besides their daily offices, were ordered to employ
themselves in studies, prayer, readings, or other good
works ; especially in the instruction of boys in spelling,.
reading, grammar, and singing. On three days in the
week they were to spend three or at least two hours
in the study of Holy Scriptures, or of some approved
doctor ; and idle priests were to be severely rebuked
and punished by their ordinaries. Schoolmasters were
to be good and Catholic men ; they were not to read
with their boys works which the ordinaries of the
·place deemed likely to corrupt their faith, or any books
by which, in the way of sport or jest, their minds
might be contaminated. It was announced that a design
which had been for some time on foot would soon

be accomplished : of publishing a grammar by authority for the use of the entire Province of Canterbury.
At present the diversity of methods was a disadvantage
to the pupils.   With every new master came a new
book and plan ˙of instruction.

Some light is thrown upon. the vexed question of
the state of the religious houses at this momentous
time.   Nothing more deterred the founders of places
of religion, or those who might intend to become
founders, than to find their houses maintaining a
smaller number of residents than according to their
original foundation or present income they ought to
maintain.   It was enjoined upon the ordinaries and
extraordinaries (whose united jurisdiction would include
all such places) that a proper number should be made
up, and kept up perpetually.   Unquestionably one of
the signs of the decay of the monastic system was the
tendency of the monks to aggregate themselves in
their great houses, where they had more society and
comfort, to the neglect of their remoter dependencies,
from which they drew the rents without affording the
benefits of their presence.   It is probable also that the
actual number of the religious was decreasing : and in
their general tone the ordinances which we are considering seem to acknowledge the decline of monasteries.
For the reformation of them it was ordered that a
sufficient instructor in grammar and the other primitive
sciences should be maintained in every religious house;
that the more apt of the religious should be regularly
sent to the Universities; and that the abbots and
priors should carefully train their subjects in the rules,
constitutions, and ceremonies of their order, and appoint them their offices, according to ability and disposition, whether within the cloisters or out of doors.
That the superiors had not always an easy task may

be judged from the following article : Apostates, or runaways who had lapsed into the world, were to be received back with all charity, if they repented, with the somewhat surprising exception of those who appeared to the ordinary of the place " from vehement signs and tokens," to have conspired against the life of their superiors or brethren, or to be likely to conspire in future. No religious person who had broken the three vows was to be allowed to leave his monastery, or to accept any benefice, charge, or chantry, through any dispensation, were it even of the Apostolic See, were it even granted under the bull of lead, unless it were proved to the ordinary to have been granted upon true and just grounds.

A list was added of seditious and heretical books which were condemned and proscribed. They included those that had been condemned previously by the Commission of the year 1530, with many that had appeared since : the works of the German heretics, and those of the active Tyndale and his coadjutors. Among them was the first work of John Frith, the future martyr, entitled, "The Disputation of Purgatory:" and the list was closed, memorably enough, with the Confession of Augsburg.

The examples above gathered from these statutes or ordinances of the clergy, may be sufficient to show that the clerical reformation was not intended to have been slight or partial. The worst evils were boldly handled : the most solemn admonitions might have armed with more active zeal the ordinaries to whom was committed the keeping of the Church. On them, indeed, depended all ; but their hands might have been strengthened, while their authority was maintained, by the opinion of the laity, expressed in Parliament or elsewhere, if no more had been within the compass of

the times than the restoration of the pristine discipline.
The declining power of the Pope, to whom the clergy
showed themselves little disposed to pay a blind obedience, the partial recovery of the Church from the intrusion of foreigners, which had troubled her ever since the
Conquest, and the peace of the country, now respiring
after the long civil wars, might have given the prospect
of a moderate and steady reformation.   But while the
clergy were exhorting the ordinaries to do their duty,
they were startled from their dreams of self-government
by the arrival of the Supplication of the Commons
against the Ordinaries.

This important accusation was received by the
Archbishop on the 12th of April, with an intimation
that the King required it to be answered speedily.   It
was therefore sent down to the Lower House of Convocation, in which, indeed, there sat more ordinaries
than in the Upper House;* and an answer was expected to be ready by the next session, April 15.   On
that day several answers were read in the Upper House,
which had been conceived in the Lower, to the Preamble
or Preface of the Supplication; or rather, perhaps one
answer to the several parts of the Preface: and, along
with this, answers to two portions of the first article of
the Supplication itself.   The clergy seem to have had no
time to frame a formal answer to the whole; nor indeed
was this necessary, since the true meaning of all was
comprised in the first part, in which the independence of
their Convocation as a Synod was attacked.   Gardiner,
Bishop of Winchester, read the answers, and corrected
them: from which he has obtained the reputation of
being the author of them.†

* Hook, Lives of Archbishops, vol. vi. p. 403.

† "Quo die (15 Ap.) lectis per episc. Winton. prooemio libelli supplicis
per communitatem Parliamenti Regi facti, cum quibusdam conceptis
responsis, duabusque particulis articuli primi libelli ejusdem, cum duabus
responsionibus ad easdem, vota et suffragia episcoporum et praelatorum

These answers were unanimously approved by the Upper House, and received the assent of the Lower House at the next session, April 19. They compose the First Answer of the Ordinaries to the Supplication of the Commons.

General assertions, unsupported by proofs, can only be met by general denials and the demand of instances. The Commons had declared that there was a great and daily widening breach between the temporal and spiritual subjects of the King: discord, strife and variance, of which there seemed like to be no end. To declare a breach is to make one: and this has been the favourite device of agitators from that day to this. The clergy answered that upon their hearts and consciences there was no such breach, debate or variance on their part: the King's subjects were their ghostly children, whom they loved, and ever should love, with hearty affection, never intending harm to their souls and bodies, nor having enterprised against them any-

unanimiter assententium collegebantur."—*Wilkins*, iii. 748, *Ex Regist. Convoc.* All this relates to the First Answer of the ordinaries, which only extended formally to the preface and first article, or part of the first article of the Commons' Supplication. But of this First Answer there are three manuscripts, somewhat different: 1. The shortest is in the Cotton Library, Cleop. F. 1 fol. 96, which has been partly transcribed by Atterbury (Rights, App., iii.). 2. The one taken by Wilkins (iii. 750), from the Register of Convocation, contains two additional clauses in answer to that part of the first article of the Commons in which it was alleged that the spiritual laws touched the King in his person, liberty, prerogative, lands, and possessions. This probably is a copy of the answer which was actually presented to the King. 3. A complete and much longer answer to the whole Supplication has been printed by Mr. Froude from the Record Office (Froude, i. 223). This runs parallel with the others (though with considerable differences) so far as they go, and then proceeds to consider all the other articles or items in the Supplication. It was probably composed more at leisure, and never presented to the King. This MS. is bound among a number of others, which are entitled "Tracts, Political and Theological." It contains several items which Mr. Froude has omitted in his transcript, unless, indeed, he found another document in the office.

thing of trouble, vexation or displeasure. It was true that they had exercised the jurisdiction of the Church, as they were bound to do, upon 'certain evil-disposed persons, utterly corrupt with the pestilent poison of heresy; but the Commons had admitted the frantic and seditious behaviour of such persons, and their fantastic opinions, taken out of the books imprinted in English in the parts beyond the sea. They were very sorry for the fall of such men; and trusted to make it appear that they had not been so great occasion of variance in exercising their spiritual jurisdiction as was surmised by the Commons.

In a multitude some might at times fall into light and evil behaviour; but they trusted that there was no such number of evil-governed persons among the clergy that the whole body of them should be charged with the variances and debates of the time. Many matters in the Supplication might have been brought to the Commons by misinformation: many were derived from rejected Bills, which had been devised by some who bore little favour to the clergy, and who now importunately prevailed to have the matter of these Bills formed into a Supplication, for the hindrance of the King's favour towards them. There were as many well-disposed and well-conscienced men among the Commons as ever were known in any Parliament; but "sinister informations and importune labours and persuasions of evil-disposed persons, pretending themselves to be thereunto moved by the zeal of justice and reformation, may induce right wise, sad, and constant men to suppose such things to be true as be not so indeed." *

* It is remarkable that all this criticism on the Commons is omitted in the MS. in the Record Office, with the exception of the acknowledgment that they were well-disposed and well-conscienced men. The clergy had reason to observe the rejected Bills. I have noticed above that the part of the Supplication which referred to the proctors of the spiritual courts

To the capital accusation that they made sanctions or laws in Convocation, without the royal assent, and without the knowledge of the temporal subjects, the answer of the clergy consisted in a vindication of the position which they had held from immemorial antiquity. There was one fountain of all law, the Scripture of God, and the determinations of Holy Church. From this were drawn their spiritual laws, and not less the temporal laws of the realm, which had been made by Christian princes and people; and if the same were sincerely interpreted after the good meaning of their makers, there would be found no contrariety nor repugnancy, but the one would be seen aiding, maintaining, and supporting the other. But, if it should otherwise appear, they were always ready to correct and conform their ordinances to the determination of Scripture and Holy Church; and if the laws of the realm were tempered accordingly, there would ensue "a most sure and perfect conjunction and agreement, as God being *lapis angularis* to agree and conjoin the same."*

As to the royal assent being required to authorise the laws made by them and their predecessors, the King must know, said the clergy, from his learning and

seems to have been made up out of the draft of a Bill of 1529. Among Darcy's Memoranda for Parliament Matters of the same date (a paper now printed in Brewer's Lett. For. and Dom., iv. p. 2553) is found: "Item, that all knights' fees, baronies, and earldoms be viewed, and how many of them be in spiritual hands. Item, to see what of all temporal lands the spiritual men hath, and by what titles, and for what purpose, and whether followed or not. Item, that it be tried whether the putting down of all the abbies be lawful and good or no, for great things hang thereon."

* It is a mistake to make the clergy ask that "if there be disagreement between the canon law and the laws of the realm, it may please the King to alter the laws of the realm." (Froude, i. 224.) They asked that both sets of laws might be referred to Scripture, and the determinations of holy Church as a "rule and square to try the Justice of all laws, as well spiritual as temporal." If their own laws were contrary to these, they would correct them, and they hoped that the King and people would do the same with their laws.

wisdom, that they could not submit the execution of their charges and duty to his royal assent. They might not so restrain the doing of their office in the feeding and ruling of Christ's people, his Grace's subjects   But if, as heretofore had been done, the King would show them his mind and opinion they would most gladly hear and follow it with all submission and humility.   And they besought him to follow the steps of his most noble progenitors, and, conformable to his own acts, to maintain and defend such laws and ordinances as they, according to their calling, and the authority of God, should make to the edification of virtue and the maintenance of Christ's faith, whereof his Highness was Defender in name, and had been hitherto in deed a special protector.   As to what was said by the Commons, that certain of the laws of the Church extended in certain causes to the person and prerogative of the King, and the interdiction of his lands and possessions, they answered that having already, in the former part of their answer, submitted their laws to be judged by God's law, which gave the measure of power to all emperors, kings, princes, and potentates, they thought better of his Highness's goodness and learning than to believe that he was misled by persons, not so well learned as himself, pretending that they presumptuously extended their laws to the King's person, prerogative, and realm.   This was done to bring them into displeasure and indignation with his Grace; but they prayed him to deliver them from that envy, when it should appear that their laws were conformable and maintainable by the Scripture of God and the determination of the Church, without which no laws could stand.*

* Since I have concluded that the answer which was actually presented to the King ended here, I do not consider it necessary to follow

The defence of the clergy was composed with dignity, moderation, and even eloquence. It was unanswerable, if the ancient constitution were to be maintained; and hard to answer, if good reasons were to be given for altering it. But it received no answer whatever. The King, in placing it in the hands of the Speaker of the Commons, observed, "We think this answer will scantly please you, for it seemeth to us very slender;" and encouraged the House to continue the controversy, concluding, "You be a great sort of wise men : I doubt not you will look circumspectly in the matter, and that it will be indifferent between you." * But he was so far from requiring the Commons to produce any evidence for their sweeping accusations, that he virtually refused further consideration to the

further the longer original which is accessible in Mr. Froude. It goes into every article of the Supplication of the Commons, and the general burden of the defence is the same—Let proofs be produced, let the cases be given ; it is unfair to condemn all for the acts of a few ; if such acts there be, they would be condemned by all : the clergy were bound to execute the laws committed to them : if they executed them properly, they did well ; if they exceeded them, or showed sinister motives, they did ill. He, for example, who exacted more than he ought for presenting a person to a benefice did ill ; but to take the usual fees was no offence : and they had never heard any priests complain of any excess therein. As to heresy, the discharge of their duty was costly, dangerous, and troublesome, and if God would release them of it, and make that plague to cease, they would be right glad : but they blamed the Commons for demanding severer laws for the repression of heresy. They complained of the treatment which some of them had received from seditious persons: they had been injured in their bodies, and thrown into the kennel in the open streets at midday. The character which they gave of their enemies was in great measure true enough. No notable person, they said, had fallen into heresy ; but "certain apostates, friars, monks, lewd priests, bankrupt merchants, vagabonds, and lewd idle fellows of corrupt intent, had embraced the abominable and erroneous opinions lately sprung up in Germany ; and by these some had been seduced in simplicity and ignorance." The worst enemies of the clergy have ever been renegades from their order.

* Hall.

defence, and demanded of the clergy a second answer.
And he deemed it decent to testify, through Edward
Fox his almoner, his displeasure against Gardiner for
the share which he had in the authorship. He might
indeed perceive in this remarkable document, amid
the phrases of decorous courtesy, a breath of freedom
which he seldom inhaled, and a tone of grave remonstrance which was little to his liking.

Gardiner, on receiving the tidings of the royal displeasure, hastened to vindicate himself in a letter to
the King, which was not unworthy of a place in the
records of a great controversy. With well-veiled
irony he said that, though he depended upon nothing
but his highness's favour to weigh rightly what he had
done, what he should have done, and what he might
do; though in correcting the answer of the Ordinaries
he had believed so great a number of learned men
who affirmed what was there written concerning God's
law to be precisely true; yet he had thought also that
he was supported by the King himself in his book
against Luther, which in his judgment clearly approved the position taken by the clergy. That book,
written in his grace's cause, and translated into
English, seemed to allow it; and the Council of Con-
stance, condemning the articles of Wickliffe, manifestly
decreed it. If his grace could now prove the contrary, he himself was not to be blamed, since he could
know nothing of his grace's proofs, and was not
learned in divinity. When he should know what he
knew not then, he would speak thereafter. If the
jurisdiction for which they contended were God's authority committed to the clergy, though they might
not use it condignly, yet they could not give it away
without danger to the receiver no less than to the
giver. Meanwhile he prayed for more knowledge;

and would willingly confer with any of the King's council on the matter.*

At the same time the Convocation was proceeding with a second Answer to the Commons, which was to be framed by the Lower House. Four sittings had been consumed, when, May 8, the rough-tongued Duke of Norfolk, the uncle of Anne Boleyn, informed the Bishop of London, who now acted as commissary for the infirm Archbishop, that they were to make it their first business to grant a new subsidy for the King's necessities, that they were to be prompt with that, and afterwards return to his Majesty with their answers. In truth, "the duke, the father, and the lady," and with them the convenient Crumwel, now governed all about Henry. The clergy hereupon sent their answer by the hands of the Bishops of London and Lincoln, of the Abbots of Westminster and Burton, of Sampson, Dean of the Chapel Royal, and Fox the King's Almoner. These deputed persons were charged to make a personal appeal to the King, to implore him of his innate goodness to aid, cherish, and support the clergy, and preserve their liberties and those of the Church unbroken, as he and his noble progenitors had hitherto done.† The attempt to soften the King was fruitless; nor was the second Answer of the clergy better received than the first. It was a memorial as firm, able, and temperate as the other in stating the case at issue, and even more admirable and coherent in phraseology.

Forasmuch, said the clergy, as the answer lately made to the Commons for their satisfaction in their bill of complaint put up to the King, failed to please or satisfy his Highness in some points concerning his

---

* Wilkins, iii. 752.   † Wilkins, iii. 748.

own particular interest, especially in the point that
concerned laws, either new to be by them made, or old
to be by them reformed, they would now specially
answer in these points. As touching the first, they
said that the laws and determinations of Christ's Holy
Church, received and used throughout all Christian
realms, were clear that the prelates of the same Church
had a spiritual jurisdiction, and judicial power to rule
and govern in faith and good manners : that they had
authority to make rules and laws tending to that purpose : which laws were of themselves binding on all
Christian people ; so that before God there needed no
temporal power to concur with the same by the way
of authority. This power of making laws, in matters
concerning the faith and good manners, all Christian
princes had hitherto held themselves bound to allow
to the prelates of their realms, no more claiming their
own consent and license to be required from time to
time, than in the giving of holy orders, or any other
act of spiritual jurisdiction. The authority proceeded
immediately from God, and from no power or consent of the prince, unless it were that consent which
came from the prince's submission to the Catholic
faith, made by his noble progenitors when they first
admitted the Christian faith and laws within this realm,
and by himself at his baptism and in his coronation
oath. This had been not only acknowledged by his
Highness himself, but with vehement and inexpugnable
reasons and authorities defended, in his book against
Martin Luther; which book they reckoned that his
Highness could not of his honour, nor of his goodness
would, revoke.

Yet, notwithstanding these considerations, not
minding to fall into contention with the King, and
having special regard to his high wisdom, great learn-

ing, and infinite goodness, they were content to make
promise to publish and put forth, as upon the lay
subjects, no constitutions, acts, or ordinances which
they should thereafter make, without his consent required ; and from time to time to suspend such acts
and ordinances, thereafter to be made, until they
should be authorised by his consent and authority,
except they were such as concerned the maintenance
of faith and good manners in the Church, or the reformation and correction of sin. Upon the refusal of
the King's consent, which they reckoned that they
never need fear, they trusted that they should be
allowed to · exercise their jurisdiction, so far as it
should be thought necessary for the maintenance of
the faith and the reformation of sin.

As for the second point, concerning laws made in
time past, contrary to the prerogative and to the laws
of the realm, as it was pretended, they said that if
they were advertised of such laws as contained any such
matter, or were not in use, or did not concern the faith
nor reformation of sin, they would gladly revoke them;
so that the Commons might execute the laws of the
realm without dread or danger of such laws, if any
such there were.*

The clergy, it will not escape the observant reader,
strove to maintain a difference between the making of
constitutions or ordinances, which they wished still to
reserve to themselves, and the publishing or enforcement of them, before which they were willing to ask
the King's consent. This, if they had succeeded in
establishing it, would have been the most satisfactory
conclusion of which the business admitted. They
would have remained free in their deliberations, as to

* Wilkins, iii. 753. *Ex* MSS. Cott. Cleop. I. fol. 101.

the matters of which they felt it expedient to treat, and able to have concluded them in the proper form of canons, constitutions, or laws of the Church; while, at the same time, all that might touch the lay subject would have been inoperative without the sanction of the King. The large exception which they made in things pertaining to the faith and to the reformation of sin would have touched their own order chiefly; or, if it were extended to the treatment of heretics, this would have made no difference, since the severities with which heresy was visited continued unabated after the loss of the jurisdiction for which the clergy were contending. Nor can it be denied, that in the maintenance of unity, it would have been advantageous both to the Church and to the nation, if the Church had retained the right of proposing and making laws, by her officers and representatives, for her own governance as a spiritual body. Every sect which afterwards broke from her possessed that right; if she had been allowed to retain it, how few the sects which would have broken from her! But in dealing with the clergy, the ordinary rules which men observe towards one another have been sometimes reversed.

The end of the struggle was not long delayed. The transactions just recorded had only occupied two days, when, May 10, by Fox the almoner, three peremptory articles were exhibited to the Convocation, to which the King required the subscription of all. These were: " First, that no constitution or ordinance should be thereafter by the clergy enacted, promulged, or put in execution, unless the King's Highness did approve the same by his high authority and royal assent; and his advice and favour were also interposed for the execution of every such constitution among his Highness's subjects. Second, that whereas divers of the constitutions provincial, which had been heretofore enacted, were thought not only much prejudicial to the King's prerogative, but also much onerous to his Highness's subjects, it should be committed to the examination and judgment of thirty-two persons, whereof sixteen were to be of the upper and nether house of the temporalty, and other sixteen of the clergy: all to be appointed by the King's Highness. So that finally, whichsoever of the said constitutions should be thought and determined of the said thirty-two persons worthy to be abrogate and annulled, the same were to be afterward taken away, and to be of no force and strength. Third, that all others of the said constitutions, which stood with God's laws and the King's, should stand in full strength and power, the King's Highness royal assent given to the same."

These sweeping requisitions formed the basis of the final Submission of the clergy. They were read by the Archbishop and prelates first in the chapel of St. Katharine in Westminster, and then in the chapel of St. Dunstan; where it was agreed that a number of either house should wait on the Bishop of Rochester, the venerable Fisher, to come to a speedy determination upon them.

At this moment the King is said to have made one of those curious historical discoveries which not unfrequently illustrated the progress of his convictions towards the goal of his desires. His former celebrated discovery of the force of the old statutes of Præmunire was followed now by the discovery that the allegiance of the bishops to the Crown was made invalid by their oath of canonical obedience to the Pope, which was sworn at consecration. This information may have been acquired from the intelligence .

of Crumwel; * but a learned prince might have been supposed to have known of the oath before. He might have heard of St. Anselm and his Peace or composition with Henry the First. He might have known that when the Pope began his claim to provide for the English bishoprics, in the thirteenth century, it was resisted by Grosseteste and other prelates before it was limited by the statuté of Provisors : that the oath of obedience to the Pope was regularly abated by the subsequent oath of fealty to the King : in which the bishop-elect renounced all engagements to the Apostolic See which might be prejudicial to the realm. He might have been aware that the Papal Provisions had long been a legal fiction, the real power of election lying with the Crown; and above all he might have been sensible that they had never touched the loyalty of the English bishops. But in truth it was time for the King to relieve the exhausted Commons in the struggle with the clergy. He sent for twelve of them, with Speaker Audley at their head, the day after he had sent his ultimatum to the clergy, May 11; and in the presence of eight of the peers, of whom one was Norfolk, declared, " That he found upon enquiry that all the prelates whom he had looked on as wholly his subjects, were but half his subjects; for at their consecration they swore an oath contrary to that which they swore to the Crown : so that it seemed they were the Pope's subjects rather than his; which he referred to their care, that such order might be taken in it, that

---

* In his romantic life of Crumwel, Fox makes his hero propound the oath of the bishops to the Pope in his first interview with the startled King; and with it their oath of fealty to the Crown. Henry is alarmed : he agrees that he is but half a king in his own realm : he despatches the new Daniel at once into the Convocation House, who reads the two oaths to the dumb-foundered traitors there assembled. But Crumwel, a layman, would not be sent into the Convocation House.

the King might not be deluded." The members returned to the House, and the two oaths of the bishops were read aloud there : the contradiction between them was manifest ; and the horrified Commons, including all the lawyers, never having noted the thing before, and never having heard of a designed, though apparently contradictory, compromise in any other part of the English system, were about to pass some severe censure on the bishops, when it was found that the plague was raging so fearfully that it would be better for them to go home without delay. On the 14th of May they were prorogued ; and the way was clear for cutting short the resistance of the clergy by proroguing them also. The brief remainder of the drama was played out between the clergy and the King alone ; and the question of the oaths was reserved for another occasion.*

Meanwhile this sudden menace, indicative of further meditation on the part of the King, may have served to alarm the bishops who were consulting with Fisher. The peers who were present when the King announced his discovery about the oaths, seem also to have been employed to shake these prelates. Nevertheless at the next session of Convocation, May 13, a warm debate took place in both Houses upon the King's Articles.† Eighteen of the Lower House voted against the first of these articles, and eight set themselves to frame another instead of it ; nineteen refused the other two articles, and seven attempted to draw up two others. In the Upper House three of the bishops

---

* Hall, Wake's *State*, p. 477. Burnet, who gives the two oaths.

† In the Register of Conv. (Wilk., iii. 749), this debate seems set down under date of May 15, the last day of Convocation. But as by that time the three Articles had been reduced to the two which compose the Submission of the Clergy, I think that it must have been held now.

consented conditionally. Standish, the Bishop of St. Asaph, proposed to add, " Provided that the King allow those constitutions which are not contrary to the law of God or of the realm to be put in execution as before." The Bishop of Lincoln, Longland, added the condition, " So that the King permit the other constitutions which have been made to be executed by the ordinaries until the matter be examined." The Bishop of London, " So that the said schedule be not against the law of God, nor contrary to the General Councils." The Bishop of Bath and Wells, Clark, dissented altogether from the Articles.

The result, however, of the debate was that the Upper House adopted an Answer to the King's demands which denoted a change of purpose.* The

* This document, which begins with the words "First as concerning," is published by Wilkins (iii. 752), as "A Reply made by the clergy to the Supplication of the Commons." But it is rather a reply to the requisitions of the King, to which in language it closely adheres. There has been, however, some difficulty among historians in deciding whether this "First as concerning" were not the second Answer of the ordinaries to the Commons: this, and not the document beginning "Forasmuch," which has been already considered. The difficulty originated with the Cotton MS. Cleopatra, F. 1, in which "First as concerning" is copied before "Forasmuch." Strype followed this wrong order (Mem. i. 199). The substance of the two documents determines their order and nature.

I am indebted to my friend Mr. Alfred Sturgeon of the Ecclesiastical Commission for a careful examination of the Cleopatra MS. F. 1, which contains this important document in several drafts. I have already observed that this document, which begins with the words "First as concerning," ought to be known as the Answer of the Clergy to the *King*, to distinguish it from their two Answers to the *Commons*. Confusion has been created by historians taking it for a third Answer to the Commons. There are three drafts or editions of it in the Cleopatra, differing somewhat from one another. The first of these (p. 97) is in a different hand from the other two. Mr. Sturgeon is inclined to think that it is a modified draft, perhaps the earliest, of the answer as returned from the Lower House. There were probably several drafts made. The other two in the Cleopatra (P. 98, 100) are both in the same hand, and follow one another without a break. The former of them is the edition given in Wilkins (iii. 752), and differs materially from the first and the third, for it omits those points on which the Lower House would seem to have especially

King's intervention in the contest was as successful as it was astute.   The prelates were not now answering

insisted; and generally breathes a more conciliatory spirit.   It is immediately followed by these words: "These Articles above written be agreed on in the above House, and the Lower House is agreed to the same, so that in the first article be added these words, *during the King's natural life*, and in the second article be added these words, *and holy Church*, with a *Proviso* at the latter end; and so the articles, as they be agreed by the Lower House, be of this form following." (Cf. Strype, M.E., i. p. 199.)   Then follows the third transcript of the whole, which includes the amendments of the Lower House.   I give it here in full, enclosing the amendments in brackets.   "First as concerning such constitutions and ordinances provincial as be to be made hereafter by your most bounden subjects, we, having our special trust and confidence in your most high and excellent wisdom, your princely goodness, and fervent zeal to the promotion of God's honour and Christian religion, and especially to your incomparable learning, far exceeding in our judgment the learning of all other kings and princes that we have read of; and not doubting but that the same should still continue and daily increase in your MaJesty, do offer and promise here unto the same, that from henceforth (during your Highness's natural life, which we most heartily desire Almighty God long to preserve) we shall forbear to enact, promulge, or put in execution any such constitution or ordinance, so by us to be made in time coming, unless your Highness, by your royal assent, shall license us to make, promulge, and execute such constitution; and the same so made shall approve by your Highness's authority.   Second, whereas your Highness's honourable Commons do pretend that divers of the constitutions provincial which have been heretofore enacted be not only much prejudicial to your Highness's prerogative royal, but also overmuch onerous to your said Commons, as is pretended; we, your most humble subjects, for the considerations aforesaid, be contented to·refer and commit all and singular the said constitutions to the examination and judgment of your Grace only.   And whatsoever of the same shall finally be found, thought, and judged by your Grace's high wisdom prejudicial and overmuch onerous, as is pretended, we offer and promise your Highness to moderate, or utterly to abrogate and annul the same, according to the judgment of your Grace.   Saving to us always all such immunities and liberties of this Church of England, as hath been granted unto the same by the goodness and benignity of your Highness, and all others, your most noble progenitors, with all such constitutions provincial as do stand with the laws of Almighty God (and Holy Church), and of your realm heretofore made.   Which we most humbly beseech your Grace to ratify and approve by your royal assent, for the better execution of the same in time to come, among your Grace's people (providing also that until your Highness's pleasure herein be further declared unto us, all manner of Ordinaries may execute their jurisdictions according to the

the Commons, but the King; and they endeavoured a compromise by offering a personal submission to the King alone. As to the King's first requirement concerning constitutions and ordinances thereafter to be made, they said that specially considering his Highness's wisdom, goodness, zeal, and incomparable learning, they would henceforth make, promulge, or execute no such constitutions without his consent.* As to the second demand, concerning constitutions and canons heretofore made, they said that, since it was pretended by the Commons that divers of them were prejudicial to the prerogative royal, and onerous to the subject, they would submit all and singular their constitutions, not to a commission of thirty-two, but to the King only; and if any of them by his wisdom were found prejudicial or onerous, as it was pretended, they would moderate or abrogate them. They saved and excepted, however, all such immunities and liberties of the Church of England as had been granted by the kings in times past, and all such constitutions provincial as stood with the laws of God and of the realm. But, on the other hand, they asked the King to ratify the same, for their better execution in time to come.

This virtual surrender on the part of the Upper House was accepted the same day by the Lower House also, though several amendments were added by the latter. Thus it came to pass that the King's Articles were accepted at first with some limitation.† On the day following, the conference was renewed between the prelates and the six or eight lay peers or

---

said constitutions, in like manner and form as they have used the same in time past)."

* This personal limitation, to Henry alone, they had attempted in their Second Answer. *Above*, p. 100.

† "Articuli a rege Synodo transmissi, examinati ac cum limitatione modica confirmati sunt."—Wilk., iii. 749.

councillors whom the King was employing in the
business; and renewed communication was had with
the King.* The result was, that though at the next
and final session of the Convocation, May 15, the
King's writ to prorogue them had been received, and
thus they were forced to an instant determination;
though the King's articles are said to have been
received "without limitation or reservation;"† yet
several of the latest stipulations made by the clergy
will be found to be included in their final surrender,
and the triumph of the prerogative royal over this part
of the ancient usages may be discovered to be less
complete than it has been given out. The peremptory
mandates which had been sent at first were recon-
structed in a more dignified form; by bringing forward
their right to be summoned by the King's writ, the
clergy contrived still to maintain the position of an
estate of the realm, though spoiled of power and
freedom; and by adding the King to the mixed commission of thirty-two persons who were to revise their
canons, they showed themselves more mindful than
the sovereign himself to preserve the venerable constitution in which the prince was supreme over the
spiritualty and the temporalty alike. Even of their
ancient jurisdiction the shadow at least seemed to be
preserved, when they themselves were admitted to the
melancholy right of aiding the King to abolish their
own ordinances; while, if the grammatical sense of the
newly framed articles were consulted, it might seem
that those ordinances only were to be called under

---

* Hook's Warham, Lives, vi. 413.

† "Sequens sessio (May 15) submissionem cleri coram domino Rege
absque ulla limitatione vel reservatione, quoad celebrationem conciliorum
provincialium, protulit, ac assensum majoris partis Convocationis ob-
tinuit."—*Reg. Conv.*, ap. Wilkins, iii. 749.

review which should be pronounced prejudicial and
onerous, and not the whole body of their laws. The
famous Submission of the Clergy finally ran thus :

" We your most humble subjects, daily orators, and
beadsmen, of your Clergy of England, having our
special trust and confidence in your most excellent
wisdom, your princely goodness, and fervent zeal in
the promotion of God's honour and Christian religion,
and also in your learning, far exceeding in our judgment the learning of all other kings and princes that
we have read of : and doubting nothing but that the
same shall still continue and increase in your Majesty,
first do offer and promise *in verbo sacerdotii* here unto
your Highness, submitting ourselves most humbly to
the same, that we will never from henceforth enact,
put in ure, promulge, or execute any new canons or
constitutions provincial, or any other new ordinance,
provincial or synodal, in our convocations or synod, in
time coming, which convocation is, always hath been,
and must be assembled only by your high commandment of writ; only your Highness by your royal
assent shall license us to assemble our convocation,
and to make, promulge, and execute such constitutions
and ordinances as shall be made in the same, and
thereto give your royal assent and authority.

" Secondarily, that whereas divers of the constitutions, and ordinances, and canons provincial or synodal,
which have been heretofore enacted, be thought to be
not only much prejudicial to your prerogative royal,
but also overmuch onerous to your Highness's subjects ; your clergy aforesaid is contented, if it may
stand so with your Highness's pleasure, that it be
committed to the examination and judgment of your
grace, and of thirty-two persons, whereof sixteen to be
of the upper and nether house of the temporalty, and

other sixteen of the clergy, all to be chosen and appointed by your most noble grace. So that finally whichsoever of the said constitutions, ordinances, or canons provincial or synodal shall be thought and determined by your grace, and by the most part of the said thirty-two persons, not to stand with God's laws and the laws of your realm, the same to be abrogated and taken away by your grace and the clergy. And such of them as shall be seen by your grace, and by the most part of the said thirty-two persons to stand with God's laws and the laws of your realm, to stand in full strength and power, your grace's most royal assent and authority, once impetrate, fully given to the same." *

---

* Wilkins, iii. 754, " Ex Regist. Warham." An attested copy is preserved in the Record Office. The Submission of the Clergy should be carefully compared with the three Articles of the King, and with the Answer which the clergy at first returned to those articles, given above. Besides the attested copy there is in the Record Office an unattested draft of the Submission of the Clergy, for the knowledge of which I am indebted to my kind helper Mr. Sturgeon. It is written in a different hand from the attested copy, and seems to be an independent document. It is evidently an earlier form than the final Submission ; and is of great importance because of the hitherto unknown fact that when, two years later, in 1534, the Act of Parliament confirming the Submission of the Clergy was framed, this draft was before Parliament, along with the Submission itself, and was recited in the Act in several instances, rather than the Submission, although the Act was professedly reciting and confirming the Submission. See next chapter. I give the draft here :—" We, your most humble subjects, daily orationers, and bedesmen of your realm of England, having our special trust and confidence in your most excellent wisdom, your princely goodness, and fervent zeal to the promotion of God's laws and Christian religion, and also in your learning, far exceeding in our judgment the learning of all other kings and princes that we have read of, and doubting nothing but that the same shall still continue and daily increase in your Majesty; First do offer and promise in verbo sacerdotii here unto your Highness, submitting ourselves most humbly to the same, that we will never from henceforth presume to attempt, allege, claim, or put in ure, or to enact, promulge, or execute any canons, constitutions or ordinances provincial, or by any other name whatsoever they may be called, in our convocation in time coming, which convocation is

It was not without boldness that the clergy had ventured to continue their debates when the King at first sent his Articles, requiring the subscription of all.

always, hath been, and must be assembled only by your high commandment of writ, but as your Highness by your royal assent shall license us to make, promulge, and execute the same, and thereto give your most royal assent and authority. Secondly, that whereas such constitutions and ordinances provincial which hath been heretofore enacted be thought to be not only most prejudicial to your prerogative royal, but also even most onerous to your Highness's subjects, it be committed to the examination and judgment of 32 persons, whereof 16 to be of the upper and lower House of the temporalty, and other 16 of the clergy, all to be chosen and appointed by your Highness, so that finally whatsoever of the said constitutions shall be thought and determined by the more part of the said 32 persons worthy to be abrogated and annulled, the same to be afterwards taken away by your most noble grace and the clergy, and to be abolished, as of no force and strength. Thirdly, that all other of the said constitutions and canons, being revised and approbate by the foresaid 32 persons, which by the most part of their judgment do stand in God's laws and your Highness's, to stand in full strength and power, your Grace's most royal assent unto. . . . and fully given to the same."

By comparing this with the Act (see next chapter), it will be seen that the Parliament departed widely from the language of the public instrument made of the Submission; in fact they played between the draft of the Submission and the Submission itself; and thus made the clergy yield much more than they had agreed to do. This is particularly to be noted in the clause which in the Submission stands simply, " We will never from henceforth enact, put in ure, promulge, or execute any new canons," &c. ; for which the Parliament substituted the double clause in the draft, " We will never from henceforth presume to attempt, allege, claim, or put in ure, or to enact, promulge or execute any canons," &c., adding however to the latter part of it the word *new* out of the Submission itself. Thus, as Atterbury remarks (Rights, 83), this part of their Submission was made to refer both to the past and to the future, both to their private and ministerial capacity, in their proceedings in their spiritual courts, and to their public and legislative capacity, as members of Convocation. On the other hand, in another place the Parliament departed not less from the draft than from the Submission itself in omitting the provision, found in both, that canons judged to be contrary to the laws of the nation should be abrogated by the King "and the clergy." Thus the clergy were deprived even of the decent mantle in which they sought to wrap their fall, the formal privilege of abrogating their own canons. Their Submission, as agreed by themselves, was a different thing from their Submission as enforced by Parliament, although the Act professedly recited the Submission.

Even when they were remodelled into their final form, they procured the consent not of all, but of the major part of the clergy. On the next day, May 16, the finally amended schedule was presented by the Archbishop to the King, walking in the palace garden. In his last public act, the troubled primate was attended by the bishops who had headed the opposition in the clergy house, St. Asaph, Lincoln, Bath and Wells; and by the abbots or priors of St. Albans, of Bury, of High Waltham, and of Merton. The Duke of Norfolk read the schedule aloud: attested copies were taken by the public notaries:* and two years later the Submission of the Clergy was confirmed by Act of Parliament: until which time we may bid the subject farewell.

If the King's discovery about the oaths of the bishops showed him disposed to press against the clergy the form and letter in which their obedience to Rome was conveyed, the clergy had already shown by one remarkable act how little their obedience to Rome altered their demeanour as ecclesiastical officers of the realm. The great Parliamentary Act of this session (to be considered after) was the abolition of Annates and other imposts which were used to be paid to the Court of Rome: and this was the first decisive stroke at the jurisdiction of Rome. But the Parliament was in this anticipated by the clergy. In a remarkable document, the clergy petitioned the King for an Act of Parliament to abolish all such payments. They represented that to pay the Annates, or first-fruits of their bishoprics, for the Pope's bulls of Provision to their sees, so impoverished the bishops of the realm, that they were often unable to repair their churches and houses in a great part of their lives, or to bestow the

* Wilkins, iii. 754.

goods of the Church in hospitality and charity, according to the minds of the donors. If a bishop died within two or three years after his promotion, he died in such debt as was to the undoing of his friends and creditors. It was contrary to the Pope's own laws against simony: and if bishops alienated the goods of their bishoprics—and the payment of these Annates was alienation—they violated the oath sworn at their consecration, and fell into perjury. It was unreasonable that the first-fruits of lands bestowed by the King's noble progenitors and other noblemen of the realm upon the Church should be applied to the Court of Rome; nor were the bishops, touching their temporalities, subject to the Court of Rome, but only to the King. Parchment, lead, and the writing of bulls were dear merchandise at Rome, if they were worth more than a hundred times their weight in gold. In the General Council of Basil (one of those which in the previous century had attempted the Clerical Reformation) it had been determined that nothing at all should be exacted in the Court of Rome for admission to any ecclesiastical or religious preferment whatever, beyond a competent salary to the writers and registers of the letters for their labour: but still the subjects were impoverished, and the treasure of the land conveyed beyond the mountains by the Annates and other exactions and expilations, and takings for indulgences, dispensations, legacies, delegacies, and other feats, too long to remember. Let the King cause these exactions to cease for ever by act of his high court of Parliament. And if the Pope thereon made process against the realm, or retained the bishops' bulls until the Annates were paid; then, since Christian men were bound to obey God rather than any man, and St. Paul exhorted to withdraw themselves from such as

it was immediately inferred by their hearers that they
meant to deny the need of a separate order of priesthood. Thus Latimer came to be regarded by the
party of innovation as a person likely to forward their
designs. On the whole he disappointed them. When
Anne Boleyn got him made a bishop, he did little in
his office, and quickly laid it down. He mourned
over the destruction which was wrought in the succeeding years of Henry's reign; and vainly strove to
save some trifle for the realm out of the wreck of the
abbeys. And in the reign of Henry's son, when
every kind of alteration, alienation and sacrilege was
in full swing, Latimer became the Jeremiah of the
Reformation.

At this time he was already a man of considerable
note. His sermons had made an impression in many
parts of the country. He had been engaged, and far
too actively engaged, at Cambridge in the disgraceful
measures which procured the sentence of the University in favour of the King's divorce. He had preached
with commendation before the King at Windsor. He
had been on the Commission which prohibited the
reading of Tyndale's versions of the Scriptures in the
vulgar tongue, and he had opposed afterwards the resolutions to which he had agreed at the time. When on
that occasion he wrote his celebrated letter to the King,
he declared himself a moderate reformer: that it was
not his will to take away the goods of the Church,
but to take away all evil persons from the goods, and
set better in their stead. In spite, or in consequence
of that letter, he was appointed one of the royal
chaplains.

Many of the Gospellers, suspected of heresy, had
been summoned of late before the bishops. In justice
to themselves, out of conscience perhaps as much as

from fear, many of them had denied and abjured the opinions imputed to them. Arthur had abjured. Bilney had abjured. But Bilney was soon in trouble again; and with him two others of the former Cambridge band, Crome, one of the most popular preachers at Paul's Cross, and Latimer, who was now settled in London. These three men were of sufficient importance to have their cases referred to Convocation in 1531; but the processes against the two former seem not to have been pursued there. Bilney went to martyrdom, and Crome recanted, under the episcopal courts of Norwich and of London; Latimer alone was judged by the highest court of the Church. The proceedings against him were marked by slowness and the desire of avoiding extremity. His case (along with those of Bilney and Crome) came up twice in March, 1531; when further deliberation was put off to another time.* After a year he was convented before Convocation again, March 11, and required by the Archbishop to subscribe to certain articles, which had been presented to him before by the Bishop of London. He absolutely refused. Requested a second and third time by other bishops and prelates to subscribe, he refused for the second and third time. He was then pronounced contumacious, and excommunicated by the Archbishop, with the consent of his brethren. But instead of being conveyed to the Bishop's prison, the Archbishop decreed that he should remain in safe custody with him in his manor of Lambeth. There, according to the custom of the time, when a prisoner was delivered to some great man who was responsible for his keeping, Latimer was allowed to converse with his custodian; and was softened by the persuasions of Warham. On March

* Wilkins, iii. 724.

21, a long debate was held in the clergy house, and
it was decided that, if Latimer would subscribe to the
articles, he might be absolved.   Latimer appeared the
following day before them, knelt down, and admitted
himself to have been indiscreet in his preaching.
" My lords," said he, " I do confess that I have mis-
ordered myself very far, in that I have presumptuously
and boldly preached, reproving certain things, by
which the people that were infirm had taken occasion
of ill.   Wherefore I ask forgiveness of my misbehaviour; I will be glad to make amends : and I have
spoken indiscreetly in vehemence of speaking, and
have erred in some things, and in manner have been
in a wrong way, as thus lacking discretion in many
things." *

The articles which he now subscribed were indeed concerning such things as a preacher might
easily handle indiscreetly without intending to be
heretical.   The abused doctrines of Purgatory, saint-
worship, and the rest, which exercised the early
reformers, might well both prompt and excuse the
outburst of honest indignation. † . There was much
idolatry, much mummery, much senseless noise and
vain repetition in the worship of the churches, to
weary the world, and provoke the zeal of simple men.
The zeal of simple men might be commendable in
itself; but it prevented them from reflecting that what
was wearisome might be harmless, and that in clamour-
ing for changes they were playing into the hands of
the avaricious and the crafty.‡

* Wilkins, iii. 747.

† See the articles in Latimer's Remains, Parker Soc., p. 218.

‡ Within a year or two Latimer was again in trouble on most of the
same points on which he now subscribed to the orthodox opinion.   He
then explained by written answers the manner in which what he said in
preaching was wrested or misunderstood.   For example, he was again

Latimer was not immediately absolved on his confession, but was ordered to appear again. Before the day appointed, he added to the indiscretions which he had confessed by writing a smart letter to one Greenwood of Cambridge, an old antagonist who had expressed some exultation at his humiliation. In this he was rash enough to say that he was not conscious of error, and had not publicly confessed error : that as to his old preaching, he would not change the verity, though he would have more respect to the capacity of the people : and that the misbehaviour of the people might be imputed to other things as well as to his preaching.* By this " foolish scribbling," as he himself truly called it, the unabsolved prisoner of Warham made it apparent that his confession of indiscretion was not meant for much. He was called up again, and required to make oath that he would answer truly what should be demanded of him. On this he appealed to the King. The King, at that moment in the hottest of his struggle with the clergy, was not yet prepared to assert his prerogative in matters touching the faith, and referred the case back to Convocation. His appeal being thus rejected, Latimer was compelled to make another confession, or recantation, in more explicit terms. than before. He appeared, April 22, before the Convocation, and on his knees he said, " That where he had aforetime confessed that he had heretofore erred, and that he meaned then it was only

accused of saying that there was no Purgatory. "None," he answered, "for such liars that will bear me in hand to say that I said not ; I shewed the state and condition of them that be in Purgatory."—(Articles imputed to Lat. by Powell ; in Fox, or Latimer's Remains (p. 225). He was not heretical but indiscreet ; both in raising questions which were made a stalking horse by the designing and ill-conditioned, and by the impetuous way in which he handled them.

* Remains, p. 356.

error of discretion, he had sithence better seen his own
acts, and searched them more deeply, and did knowledge that he had erred, not only in discretion, but
also in doctrine: that he was not called before the
said lords but upon good and just ground, and had
been by them charitably and favourably intreated.
And where he had misreported of the lords, he knowledged that he had done ill in it, and desired them
humbly on his knees to forgive him: and where he was
not of ability to make them recompense, he would
pray for them." *   On this he was fully absolved and
restored, and lived to reproach, not to say revile, his
judges.

Such was the kind of business which slowly wound
its way through the last free Convocation of the
English Church, mingled with the struggling Submission of the clergy to the King.   The raising and
burning of the body of Tracy, and the recantation
forced upon Latimer, are cited by the modern writers
as flagrant examples of the bigotry of priests.   The
provocations which gave rise to those proceedings
are kept out of sight: the slowness and pain with
which discipline was administered is forgotten: but
because discipline was administered, and because there
was a discipline to administer, the most senseless abuse
is lavished on those who administered it.

The session during which the Parliamentary estates
thus closely engaged the Convocation of the clergy,
lasted from Easter to the middle of May.   It was
rendered notable by several important laws, the
operation of which was to abolish the former privileges
of an obnoxious caste, and abridge the jurisdiction of
the Papal see.

The first of these was concerning benefit of clergy.

* Wilkins, iii. 748.

To a people long accustomed to an uniform system of criminal law it occasions surprise and sometimes indignation to reflect that during the greater part of their national history a considerable class of persons within the realm enjoyed an exemption, in certain kinds of offences, from the ordinary process of justice.   But this impression may be corrected by remembering that what is bad in one age may be good in another : and that, as this country was never remarkable for a tame submission to injuries, a state of things which endured so long cannot have exerted at any time a great pressure upon the public patience.   From the oldest times, under the somewhat indeterminate name of clerk, not only the ministers of the Church, the "servants of the altar," and religious persons in general, but apparently every one who could read or write, might be exempt from inquest before the temporal judges in petty treason and felonious offences.   Such persons might plead their clergy, and be demanded by the ordinaries of the Church to be surrendered to them, as subject to their jurisdiction, not to the King's justices. When they were delivered to the ordinaries, they were kept by them in their prisons.   If they desired to clear themselves, they did it by canonical purgation : they chose a number of compurgators, who might be able to prove them innocent.   If they failed in this, they underwent "the bishop's doom :" the sentence which the ordinary pronounced.   This franchise had origin, in the rude military ages, in the opposition of the Church to the barbarous trial by ordeal, by which offences of violence were decided.   In those times clerkship was possessed by few who were not ministers of the Church : and the ministers of the Church were the least fitted for the trial by ordeal, and the last who could decently undertake it.   This franchise, and the

process of purgation ought to be held in respectful
memory by the English, as the origin of trial by jury.
It was allowed and confirmed by the greatest of our
kings, from Alfred to Canute, from Canute to the
Edwards. Nevertheless it was not an undisputed part
of common law: and as time went on, it grew to
be regarded more as an encroachment than a right.
Disputes often arose between the justices and the
ordinaries. The former sometimes refused the plea
of clergy, and hanged and quartered convicted clerks
by course of law. They alleged that the bishops
made their prisons too commodious for felons: that
they discharged them without due purgation, on the
testimony of persons ignorant of their misdeeds, or for
the sake of lucre: to the encouragement of evil doers.
On the other hand, the ordinaries complained that the
privilege was not respected by the justices, who often
remanded clerks to gaol who had been demanded by
them, under surmise that there were other charges
against them: and even pretended that it was ambiguous whether a clerk were to be claimed by his ordinary
before or after he had been tried in the court of justice.
The allegations of the justices might be supposed to
have prevailed with the kings, who lost the forfeiture
of the goods of clergyable persons: but yet the
greatest legislators among the kings were those who
most emphatically confirmed, and in doubtful cases
extended, the privilege of clergy. In the sixteenth
century, however, there can be no doubt but that the
privilege required to be restrained. The invention of
printing was changing the face of the world: the
number of persons able to claim clergy according to
the old qualification must have increased, and bidden
fair to increase, far beyond the original proportion.
The statute now to be considered did little more than

limit clergy to the actual ministers of the Church : but
it led the way to other statutes by which the privilege
was altogether taken away.   It was passed at a time
when the justices were killing men at the rate of two
thousand a year.   Progress is glorious, uniformity is
beautiful : but dejected pity may heave her sigh in
thinking of the hundreds nay thousands of venial offenders who lost their only chance of escape from death,
during the bloody rigour of the English criminal code
under the Tudors, the Stuarts, and the early Brunswicks,
after the loophole of privilege of clergy was stopped.

In their new bill the Commons went a long way
back for a grievance.   In one of those tortuous
preambles which form so striking a contrast with the
plain brevity of our earlier laws, they complained that
the Archbishop of Canterbury in the time of Henry
the Fourth, Arundel, had promised to make a Constitution Provincial for the safe keeping of clerks
delivered to ordinaries : which Constitution was to
have been in accordance with a Letter or Mandate
made by Islip, who was Archbishop under Edward the
Third.   This had never been done, and continually
from that time thieves and murderers, having been
delivered to the ordinaries as clerks convict, were by
them speedily set at large without due purgation, for
corruption and lucre, or because the ordinaries would
not take the charges of keeping them.   "And by such
fraud they annul and make void all the good and
provable trial that is used against such offender by the
King's laws, to the great slander of such as pursue
such misdoers, and to the pernicious example, increase,
and courage of such offenders, if the King's highness,
by his authority royal, put not speedy remedy in the
premisses."*

* 23 H. VIII. 1.   The Letter of Simon Islip, to which the Commons
referred, was strict enough.   (*Wilkins*, iii. p. 13.)   In Arundel's time the

They therefore enacted that benefit of clergy should be restricted to persons within holy orders; that is, of the orders of subdeacon or above.* And that no convict person within holy orders should be allowed to make canonical purgation, unless he found two sureties of good estate, by recognisance before two justices of the peace, for his good clearing. Otherwise he was to suffer perpetual imprisonment in the prison of the ordinary who claimed him. Every ordinary might, if he saw fit, degrade a convict clerk who had been delivered to him, and send him back to the justices to be condemned to death. This Act would not have been injudicious as an adjustment of the long-standing contest between the justices and the ordinaries. But it was only to continue to the end of the next Parliament.

This Act was supplemented by another, "for clerks convict breaking prison." Divers clerks, it seems, convict of murder or felony, broke the commodious prisons of the ordinaries, to whom they had been delivered, and went their way, "doing and committing great, horrible, and detestable offences:" and for this there had been hitherto no great punishment assigned. It was now made felony, with loss of life and goods, and without further benefit of clergy. But the same distinction as in the former Act was made between other clerks and those within holy orders. Offenders of the latter class were returned to the ordinary, to be

clergy complained to the King of the continued invasion of their jurisdiction by the justices, and the reasonableness of their complaint was allowed, but they were required to make a Constitution for the stricter discharge of their jurisdiction. This they promised to do, but never did. Things went on as before between them and the justices, and a few years afterwards they were complaining again, this time in Convocation.— *Wilkins*, iii. 335.

* Mr. Froude (i. 349) strikingly labels this : "No person under the degree of subdeacon allowed to commit murder with impunity." Our poor forefathers !

by him imprisoned without purgation, that is, perpetually; unless indeed the ordinary chose rather to
degrade and send them to the King's Bench to suffer
judgment of death without further ceremony.*

Another Act provided that no person should be
cited out of the diocese in which he dwelt, except in
certain cases. Great number of the King's subjects,
it was alleged, were called by citation to appear in the
Arches, Audience, and other high courts of the Archbishop, far out of the dioceses in which they dwelt,
upon surmised or feigned causes, such as defamation,
or withholding of tithes : and if they failed to appear,
they were, upon the certificate of the summoner,
apparitor, or any such "light literate person," excommunicated, or at least suspended from all divine
service : and thereupon compelled not only to pay the
fee of the court to which they were summoned, but
also two pence to the summoner for every mile that
they should have travelled to reach it.   It was therefore enacted that no person should be cited out of his
diocese except in various cases of appeal which were
specified, upon pain of double costs to be recovered
against the officers of the court, and a fine of ten
pounds to be divided between 'the King and any
person who sued for the same in any of the temporal
courts.   Heresy, however, and probate of testaments
were excluded from the operation of this statute.   It
still remained lawful for the archbishops to summon
for heresy any person dwelling in any diocese within
their provinces, either with the consent of the bishop,
"or if that the bishop or other immediate ordinary
did not his duty in punishment of the same."   And to
the Archbishop of Canterbury the prerogative was
confirmed, or rather enlarged, of summoning out of his

---

* 23 H. VIII. 11.

diocese any person " for probate of any testament or testaments." *

This may have been a good law, although the grievances for which it provided had never given occasion for legislation before, and may perhaps have been exaggerated in the terms in which it was stated. By it a general confirmation was given, though indirectly, to the jurisdiction of the diocesan bishops, as against their metropolitans. The jurisdiction of the Archbishop's courts was reduced to causes which devolved to them by way of appeal, no longer, as heretofore, including causes which might come before them by way of querimony or complaint. But on the other hand, the long-standing dispute between the Archbishop of Canterbury and his suffragans as to probate of testaments, which had been raging the greater part of Warham's time, was decided without qualification in favour of the Archbishop. And yet the citations out of distant dioceses must have been more numerous from the necessity of proving wills in the Archbishop's courts than from any other cause ; and the Commons, from their first meeting, had made a special grievance of the expenses of probate in those courts. The other exception which has been noticed in the Act was not less remarkable. The case of heresy was left as it was before : and the Commons, who in their famous Supplication complained against the Ordinaries for extreme and uncharitable dealing with heretics, are here found providing against the unwillingness of the Ordinaries to act. Nor ought it to escape notice that at the very time when the Commons were drawing up their Supplication against the Ordinaries, they had already made this law for restraining citations ; although in their Sup-

* 23 H. VIII. 9.

plication they made the citations, against which they had just legislated, a separate article of petition, as if they had never exerted against them the plenitude of legal power.*

The word alienation has acquired since the Reformation the almost distinctive meaning of the diversion of lands from ecclesiastical or religious to secular ownership. Before the Reformation it was more often used in law to signify the conveyance from secular holding to religious, from feudal tenures to frankalmoigne. Under the old system of tenures, lands were held of lords, under obligations which were burdensome and often odious. There was military service, and other service, to be done by the tenant: and at every va-

---

* This appears, not from the imperfectly preserved Supplication itself, but from the Answer of the Ordinaries, in which indeed several other Articles of the Supplication which are now lost are enumerated and formally answered. The one in question is particularly interesting because instead of a general answer by all the Ordinaries, Warham replies personally, his own courts being most concerned. He touches upon the points noted in the text. He reminds the Commons of his own recent reforms in his courts, which took away the ground of some of their objections; he had brought down some of the fees to halves, some to the third part, and some he had wholly taken away: and he was willing to go further to content them. He was at the point to depart out of this world, and had no penny of advantage by his courts, but spake for the good of the King and his realm. He foresaw the decay of the faculty of civil law; the doctors of which faculty had done much service in treaties and confederations with outward princes. There was an Act passed already by the Lords and Commons of Parliament in the matter depending in the Supplication; and though the spiritual prelates had consented to the said Act for divers great causes, yet the Archbishops of Canterbury and York were bound to intercede for the rights of their churches. For the space of four hundred years it had appertained to them to have spiritual jurisdiction over all subjects dwelling within their provinces: not only by way of appeal, but by way of querimony or complaint. This right belonged not only to the persons of the archbishops, but to the pre-eminence of their churches. There was danger to those who studied to take away the liberties of the Church. Neither the Pope who had granted that privilege of their churches, nor any other (the honour of the King ever except) might justly take away the same, even if it had been abused. But they trusted they had given no cause to lose that privilege. *Froude*, i. 235.

cancy there were incidents, such as wardship, escheats, relief, and the like, falling either to the Crown or the lord of the fee. To avoid these was greatly in the interest of the freeholders and other tenants; and the most usual mode of effecting this was by giving their lands to the churches or the religious houses. Lands thus given were said to be aliened in mortmain. Being held by the religious houses in frankalmoigne, in pure and perpetual almesse, they owed no military service; and being continued in unchangeable perpetuity, they were not subject to the incidents or casualties. Such donations therefore were very numerous in old times, and especially about the twelfth and thirteenth centuries, during the great growth of the monastic establishments. Sometimes, indeed, they were real, and must be attributed to piety or superstition, but more frequently they were made fictitiously, to escape the multiplied obligations of tenure. A tenant holding under a chief lord might give his lands to a religious house, and take them back again to hold of the same house free of obligation. He changed his landlord by the process, and had a much easier holding under the monks than he had under a feudal superior. Thus the churches, and more especially the monastic houses, continually mitigated the rigours of the feudal system. The state of the times, and the commodity of the tenants permitted this; and if there was craft and engine in these fictitious grants, it was employed on the part of the tenants or lessees not less than on the part of the clergy and the heads of the religious houses. The lands thus thrown into mortmain were let on terms encouraging to cultivation, and the abbots and priors, the parsons and churchwardens, had the reputation of the best of landlords.

On the other hand, it was the policy both of the
Crown and of the tenants in chief to preserve the fruits
of tenure ; and the whole series of statutes of mortmain,
with which the statute book almost begins, was directed
to this end.   When these statutes were made, the
time had gone by in which kings gave endowments to
religion, and their object was to get back what had
been given, and prevent further benefactions.   The
Magna Charta not only made it unlawful for any to
give his lands to a religious house, and receive them
back to hold of the same house, or for any religious
house to take lands, and lease them to him of whom
they were received ; but also forbade all donations of
land whatever to religious houses.   All such gifts were
declared henceforth void, and to accrue to the lord.
This was confirmed in the fullest manner by the famous
statute of mortmain of Edward the First, by which it
was enacted that no land should be aliened in mortmain, under pain of forfeiture of the same.   But craft
and engine, it seems, were able to elude this peremptory enactment, as soon as it was made.   If a person
designed to alien lands in mortmain, the religious or
ecclesiastical persons to whom he designed to alien
them, brought by collusion an action to recover the
lands ; and recovered them by default.   Upon the legal
maxim that, as recoveries were prosecuted by course
of law, they were lawful, these collusive suits were held
to be beyond the danger of the statutes ; nor were they
stopped before another Act was passed by Edward, by
which a previous inquiry before a jury was allowed
into the right of the thing demanded or sought to be
recovered.   But if by this a check was given to collusion, the whole good of lands in mortmain would have
been taken away by another law of the same monarch, if it could have been rigidly enforced.   It was

enacted that if religious persons or bodies aliened the lands which they held already, that is, if they sold or leased them, the purchaser should lose both them and the money that he paid for them; and the lands were to revert, not to their former holders, but to the original donor of them, whether he were the King or a great man, to be holden at pleasure. This would tend to make the religious houses afraid of dealing out their lands to small tenants; and if, as it is often said, land accumulated in mortmain ever lay idle and unproductive, the evil must not be imputed to the religious bodies, or to them only, but to legislative interference in the natural devolution of property. By another enactment of the same vigorous reign it was ordained that no lands held in fee simple should come into mortmain by sale or purchase.*

These severities of legislation seemed to forbid the growth of religious establishments, and to tie them up in withering fixity. They were, some of them, a part of the remarkable legislation of the greatest of the Edwards, by which much of the old system of tenures was done away, and among the rest the tenure of frankalmoigne. The two last-mentioned enactments, however, seem to be at variance with the general spirit of his laws. But in the subsequent times of foreign and civil wars and troubles all these careful provisions were eluded by the great extension which was given to the doctrine of uses. It was found that feudal holders were legally able to escape the ruinous fines, forfeitures, and exactions to which they were liable in the general insecurity, if they conveyed their estates to nominal feoffees, to the use of themselves and their heirs. Such feoffments were judged good in law;

* 7 Ed. I. De Religiosis: 13 Ed. I. 32, 33, 41: 18 Ed. I. 3. Comp. Finlason's Reeve's Eng. Law, ii. 66.

and the feoffees were held bound to account to those who thus held the use for the rents and emoluments of the estates, though the seisin, or actual possession, remained with them. A distinction was thus made between use and possession; or rather a new kind of property was created. Although the age of the great growth of religious establishments was long passed, yet the Church and religion came in for their share of the advantages of this new practical manner of conveyance; and feoffments were made to their use, whether by pious laymen, or perhaps more frequently of their own lands, by members of their own bodies, which thus escaped the danger of the statutes which, under the pretence of alienation, made it mortmain for them to sell or lease their own estates. But in no long time the jealous spirit of the legislature was aroused again by their participation of the general benefit; and a statute of Richard the Second made it mortmain to be seised of lands to the use of religious or spiritual persons.*

Neither by these former statutes of mortmain and of uses was it pretended that anything else was sought but the preservation of the rights and profits of the Crown and the great lords; nor now, when the Parliament of Henry the Eighth undertook to add to the number of such statutes, was any other motive alleged. The King, and other lords and subjects of the realm, it was declared, suffered the same losses and inconveniences by reason of feoffments, fines, recoveries, and other assurances made to the use of parish churches, chapels, churchwardens, guilds, and fraternities, as they would have suffered if the lands and tenements thus given had been aliened in mortmain. Sometimes these dotations were made by

---

* 15 R. II. 5. Blackstone, Bk. ii. c. 18 and 20.

common assent of the people, without any corporation. Sometimes with the intent " to have obits perpetual, or a continual service of a priest for ever, or for three-score or four-score years." It was therefore enacted that no such uses or assurances thereafter made should continue for more than twenty years.*

Such was the way in which Henry and his Parliament opened their great attack upon corporate property, and more particularly upon the property of the religious bodies and of the churches. From the language of the Act it would seem that the chantries, or lands devoted to obits and the maintenance of priests to sing for the soul of the donor, were designed to have fallen first; and in truth this Act is the foundation of the subsequent distinction which arose between pious and superstitious uses. But, as events turned out, the storm fell first upon the monasteries; and the chantries were left to the last ferocity of Henry, and the destructive avarice of the following reign. For two centuries the course of legislation had been against corporate property, although the founding of corporations, and the favour shown them by earlier kings, had created the people and the liberties of England. But none could now have foreseen the violence of the impending revolution, nor the rapidity and success with which it was to be carried. The success was great; but yet it was less than was intended. The religious establishments were swept away, the Church was beggared; but the mighty revolution, in which the first movement was now made, rose at one time to menace every existing corporation in the realm.

---

* 23 H. VIII. 10. This statute was followed by 27 H. VIII. 10, for making persons who had only the use of their lands the actual possessors, which was felt as a heavy blow to the old system of tenure. See Ch. VI. of this work.

It would seem again, from the language used in the Act, that the old statutes of mortmain had produced their full effect in checking the alienation of lands, while those for limiting uses had failed in their operation. But the complaint of the King and the great lords was a mere pretext, and would have remained a mere pretext if the case had been reversed. Military service, the greatest of the feudal obligations, was becoming obsolete, being commuted for money payment; and with the feudal militia had disappeared the original mischief of mortmain. As to other feudal profits, which may still have survived, they were not affected by trusts and uses. The feoffees who held lands to uses were the legal holders, and were bound by law to discharge whatever obligations might exist upon the lands which they held; while to the uses to which they held they were only bound by the secondary claims of equity.* The new statute, devised under this pretence to put an end to the perpetuity of endowments, was the well-tuned prelude of spoliation; for the perpetuity of endowments has been ever the grievance of sacrilege.

But the most celebrated enactment of this session was for the abolition of Annates, or the first-fruits of bishoprics, paid on every vacancy to the Apostolic See. As this measure, if it had been passed by Parliament and sanctioned by the King at once and without reserve, would have appeared to be an abrupt and decisive act of hostility to Rome, a remarkable degree of secresy and caution was displayed in the management of it. The Papal nuncio was unable to give his master any exact account of what was being transacted within the walls of Parliament. The Bill

* Finlason's Reeve's Eng. Law, iii. 269.

remained unpublished for a year, a special clause
being inserted that the royal assent might be delayed
until the King had exhausted all efforts to bring the
Pope to a good understanding. Then only was it
ratified, and declared a statute by letters patent.*
In the terms of the Act themselves the same caution
was observed. The Lords and Commons declared,
indeed, that they were no longer willing to support
exactions which impoverished the kingdom. They
computed the sum which had been paid for first-
fruits since the second year of Henry the Seventh;
a hundred and sixty thousand pounds in less than
fifty years paid for lead and parchment; and they
represented that the age and infirmity of many of
the prelates rendered it likely that other large
sums would be inveighed to Rome anon. All
such payments were ordered to cease, except five
pounds for every hundred of the yearly value of
the bishopric: a considerable impost, which, however, was not to be paid as Annates, but for the
writing and sealing of the bulls of the bishop elect.
If the Pope refused to send his bulls before Annates were paid, then the consecration and instal-
lation of the bishop were to proceed without them.
A bishop was to be consecrated by his archbishop,
having first been nominated by the King; and
an archbishop by two bishops to be appointed by
the King; as in old times divers bishops and archbishops had been consecrated within the realm. If
the King failed to conciliate the Holy See, and the
Pope laid the kingdom under an interdict, the efforts

---

* 23 H. VIII. 20. It was ratified July 9, 1533. The Act, it may be
observed, omitted all the clerical arguments which were brought against
Annates in the Petition of Convocation (above, p. 113), and only alleged
the inconvenience to the realm.

of his displeasure were to be disregarded altogether. But at the same time it was emphatically declared that the King and his subjects remained obedient and Catholic subjects of Holy Church ; that the Bill was only a provisional regulation. Gentleness and courtesy were to be tried before extremity, and the royal assent to be delayed until the King had endeavoured to bring the Pope to terms.

In this cautious and gradual manner was the first of the great Roman cables cut away. It seemed, indeed, not improper for payments to be made out of the various realms of Christendom to maintain competently the great chancellery of Christendom ; and not unreasonable that these payments should come from those hierarchs who were bound above all others to uphold the Catholic system. But the exactions of Rome had become intolerable ; new officials were created, and the levies of money increased continually ; and the city of Julius and Leo shone as the glorious centre of art and luxury, while the churches of the nations were impoverished to feed her splendour. The Council of Basil had reprobated the payment of Annates ; the clergy of England had, as we have seen, petitioned against them in the most outspoken manner ; and now the English legislature, in repeating much of the language of the clergy, seemed to be doing them great justice in putting a limit to an oppressive burden. But the griefs of inferiors are seldom remedied by a contest between their superiors. To the bishops it would have made no difference if the Act about Annates had never passed. Their distresses were alleged, but their relief was never designed ; while to the body of the clergy the stirring of the question proved a more fruitful source of misery than anything else that was done in this age of spoliation. The term Annates, or first-fruits, was suggestive; after a couple of sessions of Parliament, the first-fruits not only of bishoprics, which used to go to the Pope, but the first-fruits of all benefices whatsoever, were transferred in one monstrous sweep to the Crown.*

The foreign history of the Bill is somewhat curious. The diplomatic efforts which Henry was engaged to make seem to have been directed rather to keep the Pontiff in the dark than to conciliate him by showing the justice of what had been done. The King's ambassadors at Rome were furnished with a copy of the Bill; but they were ordered to keep it to themselves, and by no means communicate it to others, until some occasion should arise when it might produce an effect. If mention were made of the matter among the Pope and Cardinals, they were to secure the King's position, assuring them that he had dili-. gently procured all to be submitted to his own judgment and determination, notwithstanding the persistent outcry of his subjects to have the statute promulgated without delay. They were to extol the friendship of the King towards the Holy See, which had led him to this course; and to assure them that what was done, had been done in a manner so secret that none of the other princes of Christendom knew of it. If the Pope and Cardinals complained that such a question as payment of Annates had been brought forward and discussed, then the ambassadors were to

* The Act only deals with the first-fruits of bishoprics, not of all benefices; perhaps because the bishops got the first-fruits, which went to the Pope, out of the clergy, as the priests got tithes out of the tithes of the Levites under the Mosaic law; and so the first-fruits of all benefices were virtually included in those of bishoprics. But I am not sure. Under Edward I. first-fruits of benefices were transferred to the Crown for two years. All first-fruits whatever went to the Crown under Henry VIII. See Ch. V.

say that discussion was free in the English Parliament, and could not be hindered by the King; but that he had consulted both the justice of the case and his friendship for the Pope and Cardinals, in procuring that nothing should be done against them suddenly and immediately, or without due warning; that he would preserve the tenor of the statute, examine into the truth, consult justice, and regard friendship. The ambassadors were to allow the Pope and Cardinals neither to hope too much, nor to despair too much. Vain hope the King would not feed; despair they need not feel, because nothing was decided or promulgated yet, but all was referred to him. If, however, they shewed themselves disposed to doubt the protestations of so true a friend, then it might be represented to them of how serious detriment it would be to Rome if the King should be driven to proclaim openly that which was done in secret, and by his example lead the other princes of Christendom to make a similar edict for the abrogation of Annates in their dominions.*

The agents of Henry—Ghinucci, Benet, and Cassale —were equal to the occasion. Perceiving that there was nothing said about Annates in conversation at Rome, they thought it good to bring the matter up before the Pope themselves, and give it the colour which the King desired. They asked him therefore if he had any news from England. He answered that his Nuncio had informed him that something against the Apostolic See had been done in Parliament, but that he could not find out what it was. They answered that it was probably the abolition of Annates, of which they had lately heard from the King; and went on to

* State Papers, vii. 360.

relate so much of the affair as their instructions allowed; setting forth the benignity, friendship, and justice of their master. The Pope expressed himself satisfied that the King had reserved the matter for his own discretion ; and the ambassadors told him nothing further, lest they should irritate him to speak of it in the Consistory, and it should come to the ears of the Cardinals and damage the King's cause.* Thus the Annates of English sees were lost to Rome, without exciting much attention there. But Rome had hardly time to notice the loss of English Annates, for scarce a vacancy occurred for which they might have been demanded, before in the onward rush of the revolution England was lost to Rome altogether.

On the same day that the Submission of the Clergy was signed before the King, Sir Thomas More resigned the Great Seal. The liberal temper of the author of Utopia had given way to some severity under the pressure of the times ; and some of the heretics who were disturbing the public peace had felt the weight of his office. But whether he outran the law against them, as it has been alleged, may be the subject of future inquiry. It is the effect of lengthened controversy to cause even men of large and genial nature to take their stand at length : the sense of public necessity may turn a philosopher and a wit into a stern official. Before he took office, More had learned that concessions never satisfy a revolution. From the day that he succeeded Wolsey he had been pursued by the hatred of Anne Boleyn and her faction ; they, with the King's connivance, had now carried matters to a point beyond which he conceived that he could neither interfere with effect, nor yield with credit. The independence of the clergy under the jurisdiction

* Ibid.

of the Pope was gone; and, in his apprehension at
least, the jurisdiction and the primacy of the Pope
was necessary for the avoiding of schisms.* Foreseeing alteration without end, he resigned. His career
as a minister was too short to be well compared with
that of his predecessor Wolsey; but, so far as it went,
it offers no uninstructive contrast. The sagacity of
both enabled them to understand the full meaning of
the revolution which they witnessed. They were both
zealous reformers of the abuses of the old system
which they defended: but while Wolsey was lenient
and silent, More was severe; and to his severity as a
minister he added his power of ridicule as a writer.
Not content with imprisoning the heretics, he laughed
at them. In this he stands alone among the more
eminent supporters of the Old Learning; and to this he
owes no small measure of the malignity with which his
memory has been pursued. He, and he almost alone,
showed that he understood the force of a literary agitation; and knew that the libels which were circulated
by thousands to change the mind of the people towards the clergy must be answered in their own
fashion. When he was Chancellor of the Duchy of
Lancaster, he had condescended to answer the atrocities of Simon Fish; when he became Lord Chancellor of England, he bent the wit which rivalled Erasmus
to the confutation of Barnes and Tyndale. Far more
than the prison or the stake his enemies dreaded the
caustic scorn which refuted their cavillations, unmasked
their motives, and not unfrequently exposed their
characters. The boldest of them only uttered with
bated breath the ready imputation that the champion
of the Catholic faith was the hireling of the bishops.

---

* See his Letters to Crumwel, Strype's App. 48.

His spotless integrity was proved by the poverty into which he retired after innumerable opportunities of enriching himself, amid the universal example of corruption. He continued unto death the controversial warfare upon which he had entered. His retirement, like the disgrace of Wolsey, was the sign of a new change in the times; and his successor in his high office, Audley, was a man completely to the mind of the King, the courtiers, and the party of progress.

Three months after this, at the age of fourscore years and more, died William Warham. A man of virtue, ability, and eloquence, he had been at the head of the Church almost from the beginning of this troubled century. The last public act in which he was engaged, the Submission of the Clergy, broke his heart: and before he died, he committed to writing a solemn protestation against any statutes hitherto published, or thereafter to be made by Parliament, in derogation of the Roman Pontiff and the Apostolic See, or in diminution of the ecclesiastical power, or of the rights, privileges, customs, and liberties which belonged to the prerogative of his Church of Canterbury. "We," he said, "Archbishop of Canterbury, Primate of all England, and Legate of the Apostolic See, protest publicly and expressly, for ourselves and our metropolitical Church of Canterbury, that we cannot consent to such statutes: we dissent from them, cry out against them; contradict them."* But this weak exprobration itself was the last instrument of an English primate who died legate of the Apostolic See: and when the hand that wrote it, stiff in death, but wearing still in funeral state the consecrated glove in which it had oft been raised to celebrate the great mystery of the Catholic

* Wilkins, iii. 749.

faith, was pressing to the yet unburied breast of the writer the golden cross of Canterbury, the proud dominion of a thousand years was already gone for ever. The scene was clearing for the new actors. The King had already some time been possessed of his new minister and counsellor in chief. He now got, within a few months of one another, his new Lord Keeper, his new Archbishop, his new wife, his new father-in-law, and all that belonged to them.*

* Since this chapter was written it has been denied that the Petition or address to the King against Annates was issued by Convocation, and Strype has been censured for calling it "an Address from Convocation to the King" (see above, p. 115). Certainly in the Cotton MS. Cleop. E. vi. p. 263, from which he first printed it, it has no title at all. And in the Cotton Catalogue it is simply called "A paper against the payment of Annates." It is now, however, asserted that this important document is parliamentary. In 1880 Mr. Gairdner of the Record Office boldly gave it a title opposite to that of Strype, calling it "A Petition from Parliament to the King," and placing it fifth in a batch with a dozen other documents undoubtedly parliamentary. *Letters and Papers*, v. 344. From some published correspondence which ensued it seems that the only reason Mr. Gairdner has given for this decision is that the Petition speaks of "this Parliament," "this present Parliament." But such language might be used by a body sitting concurrently with Parliament. The arguments used in the Petition shew its origin clerical : that Annates were simony, were alienation, had been forbidden by the Council of Basil; that they reduced bishops to poverty and borrowing. That the Petition was not parliamentary but convocational is proved by a letter of the King to his ambassadors at Rome, 21 Mar. 1531(2), in which he says that "all the bishops" had complained to him about Annates, and uses some of the arguments contained in the Petition. His ambassadors were to tell the Pope "Annatarum questionem veterem esse, et illarum solutionem in Concilio Basiliensi reprobatam : deinde novis officiariis Romae creatis, et estimatione pecuniae aucta, in tam immensam exactionem crevisse, ut de eo Nobis gravissime conquesti sint omnes Episcopi. Nuperime autem querela apud populum suscitata est quod Ebor. et Winton. Episcopi a suis amicis pecuniam, quam presentem non habebant, mutuo accipere coacti sint," &c. *State Papers*, vii. 361.

CHAPTER III.

A.D. 1533, 1534.

THE public business of the two following years was coloured by the King's matter. Five years had now rolled away since Henry first began to move for a divorce : and he seemed little nearer to the attainment of his wishes. At the beginning therefore of 1533, he broke the long suspense by secretly marrying Anne Boleyn, whom he had made Marchioness of Pembroke, granting her a yearly provision of a thousand pounds out of the revenues of the see of Durham. His wavering ally the King of France was informed of what he had done: and undertook to keep the secret, and to see and conciliate the Pope. But neither by the course of nature nor of policy could the fact remain concealed until the proposed interview between the Pope and the French King had passed. The consequences of marriage soon became apparent; and on Easter Eve the bride was ordered to receive the honours due to the consort of the King. The consequences of an appeal by the rightful Queen against the bigamy were to be anticipated : and Parliament, meeting in February, passed the famous Act for restraining appeals to Rome. From this time the negotiations of Europe, involved in the Divorce, became an intricate web of mutual mistrust, indecision, and contempt. Concessions were made and withdrawn by England, France, and the Pope : interviews were arranged, but never passed, or came to nothing; while on the other hand, behind the shifting clouds of foreign diplomacy, the processes begun within the realm, both civil and ecclesiastical, moved steadily and swiftly forward to the total abolition of the authority of Rome.

The Act for the restraint of Appeals has acquired and deserved the fame of being the first decisive blow struck by the English legislature against the power of the Pope. In the most important branch it put an end to his authority altogether. Legislation, hitherto, both in this and former reigns, had aimed no further than to check and limit his authority. It was one thing to regulate the licenses of the Pope, or to diminish the revenue which he drew out of the realm : and another thing to abolish his appellate jurisdiction within the realm. The former had been the object of law hitherto, from the statute of Provisors to the statute against Annates : and the statute against Annates, the last of the kind, contained an explicit declaration that the King and his subjects remained still in the obedience of Holy Church. No such declaration will be found in the Act about appeals, nor in any subsequent Act of Parliament. Henceforth the object of legislation was not the limitation but the destruction of the Papal power.

But though the object and operation of the laws became different from what it had been, yet their nature and principle remained the same as they had ever been. The former laws had sought to remedy a mischief. The Act of Appeals and the great Acts which followed it in the separation of England from Rome sought to remedy the same mischief. By the one no less than by the other the power of the Pope within the realm was treated as an usurpation, which on the one hand was suffered, and on the other hand repudiated. Alike they spoke of it as an annoyance, an inquietation, and an inconvenience. Against it they both asserted the independence of the realm. The former laws held the Pope in check within the realm: the latter drove the Pope away. The latter, in the strenuousness of their action, asserted the independence of the realm by asserting formally the supremacy of the King. But this supremacy had always existed, and was implied in every one of the former statutes. Within the realm the King was always supreme. But the latter statutes—the statutes of the Reformation—which affirmed the supremacy of the King, never went on to deny the supremacy of the Pope, for the reason that no such supremacy had ever existed. They spoke of the annoyance which the prerogatives, liberties, and privileges of the Crown, or in one word the royal supremacy, had received at various times from the authority of the Pope : but they never acknowledged that the Pope had been supreme in England, and that there was one supremacy impugning another. What the Pope had was not supremacy but primacy; and they deprived him of whatever internal jurisdiction or authority he had acquired in the realm from his pre-eminence as prime patriarch of Christendom. Having driven him out of the realm, they pursued him no further at first. They allowed his primacy to begin where the supremacy of the Crown ended; or the supremacy of the Crown to begin where his primacy ended. The internal independence of the realm, and of the Church of England as the realm in the spiritual capacity, was finally asserted. But it would be impossible to gather out of the various enactments in which this was now declared a single word to the effect that England denied the primacy of Rome.

Regarded in the immediate object, the Act for Restraint of Appeals appears a base aggravation of injury. Queen Katharine had married the King under a dis-

pensation from the Pope. After all that had passed—
the King's appeals, the trial, the negotiations—the height
of cowardly barbarity seemed to be reached when she
was cut off from the right of appeal, because the King
had married another woman, the suit yet depending:
and the legal device by which the King covered his
bigamy is of a piece with his inconsistent craft in punishing Wolsey for holding the Pope's commission, after
procuring it for him. But this miserable piece of
retrospective legislation is, nevertheless, the great
declaration of the internal independence of England,
uttered in language worthy of the matter. It would
be impossible to find a more admirable exposition of
the constitution of the realm than that which is given
in the preamble of this statute. The old imperial theory
of the realm—that England is an empire—is renewed;*
the King is declared to be the supreme head of the
realm, to whom the subjects owed obedience next to
God: and the subjects compose the body politic, which
is in one capacity termed the spiritualty, in another the
temporalty; consisting of the same people, governed

---

* From the days of Athelstan, it is the observation of Mr. Freeman,
the kings of the English assumed the title of Emperor of Britain, meaning
thereby to assert the independence of the English Crown upon any foreign
superior, and also the dependence of all the other powers of Britain
upon the English Crown. "It was meant to assert that the King of
the English was not the homager but the peer alike of the Imperator
of the West and of the Basileus of the East: and it was meant to assert
that Scots, Welsh, and Cumbrians owed no duty to Rome or Byzantium,
but only to their Father and Lord at Winchester."—*Norm. Conq.*, i.
p. 142. It was meant indeed to assert that Britain was the third imperial
division of Christendom.

To this theory, or rather to this important fact, the ecclesiastical
division anciently agreed. The Britannic churches constituted a separate
Patriarchate. Archbishop Anselm received from the Pope at the Council
of Bari, the title of Pope—Papa alterius orbis: that is to say, the Primate
of the English Church was acknowledged to be a patriarch, owning indeed
the primacy, but not the supremacy of Rome; Just as the Constantino-
politan patriarch owned the primacy but not the supremacy of Rome.

under the King, in either capacity, by the proper officers.* All causes of the law divine, or of spiritual learning, that arose within the realm, were declared to have been determined hitherto, and still to be determined by the English Church, or the spiritualty; and all causes for property and goods, and for the preservation of peace, to be administered, adjudged, and executed by the ministers and judges of the temporalty.†

---

* "In divers sundry old authentic histories and chronicles it is manifestly declared and expressed, that this realm of England is an empire, and so hath been accepted in the world, governed by one supreme head and King, having the dignity and royal estate of the imperial crown of the same: unto whom a body politic, composed of all sorts and degrees of people, divided in terms and by names of spiritualty and temporalty, been bounden and owen to bear, next to God, a natural and humble obedience: he being also institute and furnished, by the goodness and sufferance of Almighty God, with plenary, whole, and entire power, pre-eminence, authority, prerogative and jurisdiction, to render and yield justice and final determination to all manner of folk, resiants or subjects within this his realm, in all causes, matters, debates and contentions happening to occur, insurge, or begin, within the limits thereof, without restraint or provocation to any foreign princes or potentates of the world: the body spiritual whereof having power, when any cause of the law divine happened to come in question, or of spiritual learning, then it was declared, interpreted, and shewed by that part of the said body politic, called the spiritualty, now being usually called the English Church, which always hath been reputed, and also found, to be of that sort that both for knowledge, integrity, and sufficiency of number, it hath been always thought, and is also at this hour, sufficient and meet of itself, without the intermeddling of any exterior person or persons, to declare and determine all such doubts, and to administer all such offices and duties, as to their rooms spiritual doth appertain: for the due administration whereof, and to keep them from corruption and sinister affection, the King's most noble progenitors, and the antecessors of the nobles of this realm, have sufficiently endowed the said Church both with honour and possessions: and the laws temporal, for trial of property of lands and goods, and for the conservation of the people of this realm in unity and peace, without rapine or spoil, was, and yet is, administered, adjudged, and executed by sundry Judges and ministers of the other part of the said body politic, called the temporalty; and both their authorities and jurisdictions do conjoin together in the due administration of justice, the one to help the other."—24 H. VIII. c. 12.

† It is very remarkable that in this important statute while we read,

To return, therefore, to genuine English antiquity, it was enacted that all causes determined by spiritual jurisdiction—all causes testamentary, causes of matrimony and divorce, rights of tithe, oblations and obventions—should be adjudged within the King's dominions; and no appeals used out of the realm. The prelates of the realm, the ministers and curates, were desired to execute all sacraments, sacramentals, and divine services, in spite of any fulminations of interdicts, inhibitions, or excommunications, on pain of a year's imprisonment. Any person procuring sentences or processes from Rome was to incur the forfeiture of Præmunire. Appeals were to go no further than the archbishops of the King's dominions : but if any cause should arise touching the King himself, it was to be determined by the Upper House of Convocation, assembled by the King's writ.

This memorable declaration of the independence of the English Church was made, however, at the very time when her ancient liberties were being taken away, and the jurisdiction of her highest court was already impaired. But an illusive spectacle both of the decayed dignity of the Convocation, and of the vanishing power of the Pope was presented, when the clergy of the southern province were assembled, March 26, to hold debate and give sentence on the matter agitated between the King and Queen. It would seem that the Act about Appeals was not yet gone through Parliament when the clergy met, since the first question asked among the prelates, when the King's business was laid before them by the

both of the temporalty, and the judges and ministers of the temporalty on the one hand, we read only of the spiritualty on the other hand, and nothing of the officers of the spiritualty, that is of the ordinaries of the Church, or the clergy in their official capacity. To complete the balance of the scheme this was needed : and the omission could not have been accidental in so carefully worded an instrument. It shows the leaven which was working.

Lord President, the Bishop of London, was, whether they could dispute in the case while it lay undecided before the Pontiff. To satisfy their scruples the transumpt of a Papal Breve, three years old, was exhibited by Stokesley, in which it was contained, among other things, that the Chief Pontiff desired every one to declare his mind and opinion openly and fearlessly.*

---

* "Tum quæstio vertebatur, an liceret disputare in negotio regio, eo quod negotium pendebat coram summo Pontifice indecisum : et dominus præses respondebat ostendendo quoddam instrumentum confectum super transumptione cujusdam brevis apostolici, in quo inter alia continebatur quod summus Pontifex voluit unumquemque declarare mentem suam et opiniones suas in dicta causa libere et impune."—*Wilkins*, iii. 756.

"Keep a thing, its use will come." The history of this Papal Breve is curious. Ghinucci, the able Bishop of Worcester, one of Henry's ambassadors at Rome, sent a letter to Stokesley, who was at Bologna, in 1530, telling him that he had been to the Pope to ask him to modify a Breve which had been issued on the King's business, so as to allow the Universities and certain persons named by the King to give their opinion freely and fearlessly on the King's cause : the Pope answered that in the Breve he had exhorted men to have God before their eyes, and speak their minds honestly ; and that this was enough. Ghinucci replied that men should be informed that they might write their opinions, for that many feared to write, lest they should displease his Holiness ; and he furthermore requested that whereas the Breve only referred to canonists, and seemed to exclude theologians, his Holiness would at least write to his Nuncio at Venice (whither the Breve had been sent), that he would have no displeasure if certain men to be nominated by Henry's ambassador there, should without fear or respect declare their opinion of the King's cause. The Pope replied that he would order his Nuncio to do all that ought to be done, and would gratify the King's party in all that he could with honour. Of this letter from Ghinucci, Stokesley made a copy with his own hand, and sent it to Henry. It may perhaps be questioned whether a copy or transcript of the Breve itself was procured by Stokesley, or whether it was so altered by the Pope as to give the authority to speak freely which it was pretended to give. This cannot have been the celebrated Breve which was sent by the former Pope Julius into several countries, but not into England ; the authenticity of which was disputed by Henry's advisers. Stokesley now remembered the affair, and, to quiet the scruples of the clergy, produced an instrument made on [super] a transumpt of the Breve, or perhaps the Breve corrected according to Ghinucci's letter. *State Pap.*, vol. vii. 239. A definition of transumpt, the word lately revived in the State Papers for a copy made by authority, or an attested copy, may be acceptable : "Quæ in primis tabulis

Nor was the debate on the King's business restricted to the prelates, as the statute ordered: the solemnities of discussion were enacted in both the Houses of the clergy. In imitation of the Roman Consistory, in imitation of the foreign Universities, they were divided by the experienced Stokesley * into the two bodies of the theologians and the jurists, or canonists; and to either of these bodies was submitted a question appropriate to their studies. The theologians were to determine whether marriage with the widow of a brother dying without children were forbidden by the laws of nature and of God, so that it lay beyond the dispensation of the Chief Pontiff. The sentences which had been procured from the Universities of Europe were laid before them, and they were required to frame their answer according to the model of the theological faculty of Paris. This was indeed the point which made the King's great matter the crucial question of the age in England: whether the spiritual power of the Chief Pontiff extended over all controversies of faith and morals: if it were denied in such an instance, it must fall altogether. The controversy was keen; Stokesley of London leading on the one side, and Fisher of Rochester on the other. At length the former party carried the day; the Bishops of London, St. Asaph's, and Lincoln, with thirty-six abbots and priors, giving sentence according to the determinations of the Universities and the wishes of the King. To these the six abbots

transcripta sunt, solemnitate juris adhibita, dicuntur transumpta, et actio ipsa transumptio." *Calepini Dict.*

* Stokesley had witnessed the ceremonious procedures of Bologna and Padua in the King's business, where the doctors were divided into jurists and theologians. *State Papers*, vii. 253. According to the original Breve (see last note), the Pope seems to have restricted the question to the former Faculty; no mention was made in the Breve of theologians, but the omission escaped not the acute Ghinucci.—(*Ib.* 239.)

of Gloucester, Thorney, Bermondsey, Vallacrux, Croyland, and Lilshul soon afterwards adhered, adding however the important provision, " Si dicta relicta prius erat carnaliter cognita a fratre mortuo." The number of dissentients was nineteen.* In the Lower House the theologians were still less unanimous. Fourteen answered in the affirmative, seven in the negative, one remained doubtful, and one recorded his opinion that the case belonged to the divine and moral law, but was dispensable by the Pope.

The question propounded to the canonists was, whether the marriage of Prince Arthur with the Lady Katharine had been consummated. The Lower House, who reached their determination before the other, gave sentence that the proofs were sufficient that it had ; but several among them put in protestations to the contrary. The canonists of the Upper House were the Bishops of Winchester, Exeter, and Bath and Wells and three other bishops who voted by proxy. The two former of those who were there agreed in the affirmative ; the latter, the inflexible Clark, stood negative.†

---

* Compare the Reg. Conv. (Wilkins, iii. 756) with the public instruments made out of the Acts by the notaries (Rymer, xiv. p. 454). From the latter it appears that the total number of theologians present was sixty-six, and that the number of proxies was one hundred and ninety-seven. I suppose that it was from this document that Burnet was led into his absurd theory that "in the days of popery" the deans and archdeacons sat in the Upper House, and the Lower House consisted only of the proctors of the clergy. He supposes that the theologians enumerated were all of the Upper House, and is puzzled to account for so large a number there. But in fact the notaries, whom the King sent, never condescended to make an exact copy of the Acts of Convocation ; they made a rough compendium, and lumped the clergy of the two Houses all together. Their numbers refer to both Houses. Collier elaborately confutes Burnet, but might have spared his labour. The total number of canonists present (in both Houses) was forty-four.

† Wilkins, iii. 756–7.

These proceedings occupied a week, from the opening of Convocation to the 5th of April. At the end of them Doctor Tregonwell, a lawyer whose name became well known afterwards, appeared, and in the name of the King and the nobles demanded to examine the Acts of the assembly, that their determinations might be reduced to a public instrument. In the middle of the session, April 1, the Bishop of London resigned his place of president; and for the first time the uneasy throne of the Most Reverend was filled by the new Archbishop, Thomas Cranmer.

Every great revolution bears along with it well-meaning men who would never have had the desire or the power of setting it in motion; who follow it, with alternate hope and fear perhaps, but without resistance. Revolution may have her fictions and her puppets not less than royalty; and it may chance that a man of this kind, from parts, virtue, or dexterity, may appear the most conspicuous figure to the general eye, may almost give his name to his era, and yet be little more than the tool and plaything of the real authors of change. The log rises to the surface, rides the waters, and enables us to judge the rate of the current; but the waters carry the log. The poor optimist who at this time entered on his troubled·career was a memorable mixture of strength and weakness. To the astonishment of the world* he was lifted into the vacant throne of Warham, over the heads of all the Bishops, on whose bench he had never sat. He was advanced above Gardiner of Winchester, on whom the general expectation rested: a man whose public services had been greater and longer, and whose abilities were at least equal to his own. But Gardiner, though worldly and pliable in comparison with such men as

* " Præter opinionem et sensum multorum." *Antiq. Brit.*

Fisher, or even Clark or Standish, had lately shown a certain severity of intellect and conscience which could not be tried beyond a certain point. The instinct of Henry and Crumwel taught them that a man of different mould was needed to complete their triumvirate. Cranmer had a greater capacity than either Henry or Crumwel: he had much of the dispassionate quality of the statesman; but withal an indecision and want of readiness which laid him at the mercy of inferior men, and often produced duplicity in his own conduct. He joined innocency with a disposition to deal tenderly with himself, painfulness with love of ease, the solemnity of virtue with a morbid conscience and a tremulous sensibility to every current of opinion. This large, timorous, and unwieldy nature was needful to the men of violence and craft who now held in their hands the destinies of the country and the Church. He became their scribe, their tool, their voice. It is the misfortune of a nation when such a character is discovered and so used. Such a character may rise into offices and dignities which were created for one purpose, and may turn them to another. Such a character may commit the deepest treason with a clear conscience. Under cover of the reputation of such a character, the vilest and most unscrupulous may eat their way into institutions which would have defied their open approach, and may find their worst deeds consecrated in the eyes of posterity. The virtues and the reputation of Cranmer must not blind us to the tragedy which was acted under his primacy; nor cause us to forget that he was the slave first of Henry and Crumwel, afterwards of Somerset, Paget, and Northumberland: that under him the Church of England fell from wealth into poverty: that he offered no resistance to the enormous sacrilege of this and the following reign, from which indeed his own hands were not altogether clean; and that nothing was more convenient to the spoilers of the Church than that he should have been the highest of her Bishops. In doctrine he ran from one position to another with the whole rabble of innovators at his heels, until at last he seemed ready to surrender the Catholicity of the Church to the Sacramentarians. And yet there was neither any rapine committed nor any alteration effected in the sixteenth century which had not been proposed a century before, and which might not have been carried out, if Archbishop Arundel had not been a different man from Archbishop Cranmer.

Before his sudden elevation, Cranmer had only been known for his zeal in the King's matter. He had passed twenty-five years as an undistinguished student in his University, when accident recommended him to the King as an advocate for the nullity of the marriage with Katharine. It is improbable that he deserved the fame which he has acquired of being the author of the scheme of submitting the question to the universities of Europe. But he was employed by the King to write an official defence of his case; and he performed his task in Durham House, the town residence of the father of Anne Boleyn. He read and expounded his own performance before the two English Universities: he was in the commission with Gardiner and the King's Almoner Fox, which coerced the Universities into giving a favourable sentence. He was then employed in the various embassies to advocate the royal cause in France, Italy, and Germany. When he went to Rome the Pope made him Pœnitentiary of England: an important and lucrative office, since all the dispensations and licenses passed through the hands of him who held it. This mark of con-

fidence was but ill repaid by Cranmer, when he was
recalled from his foreign travels to the primacy of all
England.

It is probable enough that he was unwilling to
accept so vast an advance of dignity. The long habits
of studious retirement were hard to break. And he
had in Germany contracted his second marriage. The
scandal of a married archbishop sitting, for the first
time in history, in the see of Becket and Chicheley,
would be great: the only means of diminishing it
would be separation from his wife. But it was
dangerous to resist the determination of the King.
The necessary measures were hurried forward, and
there are few instances of the see of Canterbury being
so rapidly filled after a vacancy. Warham died at the
end of August in 1532. Before the end of the next
January, Cranmer, though still absent in Germany, was
elected by the prior and convent of Christ Church in
Canterbury. Eleven bulls, authorising the various
parts of the appointment, were expedited from Rome,
at the King's instance, in less than as many days, the
last bearing date of March 2. At the end of the same
month the new Archbishop was consecrated.

On the day of his consecration he proved his fitness for the work for which he was designed. Before
taking the customary oath of obedience to the Pope,
he made a Solemn Protestation in writing that he took
it more for form than in reality, and held himself
bound thereby to nothing against the laws of God and
the King: that he remained free to consult and devise
for the reformation of religion, the government of the
Church of England and the prerogative of the Crown.
He protested furthermore that whatever oath his proctor at Rome had exhibited in his name, it was not his intention to give him authority to promise anything in his

name contrary or repugnant to his oath which he was
to make to the King.   And if his proctor had already
exhibited such an oath, it was without his knowledge
or authority, and therefore invalid.*   This extraordinary procedure would have been more to his
honour if he had informed the Pope by his proctor of
what he was about to do, before procuring his bulls.
When he took the oath, or oaths, of obedience to the
Pope he made many omissions : and then with an
easier conscience proceeded to the oath to the King for
his temporalties.   This also he altered somewhat from
the ancient form, though in the ancient form it had
been held sufficient to annul whatever might be prejudicial to the realm in the oath to maintain the
Papacy.†

---

* Strype's Cranm., App. No. 5.   It seems doubtful whether this
Protestation was ever made in public. Fuller, Strype, and Burnet say
that it was twice repeated on the day of consecration, before witnesses,
and that authentic copies were made of it : so that "it was plain," says
Burnet, "that he intended no cheat, but to act fairly and above board."
And yet the historian throws the responsibility on "some canonists and
casuists," who, he says, advised Cranmer to do a thing "that agreed better
with their maxims than his integrity." In his Examination in 1555
Cranmer gave some particulars that confirm this. See vol. iv. p. 417
huj. op.   The Protestation is given by Fuller.

† If the reader will compare the old Oath of Canonical Obedience to
the Pope, which Burnet gives in English (Bk. ii. ann. 1532), with the
same Oath as Cranmer took it, given in Strype's Cranm. App. 5, he will
find that Cranmer qualified the promise to defend the Roman Papacy,
the rules of the Holy Fathers, and the Regality of St. Peter, by inserting
a "salvo meo ordine," and omitting "the rules of the Holy Fathers." He
also omitted the following clauses : "The rights, honours, privileges,
authorities of the Church of Rome, and of the Pope and his successors
I shall cause to be conserved, defended, augmented and promoted. I shall
not be in council, treaty, or any act, in the which anything shall be
imagined against him or the Church of Rome, their rights, sees, honours,
or powers. And if I know any such to be moved or compassed, I shall
resist it to my power, and as soon as I can, I shall advertise him, or such
as may give him knowledge. The rules of the Holy Fathers, the Decrees,
Ordinances, Sentences, Dispositions, Reservations, Provisions, and
Commandments Apostolic, I shall keep to my power, and cause to be

The new Archbishop, having thus placed himself wholly in the King's hands, was soon abundantly employed. He was to use his office to prepare the nation for the formal divorce of the Queen: he was to create a state of public feeling which might endure the scenes which were to be enacted that she might be put away: and from his tribunal was to sound the sentence of her degradation. A few days after his first appearance in Convocation, he sent, April 12, two letters, of the same import but of slightly various language, to the King. In both of them he informed the King that the great cause was much in the mouths of the rude and ignorant, who talked of the danger of an uncertain succession: he alleged that the clergy, and more especially the heads and presidents of the clergy, were falling into increasing obloquy because they provided

---

kept of others. Heretics, Schismatics, and Rebels to our Holy Father and his successors I shall resist and persecute to my power." The Oath to the King, as he took it, ran as follows (the italics are to show the Cranmerian humility):—"I renounce and utterly forsake all such clauses, words, sentences and grants which I have of the Pope's Holiness in his Bulls of the Archbishopric of Cant. that in any manner was, is, or may be hurtful or prejudicial to your Highness, your heirs, successors, estate, or dignity royal. Knowing myself to *take* and hold the said Archbishopric *immediately* and only of your Highness, *and of none other*: most lowly beseeching the same for the restitution of the temporalties of the said Archbishopric: professing to be faithful, true, and obedient subject to your said Highness, your heirs and successors, during my life. So help me God and the Holy Evangelists." The old form was the same with this down to the word royal. It then proceeded, "And also I do swear that I shall be faithful and true, and faith and truth I shall bear to you my Sovereign Lord, and to your heirs, kings of the same, of life and limb and yearly worship above all creatures, for to live and die with you and yours above all people. And diligently I shall be attendant to all your needs and business after my wit and power: and your counsel shall I keep and hold, knowledging myself to hold my bishopric of you only, beseeching you of restitution of the temporalties of the same: promising as before that I shall be a faithful, true, and obedient subject to your said Highness, heirs, and succe sors, during my life; and the services and other things due to your Highness for the restitution of the temporalties of the said Bishopric I shall truly do and obediently perform. So help me God and all saints."

no remedy for the dangers which the rude and ignorant thought to be imminent: himself he owned to be "a poor wretch and much unworthy," but nevertheless he humbly besought to be allowed, according to his office, to proceed to the examination and final determination of the great cause. Both the letters were humble enough: but one of them was written in a somewhat humbler strain than the other. Where in the one he requested the King's favour and pleasure, in the other he asked the King to license him to proceed. In the one he attempted some imitation of the style of former primates, talking of "the laws of God and Holy Church," and of his duty to relieve "all manner griefs and infirmities of the people:" in the other he omitted this passage. In the one he preferred his requests "most humbly on his knees:" in the other "prostrate at the feet of his Majesty." Henry selected the more servile of the two for an authoritative answer of consent: and in his answer he rolled his creature in the dust. He recapitulated the humble expressions of the Archbishop: he reminded him that he was nothing more than the principal minister of the spiritual jurisdiction belonging to the Crown; and that the sovereign recognised no superior but God, and was not subject to the laws of any earthly creature. But he refused not the humble petition; and by letters sealed with his seal and signed with his sign manual, he licensed him to proceed in the great cause.*

In pursuance of this mandate, the Archbishop, May 8, proceeded to Dunstable, a place within four miles of the Queen's residence of Ampthill, and set up his court in the Lady chapel of the convent there, of which the prior, Markham by name, was a zealot of the King's

---

* State Papers, i. 390: or Cranmer's Rem., Park. Soc., 237.

party. The diocesan, Longland of Lincoln, who was the King's confessor, was his assessor on the bench.* Bishop Gardiner, Dr. Bell, Dr. Claybroke, Dr. Tregonwell, Dr. Hewis, Dr. Olyver, Dr. Brytton, and Archdeacon Bedyl,† were among the counsel for the King. Sir Francis Bryan, the cousin of Anne Boleyn, along with Sir Thomas Gage and Lord Vaux, was delicately selected to summon the Queen; an office which he executed with sufficient insolence. On her refusal to appear, she was pronounced contumacious, and no further notice was taken of her throughout the trial. Nor even when the sentence was pronounced was she called to receive it. With characteristic timidity the Archbishop, fearing lest she should be moved at last to appear before his tribunal, and " do that thing therein which peradventure she would not do if she heard little of it," concealed the day on which he meant to pronounce sentence from all but the King and Crumwel, imploring both to keep the secret until all was over.‡ In the elaborate sentence of divorce which at length he fulminated against her, he embellished the record of her contumacious absence with

---

* Holinshed, Strype, and Mr. Froude (i. 439, 444) repeat that the Bishop of Bath and Wells, the inflexible Clark, was associated with Cranmer on the trial of the Queen. Cranmer himself in his letters enumerated his coadjutors, but not Clark, nor is it likely that he was there.

† Bedyl was clerk of the Council, and reported the proceedings of each day to Crumwel. See his letter in *State Papers*, i. 395. Some say that Crumwel set him to watch Cranmer. But no; Cranmer needed no watching. It is true that Bedyl says that Cranmer conducted himself at Dunstable so as to give "no evident cause of suspicion;" but that is " of suspicion to be noted in him by counsel of Lady Katharine, if she had had any present here," which she had not. It was praise of Cranmer's dexterity that Bedyl meant to bestow; not of his fidelity to the King, which was above praise. If Crumwel had set Bedyl to watch Cranmer, Bedyl would have found Cranmer suspicious enough. Crumwel afterwards gave Bedyl plenty to do.

‡ Letters, Parker Soc., p. 242.

the pious prayer that it might be compensated by the divine presence.*

The sentence of divorce was pronounced on the 23rd of May. On the 1st of June the new Queen was crowned. In the short intervening period the Archbishop had to complete his work by holding another court at Lambeth : where he officially pronounced Henry and Anne to be joined in lawful matrimony, their marriage to have been public and manifest, and to be now confirmed by his judicial and pastoral authority.† A confirmation equally important was next procured from the clergy of the northern province.. To them in Convocation assembled the same questions had been submitted which had been exercising their brethren of the south. Divided into the same classes of theologians and canonists they had held disputations on the King's matter, and had arrived at the same determination with a more general consent. Out of fifty-one theologians, of whom, however, twenty-four appeared only by proxy, there were no more than two who dissented from the conclusion that the case was indispensable by the Pope. Two only out of forty-four canonists who were personally present, and to whom are to be added five or six proxies, were found to deny that the marriage of Arthur and Katharine had been consummated. The names of the dissidents, the particulars of the discussions, are unknown. At the end, an emissary of the King, Doctor Roland Lee, had duly appeared, May 13, and demanded in the name of the King and the nobles to examine the Acts, and reduce them to a public instrument. But this not being thought sufficient, another royal commissary in Doctor Olyver

---

* " CuJus absentia divina repleatur præsentia."
† Lingard, Collier.

appeared, June 13, before the Archbishop of York, to cause another search and new copies of the public instrument to be made, which were to be dispersed abroad, that their contents might be known to all the faithful in Christ.* It is remarkable that the several instruments promulgated on the Divorce by the arch-bishops, by which in effect the power of the Pope was made void, were the last public documents in which the primates of England wrote themselves legates of the Apostolic See.

Meanwhile the heretics were not idle. In spite of his former submissions and promises, Latimer was at it again. In the pulpit at Bristol he again de-claimed against the received doctrines concerning Purgatory, the worship of saints, and pilgrimages to their images : and, as soon as it met, the Convocation of Canterbury, before proceeding to the King's matter, was compelled to consider the relapse of an imprudent orator. Their decision was wise and merciful. A copy of Latimer's former submission was ordered to be sent down to the parts which he was infesting, or should infest hereafter; and it was hoped that this record of the past, ready to be produced against him, would reduce him to moderation in the future. No higher measure was taken against him ; but this seems to have been of little effect, since in October he was inhibited by Stokesley from preaching within the diocese of London.†

These light doings hang in the balance against the heavy tragedy of John Frith, which was enacted in full painfulness in the midsummer of the year. John Frith was the most genuine martyr of the English Reformation. Whatever qualities, give dignity to

* Wilkins, iii. 765 ; Rymer, Fœd., xiv. 474.
† Wilkins, iii. 756, 760.

voluntary death were united in him.   Constancy,
intellect, deliberation, learning, and piety, combined
with youthfulness of years to grace the costly offering
which he made to his convictions.   At first the pupil
of Gardiner at Cambridge, he had been among the
young men of that University whom Wolsey, for their
parts and promise, transplanted to his magnificent
foundation in Oxford.   There he fell in with the new
learning ; and, along with many other members of the
foundation, gave himself to the study of the forbidden
books of the Lutherans.   On the charge of heresy he
was thrown into prison by the infamous Doctor
London ; and lay, with Sumner, Clerk, Bailey, and
others, in the cellar where the salt fish of their college
was stored, their only atmosphere, and almost their
only food, for many months.   Under the severities of
this captivity three of his companions who have been
named died.   When the survivors were released by
the lenity of the great Cardinal, Frith betook himself
to London, where he formed the acquaintance of
Tyndale.   He then went into Flanders, where he
married.*   In Flanders he published his first work,
a treatise against Purgatory, written partly in answer
to More's celebrated Supplication of Souls.   His tract
is a model of polemics ; close, severe, and learned ;
merciless to his great opponent, and yet free from that
unmeasured vituperation which disgusts the unpre-
judiced reader of Fish or Tyndale : and More, who
feared few adversaries, allowed it to pass in silence.†
Afterwards returning to England, Frith met with

---

* *State Papers*, vii. p. 302. Fuller.

† It is possible that More never saw it within a time when an answer
might have been expected. He observes that the Christian Brethren
took pains to prevent their books from coming into his hands.—" Answer
to a nameless Heretic," Works, p. 1035. But Frith's qualities had drawn
the attention of the King.—*State Papers*, as above.

many curious adventures, until at length he was betrayed and lodged in the Tower, chiefly, as Fox asserts, through the great hatred and deadly pursuit of the enemy whom he had provoked. But in truth he had become a member of the secret society of the Christian Brethren; a society formed to disseminate the prohibited books of the heretics; and his fearless activity exposed him easily to danger. It may be regretted that so fine a nature should have fallen into an association which, along with some men of sincere religious zeal, embraced the lightest of those heady characters which swim to the top in a revolution. The runaways of monasteries, clerical vagabonds and renegades of every kind, broken merchants, and printers who drove a roaring contraband trade in heresy, at the peril of bolder men than themselves, were among the brethren with whom this learned and godly youth joined fellowship. They repeatedly betrayed him. He was betrayed into prison; and in prison he was betrayed again. At the request of one of them he wrote, without intending to publish it, a brief discourse on the Sacrament. Another of them delivered this into the hands of More; and it became both the eventual cause of the death of the writer, and the immediate occasion of another brush between him and the old champion of the old learning. More wrote in answer to it his "Letter impugning the erroneous writing of John Frith against the blessed Sacrament of the altar." In this piece he affects to treat his antagonist as still a very young man, though he was now about twenty-five years old; and by lamenting the difficulty of procuring Frith's earlier writings, seems to indicate a reason for his own silence under his former attack. But he unconsciously extols him, when he says that he "teacheth in a few leaves shortly, all the poison that Wickliffe, Œcolampadius, Huskin, Tyndale, and Zuinglius have taught in all their books before." Frith instantly replied in his book on the Sacrament. This remarkable work may claim to be the beginning in England, in this age, of the terrific controversy on the nature of the Presence in the Sacrament, which was already convulsing the continent, and was destined to fill all Europe with blood and flame for a century to come. It is the first systematic refutation of the tenet of Transubstantiation which the English language contains. It is a store of arguments and authors, from which Cranmer borrowed most of the learning which he afterwards displayed against Gardiner. To Frith himself it proved fatal : and he knew that it would be so. " I took upon me," he wrote in the preface, "to touch this terrible tragedy, and wrote a treatise which, besides my painful imprisonment, is like to purchase me most cruel death, which I am ready and glad to receive with the spirit and inward man, although the flesh be frail, whensoever it shall please God to lay it upon me."

Frith had been in prison several months, when he was sent to Lambeth to be examined before the new Archbishop of Canterbury. In the same letter in which Cranmer describes the divorce of Katharine and the coronation of Anne, he gives his correspondent Hawkins the news of "one Frith" who was ordered by the King to be examined before himself, Gardiner, Stokesley, the Duke of Suffolk, Lord Chancellor Audley, and the Earl of Wiltshire. The laymen on this mixed commission were afterwards very notable maintainers of the Reformation ; and the whole tribunal must sustain the burden of the condemnation of Frith. But there appears to have been no disposition to deal harshly with him. Cranmer was kind ; and sent for him three or four times to persuade him to leave his opinions. His old tutor Gardiner showed him all the favour that he could.* Frith himself never complained of the way in which his examination was conducted. Some attempt had been made previously to interest Crumwel in his behalf: and Crumwel might perhaps have prevented the examination if he had chosen. But Crumwel seems not to have interfered; and the examination being held, could only end in one way.†

He was examined but upon two articles—those in which he had most stood out in controversy—Purgatory and the Sacrament of the altar. But what his opinions were on these questions, and especially on the latter, whether he were a Lutheran, or, as both More and Cranmer thought, he went far beyond Luther,‡ needs not to be enquired. Many died after him for the opinions which he held: and he was doubtless ready to have died for them; but he died neither for denying the " Pope's Purgatory " nor the dogma of Transubstantiation. He resisted upon another principle, which makes him far more memorable. The friend of Tyndale, the disciple of Œcolampadius, the stubborn antagonist of More, laid down his life in the cause of religious liberty. He died to establish the difference between a necessary article of faith and a thing which may be left indifferent. When he was examined on Purgatory, he gave his opinion freely and

---

* Gardiner's kindness was noticed in this case. Fox of course ascribes it to hypocritical cruelty.

† Sir E. Walsingham, writing to Crumwel about the prisoners in the Tower, says:—" Two of them wear irons, and Frith weareth none. Although he lacketh irons, he lacketh not wit nor pleasant tongue. His learning passeth my judgment. Sir, as ye said, it were great pity to lose him, if he may be reconciled." *Froude*, i. p. 477.

‡ "Not only affirming it to be very bread still, as Luther doth, but also (as these other beasts do), sayeth it is nothing else." *More*. The " other beasts " were Wickliffe, Œcolampadius, Tyndale, and Zuinglius.

denied the common opinion ; but added, " Nevertheless I count neither part a necessary article of our faith, necessarily to be believed under pain of damnation, whether there be such a Purgatory or not." On Transubstantiation he said, " That this should be a necessary article of the faith, I think no man can say it with a good conscience, although it were true indeed."

There is not a more glorious writing in the English language than that from which these sentences are taken : the " Articles wherefore john Frith died." To make all dogmas equally binding, to abolish the distinction between an article of faith and a thing indifferent, was the great tyranny of Rome, and the mother of the calamities of the world. We shall soon be called to observe that the first touch of true reformation was the restoration of this lost distinction, though the line was far from being drawn where Frith would have laid it. Meanwhile we may admire the greatness of the man who first died for freedom of conscience, and in sweet and touching words justified himself in laying down his life upon that ground.*

* " I think many men wonder how I can die in this article, seeing that it is no necessary article of our faith, for I grant that neither part is an article necessary to be believed under pain of damnation, but leave it as a thing indifferent, to think thereon as God shall instil in every man's mind, and that neither part condemn other in this matter, but receive each other in brotherly love, reserving each other's infirmity to God.

" The cause of my death is this : because I cannot in conscience abjure and swear that our prelates' opinion of the Sacrament (that is, that the substance of bread and wine is verily changed into the flesh and blood of our Saviour, Jesus Christ), is an undoubted article of the faith, necessary to be believed under pain of damnation.

" Now, though this opinion were indeed true (which thing they can neither prove true by Scripture nor doctors) yet could I not in conscience grant that it should be an article of the faith necessary to be believed : for there are many verities which yet may be no such articles of our faith. It is true that I lay in irons when I wrote this : howbeit I would not have you to receive this truth for an article of our faith ; for ye may think the contrary without all jeopardy of damnation." These Articles, as given in Frith's works (Russel's Ed. vol. iv. p. 450), are marvellously different from the version of them which Fox gives.

Frith went to the fire on July the fourth. His ordinary, Stokesley, to whom he was left by the commissioners, gave sentence with expressions of regret which we need not reckon insincere, and delivered him over to the secular arm at least a fortnight before his execution. His sufferings, which were prolonged, are said to have been aggravated by the ribaldry of some vile friar. His patience and courage were, as might be expected, unmoved and immovable. Bound to the same stake with him was a still younger sufferer, Andrew Hewett, a poor simple London tailor, whose general answer to the questions put to him in his examination was that " he thought as Frith thought."

The blame of such miserable scenes is always charged to the prelates of the Church : and on the favourite theory that there is something in the nature or training of ecclesiastics which renders them more cruel than laymen, there the blame is like to rest. But in truth the laws of the land, and the King whose rigorous Proclamations called for the execution of those laws, ought to bear the greater share of censure. The spiritual officers were forced into action by the King. With them laymen were often joined in commission, and took part in whatever was done. If the work had been entrusted to laymen alone : if the spiritual jurisdiction had been transferred to the justices, the laws remaining the same, would it have fared better with the heretics ? On the contrary, the whole power of the laws would have been exerted to put down heresy, as it was exerted to put down vagrancy and felony, or any other disorder : and the King's courts would have been crowded with spiritual offenders. For every fire that was lighted under the bishops, fifty would have been kindled by the new ordinaries of the Church. In the witch trials, the most horrible episode in the whole

story of human folly, which began their fearful activity
with the Reformation, the victims were one hundred
times more numerous than those who perished for
heresy from first to last in England.   The punishments were as cruel:* the alleged crime was even more
remote from human reason : the accused persons were
even more commonly of the classes which most appeal
to human pity.   And the witch trials were held before
lay tribunals in this country.   But the justices have
lacked their Fox.   As for the bishops, though of
course there were individual differences amongst them,
and a Stokesley was not so mild as a Tunstall ; yet as
a body they seem to have been averse from severity,
and slow to put themselves in motion against the
heretics.   When a martyr was brought before them,
they usually did all that lay in their power with him
in the way of persuasion : and the martyr in return
sometimes insulted them outrageously.   In fact they
regarded the processes against heretics as the most
distressing part of their office ; as an insupportable
burden, of which they would have rejoiced to be rid :
and, if Sir Thomas More is to be believed, many·
heretics who were worthy of the extremest penalties,
escaped through the leniency of the ordinaries.†

To make the best of the worst is both the wisdom

---

* Because, though witchcraft was felony, and the penalty of felony
for men was hanging, the offenders were mostly women, and for them the
penalty was burning.

† "And some of them let not with lies and perjury to defend them
self, and some to stand in defence of their errors or false denying of their
own deed, to their great peril of the fire, if their judges were not more
merciful than their malice deserveth.   And all this done, because (as
them self doth at last confess) they think, if they abjure, they shall after
be suffered to preach again.   Such a scabbed itch of vain glory catch
they in their preachings, that though all the world were the worse for it
and their own life lie therein, yet would they long to be pulpited," &c.—
More, Dial. on Her., bk. i. c. 22.

and the duty of those who are entrusted with any
portion of the heavy burden of the state: some of the
prelates who had opposed to the last the divorce of
Katharine, appeared at the coronation of Anne. But
the indignation of the lower clergy was not so easily
suppressed. Bold language, in the pulpit or in conversation, was heard everywhere; piercing even the
ears of the new court, and interrupting the splendour
and hilarity which insulted the sorrows of the dowager
queen. Cranmer had a strong remedy ready. Throughout his diocese he forbade all preaching; and ordered
all the other bishops in his province to do the same,
or nearly the same thing. They were to withdraw all
licenses to preach; and only to grant new ones under
an injunction that they who had them should "in no
wise touch or intermeddle themselves to preach or
teach any such thing that might slander or bring into
doubt and opinion the Catholic and received doctrine
of Christ's Church, or to speak such matters as touch
the prince, his laws, or succession." This restraint
of preaching continued a year. It was an expedient
hitherto unprecedented; but repeated in after times by
him who now devised it. Cranmer was at this moment,
through his share in the Divorce, the most detested
man in England. When he held a visitation at Canterbury in the autumn, his very life was in danger. He
was obliged to seek the protection of Government;
and a writ was issued to the nobility and gentry, requiring them to protect the Archbishop in the visitation
of his own Church.*

The foreign negotiations, which arose on the Sentence of Divorce, exhibited the trepidation and duplicity of Henry. He created a whirlwind of diplomacy.
His agents and ambassadors flew about, perpetually

* Hook's Cranm., Lives, vi. p. 478.

driven by fresh instructions ; and while he feared the indignation of others, he strove to give alarm by shadowy machinations on his own part. The first danger which he apprehended was a combination of the Catholic powers, the beginning of which he expected in a long-projected interview between the Pope and the King of France. To his ambassador Norfolk, he wrote therefore, to " disappoint the interview," to detach the French King by the offer of aid for a war in Piedmont, and to invite him to erect or declare in France a patriarchate, as he himself was doing in England. His next step was to make in the presence of the Archbishop of York, at Greenwich, June 29, a formal Provocation or Appeal from the Pope to a General Council. A few months previously he had refused a General Council when it was proposed by the Pope. He now allowed his appeal to remain unpublished, holding it in reserve as a weapon to be launched in reply to the expected fulmination of the Vatican. On the other side the Pope also prepared and reserved his thunderbolt. A Breve, declaring against Cranmer's Sentence of Divorce, was drawn up, but not to be published before the end of September ; and when that term arrived, it was suspended again. Meanwhile, as before, Henry stood cited to appear at Rome by proxy.

The King of England was unable to prevent the interview between the Pope and the King of France, which passed in November at Marseilles ; but his fears of a league against himself seem to have been groundless. It was impossible to unite Charles and Francis, the haughty rivals who divided Europe, against the Lutherans of Germany, much less against the Catholic realm of England. Nor seems this to have been attempted. But Henry deemed the occasion come for delivering his blow : and from his emissary Bonner the Pope received at Marseilles the Appeal to a General Council. The reception which it met showed the weakness of the power opposed to Henry. The Pope, dissembling his chagrin, returned a conciliatory answer to Bonner; in which he strangely said that he was satisfied that the cause of the King was good, and that if he would make some kind of submission to the Holy See, he should have sentence given in his favour.

This weakness of the Holy Father determined the course of Henry. He held a meeting of his Council December 2; when it was resolved to procure the opinion of the bishops whether or not the Pope were superior to a general council: and, if they could prove that a general council was of paramount authority, it was to be preached and taught, not only by the prelates and the secular clergy, but by the religious in their houses, that the power formerly exercised by the popes in the realm was a breach of the divine law and an invasion of general councils; and that this usurpation got footing here only by the connivance of princes. The provincials and rulers of the four Orders of Friars were specially commanded to cause all their preachers to preach the same; and the Friars Observants, or reformed Franciscans, of the realm, the order most obnoxious to Henry, were to be practised with, and commanded to preach in like manner, or else stayed from preaching. It was ordered that the whole Act for restraint of Appeals to Rome should be transumed and set up on every church door in England: that the King's Appeal from the Pope to a General Council also should be printed, and affixed to every church door throughout England; and that copies of the same should be transmitted into all parts of Christendom, especially into Flanders, where, in the town of Dunkirk, a copy of the Papal monition against the Divorce had been already imprudently or maliciously exposed.* It was also moved to send spies into Scotland, to get information whether that nation were concerting measures with any foreign prince: to send persons of management into Germany, to endeavour to conclude a league with the princes of the empire, the Hans Towns, the cities of Nuremburg and Augsburg, and the merchants of Brabant. The regulation of the household of the dowager Princess and her daughter Mary, and the appointing of their servants, was the last concern which occupied this important assembly.†

The voice of the Church of England was easily procured in favour of the paramount authority of general councils, and the right of princes to call them. However many of them may have misliked the occasion, the spiritual advisers of the Crown had no difficulty in declaring the doctrine of antiquity: and the declaration which was made was attested by the signature not only of Cranmer, but of Fisher, of Clark, of West, and of others who had stood against the Divorce.‡ As to the Provocation or Appeal of the

---

* Fox. † *State Pap.*, i. p. 411.

‡ This early declaration is admirable and explicit, and seems to have been the foundation of the Judgment of Convocation concerning general councils, which followed in 1536. It was to the effect that when in old times the Roman empire extended over the most of the world, the first four general councils were called by the emperor, and in the same way many later councils: until the negligence of the emperor suffered the Pope to usurp that power; yet now the empire had no such dominion, but many princes had absolute power in their own realms. No one prince could call a general council, but one or more of the great princes might require any other prince, or the rest of the princes, to agree in calling one for good intent and cause. The chief causes that such councils might be called were "that heresies might be extinct, schisms put away, good order and manners in the ministers of the Church and the people of the same established." In all the ancient councils, "in matters of faith and in interpretation of Scripture, no man made definite subscription but bishops and priests, forasmuch as the declaration of the Word of God pertains unto them." The Christian prince had power over all, as well bishops

King to a General Council, which was now published, it was a temperate and dignified instrument, but not destitute of some of the peculiar touches which characterise the state papers of Henry the Eighth. He protested that he meant to say or do nothing against the Holy Catholic Church, and the authority of the Apostolic See, given by God, in any way that might be inconsistent with the duty of a good and Catholic prince. If he had divorced his wife, he was sustained by the judgment of the learned and of the Church: if he had married another, it was because he felt himself free. He had moreover made certain statutes and ordinances by the authority of his Parliament: but this was for the safety and tranquillity of his kingdom. The present Pope had treated him badly, inflicting on him wrongs which he now refused to mention, but might on occasion divulge. The present Pope was offended by the late measures, and might proceed to further injuries, to censures and other penalties of the spiritual sword, depriving him and his subjects of the use of sacraments, and cutting them off, at least in the estimation of the world, from the unity of the Church. Now he had always obeyed God, Holy Mother Church, and the Holy Apostolic See in all things lawful and honest; he had been the defender of their rights and liberties even with danger, trouble, and grievous expense; he had been their aid and helper in conquering the foes of the Christian Faith. Fearing therefore to appear in the sight of the world to be cut off from the unity of the Church, when in truth he and his people

and priests as others. Bishops and priests have charge of souls within their own cure, power to minister sacraments, and teach the Word of God; to which Word Christian princes acknowledged themselves subject; and in case the bishops were negligent, it was the prince's office to see them do their duty. This declaration was signed by nine bishops, an abbot, and three doctors. Collier, Rec. No. xxxvii.

could be cut off by no means whatever, and desiring
to retain his subjects, lest they should withdraw themselves from the obedience of the Roman Pontiff, as
a harsh and cruel shepherd ; for these reasons he
appealed from the present Pope to a General Council :
and this he did not in contempt of the holy Apostolic
See, but for the preservation of the truth of the Gospel,
and for the causes above expressed.*

But while the Defender of the Faith thus vaunted
his former services to the Catholic cause, he was
meditating a league with the Lutheran princes of
Germany. Already, in the summer, he had despatched
an envoy, Stephen Vaughan, to sound their inclinations ; but Vaughan was so ill received by the first of
them, the Elector of Saxe, that he went no farther.
The King now proposed to renew the attempt, following the Resolutions of the Council ; and began by
informing his ally, the Most Christian King, of the
scheme. Francis replied by despatching the Archbishop of Paris into England on a mission of conciliation. A general Protestant league was probably too
great an idea to have been seriously entertained by
the mind of Henry. It flitted before him now, in
a moment of furious terror : it was laid before him
afterwards in sober earnestness by the Lutherans
themselves : and if it had come to pass it would have
changed the face of Europe. But he only dallied with
the thought. Neither in his reign nor at any subsequent time has this confederation been effected : nor
probably ever will be. The lamentation of those who
hold that England missed her way in the Reformation
by not having joined in the glorious march to perfect
freedom and enlightenment may be considered : to the
liberal there is a fascination in the thought of union

* Rymer, Fœd., xiv. 476.

and amity: the innovator likes to find himself in company. But the less ardent are agreed that if England was half ruined by the passions of Henry, she was saved from a great danger through his vacillations; and that it was happy for his realm that whilst he was urging a ruthless revolution at home, his foreign politics displayed no higher quality than the most petty craft and despicable duplicity. It is hard to admire the man who was burning and banning Lutherans at home, while he was trying to ally himself with them abroad; who was boasting his achievements in defence of the Catholic cause at the very moment when he was meditating to desert it.

He and his Council were more congenially employed in the regulation of the household of the Dowager Princess and her daughter Mary. Those unhappy women were treated with a barbarity which moved the pity of Europe. The repudiated wife of Henry was maintained with a parsimony which almost equalled the destitution into which Wolsey was allowed to fall after his disgrace. Removed from one prescribed residence to another, her actions spied, her servants harassed; persecuted about the title which she refused to resign; often insulted by the ruffians whom her husband chose to convey his mandates to her, the once joyous and beautiful daughter of Grenada languished the remnant of a life of matchless dignity and patience. In the interval between her divorce and her death, she beheld her dearest friends perish violently in the rage of the revolution which had cast her from the throne. But her fate seemed almost preferable to that which befell her daughter. To describe the particulars of the treatment which Mary received from her father belongs, happily, rather to the censurer or the panegyrist of Henry than to the historian of the Church of England; but it may be observed that the sufferings which she underwent developed the nobler qualities of Mary's nature into a sort of morbid intensity. Her nature was one of strong affection. She let her love go forth whither it was drawn, and had no power to recall it. When her father made her a nursery governess to the infant Elizabeth, whom she was to call princess but not sister, neither that menial degradation, nor the insolence of her step-dame Boleyn, could check the attachment which she formed to her helpless charge. But the great objects of her love were her mother, and next to her mother her father. So long as her mother lived, she was inflexible in refusing any concession which would have dishonoured her: maintaining her own legitimacy and her right to the rank of her birth. But that mother had told her to "obey the King's commandments;" and after her death we find her bowing to the threats of Crumwel, and subscribing to words which even at this distance of time awaken a hot feeling of disgust that ever they should have been dictated to a daughter: "Item, I do freely, frankly, and for the discharge of my duty towards God, the King's Highness, and his laws, without other respect, recognise and acknowledge that the marriage heretofore had between his majesty and my mother, the late princess dowager, was by God's law and man's law incestuous and unlawful."*

The Bishop of Paris, the celebrated Bellay, to whom was entrusted the important office of making the last effort to preserve England in the obedience of the Pope, was a man well qualified for the task. He was an experienced diplomatist, formerly employed in the English affairs, and in favour with the King. His mission was to persuade the King to withdraw his

* State Papers, i. 459.

Appeal to a general council, and to submit his cause to the Roman consistory. He was able to renew the promise of a favourable sentence, and the offer of a midway place of trial: or, in other words, to declare that, if the King of England would in any way submit to the Pope, the Pope would abandon the cause of Katharine. This duplicity of Rome in her last transaction with England was well worthy of her conduct for many centuries. It was met by superior cunning. Henry yielded, or seemed to yield, the required submission; and packed off the eager advocate of peace, who seems to have been the only honest man concerned in the business, to Rome, in the depth of winter, with power to make terms and engagements for him. Bellay prevailed on the Pope to suspend his sentence for the second time until the 23rd of March; and lost no time in acquainting the King with what he had done. The King professed himself to approve, and despatched a post to confirm the agreement; while Sir Edmund Karne and Dr. Revett followed with a fuller commission to the same effect. But the post was delayed, perhaps by accident: the fatal day arrived when the King's matter was to come before the conclave: and in spite of the entreaties of Bellay for a further delay the cause came on; the voice of justice prevailed in the mouth of the Imperial party; and sentence was given against the King according to the votes of a vast majority of the cardinals. The marriage was pronounced valid and canonical: perpetual silence on the alleged invalidity of the same was imposed upon the King; and he was condemned in costs. Two days after this the delayed post arrived; but as neither Bellay nor the Pope had been able to get the hearing deferred, still less were they able to get the case reconsidered. Nor would the result have

been different if they had been able.   Nineteen
cardinals out of twenty-two, though after much double-
dealing,* had recorded their votes against the King.
The Bishop of Paris left Rome in despair.   On his
way home, meeting Karne and Revett, the English
commissioners, at Bologna, he told them that they
need go no farther.

All these negotiations, however, mattered not a
straw in determining the course of England.   They
were a solemn farce played by Henry as the most
decent means of getting rid of the interference of his
French ally.   The separation from Rome was not
caused by the sentence of the Pope against the King;
for the separation from Rome had taken place before
the news of the sentence could have reached England.
Henry in fact despatched the Bishop of Paris to Rome
on a fool's errand; and as soon as he was gone, began
in his Parliament the rapid series of enactments by
which the realm of England was severed for ever from
the see of Rome.

The Houses met January 15, 1534.   Scarce a third
of the spiritual lords were present.   Out of twenty-
six abbots fourteen were away; and of the bishops none
other appeared but Canterbury, London, Winchester,
Lincoln, Bath and Wells, Landaff, and Carlisle.†
During the session the preachers at Paul's Cross
preached every Sunday against the authority of the
Pope in England, by order of the Council.

Of the three great Acts of the session which were
directed against Rome, the first which passed bore the

---

* Bellay had sent to King Francis a list of the cardinals who would
vote for the King of England; this must have included many who voted
against him.   Bellay said afterwards that no reliance was to be placed on
them, for they spoke one way and voted the other.   *Legrand.*

† Burnet, and Lords' Journals.

title of an Act "for the restraint of Annates," or, "for
the non-payment of first-fruits to the Bishop of Rome:"
but it was also called, when it first appeared, a "Bill
concerning the consecration of bishops."* Sweeping
as it was, it must have been still more extreme in
the first draft, which the Commons sent up to the
Lords, February 7. The Lords rejected this draft,
February 27; a new Bill was framed and returned
on the same day, and this finally passed both Houses,
March 16. In this, as in the other enactments regarding Rome, a less deferential style marked the growing
alienation of the kingdom. The "Pope's Holiness" of
former statutes was constantly henceforth "the Bishop
of Rome, otherwise called the Pope." The body of
the Act may be briefly described. Whereas the Act
about Annates which was made two years before,†
reserved certain payments for bulls procured from the
see of Rome on the election of every bishop, this Act
extinguished all such payments without reserve; it forbad bulls, breves, or any other thing to be procured from
Rome, and confined the elections of bishops entirely
within the kingdom. As to the form and manner of
their election, it was least of all to be expected that the
Church of England should have recovered now her
long lost liberty in this important particular; but the
nominal freedom which she had enjoyed of old was
not disturbed unnecessarily. From remote antiquity
the theory had been that the prelates of churches and
monasteries should be freely elected by chapters
and convents, the election being afterwards confirmed

---

* In the Lords' Journals. This is the first session in which we have
the advantage of that document. The Convocations had kept journals
for ages, but the Lords only now began the practice; and, strange to say,
the Commons kept none before the reign of Edward the Sixth.

† See last chap., *ad fin.*

by the consent of the King and the council of the realm. But this theory was rarely real, the kings in various ways generally contriving to overrule the elections, whether by nominating, investing, or signifying the candidate whom they preferred. The last formal settlement of the matter had been in the time of King John, who in one of his charters conceded that the election of all bishops and abbots should be free and canonical, the King's license to elect, or *congé d'élire*, being first procured. But the charter of John was of no avail in protecting the liberty of the churches; and the last of the royal inventions had been to accompany the license to elect with a letter missive to signify to the chapter the person whom the King desired to be elected. In the Act which now passed, the old process of the license to elect, or *congé d'élire*, and the old abuse of royal nomination, in the shape of the letter missive, were both continued: but the latter was made part of the statute law of England for the first time.* If the chapter failed to elect in a certain number of days, they were placed under a Præmunire, and the King proceeded to fill the vacancy by simple nomination, without further regard to them. The Bishop elect was to make his corporal oath to the King and to none other.† This Act was completed

---

* The letter missive I venture to call an old mode of overruling the elections of bishops; but I am not sure that it is not due to the genius of Henry and Crumwel, and that the system of licenses had not fallen into disuse, till it was renewed thus as a legal fiction.

† 25 H. VIII. 20. Contending historians have affirmed or denied the prevalence of capitular, as opposed to royal, election in the early English Church. Lingard, relying on William of Malmsbury, says that in the old English time capitular election prevailed. ("Electio præsulum et abbatum tempore Anglorum penes cleros et monachos fuit."—Malm., de Pont., iii. 157; Ling. Ang.-Sax. Ch., i. 80.) But Inett denies that a single instance of capitular election can be brought from any contemporary authority. (Orig. ii. 454.) Certainly whenever the circumstances of

by another, "The Act concerning Peter-pence and dispensations," called also "for the exoneration from

an election are recorded in the English Chronicles, the consent of the King, or of the King and witan, is mentioned; but it need not be supposed from this that there was no previous election by the chapter. Traces of capitular election are to be found from the time of Archbishop Theodore (Stubbs, Sel. Chart., 130; Freeman, Norm. Conq., ii. 66): and yet that great organiser of the English Church presided at elections made in the gemote, where the King and the witan were assembled. (Lingard, A. S. Ch. i. 82). The case of Plegmund of Canterbury, who was chosen of God "and eallen his halechen" according to one of the English Chronicles, is brought by Lingard to prove capitular election. But all the rest of the Chronicles say that Plegmund was chosen "of God and of all the *folk*" (anno 890). Archbishop Ælfric, according to one of the Chronicles (anno 995), was elected "by the King and all his witan," and the chapter of Christ Church vainly opposed his election. Both parties went to the Pope: and the Pope supported Ælfric on the ground that he had been elected by the King and people: and rejected the petition of his opponents. "The Pope would not do that, because they brought no writ from the King or from the folk: and bad them go, lo! where they would." Ælfric returned in triumph, expelled the secular priests of Christ Church, and filled their places with monks. In the time of Dunstan an attempt was made by the Council of Winchester to allow the monks, who had in so many cathedral churches displaced the secular canons, to elect the bishop from their own number, or, if not, from some other well-known monastery, the consent of the King being obtained. (Selden's Eadmer, 149; Lingard, A. S. Ch., ii. 303.) Thus capitular election was restored by the reformation of Dunstan. But these regulations were soon broken; and throughout the later English period we have instances in which the King alone made the appointments to bishoprics. (See the Chronicles, annis 1044, 5, 6, and 7.) Under Canute and his successors the practice of investiture with the ring and staff or crozier seems to have been begun. Those emblems of episcopacy were sent by the chapter to the King, when a vacancy occurred, and were returned by him with a notification of the person whom he appointed. Edward the Confessor used to notify the appointment of a prelate by charter, without reference to an election; and it is well known that the disregard of capitular election in the case of Archbishop Stigand was one of the pretexts on which William the Conqueror invaded England. After the Conquest, St. Anselm prevailed with Henry I. to give up the system of investiture with ring and staff; and freedom of election was promised and confirmed to the Church by all the great charters of liberties of the twelfth century, the elect prelate of course doing homage to the King for the temporalities. By the Constitutions of Clarendon it was ordered that elections should take place in the royal chapel, subject to the approval of the King and chief persons of the realm. It is thought, however, that

exactions paid to the see of Rome ;" but which seems
at first to have borne the franker title of "a Bill for
the abrogation of the usurped authority of the Roman
Pontiff." This was read in the Lords, for the first
time, March 13 ; for the second time, on the next day,
and committed to the Lord Chancellor. On March 19,
it was read for the third time, with a provision which
had been added ; for the fourth time it was read on the
20th, sent down to the Commons, and by them passed
and returned. On the 30th it was finally passed by
the Lords. This was the statute which the lawyers
describe as discharging the subject from all dependence
on the see of Rome. It bore the form of a petition
or supplication to the King, to whom it set forth
the intolerable exactions which the Bishop of Rome,
otherwise called the Pope, and his chambers, which he

the elections were more nominally than really free; and the long vacancies,
caused by the delays of the kings in doing their part, that they might
enjoy the temporalities meanwhile, were a great evil. The process of
congé d'élire, or the King's license to elect, granted to the chapters, is
said to have been begun by King John. (Godolphin's Abridgment, 42.)
He promised freedom of election, his license being first gotten, which he
would neither refuse nor defer. If the license were refused or deferred,
the electors were to proceed to make a canonical or capitular election,
and afterwards require the royal assent. But it is certain that the kings
soon returned to the old practice of nomination in a form accommodated
to this process, and accompanied their license with a letter missive
requiring the chapter to elect whom they signified. (See the case of Archbishop Bouchier, about 1433, in Hook's Lives, v. 276.)

On the whole it may be concluded : 1. That free election by the
chapters, followed by the consent of the King and realm, was the right
thing. 2. That the interference of the King in the first instance, by
signifying to the electors the person whom he would have them choose,
was an abuse. 3. That freedom of election, though repeatedly promised,
was only secured at rare and brief intervals by powerful ecclesiastics,
such as Theodore, Alcuin, Dunstan, Anselm, and Langton : the kings in
different periods ensuring the return of the persons of their choice, whether
by a charter of nomination, by investiture, or by letters missive to the
chapters. 4. That the liberty of the Church was finally destroyed, and
the abuse perpetuated in the form of law, by Henry the Eighth.

called Apostolic, took out of the realm by usurpation and sufferance. There were "pensions, censes, Peter-pence, procurations, fruits, suits for provisions, and expeditions of bulls for archbishoprics and bishoprics, and for delegacies and rescripts in causes of contentions and appeals, jurisdictions legantine; and also for dispensations, licenses, faculties, grants, relaxations, writs called perinde valere, rehabilitations, abolitions, and other infinite sorts of bulls, breves, and instruments of sundry natures, names, and kinds, in great number;" of which the catalogue seemed swollen by the zeal of recitation.* It was, however, no doubt true that the Pope got much money out of England; more perhaps than from any other country: and that the English nation had been treated formerly by the popes with far less consideration than they deserved by their piety. The remonstrances of the English nation against the intolerable and incessant exactions of the Pope had been heard even in the highest day of Papal domination: all orders of men in the kingdom had joined in these representations; and by the heads of the religious houses especially the High Pontiff had been warned that his conduct would eventually cause a schism.† This ancient prediction was fulfilled at

---

* 25 H. VIII. 20.   Stat. of Realm, and Lords' Journals.

† Matthew Paris has preserved a letter addressed in 1247 to Pope Innocent the Fourth in the name of the clergy and people of the Province of Canterbury. He introduces it by telling how the Archdeacons of England and a large part of the Clergy of the whole realm assembled together with the nobles, and made common complaint of the exactions of the Pope. The Commonwealth was concerned, the interests of the whole realm were involved, clergy and people were alike distressed. They laid their complaints before the King as the guardian of the realm; and at length by common consent, "ex parte communitatis totius cleri et populi Anglicani," wrote letters of grievance both to the Pope and to the Cardinals. The letter to the Cardinals is the longer, and goes into the particulars of the extortions of the Holy See: both are firm in tone, but very respectful in language to the Mother Church. (Matt. Par. 721 *Wals.*

length; and from the venerable contribution known as
Peter-pence* down to the latest paper figment of the
Apostolic Chamber, all payments to the see of Rome
were swept away for ever. It was declared that the
realm was free from any laws of man, but such as had
been devised within the same : and that it lay with the
King and the Parliament, the "lords spiritual and temporal, and the Commons, representing the whole state
of the realm, in the most high court of Parliament," to
abrogate, annul, alter, or diminish all such laws : and
"not only to dispense, but also to authorise some elect
person or persons to dispense with those and all other
human laws of the realm, as the quality of the persons
and matter should require." The spiritual jurisdiction,
therefore, which had been usurped by the see of Rome
was transferred to the see of Canterbury. All licenses,
dispensations, and other instruments which were needful were to be granted henceforth by the Archbishop
of Canterbury, under restrictions which were elabo-

Freeman's Growth of Eng. Const., p. 77.) In the two previous years
there were two other letters sent to Rome, which are even better worth
reading. The former was in the name of the "Magnates et Universitas
Regni Angliæ;" it remonstrated very sternly on the infringement of the
rights of patronage by filling the livings with wolfish Italians, who did
nothing, resided abroad, and took large sums out of the kingdom. The
other letter was in the name of Simon de Montfort, "Et alii totius Regni
Angliæ Barones, proceres, et magnates, et nobiles portuum maris habi-
tatores (Barons of the Cinque Ports) necnon et clerus et populus universus."
It was supplemented by a letter from the Abbots of England, in which
they warned the Pope against causing a separation between the kingdom
and the priesthood, to the ruin of the Church.—(Matt. Par. 666, 699,
700.)

* The old payment called Peter-pence, from the days of the Mercian
King Offa, was originally made for maintaining an English college in
Rome. Baronius and other Roman writers misrepresented this payment
as a quit-rent for the kingdom, and an acknowledgment of dependence
on Rome. They have been sufficiently confuted by Spelman and Collier.
Edward the Third stopped the payment in 1366; but only for a time.—
Collier, iii. 129 (Barham's Ed.).

rately specified in the Act. The laborious language employed sufficiently indicates that the framers of the Act understood and desired to maintain the distinction between the spiritualities of a bishop and his high priestly office : the former only were termed "human laws," subject to the control of the powers of the realm : and nothing pertaining to a bishop was regarded therein but that spiritual jurisdiction which can be exercised by that ecclesiastical officer, called "the guardian of the spiritualities," whom the law provides during the vacancy of a see.* It was this spiritual jurisdiction only which was, or could be, transferred from the Bishop of Rome to the Bishop of Canterbury, because it was this only which had been, or could have been, usurped by the Bishop of Rome.† And therefore it could be added‡ that the King, his nobles and subjects, intended not "to decline or vary from the congregation of Christ's Church in any things concerning the very Articles of the Catholic faith of Christendom, or in any other things declared by Holy Scripture and the word of God necessary for their salvation : but only to make an ordinance by policies necessary to repress vice and for the good conservation

---

* The spiritualities of a bishop, in the legal and technical sense, mean not his spiritual offices or functions, such as ordination, consecration, or confirmation; but such parts of his jurisdiction as institutions, admissions, and the like ; for the administration of which the law provides an officer, called "the guardian of the spiritualities," when the see is vacant: and a bishop cannot exercise the spiritual Jurisdiction before his election be confirmed by the Crown. The temporalities are all such things as a bishop gets by livery from the King, as lands and houses. Hence a bishop is said to hold both his spiritualities and temporalities of the Crown, without any reference to his spiritual or apostolic office.

† Whence it was provided that "all such manner of licenses, dispensations, faculties, instruments, rescripts, and other writings," which under the authority of the Act might be granted by the Archbishop of Canterbury, might, during the vacancy of the see, be granted by the guardian of the spiritualities.   Sec. 16.   ‡ Sec. 19.

of this realm in peace, unity, and tranquillity, from
ravin and spoil, ensuing much the old ancient customs
of this realm in that behalf: not minding to seek for
any relief, succours, or remedies, for any worldly
things or human laws in any cause of necessity, but
within this realm, at the hands of his Highness, his
heirs and successors, which had and ought to have
an imperial power and authority in the same, and
not obliged in any worldly causes to any other
superior."

Indulgences and all manner of privileges, and the
abuses of them, the fatal shame of Rome, were specially
ordered to be reformed by the King in council. But
the good that this Act wrought was far outweighed by
the evil. The true meaning and intent of it all was
contained in the clauses by which all the exempt abbeys
and monasteries were placed at the mercy of the King.
The Act, as we have seen, transferred a great deal of
the spiritual jurisdiction usurped by the Pope to the
Archbishop of Canterbury. It might be supposed that
it would have transferred to the Archbishop of Canterbury, among the rest, that important part of the Pope's
spiritual jurisdiction which related to the religious
houses. There were religious houses, abbeys, priories,
colleges and hospitals, which were exempt from the jurisdiction of the English primate or any of his suffragans.
They might not be visited by him, the election of their
officers required no confirmation from him, their
privileges and liberties were neither granted nor confirmed by his authority. They were dependent on the
Pope in regimen : and some of them—the various sorts
of Friars—were associated in Congregations which held
their assemblies out of the realm. There had been
struggles in all times between these exempt communities
and the ordinaries of the Church of England : and now

that the authority of their foreign superior was being taken away, it seemed the proper thing to place them under the control of the English primates and bishops. Instead of which, there was a provision made that neither "the Archbishop of Canterbury, nor any other person or persons," should have power to "visit or vex" them. That dangerous jurisdiction was to be entrusted to the tenderer hands of the King, and of such persons as the King might appoint by commission under the great seal. The confidence which his Parliament reposed in the King was indeed visibly increasing. The servile spirit which soon afterwards surrendered the safety of the subject by the Act about verbal treason, and betrayed the constitution itself in the Act of Proclamations, was manifested almost as strikingly in this Act also. With the humility of a Roman Senate towards a Roman Emperor, the Parliament of England ordained that if the King wished their Act to take effect earlier than they had fixed, or if he chose to annul the whole or part of it before it took effect, he might issue his letters patent in those behalfs.

The Submission of the Clergy had been already extorted from Convocation under the severe pressure of tyranny; and appeals to Rome had been already abrogated, in order to deprive the dowager princess of her last resource. To invest the one with the force of statute, to confirm the other by a new enactment, and join the two together in a single Act of Parliament, was to raise a legislative monument which should eternally proclaim the causes and the nature of the English Reformation. For this solemn work the Commons appeared in the House of Lords, March 27, with a Bill which was read twice. Next day the Bill was returned from the Commons with a provision which the Lords had added; and it passed the Lords. On the last day of the session, March 30, it passed the Commons, and "after dinner" received the signature of the King. This was the "Act for the Submission of the Clergy, and Restraint of Appeals."* It was ordained that the Clergy, according to their Submission, were neither to execute their old canons or constitutions, nor make new ones, without the assent and license of the King, on pain of imprisonment and fine at the royal pleasure: that their Convocations were only to be assembled by the authority of the King's writ: that the King should have power to nominate Two and Thirty persons, sixteen of the spiritualty and sixteen of the temporalty, to revise the canons, ordinances, and constitutions provincial; and that in the meantime such of the canons which were not contrariant to the laws of the realm, nor prejudicial to the prerogative royal, should still be used and executed as heretofore. The flame of controversy has raged round every letter of this celebrated Act: how far it forbad or permitted the clergy to move, to treat, to debate, or to legislate in their assemblies; whether it respected one kind of Convocation or more; and whether there were more than one kind of Convocation which it could respect: these and other questions have been disputed with more than the usual acrimony of theological warfare, and with incredible closeness of research.† But for the purposes

---

* 25 H. VIII. 20. Lords' Journ.; Wake's State of the Church, p. 479.

† I allude to the controversy between Atterbury and Wake at the beginning of the eighteenth century—one of the bitterest that ever was waged. The heat of Atterbury in his Rights of Convocation kindled to the full the ophiophagous temper of Wake, who pursued him in a folio treatise of near a thousand pages, the State of the Church and Clergy. They both displayed immense erudition and unwearied labour. For instance, the Act of Parliament which we are considering consists but of a few paragraphs, and yet in their volumes the discussion of it occupies countless pages. The meaning of every word, the punctuation, and division into periods, not less than the tenor of the whole, are fought over with unyielding obstinacy. The controversy did good to the Church.

of history it is enough to observe that the intention of the Act was to discourage the clergy from debating, not less clearly than to forbid them to make new ecclesiastical laws without the King. They could never be certain at what point of their proceedings the King's authority and license might be needful; how far they might go without it: what kind of matter might require it and what not. All was left undetermined; and if they attempted anything whatever, they might find themselves clapped into prison and heavily fined, as having fallen again into a Præmunire. As for the plan of examining and revising the old canons and constitutions by a commission of thirty-two persons, this was never carried out. The King seems indeed to have nominated them;* but he took no further notice of them or their work: and the ecclesiastical laws meantime remained in abeyance. It is true indeed that there was a provision added to the Act, that those canons which were not contrariant to the laws of the realm and the prerogative of the King should be executed as heretofore, until the proposed revision should be made: but who was to determine which of the canons were meant?† And who was to define a prerogative royal

---

* See a remarkable letter of Cranmer to the King, written in 1544. Burnet Coll. to Edw. VI. Bk. i. No. 61.

† This provision, which is the last in the Act, was added by the Lords. (Wake's State, p. 557.) Poor Wake dreams that it was the design of Parliament to restrict Convocation to the business of the *State*, and so create a necessity for the frequent holding of Provincial Synods and Diocesan Synods for the business of the *Church*. He also denies that they suspended the old canons and constitutions by this Act (p. 553 *sq.*). I venture to think with Atterbury that they did, at least virtually.

I have pointed out already in the last chapter that in this Act the Commons (for it originated with them) did not adhere to the attested Submission of the Clergy, but recited and enacted an earlier draft of the same. To show this fully, I give the Act, which may be compared with the documents given in the last chapter:—"Whereas the King's humble and obedient subJects, the clergy of this realm of England, have not only knowledged, according to the truth, That the Convocations of the said

which was growing greater every day ? The clergy
might perhaps have shown that none of their canons

clergy are, always have been, and ought to be, assembled by the King's
Writ; but also, submitting themselves to the King's Majesty, have
promised *in Verbo Sacerdotii* that they will never from henceforth
presume to attempt, allege, claim, or put in ure; or to enact, promulge,
or execute any new Canons, Constitutions or Ordinances, Provincial or
other, by whatsoever·name they shall be called, in the Convocation, unless
the King's most royal Assent and License may to them be had, to make,
promulge, and execute the same; and that his MaJesty do give his most
royal Assent and authority in that behalf. And where divers Constitutions, Ordinances and Canons, Provincial or Synodal, which heretofore
have been enacted, and be thought not only to be much prejudical to
the King's Prerogative royal, and repugnant to the laws and statutes
of the Realm, but also over much onerous to his Highness and his
Subjects: The said Clergy hath most humbly besought the King's
Majesty that the said Constitutions and Canons may be committed to
the examination and judgment of his Highness and of Two and Thirty
Persons of the King's Subjects, whereof Sixteen to be of the upper and
nether house of the Parliament, of the Temporalty, and other sixteen to
be of the Clergy of this Realm; and all the said Two and Thirty Persons
to be chosen and appointed by the King's Majesty: and that such of
the said Constitutions and Canons as shall be thought and determined
by the said Two and Thirty Persons, or the more part of them, worthy
to be abrogated and annulled, shall be˙ obsolete and made of no value
accordingly: And such other of the same Constitutions and Canons as
by the said Two and Thirty, or the more part of them, shall be approved
to stand with the Laws of God, and consonant to the Laws of this Realm,
shall stand in their full strength and power, the King's most Royal
Assent first had and obtained to the same.

" Be it therefore now enacted by the authority of this present Parliament, according to the said Submission and Petition of the said Clergy,
that they, ne any of them, from henceforth shall presume to attempt,
allege, claim, or put in ure, any constitutions or ordinances, provincial or
synodal, or any other canons; nor shall enact, promulge or execute any
such canons, constitutions or ordinances provincial, by whatsoever name
or names they may be called, in their Convocations in time coming
(which always shall be assembled by authority of the King's Writ) unless
the same clergy may have the King's most royal Assent and License to
make, promulge, and execute such canons, constitutions and ordinances
Provincial or Synodal, upon pain of every one of the said clergy, doing
contrary to this Act, and being thereof convict, to suffer imprisonment
and make fine at the King's will.

"And forasmuch as such canons, constitutions, and ordinances as
heretofore have been made by the clergy of this Realm cannot now at
the session of this present Parliament, the reason of shortness of time,

were repugnant to the laws of the realm, if it had ever come to that; but they could never have been safe against the royal prerogative. We find the bishops, in their uncertainty after the passing of the Act, taking out licenses for the execution of their functions as ordinaries of the Church.* We shall find this com-

be viewed, examined and determined by the King's Highness and Thirty-two Persons to be chosen and appointed, according to the petition of the said Clergy, in form above rehearsed :

"Be it therefore enacted by Authority aforesaid, That the King's Highness shall have the power and authority to nominate and assign at his pleasure the said Two and Thirty of his subjects, whereof sixteen to be of the clergy and sixteen of the temporalty, of the upper and nether house of the Parliament. And if any of the said Two and Thirty shall happen to die before their full determination, then his Highness to nominate other, from time to time, of the said two houses of the Parliament, to supply the number of the said Two and Thirty. And that the same Two and Thirty by his Highness to be named, shall have power and authority to view, search and examine the said canons, constitutions and ordinances provincial and synodal heretofore made ; and such of them as the King's Highness and the said Two and Thirty, or the most part of them, shall deem and adjudge worthy to be continued, kept and obeyed, shall be from henceforth kept, obeyed and executed within this realm, so that the King's most Royal Assent, under his great Seal, be first had to the same : and the residue of the said canons, constitutions and ordinances provincial, which the King's Highness and the said Two and Thirty persons, or the most part of them, shall not approve, or deem and judge worthy to be abolite, abrogate, and made frustrate, shall from henceforth be void and of none effect, and never be put in execution within this realm.

"Provided always that no canons, constitutions or ordinances shall be made or put in execution within this realm, by authority of the Convocations of the Clergy, which shall be contrariant or repugnant to the King's Prerogative Royal, or to the Customs, laws, or Statutes of this Realm, any thing contained in this Act to the contrary hereof notwithstanding. . . .

"Provided also that such canons, constitutions, ordinances and synodals provincial being already made, which be not contrariant or repugnant to the laws, statutes and customs of this realm, nor to the damage or hurt of the King's Prerogative Royal, shall now still be used and executed, as they were afore the making of this Act, till such time as they be viewed, searched, or otherwise ordered and determined by the said Two and Thirty persons, or the more part of them, according to the tenor, force, and effect of this present Act."

* Wake, p. 557.

mission of thirty-two again and again promoted by Act
of Parliament in the course of the Reformation, and
again and again brought to nought.   What came of it
eventually will be seen in due time.   With regard to
appeals, the Act confirmed the measure of the year
before in transferring them from Rome to Canterbury
and the other arch-sees of England; but it gave a
further and final appeal from the Archbishops into the
Court of Chancery.   And it so happened that monasteries and other places, exempt were here again excepted from the general tenor of the law.   The appeals
from all such places, which were wont to be made to
Rome, were ordered not to be made to the Archbishops, but immediately into Chancery.   Thus was
the axe laid to the root of the monastic tree.

Besides these momentous statutes, which transferred the jurisdiction of the Pope to the Crown and
the primates of England, there were two Acts which
concerned the general state of the Church.   Benefit of
clergy had been taken from malefactors, who were
arraigned before the justices instead of answering to
their ordinaries, as we have seen before.   But some
offenders eluded the law by standing mute, or answering
indirectly when they were arraigned, instead of pleading not guilty; or sometimes they would " peremptorily
challenge above the number of twenty " persons on the
jury, and escape by that means.   These evasions were
now taken away.*   A far more important Act was
concerning the punishment of heresies.   This was
couched in the familiar form of a supplication to the
King from the Commons.   His loving and obedient
subjects the Commons shewed in most humble wise to
their sovereign lord that the Clergy of the realm had
obtained " upon their suggestion" by authority of Parlia-

* 25 H. VIII. 3.   Conf. 22 H. VIII. 14, and 32 H. VIII. 3.

and convented to answer to the ordinary in an open place. If the person thus examined were convicted, he was to abjure and do reasonable penance, or else be burned, the King's writ De heretico comburendo being first procured. The ordinary might admit to bail an accused person : or, if he refused, it might be done by two justices of the peace. Nothing that might be said or done against the Pope or his decrees was to be accounted for heresy.

By this beneficial Act the ordinaries were some-what relieved of the most burdensome and odious part of their duties. The Commons, however, acted not from the enlightened conception that religious opinions are not any object of legal coercion : but because they held the powers which had been granted by their own forefathers to the ecclesiastical authorities to be oppressive to the subject. They therefore mixed the temporal with the spiritual jurisdiction : and this they did by returning in part to the more ancient system of the writ De heretico comburendo, which was originally part of the common law. By that milder system no person could be convicted of heresy by the opinion of an ordinary or in the smaller spiritual courts, but only before the Archbishop himself in a synod of the province : and when he was convicted might still be pardoned by the King, since the writ was not a writ of course, but issuing only by the special pleasure of the King in council.* In their renewal of this system, the Commons seem to make sheriffs in their leets answer for the provincial synod. It was advantageous, moreover, that many heresies concerning the Pope

---

* Blackstone, bk. iv. c. 4. It is to be regretted that an historian should have transferred the title of this old writ to the famous Act of H. IV. against the Lollards, (2 H. IV. 15) which in fact superseded it. Mr. Froude has done so : ii. 20.

were taken away by this Act: but the Commons showed what manner of spirit they were of, when six years later, following the changed humour of the King, they made the denial of Transubstantiation, the most contested point of Roman doctrine, to be heresy and punishable by fire.

The numerous Acts of this diligent session which struck at particular persons shewed a desire to get the machinery of the revolution to work as fast as it was erected. The Commons had not sat long before they sent up a complaint made by one Thomas Philips against the Bishop of London, for having kept him long time in prison upon suspicion of heresy. The articles which had been objected to the alleged heretic, and his answers to the same, were read before the Lords: but the business was considered frivolous, and the Bill was sent back to the Commons. On this the Commons sent a deputation to the Bishop, to require him to answer immediately in writing to such things as were charged against him by Philips. The Bishop reported this next day in the House of Lords: and the Peers with one voice declared that it was not to be granted that one of their House should make answer to any person in that place. This question of privilege is one of the earliest instances of a collision between the two Houses.*

---

* The case of Philips, according to himself, was a hard one. He was kept three years in prison on suspicion of heresy, because he neither made his purgation nor would abjure canonically. According to Fox (List of persons abJured), he offered an abjuration which did not satisfy the bishop. Mr. Froude (ii. 77) says, following the Petition which Philips sent to the Commons, which is in the Rolls House, that he fully cleared himself, and yet was illegally detained. It appears from Fox, however, that he was one of the Christian Brethren, and that heretical books, such as Tracy's Testament, were found on him. Mr. Froude expends some eloquence on the case, with the view of inculpating Sir Thomas More: but he seems to fail therein. I. He owns that More, who first arrested Philips, delivered him

There passed a private Act for the depriving the two last of the long succession of foreign bishops who had drained the English sees of their wealth and impaired their dignity from the time of the Norman Conquest. These happened to be Cardinal Campeggio and Jerome de Ghinucci, who held the bishoprics of Salisbury and Worcester. The part which the former of these non-resident aliens had played in the Divorce had probably roused against him the resentment of the King: the other however had been for years his skilful agent at Rome, and been recommended by him about a year before for a cardinal's hat. Their deprivation put an end to an abuse against which the

to the ordinary within ten days, as the law required. 2. He adds, however, that More, along with the ordinary, examined him privately from time to time, which private examinations were against the law. For this he refers to Fox. Fox says only that "he was oftentimes examined before Master More and the Bishop," which would surely be in the Bishop's court, not in private. In the very next sentence Fox relates that "one Stacy first bare witness against him, but after *in the court openly* he protested that he did it for fear." The case may prove that the law was bad, but it does not prove that either the chancellor or the diocesan exceeded the law. On Philips cf. Hall, p. 827.

There is another case, that of one John Field, which is also cited at length by Mr. Froude to criminate More: but I cannot find from anything that appears that this was a case of heresy at all. At least it never came under ecclesiastical cognisance. More kept Field in prison eighteen days and then set him free, binding him to appear before him eight days after in the Star Chamber. He then sent him to the Fleet for two years, and after that time he was again imprisoned by the Duke of Norfolk, at the instance, as he says, of More, who had then quitted office, and by means of representations made by More through the Bishops of Winchester and London. All that time there was nothing laid to his charge. Now, if the case had been clearly spiritual, More was bound by 2 H. V. st. 1, ch. 7 to have delivered his prisoner to the ordinary within ten days (as he delivered Philips): but this was "in case the person be not indicted of any other thing, whereof the cognisance belongs to the secular judges and officers:" in that case he was to be examined before the secular Judges before he was delivered to the ordinary. More's procedure seems to show that Field was under suspicion of some secular offence: but we know nothing of his case but what he tells us himself. ·

nation had protested forages ; but their deprivation by
Act of Parliament, without the intervention of a synod,
has been remarked as an infringement of the liberties
of the Church of England.*　　They were succeeded by
Shaxton and Latimer after a year.

Latimer meanwhile had been preparing for the
episcopal office by work of another kind.　　Rising in the
King's favour almost to the height of Crumwel and
Cranmer, he had been associated with those powerful
ministers to form a commission for investigating the
wretched business of the Holy Maid of Kent, whose
attainder of high treason is one of the most striking
acts of this session.　　The story of that personage is
briefly this.　　A poor servant girl in a village in Kent
had fits, or some such infirmity, in which she was wont
to utter many foolish and idle words.　　The parson of
the parish, through folly or covetousness, treated these
visitations of disease as inspired trances : rode off to
Warham, who was then Archbishop of Canterbury,
and told him a longer story about them than he could
justify, or the Archbishop believe.†　　He persisted however in his design of magnifying them, in order to
increase the credit and profit of his chapel : and he
found an able coadjutor in a monk of Canterbury.　　The
poor girl was persuaded to continue by simulation the
contortions and ejaculations which had an involuntary
origin : she became a professed nun, and the complete tool of a gang of designing monks and friars.

---

* Collier.

† Warham's conduct in this curious business has been much questioned.
In the bill of attainder he is said to have countenanced the Maid of Kent,
though at first he seems to have contemned her.　Fisher also spoke of
the high opinion which the Archbishop imbibed of her pretensions to
inspiration.　He had a book of her prophecies, which had been written
down.　But he was so far from concealing this from any traitorous
designs that he showed it to the King, who gave it to Sir T. More to
look at.

The thing succeeded: her fame spread, and her utterances acquired a character which was gravely assumed to imperil the safety of the King and the peace of the realm. Among other things she declared that the King should not survive his second marriage a month, or six months, that in the reputation of Almighty God he should not be a King a day nor an hour, and should die a villain's death. All this had been going on long enough: and it might have been thought that as the King had survived the various terms prefixed for his destruction, he would have been content to let the drivel of a deranged woman and a pack of disreputable friars sink into contempt, or check it at most with a disdainful reprimand. But there were other women whom he had wronged and whom he feared, though with little reason. His divorced wife and her daughter were rousing in his mind one of those blind fits of rage and dread which in his later years so often defiled with blood the page of history. No blood had yet been shed in the business of the Divorce: the attainder of Elizabeth Barton and her adherents began the copious shower. Already the King had made a Star Chamber business of it, before the legislative powers of the realm were evoked to his assistance. Crumwel, Cranmer, and Latimer sat upon it: the monks and friars concerned were examined, and driven to confession, as it is believed, by torture: the depositions of anonymous witnesses were taken against them,* and they, with the nun herself, had been put to open penance at St. Paul's Cross. The thing should have ended there. But instead of that, a mighty charge of conspiracy, implicating some of the highest persons in the land, was got up: the nun and her accomplices

---

* Strype, E. M., i. 171, from the Cleop. E. 4.

were solemnly put into a bill of attainder of treason,
brought before the House of Lords, and afterwards
executed at Tyburn.   Some of her adherents were
made guilty of misprision of treason, and condemned
to imprisonment at the King's pleasure, and to lose
their goods.   Among these was Fisher Bishop of
Rochester, his chaplain Adeson, and Abel the chaplain of Queen Katharine.   The name of More was at
first inserted in the bill, but he so completely cleared
himself that it was struck out.   The names of the rest
of the persons said to be implicated were suppressed,
and they were all pardoned, as it was written in the
bill, at the intercession of Queen Anne.*

To the venerable Fisher, the attainder was rather
a miserable insult than a punishment by law.   He was
not imprisoned, and he compounded for his goods by
a fine of three hundred pounds.†   Indeed he established
his innocence of treasonable complicity so completely,
that it would have been intolerable to proceed against
him to the full extent.   Crumwel wrote to him, advising
him to confess himself guilty, and promising him the
King's pardon.‡   But this the aged prelate disdained
to do.   Unable through infirmity to present himself
before his peers, he addressed to them a long justifica-
tory letter, in which he pleaded that it was no default

* 25 H. VIII. 12. The accusations in the Act are: 1. The alleged
treasonable predictions; 2. That a great book of them was made by the
registrar of Canterbury, ready to have been printed; 3. That sermons
were intended to have been preached about them; 4. That the nun made
two false communications with two of the Pope's ambassadors, Pullyon
and Sylvester; 5. That her accomplices, Bocking, Masters, Rich, Gold,
and Dering, travelled about, making secret relations; 6. That Gold had
seen Queen Katharine; 7. That T. Gold, gentleman, had brought a
message from the nun, after she was in the Tower, to encourage her
adherents. There seems not much in all this, but a mighty deal is made
of it in the Act.

† Lingard.

‡ Wright's Suppression of Monast., p. 27.

oath which was tendered to them, and to the laymen who were sworn, was the same which was tendered to More; that is, the oath which had been sworn by both Houses of Parliament. But that was not the oath which was tendered to the religious orders, when the commissioners began to go through the country to swear them. No form of oath being prescribed in the Act, advantage was taken of this omission to administer to the inmates of the religious houses a far more severe and explicit form of oath than that which More and Fisher had refused, than that which the Houses of Parliament and the secular clergy had consented to take. They were required to swear not only that the chaste and holy marriage between Henry and Anne was just and legitimate, and the succession good in their offspring; but also that they would preach and persuade the same on every occasion. They were required to swear that they would ever hold the King to be Head of the Church of England; that the Bishop of Rome, who in his Bulls usurped the name of Pope, and arrogated to himself the primacy of Most High Pontiff, had no more authority or jurisdiction than other bishops in England or elsewhere, in their dioceses; that they would for ever renounce the laws, decrees and canons of the Bishop of Rome, if any of them should be found contrary to the law of God and Holy Scripture; and that they would adhere to all the decrees and proclamations of the King, and also to all the laws of England, and the statutes of Parliament. In their private or public addresses they were to swear that they would not presume to twist anything taken out of Holy Scripture to another sense, but would preach Christ and His words and acts simply, openly, sincerely, and according to the rule of the Holy Scriptures and of doctors who were truly Catholic and ortho-

dox. In their prayers and litanies they were to bid
the people remember first the King as Supreme Head
of the Church of England, then the Queen and her
offspring, then the Archbishop of Canterbury and the
other clergy.* In all this there was an evident in-

---

* Quum ea non solum Christianæ religionis et pietatis ratio, sed
nostræ etiam obedientiæ Regula, ut Domino nostro Henrico ejus nominis
octavo, cui uni et soli post Christum Jesum Servatorem nostrum debemus
universa, non modo omnimodam in Christo, et eandam sinceram integram
perpetuamque animi devotionem, fidem, observantiam, honorem, cultum,
reverentiam, præstemus, sed etiam de eadem fide et observantia nostra
rationem, quotienscunque postulabitur, reddamus, et palam omnibus, si
nos poscat, libentissime testemur : Noverint universi, ad quos præsens
Scriptum pervenerit, quod nos (Priores et Conventus v. Decanus et
Capitulum, &c) uno ore et voce, atque unanimi omnium et singulorum
consensu et assensu, hoc scripto nostro sub sigillis nostris communibus
in Domibus nostris capitularibus dato, pro nobis et successoribus nostris
omnibus et singulis imperpetuum profitemur, testamur, ac fideliter pro-
mittimus et spondemus, Nos, dictos . . . . et successores nostros omnes
et singulos, integram, inviolatam, sinceram perpetuamque fidem, observantiam et obedientiam semper præstaturos erga Dominum Regem
nostrum Henricum Octavum, et erga Serenissimam Reginam Annam,
ejusdem Uxorem, et erga castum sanctumque Matrimonium nuper non
solum inter eosdem juste et legitime contractum, ratum, et consummatum,
sed etiam tam in Duabus Convocationibus cleri, quam in Parliamento
Dominorum Spiritualium et Temporalium atque Communium in eodem
Parliamento congregatorum et præsentium determinatum, et per Thomam
Cantuarien. Archiepiscopum solemniter confirmatum, et erga quamcunque
aliam ejusdem Henrici Regis nostri Uxorem post mortem prædictæ
Annæ nunc Uxoris suæ legitime ducendam, et erga Sobolem dictl Domini
Regis Henrici ex prædicta Anna tam progenitam quam progenerandam,
et erga Sobolem dicti Domini Regis ex alia quacunque legitima Uxore
post mortem ejusdem Annæ legitime progenerandam, et quod eadem
Populo notificabimus, prædicabimus, et suadebimus, ubicunque dabitur
locus et occasio. Item, quod confirmatum ratumque habemus semperque
perpetuo habituri sumus, quod prædictus Rex noster Henricus est Caput
Ecclesiæ Anglicanæ. Item, quod Episcopus Romanus, qui in suis Bullis
Papæ nomen usurpat, et summi Pontificis Principatum sibi arrogat,
nihilo majoris neque auctoritatis aut jurisdictionis habendus sit quam
cæteri quivis Episcopi in Anglia vel alibi in sua quisque diocese. Item,
quod soli dicto Domino Regi et Successoribus suis adhærebimus, atque
ejus Decreta et Proclamationes, insuper omnes Angliæ leges, atque etiam
Statuta omnia in Parliamento et per Parliamentum decreta, confirmata,
stabilita, et ratificata perpetuo manutenebimus, Episcopi Romani Legibus,

tention of making the oath intolerable, to get a pretext for falling on the religious houses and destroying them. The attempt was only partially successful, for the oath was taken in almost every chapterhouse where it was tendered; and if the religious orders were the standing army of the Pope, and the light scouts of sedition, as they have been represented, never army capitulated so easily. In three instances only was resistance attempted, either among the friars or the monks; but the mere attempt at resistance gave the King the opportunity of suppressing a whole religious order. The friars appear to have been dealt with more rigorously than the rest of the religious. The visitation began with them. They, and they only, were required to add to their subscriptions a declaration that they subscribed of their own will, not upon compulsion.* It began with the various Friaries of London. The priors and convents of the Minorites, of the Friars Preachers, of

---

Decretis et canonibus, si qui contra legem Divinam et sacram Scripturam esse invenientur, in perpetuum renunciantes. Item, quod nullus nostrum omnium in ulla vel privata vel publica concione quicquam ex sacris Scripturis desumptum ad alienum sensum detorquere præsumet: sed quisque Christum, Ejusque Verba et Facta simpliciter, sincere, aperte, et ad normam seu regulam sacrarum Scripturarum et vere Catholicorum atque Orthodoxorum Doctorum, prædicabit catholice et orthodoxe. Item, quod unusquisque in suis orationibus et comprecationibus de more faciendis primum omnium Regem, tanquam Supremum Caput Ecclesiæ Anglicanæ, Deo et populi precibus commendabit: deinde Reginam cum sua sobole, tum demum Archiepiscopum Cantuariensem cum cæteris cleri ordinibus prout videbitur. Item, quod omnes et singuli prædicti (Priores et Conventus, s. q. a.) nos et successores nostros Conscientiæ et Jurisjurandi Sacramento firmiter obligamus, quod omnia et singula prædicta fideliter et in perpetuum observabimus. In cujus rei testimonium huic Instrumento vel Scripto nostro commune Sigillum nostrum appendimus, et nostra nomina propria quisque manu subscripsimus. Datum in Domo nostra Capitulari die (primo) mensis (Maii) anno Christi MDXXXIV.— Rym. Fœd. xiv. 489. [See end of this chapter.]

* "Sponte non coacte." Rym. This may be compared with the celebrated "ex animo" subscription to the Thirty-nine Articles which caused the first separation of the Puritans from the Church of England.

the Austin Friars, and of the Crutched or Crossed Friars were visited, April 17 to 20, by Dr. George Browne, the Provincial of the whole order of Austin Friars, and by John Hilsey, the Provincial of the whole order of the Friars Preachers—two men who were highly promoted not long after by Henry and Crumwel for their services. The Friars of Langley Regis, Bedford, Aylesbury, Hitchin, Dunstable, and Ware, were visited May 5 to 10; and it cannot be doubted but that Browne and Hilsey, or their deputies, or fellow-commissioners, went on visiting the houses of the friars throughout the southern part of the kingdom. Among the rest Thomas Bedyl, clerk of the Council, and Roland Lee, the new bishop of Lichfield, visited the Observants of Richmond and Greenwich about the middle of june.

The Order of St. Francis de Observantia, or reformed Franciscans, who possessed several establishments in England, were a small but vigorous and well-disciplined body. To them belonged some of the most eminent preachers of the age; as Elstow, Peto, and Forest. In the chapel of their house of Greenwich, where the King often worshipped, and where lately the infant Elizabeth had been baptized, these preachers had not feared to tell him to his face that his second marriage was unlawful, and that those preachers who justified it were men of no sincerity, who courted the King's fancy and flattered his inclination for the sake of wealth and promotion in the Church. When the King set other preachers to answer them from the same pulpit, they returned to the charge, in their turn, with so much vehemence that he himself called out to them to stop. Their boldness of speech brought them before the Council, where Crumwel told them that they well deserved to be enclosed in a sack and thrown into the Thames. But this Eastern mode of punishment seemed to have few terrors for the English friars, one of whom made answer that such sentences might frighten the court epicures, who had lost their courage in their palate, but not men who counted it honour to suffer for duty, and who knew that the way to heaven was as near by water as by land.* The time when these sallies happened, was before the second marriage was owned publicly, and so the preachers were dismissed with a reprimand: but their boldness set them up for marks in the King's eye. They and their brethren were implicated, so far as anybody was implicated, in the matter of the Nun of Kent; and when they refused the new Oath about the succession, the suppression of their whole order was determined, two years before the suppression of the other religious bodies.

Armed with letters from Crumwel and the articles from the Provincial of the Augustin Friars, the two commissioners took their way towards Richmond, where they held their first communication with the warden and one of the seniors, and afterwards with the whole convent. They bade them consent to the articles, and confirm them by the convent seal; but the warden and convent showed themselves obstinate at first in refusing. They then moved them to put the matter wholly in the hands of their four seniors, who were named " discretes," † who should have power to decide for all; and into this trap the brethren of Richmond fell. The commissioners left them, bidding the discretes come after them next morning to Greenwich with their final answer, and to bring the convent seal with them. They came, and the thing was done. But at Greenwich itself there was less success. Here the convent absolutely refused to allow the matter to be

* Stow's Annals: Collier.　　　† [Oddly printed " distrettes."]

put into the hands of the discretes, saying that as the matter concerned the souls of everyone, they would answer everyone for himself. After much debating, the commissioners were obliged to ask everyone his determination separately; and found all in one mind of contradiction and dissent, more especially on the article "That the Bishop of Rome had no more authority than any other bishop in England."* This the brethren said was clearly against their profession and the rules of St. Francis; and they brought out their rules and showed them to the visitors.† The latter made answer, first, that the rule was meant for friars of Italy, not of England; secondly, that the chapter of their rule which they adduced was a forgery;‡ thirdly, that neither the Pope, nor St. Francis, nor their rules, vows and professions could take away one jot of the entire obedience which they owed to the King. On the last topic the visitors expatiated in an eloquent, rational, and enlightened manner; but had to complain that "all this reason could not sink into their obstinate heads and worn in custom of obedience to the Pope." In vain they told them that all the bishops, prelates, and heads, including London, Winchester, Durham,

---

* [As to this Article, see end of chapter.]

† "In which rules it is thus written, as they shewed unto us: 'Ad hoc per obedientiam injungo ministris ut petant a Domino Papa unum de sanctæ Romanæ Ecclesiæ Cardinalibus, qui sit gubernator, protector, et corrector istius fraternitatis, ut semper subditi et subjecti pedibus sanctæ ecclesiæ eJusdem stabiles in fide Catholica paupertatem et humilitatem, et secundum Evangelium Domini nostri Jesu Christi, quod firmiter promisimus observemus.'"—Lee and Bedyl to Crumwel, Wright's Suppr. of Mon., p. 43.

‡ This early specimen of destructive criticism is curious enough. The chapter of the rule of St. Francis which the brethren alleged contained the word ministers: "and we shewed them that in our opinion that chapter was no part of St. Francis' rule, but was forged since, and planted into the same by some ambitious friar of that order, for, as we supposed, the name of ministers was not found out or spoken of, when their rule was confirmed."—Lee and Bedyl to Crumwel, *ib.*

and Bath, had subscribed to the same conclusion (which we shall presently see) : their final answer was that "they had professed St. Francis' religion, and in the observance thereof they would live and die."

The suppression of the whole order to which these recusants belonged followed forthwith ; but of the wholesale religious catastrophes by which the reign of Henry is distinguished, this, which is the earliest, is perhaps the most obscure. As yet there was no law of verbal treason, so that the Observants of Greenwich could not share the conspicuous fate of the gibbet with the Carthusians who suffered in the following year, when verbal treason had been invented : nor was it possible to institute a legal prosecution against men who had done nothing but refuse to subscribe articles propounded, and perhaps composed, by the Provincial of another order of friars, but required by no law. But Henry, though cautious in general of exerting his might unassisted by law, seems to have seen here a case in which he might proceed not only without scruple, but without pretence. All the Observants were expelled from their houses, which were filled with friars of the Augustinian Order ; they themselves were put in prison, or dispersed in other convents, to the number of two hundred ; and the transaction, wearing somewhat of the colour of an exchange, passed without the censure of the nation. Of the imprisoned brethren no fewer than fifty died under the rigours of their confinement. The rest, through the influence of Wriothesley, their secret friend and patron, obtained the more merciful doom of banishment, and made their way into France and Scotland.*

* Sanders, Fuller, Lingard. There is some discrepancy between these writers and Herbert, who says nothing of the imprisonment of the Observants, but that they were dispersed into other houses, and their room filled by Friars Austin. Perhaps their case has been confounded

For the rest, the various commissioners extended their loyal exertions into almost every religious or ecclesiastical foundation of the south. The cathedral churches of Canterbury, London, Wells, Lincoln, Worcester, St. David, St. Asaph, Landaff, and Norwich; the colleges of Oxford—Oriel, Baliol, Brasenose, Merton, All Souls; and a vast number of convents, hospitals, and collegiate churches, were visited and took the oath and made their subscriptions.* The Bishop of Winchester seems to have been able to preserve his diocese from particular visitations by assembling the clergy in his cathedral chapterhouse, and causing them to subscribe in a body there. This visitation, the first wave of a deluge, was probably extended over the dioceses of the northern province.† It lasted nearly to the end of the year.

with that of the Franciscan Priory of Christ Church in London, which was seized and given to Audley two years before, in 1532, the inmates being distributed into other houses of their order. The two cases exhibit Henry's first essays in the art of suppression. In the one he seized and alienated the house, but sent the inmates into other houses of their own religion. In the other he imprisoned or dispersed an entire order, but allowed their houses to be devoted to religious ends a little longer. It remained for him to combine the two processes; to seize the houses and disperse the inmates.

* The "Juramenta et Fidelitates" of one hundred and sixty-four foundations of all sorts are recorded in Rymer, xiv. 495-527. All subscribed without protestation except Baliol College, the master of which, William Whyte, and the Fellows added, "Ista Protestatione præhibita quod nos nihil agere intendimus contra legem Divinam, nec contra Orthodoxæ Fidei Normam, nec contra Sacrosanctæ Matris Ecclesiæ Catholicæ Doctrinam." [For more, see end of chapter.]

† Wharton, in his Observ. on Strype's Cranmer, says that the originals of the subscriptions of thirteen dioceses remain in the Exchequer, into which they were first returned: and that to his certain knowledge those "of the other nine dioceses are yet remaining in a certain place."— Strype's *Cranm.*, sub fin. [See end of chapter.]

Was the oath, which was for all subjects, generally administered to laymen, as it was to spiritual persons? Cranmer, in one of his letters, speaks of his own "commission to take oath of the King's subjects for his highness' succession," and also speaks of commissions

The next case in which serious opposition was attempted was that of the Charterhouse of London. Under the rule of John Houghton their prior, the Carthusian monks of the House of the Salutation of the Blessed Mary of London had not declined from the ancient discipline which had made their order renowned throughout the world. Their strict lives, their spare diet, their constant exercises, and the works of charity and mercy to which they were devoted, rendered them worthy representatives of the best days of monasticism. No treasonable designs, no political machinations, had ever been imputed to them: they had taken no part in the agitation caused by the Nun of Canterbury:* no expression of opinion concerning the doings of the King and Parliament was known to have proceeded from them. They appear to have desired simply to keep their vows, and to live in peace. Early in April this pious fraternity was visited by Lee and Bedyl. When the oath was tendered, the prior made answer, "that it belonged not to him nor any of those under him to meddle with the King's business, nor concerned it him whom the King would divorce, nor whom he would marry." The Visitors insisted however that he should call the convent together

being issued to justices of the peace to take the same oath. Cranmer says that he let "those who could not write make their sheep-mark, or some other mark, as they could scribble."—*Rem.*, p. 290. Strype (*Cranm.*, p. 26, fol. ed.) says that Crumwel, Audley, the Abbot of Westminster, and others along with Cranmer, were appointed commissioners to tender the oath: and that the nobility and gentry took it, subscribing their names in a long list. But this seems to refer to the swearing of the Parliament before they separated. So also Latimer says, in a letter to Crumwel, that he thought "that gentlemen of lands and arms should so swear to the King's issue that their oaths and also names be registered, &c. so that you should soon know who were sworn, and who not."—*Remains*, p. 367.

* She had, however, visited them. "Having gone her Perambulations to the Charterhouse of London and Shene, then to the Nunnery of Sion, and thence to the Friars of Richmond, Canterbury and Greenwich, she came to the King himself."—Bailey's *Fisher*, p. 135.

immediately: on which he said that "for his part he could not apprehend how the former marriage, celebrated according to the rites of the Church, and so long continued, should be void." This was enough for the Visitors: Houghton was sent to the Tower, accompanied thither by Humphrey Middlemore, the procurator of the house, who had manfully stood by his superior. When the two had been a month in the Tower, however, they were persuaded by Stokesley, Bishop of London, Lee of York, and "certain other good and learned men" who visited them, that the present controversy was not a lawful cause for which they should expose themselves to death. So they promised to yield to the King's commandment, and were sent home. As soon as they had returned, they called together the brethren in the chapterhouse, and Houghton told them of the submission which he had promised to make, adding that he was conscious that he had only delayed the danger which threatened them, not averted it. "Our hour, dear brethren," he said, "is not yet come: but in the same night that we were set free I dreamed that I should not escape thus. Within a year I shall be brought again to that place, and then I shall finish my course." The monks, influenced by these prophetic words, at first resolved not to purchase a useless delay by a pretended submission; and when the commissioners soon afterwards came to propound the oath, they refused it. The commissioners, however, came again, with the Lord Mayor and officers to carry them to prison, May 4; and then they submitted and took the oath with this condition, "so far as it was lawful." This not being enough, they were visited again, May 29, by Lee and Bedyl; when fourteen subscribed, among whom were Houghton and Middlemore themselves. Lee came again, june 6, accompanied not by Bedyl (who was further afield) but by another Visitor named Thomas Kytson; and, armed with new letters patent, exacted the oath from the rest of the fraternity. Among those who subscribed on the latter occasion were William Exmew, a priest, and Sebastian Newdigate, a professed monk: both of whom afterwards suffered martyrdom. It is touching also to read the name of poor Maurice Channey, the less resolute brother, to whom we owe the narrative which reveals so much of the inner life of the convent in those days. Such was the first act in the tragedy of the Charterhouse.*

We must follow now the adventurous Bedyl a little further, to be introduced to the third religious body which offered resistance to the King and Parliament; though the fitful opposition of the friars of Sion was scarce worthy to be compared with the deliberate resolution which animated the Observants and the Carthusians. The sharp tool whom Crumwel drove found himself reposing in Cranmer's manor of Otford in the latter end of August, after many toils. From that place he wrote to his master a recital of his exertions, which is of historical value, because it contains the first hint of the policy, which was pursued soon after in the suppression of the religious houses, of killing off the best of the monks and friars, and scattering the rest. He had found, said Bedyl, divers of the religious men ready to hazard their souls and bodies, and the suppression of their houses, for the Bishop of Rome. It made no great matter, indeed, what became of such men, provided that their souls were saved; and for his part he wished them dead by God's hand, that men

---

* Cf. Historia Martyr. Angl., c. 9; Rymer, xiv. p. 491: Strype, E. M., i. p. 399. [Houghton was a severe ruler: see Gairdner, Lett. and Pap. vi. 409.]

might escape the obloquy of punishing them;* for some persons had an opinion of their apparent holiness, which was for the most part hypocrisy. He had already taken pains to reduce them from their errors for the charity which he owed their souls and bodies: and, for his caution seems to have been equal to his charity, he waited now for orders to take more pains. He had taken pains with the monks of the Charterhouses, especially of London; and he had taken pains with the friars of Sion. But he found these friars no less ready than the rest to offer themselves in sacrifice to the great idol of Rome; for which they were doubtless accursed of God, because they trusted in man concerning everlasting life.†

The Brigitites, or reformed Austin Friars, possessed, their only English establishment, the large and celebrated foundation of Sion, in Brentford. Of this order the sisters, to the number of sixty, were of irreproachable conduct: the twenty-five brethren, half of whom were priests, were of mingled character. Their superior under the name of Confessor, enjoyed the dignity of a prior. He who held the office at this time professed extreme loyalty to the King when the visitation began; but at the same time, if the deposition of a treacherous penitent be to be believed, he was counselling those who sought him in confession to hold by the Pope, to beware of the heretics, and

---

* Aspirants are numerous: but the topmost peak of the necessitarian sublime has been reached perhaps by Mr. Froude with the aid of the great Bedyl. Bedyl said that he would that all such obstinate persons as the friars of Sion "were dead indeed by God's hand, that no man should run wrongfully into obloquy for their just punishment."—*State Pap.*, i. 422. Mr. Froude has touched this into perfection when he says that Bedyl said the friars "would confer a service on the country by dying quietly, lest *honest* men should incur unmerited obloquy in putting them to death."—ii. 342.

† State Papers, i. 422.

to expect the restoration of the papal authority.* Under such a head the conduct of the brethren was various, and the discipline perhaps relaxed. Bedyl (for we return to the narrative of his letters) visited them for the first time in July, along with the Bishop of London, and found the sisterhood conformable: of the brethren he said that the saddest and best learned and most honest were the Father Confessor and Father Carson, who might bring the rest to good con-formity, though there were two of the brethren who were somewhat seditious and must be weeded out, since they were infecting the rest: the surveyor of the lands of Sion, Master More, was also a right honest man, and a faithful to his prince. Of his fellow-visitor, the Bishop of London, Archdeacon Bedyl was able to report to his master that he had spoken for the King's title and against the Bishop of Rome, in such manner and fashion as was excellent and singular. He departed for Otford, after giving orders to the Confessor to declare the King's title in his sermon on the following Sunday, and engaging the honest More to come to him in the place of his repose, and report whether the Confessor had obeyed. The honest More came, after an interval of several weeks, and made a full report of the affairs of Sion. The Confessor had done his duty fully, for he had preached twice and declared the King's title: nor had Father Carson failed, though in the very act of declaring the title he had brought out the words "mea culpa" in a strange manner, but perhaps unadvisedly, since it was a term often used. But of the rest there was no good to report. One preacher named Whitford, who was a man of small learning and a great railer, preached in his turn, but

* "Deposition concerning the popish conduct of a priest. Rolls House MS."—*Froude*, ii. 316.

said not a word of the title.   Another, named Ricot,
when he preached, declared the title, but added that
he who commanded him so to preach should discharge
his conscience.   And as soon as Ricot began to declare the title, eight or nine of the friars departed from
the sermon, contrary to the rule of their order, and to
the great slander of a large congregation.   Those who
departed were Coppinger, Lache, a very wilful and
seditious person, Little, Bishop, Parker, Browne, Tur-
lington and Bowell.   It would be well, recommended
Bedyl, either to suspend all preaching for a time, or to
take some order with these persons, and to begin with
Whitford and Lache : for the Confessor could do no
good with these two, and feared for his life.   Perhaps
it would be advisable that some of the King's servants
of the neighbourhood should be present at sermons,
and bring those who misbehaved to prison.   It was
thought that some of the friars were like to escape out
of their cloister, and it would be no great loss if they
did, so that no more were heard of them.*

After this ill report, the cloisters of Sion were much
favoured by official visitors.   The author of the new
loyalty, Crumwel himself, came, and held a conference
with the Confessor.   As he left the Confessor's
chamber, one of the brethren, a " foolish fellow with a
curled head," knelt in his way, probably with the
notion of making some remonstrance ; but nothing
came of it.   One of Crumwel's most notorious instruments, Dr. Layton, came next, and seems to have
taken up his quarters in Sion for some time.   He
presently reported to his master that on Sunday,
December 12, one of the recusant brethren, Bishop,
declared the King's title very well, when he preached,

---

* State Papers, i. 422.   It may be added that the honest More fell into
suspicion a few months later. *Ellis*, 11, 2, 85.

and the church was full of people. But the same foolish fellow with the curled head openly called Bishop a false knave, when he did it. As to Bishop himself, Layton said that in questioning the lay brethren he had heard many enormous things of him. Bishop wanted to go out by night with two of the brethren in secular apparel, but they had not money to buy the apparel. He wanted one of the lay brethren who was a smith to make him a key for the door. He wanted the same brother to pull a bar of iron out of one of the windows. He persuaded the sexton that he wanted to be in contemplation in the church by night, and there he talked with one of the nuns at the grate of the nuns' choir. This nun seems to have been the only frail one of Sion. Bishop was her confessor. Besides the nun there was a wife of Uxbridge. He found many brethren right weary of their habit, and willing to depart thence. From such religion and pre-tended sanctity God save Layton! He concluded his information with a curious insinuation, or compliment, concerning the other Visitor, Bedyl. God had given Mr. Bedyl such capacity, said Layton, that if he had been a friar, and of Bishop's counsel, he would have helped him without any breaking of grates or counter-feiting of keys.

Two days after this Dr. Buttes and the Queen's Almoner came to Sion to convert Whitford and Little. On the next day came Dr. Aldrich, Dr. Curwen, Dr. Baugh, and Dr. Morgan, sent by the King on the same errand, but without effect. Then, or else before, came Bedyl again, and dealt with Whitford in the garden both with fair words and foul, telling him that his irreligious life might bring him to public shame, and his indecent words when he heard ladies in their confessions, might bring shrift to an end in England.

But Whitford had a forehead of brass.   However, the eloquent Visitor reformed a lay brother named Matthew by the hope of liberty, or release from the cloister.   Whitford, Little, and a lay brother named Turbington, who was very sturdy against the title, were commended to Crumwel's special consideration. The two former had been sequestered by the Visitors from hearing the confessions of the ladies : and Bedyl advised that the place where those friars had been wont to hear utterward confessions, or the confessions of all comers at certain times of the year, should be walled up, and that use fordone for ever, for these utterward confessions had been the cause of much evil and treason in the matter of the King's title.   The ladies desired that Bishop and Parker might be discharged from the convent ; and Bishop and Parker desired the same. There had been some trouble among the ladies about the King's title; Lord Windsor had come thither, and laboured much to convert his sister and some of his kinswomen there : and the Bishop of London came the next day, and he and the loyal Confessor had the ladies into their chapterhouse, and told them, upon their consciences and the peril of their souls, that they ought by God's law to consent to the title.   The ladies were much comforted : and when the Visitors willed all who consented to the title to sit still, and all, who would not consent, to leave the chapter house, there was not one that departed.   Nevertheless, there was one sturdy and wilful sister, Agnes Smith, who was trying to prevent the Visitors from getting possession of the convent seal ; but they trusted to get it that morning, with the subscription of the abbess for all her sisters : which was the best fashion that they could bring it to.*

* Wright's Supp. of Mon., pp. 47, 48.

Such were the scenes, such was the work, that was rendered necessary by the new loyalty.

The summer of this eventful year was illustrated by several declarations extorted from the clergy and the Universities against the usurped power of the Pope. The northern bishops and clergy were suspected beyond their southern brethren of reluctance in complying with the changes made by the King and Parliament ; and it was deemed expedient to exact from them, before their Convocation separated, an explicit declaration that the Pope had no power in England.   The royal breve was laid before the northern synod, May 5; requiring them to deliberate and determine upon the single point, whether by Holy Scripture the Bishop of Rome had greater jurisdiction in the realm of England than any other bishop. The limitation of the question to the text of Holy Scripture, to the exclusion of ecclesiastical history and tradition, might have been remarked as curious in the Defender of the Faith ; but it simplified the task of the clergy.   They searched the Scriptures; and finding there nothing about the relations between Rome and England, returned with one consent, June 2, a Declaration according to the wishes of the King.   In this distinct sentence against the Pope, so far as it went, the northern clergy had the honour of preceding their brethren of the south.*   The same question about the same time was propounded by the same authority to the two Universities, and the same answer was returned by both.†   No other answer could be given.   But, if the question seemed stolid to the learned, it was artful in the proposer.   The limitation under which it was pro-

* Wilk., iii. 782.   This is the earliest document in which I have found the word supremacy applied to the papal authority.   The register of Convocation, quoted here, describes the sentence as being " adversus suprematum Papæ."

† Wilk., iii. 772, 776.   State Pap., i. 425.

posed was forgotten; and the vulgar would only remember that it had been unanimously concluded by the Clergy and the Universities that the Pope had no more power in England than any other foreign bishop. Before the end of the year the same answer was obtained from the southern clergy also.

After an unusually short interval, the Houses of Parliament assembled again in the beginning of November. Their first Act was to declare that the King ought to have the title and style of Supreme Head of the Church of England.* The brief declaration in which this was embodied was of little more than formal importance. It neither made, nor professed to make, any change in the Constitution. The King was already Supreme Head of the Church of England; and the Act began by saying that he was so already. The King had been already acknowledged by the clergy of the realm in their Convocations to be the Supreme Head of the Church of England; and the Act went on to rehearse that the clergy had acknowledged him already. But it seemed desirable "for increase of virtue in Christ's religion, and to repress and extirpe all errors, heresies, and other enormities and abuses," to authorise him to have the title and " all honours, dignities, pre-eminences, jurisdictions, privileges, authorities, immunities, profits, and commodities" belonging thereto. The honours and dignities, it may be observed, he had already, because he was Supreme Head; the jurisdictions, privileges, authorities, and immunities which were usurped by foreign power had already been restored severally; and with them the profits and commodities which pertained to the same high office of right. But the Houses of Parliament meant to augment very largely the profits and commodities, if they added

* 26 H. VIII. 1.

nothing to the dignity of the head of the realm by a
mere declaration of his title. The King, they added,
was to have power and authority " to visit and reform
errors, heresies, contempts, and offences." He had
such power already as the Supreme Ordinary, and
could have exercised it at any time through his spiritual officers; and in a constitutional point of view the
clause which thus empowered him was merely declara-
tory, like the other parts of the Act. But it was a
declaration made with a terrible intention. He took
the advantage it was meant to afford, and proceeded
to ruin the monasteries, and half ruin the Church, for
his own profits and commodities.

It has been seen that when the clergy, two years
before, acknowledged the King for their Supreme
Head, they represented the distress to which they
were reduced by the Papal exactions of Annates, or
Firstfruits; and petitioned him for the abolition of
those oppressive impositions. Now that the Lords
and Commons in their turn acknowledged the King
for their Supreme Head, they celebrated the occasion
by annexing the firstfruits of all spiritual promotions
to the Crown. It might have seemed proper, since
the Pope was gone, that his exactions should go after
him. But the profits and commodities of the Supreme
Head were to be augmented. From the ecclesiastical
laws of this reign, monuments of adulation and hypocrisy, it would be impossible to select a more perfect
specimen of cunning baseness than the Preamble of
the Act by which this great injury to the Church was
perpetuated. With cumbrous verbiage it was set forth
that " it was, and of very duty ought to be, the natural
inclination of all good people, like most faithful, loving,
and obedient subjects, sincerely and willingly to desire
to provide, not only for the public weal of their native

country, but also for the supportation, maintenance, and
defence of the royal estate of their most dread, benign,
and gracious sovereign lord, upon whom and in whom
dependeth all their joy and wealth, in whom also is
united and knit so princely a heart and courage, mixed
with mercy, wisdom and justice, and also a natural affection joined to the same, as by the great, inestimable, and
benevolent arguments thereof, being most bountifully,
largely, and many times shewed, ministered, and approved towards his loving and obedient subjects, had
well appeared; which required a like correspondence of
gratitude to be considered, according to their most
bounden duties: wherefore the said humble and obedient subjects, as well the lords spiritual and temporal
as the Commons, in Parliament assembled, calling to
their remembrance not only the manifold and innumerable benefits administered by his Highness to them
all, and the residue of all other his subjects of this
realm, but also how long his Majesty had most victoriously by his high wisdom and policy protected,
defended, and governed this his realm, and maintained
his people and subjects of the same in tranquillity,
peace, unity, quietness, and wealth; and also considering what great, excessive and inestimable charges
his Highness had heretofore been at and sustained
by the space of six-and-twenty whole years, and
also daily sustained, for the maintenance, tuition, and
defence of his realm, and his loving subjects of the
same, which could not be sustained and borne without
some honourable provision might be made, found,
provided, and ordained for maintenance thereof; did
therefore desire and most humbly pray, that for the
more surety of continuance and augmentation of his
Highness' royal estate, being not only now recognised
(as he always indeed had heretofore been) the only

Supreme Head in earth, next and immediately under God, of the Church of England, but also their most assured and undoubted natural sovereign liege lord and King, having the whole governance, tuition, maintenance and defence of that his realm——" * for these many, manifold, and multiplied considerations they besought him to accept the firstfruits and profits for one year of every spiritual benefice, from archbishopric down to free chapel; and a yearly tenth of the same. Commissioners were to search for the value of every benefice. We shall find them at their work anon. The penalty for default of payment of the tenths was deprivation. The charge of collecting them was thrown upon the bishops. This seemed a ready mode of discharging the inestimable obligations which his Majesty's faithful subjects in Parliament assembled owned so copiously. Some grains of mercy were added. No firstfruits were to be taken from a living of less than eight marks a year, unless the incumbent remained in it above three years from his presentation; but if he lived in it so long as that, firstfruits were to be levied. The fifth part of the enormous fine which the clergy had incurred under the Præmunire two years before was remitted, in consideration of the yearly payments which they were henceforth required to make. To prevent the Act from cutting both ways, another Act

---

* 26 H. VIII. 3. It may be observed that if the notion of the lawyers that there were two supremacies, and that the Pope's supremacy was taken away in order to establish the royal supremacy, had any foundation, it would have been found in this Act, which has been called the natural sequel of the Act conferring the title of Supreme Head. This latter is vulgarly called "the Supremacy Act," as if the King now took the Supremacy from the Pope; and for the first time became Supreme Head of the English Church, and then consequently took what revenues had belonged to the former Supreme Head or governor. This view never struck those who did the deed. In documents of the time it is called the "Act of Supreme Head," but never the Supremacy Act.

was passed. There were many lands belonging to spiritual owners which were let, it might be, to temporal persons. Therefore, " for certain reasonable and urgent considerations moving the King's high court of Parliament," it was ordained that the farmers or lessees of such lands should not be liable to pay firstfruits or tenths on them; but that the payment should fall on the spiritual owners.*

Twenty-six towns were named, in another Act, for the sees of as many suffragan bishops, who might be appointed at the request of diocesans requiring aid.† The relief was accepted by at least half that number of diocesans within the next five years: but it must not be supposed that there was an unmitigated evil previously in the vastness of dioceses and the paucity of bishops. Seeless suffragans, with imaginary titles generally taken from some foreign town, were appointed under the old system by those diocesan bishops who chose to have them. A succession of bishops of Sidon had been the assistants of the archbishops of Canterbury: the bishop of Negropont was the suffragan of York: the Athenian town of Reonen gave a title to the episcopal coadjutor of Salisbury; and the Bishop of Hippolitanum assisted in the ordinations of Cranmer. The new Act for the nomination of suffragans put an end to this ancient system; but it was not the first remedy applied to a long-standing defect.‡

In the previous session an Act of Succession had been passed, to which all subjects were required to

* 26 H. VIII. 17.

† Thetford, Ipswich, Colchester, Dover, Guildford, Southampton, Taunton, Shaftesbury, Molton, Marlborough, Bedford, Gloucester, Leicester, Shrewsbury, Bristol, Penrith (Landaff), Bridgewater, Nottingham, Grantham, Hull. Huntingdon, Cambridge, Penrith, Berwick, St. Germains in Cornwall, and the Isle of Wight. 26 H. VIII. 14.

‡ Strype's Cranm. Bk. i. c. ix.

swear; but no form of oath had been prescribed. Commissioners had tendered an oath, and punished those who refused to take it, although no power of punishment was given them by the Act. But the tyranny of Henry was ever fearful of overpassing the law, while the limits of the law were easily shifted to accommodate the tyranny of Henry. The former Act was now confirmed by another, in which it was declared that the oath taken by the Houses, before they were last prorogued, was the oath intended to be taken by all subjects: and that a certificate made by the commissioners against those who refused the oath should have the same validity as an indictment before a jury.* The offer of More and Fisher to swear to the succession, but not in the form prescribed, was thus set aside finally: and the previous imprisonment of More, Fisher, Houghton and Middlemore was brought, so far as it was possible, under the shelter of the law. These Acts for securing the succession in the progeny of Anne Boleyn were the beginning of the most miserable series of enactments that disgraces the Statute Book, the treason laws of Henry the Eighth. They made it high treason to do or procure anything to the peril of the King's person or crown, or to the slander of Queen Anne and her issue royal, by writing, or printing, or any other exterior act: misprision of treason to do or procure the like by words only. They were now improved by a new law, by which in treason verbal offences against the King or Queen were exalted to the higher degree. It was made high treason for any person to "maliciously wish, will or desire, by words or writing, or by craft imagine, invent, practise or attempt any bodily harm to be done or committed to the King's most royal person, the

* 26 H. VIII. 2.

Queen's, or their heirs apparent, or to deprive them, or any of them, of the dignity, title or name of their royal estates : or slanderously and maliciously publish and pronounce by express writing or words that the King should be heretic, schismatic, tyrant, infidel, or usurper of the crown." With these new kinds were oddly mingled some very overt acts of treason, such as rebelliously keeping the King's castles, ships, or ordnance.* It was a wonderful surrender of liberty, this law to make words high treason : and by historians who cannot understand why the guardians of the realm should have yielded such tremendous power into the King's hands, it is assumed that there was some terrific crisis, struggle, or danger impending, which was to be met by extraordinary measures. The truth is that these extraordinary measures were taken in order to create a crisis. Henry the Eighth was never in so much danger as his father incurred from Perkin Warbeck. But danger was proclaimed, and measures destructive of liberty were taken, because the King and Parliament were seeking for pretexts to carry on the revolution which they had begun. The outcries or murmurs of monks and friars smarting under injury, or rather the informations laid against them by Crumwel's spies, were to be exalted to the dignity of high treason, that some decent occasion might be found for putting an end to the religious orders and seizing their estates.† In the opinion of a great jurist, the

---

* 26 H. VIII. 13.

† Mr. Froude (vol. ii. c. ix.), to palliate the extraordinary Acts of 1534, has collected all that he can of what he calls "Catholic treasons" meditated at that time : 1. The Archbishop of York was reported to have spoken of standing against the King to death. It may be answered there were many attempts made by royal agents about this period to criminate the Archbishop of York. This one was made by Bedyl's spy, the Confessor of Sion, to whom the words were reported to have been spoken.

single crime of treason, left open to an indefinite latitude
of construction, is sufficient to turn any government into
an arbitrary power.*   The English Parliament, when
in the reign of Edward the Third they reduced that
undetermined crime to specific definition, were justly
held to have reared a second pillar, almost equal to the
Great Charter itself, in the edifice of freedom, against
the tyranny of kings and the capricious interpretation
of judges.   Those must have been no ordinary con-

The Archbishop was examined in January 1535 by Layton and Legh, two
of the King's Visitors, about the words imputed to him : but he utterly
denied having spoken them (State Papers, i. p. 453 ; Strype, i. p. 293),
and declared that he had never seen anyone at Sion since the year before
the Statute (of verbal treason) was passed, nor had he seen or spoken to
any messenger from Sion. (Ellis, 3rd Ser. iii. p. 373.) 2. The Bishop of
Durham's house (I suppose in London) was searched by the Visitor
Ap Rice, but nothing treasonable was found.   As this is taken out
of a "Rolls House MS.," no more can be said of it.   3. Some of the
friars of Sion behaved badly at sermon.   So we have seen from Bedyl's
letters to Crumwel.   4. Forest, the bold friar of Greenwich, told a
penitent that he had abjured the Pope in the outward, but not in the
inward man, that he owed an obedience to the Pope which he could not
shake off ; and that it was his use and practice in confession to induce
men to hold and stick to the old fashion of belief.   *Ex pede Herculem !*
There may have been many such dangerous confessors.   But why not as
many communicative penitents?   5. A treacherous penitent told Crumwel that the Confessor of Sion had said that the Pope had been put out
by the King and Parliament, but not for long.   That Confessor, according to Bedyl, was a loyal man ; he may very well have been too loyal to
be honest.   6. A friar named Maitland spoke very rudely of the King
and Anne Boleyn, and said that he knew by necromancy that all men of
the new learning should be suppressed and suffer death, and the old
learning be set up again by the King's enemies beyond seas.   This was
from an informer; and sounds of one.   7. In the May of 1534 two priests
named Feron and Hale were heard compassing treason in the cloister of
Sion, Hale prompting Feron in English with matter for a Latin pamphlet
to be written to the effect that three parts of England were against the
King, that the realm was being reduced to the miserable condition of
France; that there was sufficient cause for rebellion ; that Henry was the
cruellest capital heretic, and his life more foul and stinking than a sow.
There was more in this : but see next chapter for a full account of Feron
and Hale.   These were fine reasons for altering the laws of the realm !
    * Esprit des Lois, vi. 7.

siderations which induced the Parliament of Henry the Eighth not only to undo the work of the past, but to go beyond the boldest stretch of construction in the invention of treasons. But they had not gone as far as it was possible to go even now. They had extended the crime of treason to the desires of the mind expressed by the words of the mouth. We shall find them afterwards extending it to the thoughts of the heart also and the beliefs.*

An Act of attainder against Fisher and others, and an Act of attainder against More, were the closing works of a session which completed the legal machinery of the revolution. The venerable Fisher, in the former session of this year, had been attainted of misprision of treason in the matter of the Nun of Kent; but he was allowed, as we have seen, to compound for loss of goods by a fine. When baseness deals to virtue the first stab, it sometimes recoils, half afraid of the wound itself has made: but it grows bolder by repeated strokes. It is the spotlessness of virtue which makes defencelessness appear formidable; but virtue wounded soon becomes virtue sullied, even by her own blood.' Fisher was now attainted of "misprision of high treason" for refusing the oath. His former attainder and his imprisonment had made the powerful enemies, who once could not but revere him,

---

* Great debate for many days is said to have arisen on this Act : "the Commons themselves began to think it a very hard law, and full of rigour: for, said they, a man may chance to say such a thing by way of discourse, or such word may fall from him unawares, and it was a strange thing that a man should die for saying he was not head of the Church." Thereon the King sent them word that "except it could be proved that the party spoke it maliciously, the statute should not be of any force to condemn. So the word maliciously was put in, and it passed currently, which afterwards served as much purpose as the words, Quantum per legem Dei licet."—Bailie's *Fisher.* We shall see something more of this word *maliciously.*

accustomed to associate disgrace and punishment with him in their minds; and henceforth he received no mercy. All his goods were forfeited to the Crown, and his bishopric of Rochester was declared void of bishop. Christopher Plummer of Windsor, Miles Wilson and Miles Wyllen of London, Edward Powell of Salisbury, Richard Fetherstonhaugh of London, clerks, were included in the bill against Fisher: Wilson and Fetherstonhaugh for having refused the oath since May, the others for having "committed traitorously, contrary to their allegiance and duties, many and sundry detestable offences of misprision of high treason."* Wilson, Powell and Fetherstonhaugh were all doctors of distinction. The first of them is mentioned by Sir Thomas More as having refused the oath on the same day with himself: the other two had been among the counsel of the late queen in the trial before the legates. It is probable that the punishment of these clerks, like that of Fisher himself for un-specified crimes, was merely arbitrary, not in pursuance of previous proceedings at common law. The Act against More was even more invidious. The several grants of lands and tenements which the King had made to him were recounted: they had been made because the King hoped for true and faithful service and counsel from him; but he had been, said the Act, guilty of ingratitude, not only in refusing the oath, but in that "he had unkindly and ingrately served the King by divers and sundry ways, means, and conditions, contrary to his trust and confidence." The grants were cancelled, and the former confidant of the King was left to the penalties of misprision of treason.† He

---

* 26 H. VIII. 22.

† 26 H. VIII. 23. The accusation of ingratitude because More gave un-palatable advice sometimes, may be illustrated by the following anecdote :

and Fisher continued to languish in severe durance,
and at the end of the year Fisher wrote to Crumwel
a pathetic account of the sufferings which he had to
sustain from cold, hunger and nakedness, want of
books, and of the means of religious consolation.*
Such was the second part of their tragedy.

As soon as the Southern Convocation which attended this session of Parliament was gathered together,
the same question was propounded to them which
had been determined already by the clergy of the
North and by the Universities: Whether the Bishop
of Rome have by sacred Scripture any greater authority in the realm of England than any other bishop.
The number present was small, but the sentence was
less unanimous than those given by the other assemblies: and out of thirty-nine, one doubted and four
stood in the affirmative of the power of the Pope.†

"Within a while after the resigning of his office, Mr. Crumwel (now
highly in the King's favour) came of a message from the King to Sir
Thomas: wherein when they had throughly talked together, before his
going away, Sir Thomas said unto him: Mr. Crumwel, you are entered
into the service of a most noble, wise, and liberal prince; if you will
follow my poor advice, you shall in your counsel given to his Majesty
ever tell him what he ought to do, but never what he is able to do: so
shall you show yourself a true and faithful servant, and a right worthy
counsellor: for if a lion knew his own strength, hard were it for any man
to rule him."—More's *Life of More*, p. 260.

* Strype, E. M. i. p. 270. "I have neither shirt nor coat, nor yet
other clothes that are necessary for me to wear, but that be ragged and
rent too shamefully. Notwithstanding I might easily suffer that if that
would keep my body warm. But my diet God knoweth how slender it is
many times. And now in mine age my stomach may not away but with
a few kind of meat, which if I want I decay forthwith, and fall into crases
and diseases of my body. . . . May it please you that I may take some
Priest with me in the Tower . . . to hear my confession against this holy
time.—That I may borrow some books to say my devotion more effectually these holy days for the comfort of my soul. Our Lord God send
you a merry Christmas, &c." Dec. 22.

† Wilkins, iii. 769.

The next question that engaged them was the style of the Archbishop.

In the pontifical system certain great sees in several of the kingdoms of Europe had long possessed a higher official relation than others to the Apostolic See; and Canterbury and York shared with Pisa, Rheims, and Metz the privilege of inherent legatine authority. The occupiers of those sees bore the title of born legates of the Apostolic See: but it is observable that in each case this standing acknowledgment of the pontifical jurisdiction was not historically a monument of dependence, but of independence: a device to curtail the encroachments of Rome in the high day of her domination, the continual presence of a legatus natus in the realm often preventing the more active intervention of a legatus a latere.* Now, however, that the connection between Rome and England was being

---

* The first Archbishop of Canterbury who assumed the legatine title was William of Corbeuil, in the first part of the twelfth century, who became a legatus natus to avoid the dictation of a legatus a latere, and preserve the purity of English ecclesiastical law. Before his time legates a latere had occasionally appeared in England, but (except the early instance of the Council of Calcuith in 785) they had never presumed to preside over synods, or to make canons and impose them on the clergy. As soon as they did this, about 1125, Archbishop William, " considering the Church of England to have suffered a heavy scandal" (Continuator of Flor. Worc. in Hook's Lives, ii. 312), repaired to Rome, and obtained to himself and his successors the privilege of being a legate born. The expedient was successful in restraining the interference of foreigners, particularly in regard to the ecclesiastical laws. Henceforth, as a rule, no legate made canons in any national or provincial synod of England, unless he were an English archbishop: nor in any diocesan synod, unless he were an English bishop. Only three instances to the contrary can be collected from subsequent history. One was in the twelfth century, when the see of Canterbury was vacant, and the Archbishop of York sick. The other two were the notorious visits of the nuncios Otto and Ottobon in the thirteenth century, in the full tide of papal domination. The last legate a latere seen in England was Wolsey, who was an Englishman, and this consoling circumstance was particularly insisted upon by those of the bishops who welcomed the reformations which he was to have effected in his extraordinary character.

formally severed, the title, long unsubstantial, was but
a shadow.   And since the Parliament in some of their
late Church Acts had omitted it and substituted another, it was but the shadow of a shade.   Cranmer
commanded in Convocation that the title should be
disused, and the word metropolitan, already employed
by Parliament, inserted instead of it.*

For the rest the clergy examined some heretical
books, in particular one which was ascribed to the man
whom More designated "the captain of our English
heretics," Tyndale ;† and a Primer, which was submitted
by the Abbot of Northampton, and appeared to the
Most Reverend and his brethren to be suspect.‡   They
also requested the archbishop to make instance with
his Majesty that he would order all heretical books to
be delivered up within three months by those who had
them ; that he would deign to prohibit his lay subjects
from publicly and contentiously disputing on the
Catholic faith : and that he would appoint fit persons
to translate the Holy Scriptures into the vulgar tongue,
and allow them to the people according to their learning.§   The solicitude of the clergy to preserve the

---

* "Archiepiscopus, habita prius communicatione per longum tempus
de et super diversis urgentibus causis heresin concernentibus, et pro
reformatione ejusdem, voluit et mandavit quod in omnibus et singulis
procuratoriis exhibitis coram eo in hac Convocatione, sive sacra Synodo
Provinciali, et imposterum in eadem Convocatione exhibendis inferatur
hoc verbum 'metropolitanus,' et deleatur ab iisdem 'Apostolicæ sedis
legatus.'"—*Wilkins*, iii. 769.

† The book ascribed to Tyndale was undoubtedly "the poisoned book
which a nameless heretic hath named The Supper of the Lord," to which
Sir T. More wrote "The Answer" in 1533.   It is printed in Tyndale's
works (i.).

‡ The Primer, or Private Office Book, was a favourite vehicle with
the heretics, or reformers, for conveying their doctrines.   There was one
condemned by Convocation in 1530.   But I reserve the subject at present.

§ "Et quod ulterius regia sua MaJestas dignaretur decernere quod
sacra Scriptura in vulgarem linguam Anglicanam per quosdam probos

faith committed to them, at the moment when the rights and privileges, and even the existence, of the spiritual estate seemed to be destroyed or endangered, may be left to move the scorn or the sympathy of the reader.

viros per dictum illustrissimum regem nominandos transferatur et populo pro eorum eruditione deliberetur et tradatur."—*Wilkins*, iii. 770 and 776. In the latter place Wilkins quotes this " Petitio Synodi " from the Cleopatra MS. E 5, fol. 339, where it occurs before a Royal Proclamation to bring in seditious books: fol. 340 ; and Wilkins has printed them both together, as if the Proclamation followed as an answer to the Petition. I judged from internal evidence that the Proclamation must be later by some years than the Petition: and I am glad to be confirmed by Mr. Sturgeon, who says that it is in a different handwriting, and endorsed 30 H. VIII., i. e. 1538.

[Since this volume was written, two volumes, still remaining in the Record Office, of the signatures of the clergy to a declaration against the papal authority, have been described by Mr. Gairdner in *Lett. and Papers* vii. No. 1025, p. 395. They contain a large number of signatures, taken during the ministration of the Oath, in nine or ten dioceses, and may very possibly be the subscriptions to which Wharton referred (*above*, p. 218). The declaration to which they are attached is remarkably brief : " Romanus episcopus non habet majorem aliquam juris dictionem a Deo sibi collatam in hoc regno Angliæ quam quivis alius externus episcopus." The dioceses are Lincoln, Exeter, Bath, Rochester, St. Davids, St. Asaph, Landaff, Worcester, Bristol ; but there are some miscellaneous subscriptions from London and Canterbury, and perhaps elsewhere. The clergy are generally arranged by deaneries: but there are single churches mentioned, and some monasteries and colleges. The documents afford some materials for ascertaining the number of the clergy.

Mr. Gairdner has also calendared what is evidently the original draft or notion of the severer oath administered to the monasteries, and especially the friars, which I have given, p. 212 : and a special commission to Browne and Hilsey to visit all friars, " to enquire concerning their lives, morals, and fealty to the King, and reduce them to uniformity, if necessary, by aid of the secular arm " (*above*, p. 214). *Lett. and Papers*, vii. pp. 233, 236.]

CHAPTER IV.

A.D. 1535.

The first act of the Supreme Head of the English Church was to appoint a Vicar General in things ecclesiastical. There was some following of the displaced Pope in this. The Pope erewhile had had his vicar general in England, the last who exercised that high office having been Cardinal Wolsey. A bishop also has usually his vicar general of his diocese. But this observance of ecclesiastical form was only a convenient device for carrying on the tremendous designs which were now clearly meditated. The vicar general whom Henry chose was Thomas Crumwel. During the five most momentous years of her existence, the fate of the English Church was in the hands of the most unscrupulous of men. He was invested with power over life and property such as no English subject has ever wielded. Never hesitating to employ the vilest means, but always acting with a caution which ensured the approbation of the Supreme Head, he effected a revolution of which the results and consequences will be felt everlastingly. Then, having effected it, by the master whom he vainly thought that he had mastered, he was dismissed to the block.

This creation of a vicar general was the first of the various modes by which, from that day to this, the spiritual jurisdiction of the Crown has been put in commission. Hitherto in English history the spiritual jurisdiction of the Crown had been exercised by the sovereign himself, heading the hierarchy, and giving to their determinations the sanction of the realm. Henry took a new title which conferred no new powers : a title which he and his Parliament were alike anxious to define on every opportunity as conferring no new powers; but which has been understood in the opposite sense by one generation after another, and has done more to confuse English history than anything else has ever done. He took this title in the midst of the strongest personal government that has ever been exercised in England : and it might have been thought that he meant to intervene in person in the affairs of the spiritual state beyond all his predecessors on the throne. And yet the first thing that he did after this violent assertion of his spiritual jurisdiction was to delegate it to another. But Henry knew well the advantage of divided responsibility. He knew the importance of diverting public odium from himself. His foreign papers abound in instances of this device. When any of his measures were disliked at Rome, he had always the answer ready, that what was done was done in the great assembly of the English realm which was called Parliament : that Parliament was free, and its determinations could neither be controlled nor revoked by him. In the same way, now that the dissolution of the religious houses was to be effected— a prodigious responsibility—the burden was to be shifted from the monarch to his creature. Thus, a century and a half at least before England grew accustomed to see her king commit his temporal functions into the hands of a body of men called the Ministry, she saw her king begin to put his spiritual functions into commission. But of all the experiments in delegation to which the spiritual jurisdiction of the English Crown has been subjected the most unhappy was the first—the Vicar Generalship of Thomas Crumwel.

Crumwel was already Master of the Rolls and Principal Secretary of the King. By virtue of the one office a great part of the legal machinery of the country lay in his hands : but still greater power was gathered into them through the other. The office of Principal Secretary was more important than the three Secretaryships of State, which in modern times represent it, put together. The whole of the foreign and domestic correspondence of the government passed beneath his eye, and might be manipulated by him. He arranged what the King should see. Sometimes he erased parts of despatches which were received, and then caused fresh copies to be made for the King. A large part of the most important reports was addressed to him alone, and might be communicated or not to the King, as he chose. His office gave him the right or privilege of approaching the royal presence whenever he willed; and he so engrossed all personal communication with the sovereign, that the other high functionaries found their office laid aside. These accumulated powers were immeasurably increased by the new Commission which is now to be considered.

This characteristic document, composed in that florid eloquence which in Henry always clothed a dark design, began by attacking in a general manner the

rulers of the Church. They, it was said, had so abused
their office for the sake of private advantage, that
danger was that Christ should not know His spouse.
They corrected others, but from others they would
endure no correction; and yet day after day beyond
other men they did things which called for correction,
and from their corrupt manners they had caused
a scandal among the people. Heaven therefore demanded of his royal excellency, nor less his high office
laid it upon him, to purge the Church of the weeds
of vice, and stock her with the seeds and plants of
virtue. With the rulers of the Church, therefore,
would he inaugurate the Reformation; that when the
source and fountain was cleansed, the stream might
thenceforth run clear and limpid. Moved by these
high considerations, but unable to attend to all things
personally, he called others to his aid as ministers; and
hereby constituted and deputed to be his Vicegerent,
Vicar General, and special and principal Commissary
in causes ecclesiastical, to exercise all and every jurisdiction, authority, or rightful power inherent in the
Supreme Head of the Church of England, Thomas
Crumwel. Thomas Crumwel might constitute and
depute other commissioners, whom it was left to
him to name. And these commissioners—Thomas
Crumwel and the rest—had power to visit, when and
whenever they thought good, all and singular churches,
metropolitical, cathedral, and collegiate; hospitals and
monasteries, both of men and women, priories, preceptories, dignities, offices, houses, and all places
ecclesiastical, both secular and regular, exempt and
non-exempt; to make enquiries concerning the life,
manners, and conversation both of the presidents or
prelates of the same, of whatever name or dignity,

even if they shone in the archiepiscopal or episcopal splendours ; * and also of the other persons who abode there. Those whom they deemed "curious" or culpable they might punish in proportion to the fault, by deprivation, suspension, and sequestration. They might make statutes and ordinances for the good and laudable conservation or reformation of the persons and places aforesaid; and punish those who trangressed them. Whenever and wherever it seemed to them good, they might hold, continue, and prorogue synods, chapters, and convocations, both general and particular, for any cause or reason whatever; summoning the clergy and people, presiding over the assembly, and constituting and ordaining whatever they thought proper for the reformation of persons or orders, and using all means to restore them to honesty of life. All subjects of the realm, for any cause whatever pertaining to the ecclesiastical forum, might be called and cited before them : the contumacious and rebellious to be coerced as well by ecclesiastical censures and penalties as by imposition of forfeitures and the other remedies of the kingdom. By them were to be received the resignations and surrenders of churches and ecclesiastical places : by them were vacancies to be declared, and licenses assigned for the payments, fruits, and emoluments of the churches and places within their commission. If an exchange were sought, they were to effect it with proper persons requesting it; and of resigning ministers the annual pensions were to be fixed by them. In all elections of prelates they were to preside : they were to indicate who should be elected. With them lay the institution, investiture, and induction of all ecclesiastical

* "Quocunque nomine et dignitate, etiamsi archiepiscopali vel episcopali præfulgeant."

persons during the time of the visitation. Such was the death-warrant of the Old Learning.*

The unparalleled revolution in property which marked the end of the reign of Henry the Eighth was now to be begun. An animating spirit had been found under whose vigorous impulse delay was unlikely to retard it : nay, the only danger was lest wheel should outrun wheel. The commissions for ascertaining the true value of the firstfruits and tenths of all sees and benefices, which had been ordered by Parliament in the last session,† were now made out, January 30: and the clear revenue and profits of one entire year, and the tenth part of the annual revenue of every spiritual office or dignity, from an archbishopric to a free chapel, from an abbey to a chantry, were to be taken away and given to the Crown. The Lord Chancellor, Audley, sent into every county a commission, which included the bishop of the diocese, and generally contained the principal residents below the degree of baron. The art of visiting, which was carried to perfection in the Reformation, may be favourably studied in this early example. The commissioners might go in parties of no more than three, and proceed to investigate all sources of information. In the manner of many a subsequent visitation, they carried with them instructions signed by the King. They were empowered to send for the officers of the bishop

* Wilkins, iii. 784. This commission was issued probably long before the great Visitations of monasteries, which began in October 1535. In a paper of that date Crumwel is already styled "vicegerentem, vicarium generalem, et officialem principalem." (*Wilkins*, iii. 798.) It was probably, as Burnet says, the first act of the Supreme Head. It will be observed that the several titles given to Crumwel are conceived as equivalent to one another, and are in imitation of ecclesiastical phraseology. But in the following year another commission of even greater extent was issued, in which he was simply styled Vicegerent. See Herbert.

† In the Act for restraint of Annates.

and of the archdeacons, of whom they were to learn what rural deaneries there lay within the diocese : into each rural deanery they might then disperse themselves, and examine the incumbents, their receivers, and auditors on oath, searching their registers, Easter books, and other writings. All the monasteries and religious foundations were examined in the same way. It was particularly ordered that no bishop should give institution to any living until a bond had been given for the firstfruits : which was a heavy requisition, since the clergy had to travel up to London, it might be from the end of the kingdom, to give their bonds, and spend as much on the road as the firstfruits were worth.* The commissioners might, upon good cause, make deductions from the payments to which the clergy were liable : but it seems that they were very frugal in doing so.† Their returns were to be made into the King's exchequer by the Octaves of Holy Trinity; but from the magnitude of the task it may be doubted whether it could have been finished by the time appointed. To this commission we owe the extensive and valuable document known as the Valor Ecclesiasticus of Henry the Eighth.‡

* Bishop Tunstall of Durham wrote to Crumwel complaining of this hardship, and suggesting that some persons might be appointed in those parts to take the bonds. Strype, App. No. 59.

† So Bishop Gardiner complained, see his letter to Crumwel, and his "Articles wherein the Commissioners have not shewed such favours to the parties here in their allowances, as, they pretended before them, was due by the Act of Parliament in that behalf." One of these may suffice. In benefices where there were chapels, some one, some two, some three, besides the parish church, they reckoned all the profits that arose out of the chapels, but allowed no deduction for the charge of the priest who was necessary and perpetually served them. Strype, i. 327. See also the Archb. of York's Letters, *ib.*

‡ Published 1810–1825, by the Records Commission, in six vols. fol. See also Wilkins, iii. 783. Mr. Hunter believes, as he says in his General Introduction (p. v.), that the commission was executed between

The Valor Ecclesiasticus was the return of the revenue of the ecclesiastical and monastic property in England, which was made on the very eve of the violent alienation of a third of the same. It was the only complete survey of ecclesiastical property which had been made since the so-called Taxatio of Pope Nicholas the Fourth at the end of the thirteenth century, which it superseded as a standard of value.* It was not a friendly survey, but it was probably a fair one. The examination was conducted on fixed principles, by persons who acted as a check on one another, and had no inducement to exceed their instructions. It shews, as might be expected from a fair valuation, that there had been no great change in Church property at least for two centuries and a half. The gross revenue of the Church and the monasteries, according to this Valor, is said to have been three hundred and twenty thousand pounds.† The gross revenue of the Church, according to the Taxatio of Pope Nicholas,

---

January and June 1535. But Fuller says that it took some years. "Devonshire and Somerset were done in the 27th, Staffordshire and many other counties in the 34th year of Henry VIII., and most of Wales not till the reign of Edward VI." He adds that the commissioners were sent into Ireland, but never got into the county of Kerry. Ch. Hist., Bk. v. 228.

* Pope Nicholas IV. granted the tenths of England to Edward I. for six years in 1288 : this occasioned a Taxation by the King's Precept to be begun in that year; which was finished in 1292. It is commonly called the Taxatio of Pope Nicholas IV. Published by the Records Commission in 1802.

† Speed, in his elaborate and invaluable Tables, made from the Valor, gives the total value of all spiritual promotions at 320,280*l.* 10*s.* This was divided among 21 archbishoprics and bishoprics, 11 deaneries, 60 archdeaconries, 394 dignities and prebends, 8,803 benefices, 605 religious houses, 110 hospitals, 96 colleges, 2,374 chantries and free chapels. Total number of promotions, 12,474. The recent editor of the Valor, Mr. Hunter, complains that part of it is lost, especially the particulars of the returns of Berkshire, Rutlandshire, Northumberland, and part of London. These particulars, however, are supplied by Speed, who seems to have examined the Valor before they were lost.

which was made in the time of Edward the First, was
two hundred and twenty thousand pounds.* Within
the period between the two the revenue of the whole
kingdom had trebled itself. It would be a high estimation to put the revenue of the kingdom under
Edward the First at a million sterling. Under Henry
the Eighth it has been computed to have been three
millions.† If, therefore, the revenue of the Church and
the religious orders shew an absolute increase during
this interval, it shews a relative decrease. Under
Edward it was about eleven fiftieths of the whole
revenue : under Henry it was not more than eight
seventy-fifths. These authentic records may serve
perhaps to correct the common but erroneous notions
which prevail of the vast and disproportionate wealth
of the Church and the religious houses in the ages
before the Reformation.‡

* After going through the Taxatio, I have got the sum total of
218,802*l.*, of which 80,679*l.* are "temporalia," including the possessions
of the religious, the rest "spiritualia" or property attached to spiritual
functions. I do not however wish to dispute the figures of a very able
writer in the Home and Foreign Review (January 1864), to whom I am
much indebted in this part. He gives a gross revenue of 206,000*l.*: and
returns the estates of the monasteries at 51,197*l.* The same writer observes that the monastic valuation does not include the benefices held by
the monasteries—an important item, which would bring the record of the
thirteenth century more nearly to an equality with that of the sixteenth ;
for the Valor of Henry VIII. includes them. The distinction between
"temporalia" and "spiritualia" does not depend on their possessors so
much as on their origin. The former arose from *temporal goods*, as lands :
the latter from *spiritual functions*, which secured tithes, fees, &c. For
this observation I am indebted to Mr. Thomas, the author of the very
valuable Hist. of the Diocese of St. Asaph.

† Hume.

‡ Extravagant fictions concerning the property of the Church, and
indeed concerning the whole of the landed property of England, from the
time of the Conquest, have obtained almost undisputed currency. Hume
and other historians have repeated that, according to Ordericus Vitalis,
the Conqueror divided England into 60,000 knights fees. And yet Ordericus never said this. He said that the land was distributed into
knights fees in such order that the realm should always have a force of

Before he abandoned the title of Legate of the Apostolic See, Cranmer had begun a Visitation of the whole province of Canterbury. His Visitation was still proceeding now. A provincial or metropolitical Visitation had not been carried through for a hundred years.* This exercise of the Archbishop's authority was resisted by two of his suffragans, Gardiner of Winchester and Stokesley of London (both of whom had been aggrieved by his advancement), on grounds which display the confusion, uncertainty, and irritation caused by the alteration of title. Gardiner alleged that if the Archbishop had abandoned the ancient title of Legate of the Apostolic See because it was in diminution of the prerogative royal, he had for the same reason no right to the title of Primate of all England, by virtue of which he was attempting to hold his Visitation. He urged furthermore that it was hard for Cranmer to lay upon his diocese of Winchester the cost and charges of a new Visitation, when it had been visited by Cranmer's predecessor only five years before: especially now that it had to pay the new and heavy imposition of the tenths. The answer of Cranmer to

sixty thousand men. (Bk. iv. c. 7.) As to the Church, I gladly avail myself of the labours of the writer of the article mentioned above, to correct these fables. Milman, he observes, wrongly accepts that the Church under Henry IV. owned more than half the knights fees in the realm—28,000 out of 53,225. This fiction is found first in Sprot's Chronicle, compiled under Edward I.: where it occurs with the statement that the Conqueror divided the land into 60,225 knights fees, and that there were then 45,000 churches in the country. This last about the churches we can correct to some extent from Domesday Book, where the number for several counties is given—Norfolk 317, Suffolk 364, Lincolnshire 222. We may conclude that ten thousand, including every place where service was performed, would be a high estimate. As to the knights fees, the Black Book, compiled under Henry II., would give, on an average of fifteen counties, eight thousand for the whole kingdom, not including those held immediately of the King, which were 539 at the Conquest. The knights fees held by the Church would by the same calculation amount to two thirty-fifths of the whole—rather under five hundred.

* But see Wharton's observations at the end of Strype's Cranmer.

this somewhat captious objection was easy and triumphant. The Bishop of Winchester, he said, seemed to tender the King's cause, but meant to tender his own. When the Bishop of Rome was taken for Supreme Head he had Primates under him, but his supreme authority was not less esteemed. Why, then, might not the King, being Supreme Head, have Primates under him, without a diminishing of his supreme authority?* He doubted not but that all the bishops in England would gladly have both the authority and the title of the archbishops taken away, that they might all be equal together. The Diotrephes of St. john, who desired to have the pre-eminence, had more successors than all the Apostles. As to the charges of the Visitation, it was true that Warham had visited the see of Winchester five years ago when it was vacant; but Gardiner himself had laid it under a Visitation within half a year after, and that against all right, and when the clergy were paying, not the tenth, but the half of their benefices in five years to the King.† Moreover, all the other bishops had kept their Visitations, notwithstanding this provincial Visitation, while Winchester had not been visited by any man for three years, and had therefore less cause to complain than any other diocese. And if the Bishop's objections should be allowed this year, they might hold good against any Visitation whatever in time to come. For himself, the Archbishop added with truth, he cared no

---

* These inaccurate expressions shew how soon the now prevalent theory of one Supremacy displaced by another had obtained a lodgement at least in the mind of Cranmer. He may almost be called the author of the theory. The Pope never was "taken for Supreme Head" in England until Cranmer took him, and never held the Supremacy. Cranmer, with great general capacity, had a characteristic inaccuracy of mind.

† In 1523 the Convocation granted the extraordinary subsidy of half the revenue of every benefice, to be levied in five years. Wilkins, iii. 699.

more for any title, name, or style than the paring of an apple, further than it might set forth God's word and will : he laid himself and his cause at his Prince's feet : and yet he would not utterly excuse himself in the matter of calling himself Primate. He spoke only for so much as he felt in his heart. But many evil affections lay lurking in his heart, and not lightly to be espied. He did not know the bottom of his own heart.*

The resistance of Stokesley to the Visitation was grounded upon another of the Archbishop's titles. In his monition to the bishop, abbots, prior, and archdeacon of London, Cranmer called himself Legate of the Apostolic See. His monition, it is probable, was issued before he renounced that ancient title ; and his Visitation took place after. The bishop and chapter advertised him of his mistake by letters before the day of Visitation : but he took no notice of them. When he arrived in the Chapterhouse of St. Paul's, they openly protested in writing against his appearing as Legate, and declared that they would not allow or obey his Visitation or jurisdiction. He refused to admit their Protestation. Stokesley thereupon appealed to the King, of course without effect. The Visitation was held, and seems to have been spread over some months, during which the jurisdiction of the bishop, dean, and archdeacon was suspended. All that Stokesley could do was to enter in his Register several Protestations for preserving his privileges.†

It was necessary, indeed, now that the jurisdiction of Rome was taken away, to put a formal end to the obedience of the bishops to the Pontiff. Their canonical obligation had never stood in the way of their

* Cranmer to Crumwel, May 12, 1535. Strype's Cranm. App. xiv.
† Strype's Cranm. App. xv.

loyalty. In all times, as we have observed already, it had been regularly limited by their obligations to the realm. In the course of the present revolution it had been virtually abrogated. The bishops who had sworn obedience to the Pope had in Convocation gone before the other estates of the realm in moving for the abolition of the Papal impositions. They had sworn to the succession of the offspring of Anne Boleyn. They had declared solemnly in Convocation that the King was the Supreme Head of the Church. They had declared solemnly in Convocation that the Bishop of Rome had no jurisdiction within the realm. But the logical mind of the King now returned to the oath of canonical obedience, which he had formerly discovered to be contrary to his high prerogative. It was resolved to exact from the bishops the formal denial of that which they had sworn. A Renunciation of the Pope, not indeed in the form of an oath, but of an obligation, profession, or engagement, was taken of the bishops in the month of February. They promised never to take an oath of fealty or obedience to any foreign power; to maintain the King's cause and quarrel ; to observe all the laws which had been enacted for the suppression of the papacy; not to appeal to the Bishop of Rome, nor procure from him any bulls, breves, or prescripts whatsoever. They declared the papacy, or Roman patriarchate, not to have been ordained by God in Holy Scripture, but by human tradition : and they promised henceforth never to call the Bishop of Rome by the name of Pope, or Most high Bishop, or Universal Bishop, or Most Holy Lord, but to call him only Bishop of Rome, or Brother. This engagement is, I think, the first document which may be construed to deny the pre-eminence of the See of Rome in Christendom, not less than the jurisdiction and authority of Rome in England. And it was the first document which was derived evidently from Lutheranism. The pontifical titles therein denied were those which had been denied by Luther.*

This procedure was neither inconsequent on all that had gone before, nor in itself unreasonable. But it would have been unimportant if it had not formed part of a general and elaborate system of depression, devised by the Supreme Head and his Vicar General, which came into operation at the same time. In the summer of the year 1535 it was deemed desirable to humble, or at least to harass, all the prelates of the Church of England. Cranmer's Visitation and the Renunciation of the Pope were the first devices employed for this purpose; but these were followed by others far more humiliating.

To make the bishops preach to others what they had professed for themselves was therefore the next study of the Supreme Head. Letters General were sent to them all on the first of June, straitly commanding them in their proper persons to preach the sincere word of God and the new title of the King: to see that their clergy, both secular and regular, did the same every

---

* Wilk. iii. 780; Rymer, xiv. 549; Fox. It was not an Oath, but a Sponsio, or simply a Renunciatio Papæ. The important clauses which pursued the Pope across the mountains were these: "Papatum Romanum non esse a Deo in S. Literis ordinatum profiteor, sed humanitus traditum firmiter affirmo. . . . Ipsumque Romanum Episcopum modernum, aut ejus in illo episcopatu successorem quemcunque, non papam, non summum episcopum, non universalem episcopum, non sanctissimum dominum, sed solum Romanum episcopum, et fratrem (ut priscis episcopis mos erat) scienter publice afferam." Luther, in his book, De Potestate Papæ, recounted that the greatest of the Popes, Gregory, had repeatedly declared the title of Universal Bishop to be profane, sacrilegious, anti-Christian, and never to have been borne by any of his predecessors. "Quid," asked Luther, "de nomine Summi et Sanctissimi dixisset?" See Bellarmini, De Rom. Pontiff. Lib. ii. c. 31, for the controversy on the Pontifical titles.

Sunday and feast day. They were to cause all prayers, rubrics, and canons in mass-books and other books used in churches, in which the Bishop of Rome was named, to be rased out, " that the name and memory of the Bishop of Rome, except to his contumely and reproach, might be extinct, suppressed, and obscured."* This monition was followed soon after by a lengthy " Order for preaching and bidding of the beads in all sermons to be made within the realm."† All preachers were to pray, in the bidding; for the whole Catholic Church, and for the Catholic Church of the realm; for the King, only Supreme Head of the Catholic Church of England, for Queen Anne and the Lady Elizabeth, for the whole clergy and temporalty, and specially such as the preacher might name of devotion : for the souls of the dead, and specially of such as it might please the preacher to name. It was ordered that every preacher should preach at least once against the usurped power of the Bishop of

---

* These Letters General are described in their tenor in the document which Wilkins (iii. 772) mistakenly calls a " Proclamation," but which is in fact " The King's Letter to the Justices," given in Strype, E. M. ii. 209, of which anon. The rage of Henry against the Pope's name has been set in a ridiculous light by Sanders. " Per calendaria, per indices, per scripta patrum, per totum jus canonicum, per scholasticos doctores, Papæ vocabulum lituris obducebatur : imo in fronte operum D. Cypriani, Ambrosii, Hieronymi, Augustini, Leonis, Gregorii, Prosperi, ac aliorum Ecclesiæ luminum, singuli scribere coacti sunt, si quid in iis operibus inesset quod Pontificis Romani Primatum tueretur, aut confirmaret, se illi verbo, sententiæ, rationi jam nunc renunciare, nec tanti criminis reos unquam esse velle, ut quibusvis patribus aut Doctoribus in ea re consentiant." P. 89. But Henry was never less puerile than when he seemed so most.

† The Order for preaching was not sent on June 1, along with the Letters General, but on the 3rd. See Cranmer's Letters to the King, Remains, p. 325, or Strype's Cranm. App. 13. Hence Shaxton, replying on the 4th, only mentions having received " the King's most honourable letters," whereas Longland, on the 25th, mentions first the letters and then " the last declaration sent unto him last in English," i. e., the Order for preaching. See below.

Rome, and that no man should defend the same : that preachers should not contend openly in pulpit against one another, but complain to the King or the ordinary, the complainer to be punished if the complaint were not true : that for a year no preacher should preach either for or against purgatory, honouring of saints, marriage of priests, pilgrimages, miracles, or solifi-dianism : which things had hitherto caused dissensions in the realm, though those dissensions, it was boldly averred, were now well pacified. All were to preach the Scripture and pure Word of Christ, and not to mix them with man's institutions, nor believe that the force of God's law and man's law was like, nor that any man had power to dispense with God's law. The General Sentence or Curse, which used to be read in churches four times a year, was not to be used in any point contrary to the jurisdiction, the laws, the liberties of the King and realm :* and the Collects for the King and Queen were to be said on all high masses in every cathedral church, religious house, and parish church. The Order concluded with a sort of model of a sermon on the history of the Divorce, intended to furnish preachers with arguments in favour of the royal cause.†

These directions, which were evidently of Cranmer's composure, were exactly obeyed by the bishops. Some, perhaps all of them, returned prompt acknowledgments to Crumwel, and reports of their proceedings thereupon. Shaxton of Salisbury rejoiced that the King's Highness

---

* This was necessary, as the General Sentence contained many curses " on those who infringed the privileges and immunities of Holy Church, or deprived her of any of her rights and dues."—*Strype*, E. M., i. 253, ii. 188.

† Cranm. Rem., 460. This " Order for preaching " the zealous Bedyl ventured to improve by some emendations and embellishments of his own, for the assistance of the " brute curates " who might have to use it. His improved edition may be seen in Strype, E. M., ii. 213.

had written so earnestly to his bishops in so earnest
a cause, praying withal that Crumwel's wisdom, or God's
wisdom in Crumwel, would go on from one thing to
another, till the usurped power of the man of Rome
were clean abolished. Sherborn of Chichester, a very
aged man, reported that he had done the King's
commandment in his cathedral church; that his suffragan had done the same in all the populous towns of
his diocese; and that within the month he had neither
abbot nor prior, dean nor archdeacon, provost, parson,
vicar, nor curate within his limits unadvertised of the
Order; and that he would see that all did their duties.
Longland of Lincoln had not only preached and declared the title and all the rest of the Order throughout
his diocese, but caused two thousand copies to be put
in print, for the more speedy furtherance of the King's
design. Gardiner of Winchester, and his neighbour
of London, both sent satisfactory reports of their proceedings. Goodrich of Ely enjoined every master
and fellow in Cambridge to preach every Sunday and
festival in the parish church within whose bounds his
college stood, against the Pope and for the King.*
Tunstall of Durham had even forestalled the King's
commandment, for he had set forth the title of Supreme
Head throughout his diocese, and had caused the
King to be so prayed for, ever since the Act of Parliament thereon made: and on receiving the monitions
he had lost no time in preaching against the Pope's
authority. Even the suspected Lee of York, on whom
several attempts were made to fasten a charge of
backwardness, completely cleared himself.†

* In his Letters to Edmunds, Master of Peterhouse, Strype, E. M.,
i. 287.

† See their Letters, Strype, E. M., ii. 204, sq.; Ellis, 3rd Ser. ii. 336.
Gardiner's letter is in State Papers, i. 430. Tunstall complained in a

But neither the honesty or submission with which they might have been credited, nor the diligence which they displayed, availed to shield the bishops and their clergy from the insults of suspicion. A few days after the Order for preaching had been sent to them, a circular letter was sent, June 9, to the Justices of the Peace, commanding the latter to make " diligent search and suit " that the bishops and clergy executed their charge without diminution or omission : and to observe whether in executing it they " coldly and feignedly made use of any manner of sinister addition, wrong interpretation, or painted colour." If the Justices found any default or dissimulation they were to report it without delay to the Council. A threat was added to stimulate their zeal. As, said the King, upon singular trust and assured confidence he had chosen and elected them among so many for this purpose, so, if they omitted to do whatsoever should be in their power for the due performance of his mind and pleasure in this behalf, or halted or stumbled at any part or specialty of the same, they were to be assured that he, like a prince of justice, would so extremely punish them, that all

dignified way of some insinuations in the King's letter to him, that he was looking " for a new world or mutation," meaning the restoration of the Pope's power. A fair account of the several attempts to criminate the Archbishop of York is given in Strype, i. 287 sq. The northern clergy were generally suspected of backwardness in complying with the changes of the times : and before this, in April, the King had set the Earl of Sussex, the Lord Lieutenant there, to watch them. Strype, ii. 208. Some of them dared not obey the King's orders for fear of the people. Strype, i. 297. With the bishops the King had begun to work the year before, when he summoned them to Winchester, and gave them some strict admonitions. Strype's Cranm. The reign of terror under which they and their clergy lived may be judged from the fact that even the intrepid Clark of Bath and Wells deemed it necessary to write to Crumwel, in February 1535, to excuse an unlucky preacher who by a slip of the tongue prayed for the King, *Katherine* the Queen, and the Lady Elizabeth their daughter, instead of Anne the Queen. *State Papers*, i. 427.

the world beside should take example by them, and beware contrary to their allegiance to disobey the lawful commandment of their sovereign lord and prince in such things: as by the faithful execution thereof they should not only advance the honour of Almighty God and set forth the majesty and imperial dignity of their sovereign lord, but also bring an inestimable weal, profit, and commodity, unity, and tranquillity, to all the common state of that his realm, whereunto by the laws of God, nature, and man they were utterly bound.*

This monition to the Justices of the Peace was next addressed, with certain alterations, June 25, to the King's Justices also. They, as the King considered, might be of good service to his cause at assizes and sessions: and he esteemed them to be of such singular zeal and affection towards the glory of Almighty God, and of so faithful and loving heart towards himself, that they would with all their wisdoms, diligences, and labours accomplish all such things as might be to the preferment and setting forth of God's word, and the amplification, defence, and maintenance of his own interest, right, title, style, jurisdiction, and authority, appertaining unto him, his dignity, prerogative, and crown imperial of that his realm. They were therefore commanded, laying apart all vain affections, respects, and carnal considerations, and setting before their eyes the mirror of truth, the right and dignity of their sove-

---

* This is the document which Fox and Wilkins (iii. 772) miscall a Proclamation. The admirers of the style of Henry's state papers are particularly enthusiastic over the verbiage of this, while they regard the issuing of it as a masterpiece of noble policy. It is certainly equal to anything that Henry, or Henry's Parliament, or Crumwel ever composed. The indirect quotations given above convey but a poor idea of it, they are so garbled. But it may be seen nearly at full length in Froude, ii. 230: though even Mr. Froude has not been able to get quite to the end of it, and perhaps some of Mr. Froude's "honest laymen" did not either.

reign lord, thus sounding to the inestimable unity and commodity, both of themselves and of other his faithful and loving subjects, not only to keep the same close watch on the bishops and clergy which was ordered on the Justices of the Peace, but always at assizes and sessions to preach, teach, and declare to the people the premisses; in order that parents and masters of families might learn and teach the same. On these itinerant servants of the crown, notwithstanding the King's high estimation of. them, it was necessary to lay the same stern threatenings which had awed their brethren of the Peace: and, since by that time the tragedy of the Charterhouse was just ended, and the head of Bishop Fisher was already rotting on London Bridge, it was added that they were at their sessions to declare to the people the treasons and secret practices of the malicious minds of the late. Bishop of Rochester, of Sir Thomas More, and others who had intended to seminate, engender, and breed among the people and subjects of the King a most mischievous and seditious opinion. Upon this they were to dilate, persuading and establishing the people in the truth, that they might thereby detest and abhor in their hearts the most recreant and traitorous abuses and behaviours of the said malicious malefactors.*

* The various documents which have been brought together in the above narrative have been separated hitherto by an unfortunate mistake of date on the part of historians. Strype, in his Cranmer, put the Order for preaching in the year 1534 "about June," though in his E. M., i. 285 he rightly puts it in 1535, calling it there "the declaration to be read to the people," which is only another name for the same thing. Fox and Wilkins put the Letter to the Justices in June 1534, and add confusion by calling it a Proclamation. All the writers, from Fox to the Parker editors, and from these to Mr. Froude, follow in the same track. It is certain that neither of these documents belongs to June 1534, since they allude to subsequent events, e. g. the confirmation of the title of Supreme Head by Parliament, which was in the November of that year, and the

By way of a last precaution to ensure their loyalty, the bishops were commanded to send up to court the sermons which they had preached on the arguments propounded to them. Having satisfied the critics who examined them, these prelections were despatched into Germany to convince the princes of the undoubted resolution of the King in banishing the Pope from his Catholic dominions.*

The oath of the bishops to the Pope having been cancelled by the Renunciation, it remained to alter conformably the oath of the clergy to the bishops. Every clergyman, on being instituted to a benefice, had sworn hitherto to be obedient to his diocesan in all lawful and canonical mandates: to preach, teach, defend, and in any way bring before the people neither the Lutheran heresy nor any other heresy condemned by the Church, but to oppose heresies and the fautors of heresies to the utmost of his power. At the instance of the Vicar General this older form of oath was re-called, and amended on a model furnished by Goodrich, who had lately succeeded the less compliant West in the see of Ely. Of canonical obedience there was no mention made in the form now propounded; the clergy swore to be obedient to their diocesans in all

Renunciation of the Pope by the Bishops, which was in February 1535. The true order of all the documents was as follows:—

Letters General to the Bishops, June 1, 1535.
Order for preaching and bidding of beads, June 3.
Shaxton's Answer to Letters General, June 4.
Letter to Justices, June 9.
Gardiner's Answer to Letters General and Order, June 10.
Longland's Answer, June 25.
Letter to Judges, June 25.
Goodrich's Letter to Heads of Cambridge, June 27.
Sherborn's Answer to Letters General and Order, June 28.
Lee's Answer, July 1.
Tunstall's Answer, July 11.

* Strype, E. M., i. 295.

honest and lawful mandates : to renounce the Pope for ever, and his constitutions and decrees, which had been condemned by the King's Parliament, or should be condemned thereafter : neither to preach, teach, nor defend them, nor in any way to bring them before the people, but to oppose them and their fautors to the utmost of their power.*

Among the religious orders the only formal opposition that had been made to the oaths and subscriptions hitherto exacted had been offered by the Observants, the Brigitites, and the Carthusians. Of these the surviving orders of the Brigitites and the Carthusians were destined this year to furnish martyrs to the falling cause. A special sessions of Oyer and Terminer for Middlesex, which opened at Westminster April 24, for the first time painted the scaffold with the blood of the religious who denied the King's new title, and of the few secular clergy who stood by them in their opinion. The first case which was brought before this tribunal was that of two secular clergymen named Feron and Hale, who were indicted of high

---

* Ego N. juro, ad hæc Sancta Dei Evangelia corporaliter tacta, quod ero obediens Reverendo in Christo Patri et Domino N. Permissione (Miseratione) Divina Eliensi Episcopo, et successoribus suis, in omnibus llicitis et canonicis (honestis ac licitis) mandatis juxta Juris exigentia (last three words omitted). Item (Juro) quod nullam Heresim Luthereanam, aut aliam quamcunque ab Ecclesia damnatam (me imperpetuum renunciaturum Papam una cum constitutionibus ac decretis suis, quæ a Parliamento Domini Regis damnata sunt, aut imposterum damnabuntur : quodque nec) docebo, predicabo, aut ratiocinando quovis modo defendam, aut pro eis, earumve aliqua (eorumve aliquo) inter conferendum auctoritatem vel rationem quamcunque, joco vel serio, animo deliberato in medium proferam : sed eas omnes et singulas (ea omnia et singula) pro ingenii mei viribus et doctrina, et carum (eorum) fautores, impugnabo. Sic ut me Deus adjuvet, et hæc Sancta Dei Evangelia. The variant parts which make up the new oath are in the brackets. *State Papers*, i. 437. It may be presumed that this was sent to all the bishops, or some such form, to be propounded to the clergy.

treason under the Act for establishing the succession. Feron was a clerk of Teddington, Hale of Isleworth, that is, of Sion. The charge made against them was that in the May of the previous year they had held treasonable conversations against the King and his marriage, when they were walking to and fro at Sion. How their conversations were overheard and reported we are not informed : but the indictment set forth that "after many false and scandalous words spoken by Feron to Hale, the said Feron asked Hale if there was no one who had written or could write against the King's evil deeds." Hale made answer that there was sufficient reason to write against the King, and urged Feron to do so, alleging that there never was so great a robber of the Commonwealth as the present King : that he oppressed and robbed the spiritualty—innocent, learned, and virtuous men—and thrust them into perpetual prison : that he did this as if he were an injured man, and the champion of the Christian faith, though of a truth he was the cruellest heretic and defacer of the Church of Christ : that he extended his oppressions to the nobles and commons, whom he impoverished and destroyed that he might enjoy his foul pleasures and increase his treasures : that he enriched strangers, and built superfluous palaces : that his life was most foul, no matron of the court safe from his lust, his wife neglected, and he living in fornication with Anne, to the shame of the realm.* Nearly a year after Hale

---

* Hale's words were, "Sith the realm of England was first a realm, was there never in it so great a robber and piller of the Commonwealth read nor heard of, as is our King. And not only we that be of the spiritualty by his wrong be oppressed and robbed of our living, as if we were his utter enemies, enemies unto Christ, and guilty of his death, but also thus ungodly doth he handle innocents, and also highly learned and virtuous men, not only robbing them of their living, and spoiling them of their goods, but also thrusting them into perpetual prison, so that it is too

had spoken these words in English, Feron wrote them down in Latin, March 10; and it may have been this translation which caused the indictment. Hale was said to have added in the same conversation that until the King and rulers of the realm were plucked by the pates and brought to the pot, it would never be merry in England; that Ireland was against him, Wales was against him; and if Ireland and Wales invaded England, it would be found that three parts of England were against him, for that the commons saw well enough a sufficient cause of rebellion and insurrection in the realm, since there was a design to reduce the realm to the same miserable condition as France.*

great pity to hear and more to be lamented than any good Christian man's ears may abide. And he doth the same, as by that means he would avenge his own injuries and the injuries of Christian faith, by whose title in a marvellous fashion he boasteth himself to be above and to excel all other Christian kings and princes, thereby being puffed with vain glory, and pride. Where of a truth he is the most cruellest capital heretic defacer and treader under foot of Christ and of his Church, continually applying and minding to extinct the same. And also the lay-fee, sometimes the nobles and sometimes the commons, without difference, upon chance and displeasance grown, or of truth forsought and feigned, he doth impoverish, destroy, and kill for none other intent but that he may enjoy and use his foul pleasures, and increase to himself great treasure and riches, enriching strangers and pilling and robbing his own subjects, and making fair houses but most superfluous. Whose death I beseech God may be like to the death of the most wicked John, sometime king of this realm, or rather to be called a great tyrant than a king: and that his death may not be much unlike to the end of that manqueller Richard, sometime usurper of this imperial realm. And if thou wilt deeply look upon his life thou shalt find it more foul and more stinking than a sow, wallowing and defiling herself in any filthy place; for how great soever he is, he is fully given to his foul pleasure of the flesh and other voluptuousness. And look how many matrons be in the court, or given to marriage, these almost all he hath violated, so often neglecting his duty to his wife, and offending the Holy Sacrament of matrimony: and now he hath taken to his wife of fornication the matron Anne, not only with the highest shame and undoing himself, but also all this realm." Third Report of Deputy Keeper of Public Records, App. ii., Baga de Secretis.

* "That in the same conversation between Feron and Hale on May 20 (1534), Hale said to Feron 'Until the King and the rulers of this realm

The prisoners thus accused were brought to the bar April 28, and pleaded Not Guilty; but the next day they severally pleaded Guilty, and seem to have tried to save themselves by inculpating others. Feron was spared, but Hale was executed at Tyburn in the company of better men.*

By the side of these culprits in their trial stood a brother of the house of Sion, who was not ranked, however, with them, but with the Carthusian martyrs whose sufferings, presently to be recounted, came to pass at the same time and place. Richard Reynolds was the intimate friend of the famous Reginald Pole. He was an eminent theologian, and, what was rare at the time, well skilled in Greek and Hebrew. He was a man of blameless life.† This Brigitite was not ac-

---

be plucked by the pates, and brought, as we say, to the pot, shall we never live merrily in England, which I pray God may chance, and now shortly to come to pass. Ireland is set against him, which will never shrink in their quarrel to die in it: and what think ye of Wales? Their noble and gentle Ap-Rice so cruelly put to death, and he innocent, as they say, in the cause. I think not contrary but they will join and take part with the Irish, and so invade our realm. If they do, doubt ye not but they shall have aid and strength enough in England: for this is truth, three parts of England be against the King, as he shall find, if he need; for of truth they go about to bring this realm into such miserable condition as is France, which the Commons see and perceive well enough, a sufficient cause of rebellion and insurrection in this realm. And truly we of the Church shall never live merrily until that day come.' To the King's contempt, and in despite of the said marriage," &c. *Ib.* I have quoted the whole of the allegations made in the indictment. As to Ireland, the reader may be reminded that these words were spoken on the eve of Fitzgerald's rebellion. As to Wales and Ap-Rice, see Froude's note, ii. p. 320.

* There can be no doubt but that Hale, as well as Feron, tried to get himself off by accusing others. In Crumwel's Memoranda is the item, "What the King's Highness will have done with such persons as do remain in prison by the accusation of Hale the priest."—Ellis' *Lett.*, ii. 120.

† "Et hic facere non possum quin unum nominatim appellem, quem ego familiariter noram: ei Reginaldo erat nomen, qui et vitæ sanctitate cum præcipuis illorum erat comparandus, qui exactiorem ad Christi normam vivendi rationem profitentur, et quod in paucissimis ejus generis

cused, like Feron and Hale, of conspiring and writing against the king: but like the Carthusians, of denying the King's claim to the title of Supreme Head of the Church of England. He had been seized and committed to the Tower some time before. He was examined by the Council April 15, when he said that he had determined to imitate the Lord Jesus before Herod, and to answer nothing. "But because you urge me," he continued, "that I may satisfy my own conscience, and the consciences of those that are present, I say that our opinion, if it might go by the suffrages of men, would have more plenty of witnesses than yours: you have but the Parliament of one kingdom, I have with me the whole Christian world, except those of this kingdom; I do not say all of this kingdom, because the less part is with you: and granting that the major part of the nation followed not my opinion, it is in external dissembling, and for fear of losing their dignities or honours, or for hope of obtaining the King's favour." Crumwel charged him, on pain of incurring the rigour of the law, to declare of whom he spoke. "Of all the good men of the kingdom," answered he, and went on: "I have on my part all the General Councils, all the pastors and doctors of the Church that have been for fifteen hundred years past, particularly Jerome, Ambrose, Augustin, Gregory: and I am sure that after his Majesty shall have known the truth of this, he will be offended

---

hominum reperitur, omnium liberalium artium cognitionem non vulgarem habebat, eamque ex ipsis haustam fontibus. Nam tres præcipuas linguas, quibus omnis liberalis doctrina continetur, probe callebat, et solus ex monachis Anglis callebat. Ad cujus sanctitatis pariter et doctrinæ laudem in omne tempus confirmandam, et ad cumulum pietatis in Christum, et in te, O Patria, caritatis ostendendam, nihil deesse videbatur, nisi ut cum aliis heroibus suo tam necessario tempore veritatis testimonium legationi sanguine suo daret."—Pole, *Unit.* Lib. iii.

above measure with some bishops who have given him his counsel." He was then asked why he, contrary to the King's authority within his kingdom, did dissuade many from consenting to the opinion of the King and Parliament. He answered that "he had never declared his opinion to any man living but to those that came to confession, which he could not avoid in discharge of his conscience : but if he had not declared his mind then, he would declare it now, because in that part he was obliged to God and his conscience ; and that in such things he could not offend justly." * When he was brought to trial before the Commission at Westminster, along with the three Carthusian priors, on the charge of high treason, and heard the sentence given against him, April 29, he said, " This is the judgment of the world," and asked his judges to give him three days to prepare for death. On being told that it lay only with the King to grant this request, he said in Latin, " I trust verily to see the goodness of the Lord in the land of the living." His petition was granted : the execution of himself and his fellows was delayed for several days. At Tyburn he exhorted the people to pray for the King, lest, having begun like Solomon, he, like Solomon, should be led astray at last by strange women. †

Meantime the temper of the Carthusians was being tried again. On his release from the Tower in the middle of the year before, the Prior of the London Charterhouse had declared prophetically that sub-mission had procured but a respite, and that within a year he should be brought again to the same place, and there finish his course. He and his brethren had

---

* Hist. Martyr. Angl. Strype, i. 304. Mr. Froude puts all this into the mouth of Prior Houghton.

† Sanders.

submitted in obedience to Stokesley, Lee, and other learned men; but Houghton had foreseen that no submission would avail to save them from destruction, the object of their enemies being to goad them into resistance by repeated requisitions. On that occasion the brethren had been urged with an oath which touched not only the Divorce and the Succession of the Crown, but also the Supreme Headship of the King, although at the time the Act of Supreme Head had not become part of the law of the land. Now that the Act was passed, it was time to work upon it with renewed vigour. In April it was signified to the Order that they were to submit again, and subscribe to the Act. The Prior called a chapter, and told them what was coming. What he feared, he said, was the dispersion of them. Some of the brethren were young: there were others whose hearts were still infirm: they were living in innocency now, but they might soon be compelled to mingle with the world, and having begun in the spirit, they might be consumed by the flesh. "What shall I say, what shall I do," he cried, "if I cannot save those whom God has entrusted to my keeping?" The brethren wept, and cried with one voice that they would die together in their integrity, calling God to witness the injustice with which they were treated. "Would that it might be so, that we might die together," answered the Prior, "but thus it will not be: me and the elder brethren they will kill, but many of you are of noble blood; these and the younger they will dismiss into the world: however, if the oath of one will satisfy them, I will expose myself to God's mercy, and be made anathema for my younger brethren, if I lawfully may, by yielding to the King's will; but if they determine to have the consent of all, God's will be done, let us all be sacrificed." He then advised them to prepare themselves by a general confession, giving them liberty to choose each whom he would in the cloister for a confessor. This touching ceremony was performed on the day following. The Prior preached in the chapel on the fifty-ninth Psalm, "Why hast thou cast us off, O Lord?" concluding his discourse with the words, "It is better that we should suffer here a short penance for our faults than be reserved for the eternal pains of hell hereafter." He then desired them to do as they should see him do; and, rising up, went to the eldest of the house, who sat next to him, and kneeling on his knees before him, asked of him forgiveness for all excesses and offences anyways committed against him in heart, word, or deed. The other did the like to him. He then went on to the next, and said the same; and so to every one, to the last. The rest followed in like manner, and all did the same to one another.

The day after this, the third day, was the Mass of the Holy Ghost. God, says the historian of these affecting scenes, made known his presence among us. As soon as the elevation was done, there came a small whispering wind, whereat every man's heart was filled with a sweet operation. There followed a sound of soft music, wherewith our venerable father was so moved that he sank down in tears, and could not continue the service for a long time. All remained stupified, hearing the sound, and feeling the marvellous effect of it on their spirits, but not knowing whence it came nor whither it went. From that time they continued instant in prayer and supplication night and day.

At this time came to London, probably on the same business of the Act of Supreme Head, Robert

Lawrence and Augustine Webster, Priors of the Charterhouses of Belleval, or Beauval, in Nottinghamshire,
and of Axholme, in Lincolnshire; and took their
lodgings in the London house. The former of these
was an old inmate of the house, where he had first
entered religion; the latter, after being professed of the
large Charterhouse of Shene in Surrey, had gone into
Lincolnshire. So completely has the monastic institute
been eradicated in England, and the memory of it
obscured, that of the thousands who know and venerate
the isle of Axholme as the birthplace of John Wesley,
it is probable that there is not one who is aware
that it was once the scene of the daily life of one of
the last and most constant martyrs of that religious
system the loss of which John Wesley sought to repair
by instituting his order of lay preachers. The three
priors, after consulting together, resolved to prevent
the coming of the King's counsellors, and to apply
for some mitigation of the rigorous requirements
which they expected. Offering themselves in behalf
of their brethren, according to the resolution taken by
Houghton, they ventured to wait on Crumwel at his
house, to explain their conscientious objections to the
Act of Supreme Head. By way of answer Crumwel
sent them from his house to the Tower: where within
a week he visited them in company with some others
of the Council, and demanded their oaths in acknowledgment of the Supreme Head. They answered that
they would consent to all things that the divine law
would allow, and so far as it would allow. Crumwel
would admit of no exception. They then said that the
Catholic Church had always held and taught otherwise,
and against that they dared not go. This gave Crumwel
what he wanted: the next day, April 27, a precept
was issued by the justices of the special commission

at Westminster, which had just found the indictment
against Feron and Hale, to bring up the three priors
and with them the Brigitite Reynolds, whose examination in the Tower had left him in the same strait : and
on the following, April 28, an indictment against all
four in common set forth the words of their mouths,
gathered in the previous examinations, as offences
against the Act of Supreme Head, and the desires of
their hearts, presumed from the words of their mouths,
as offences against the late Acts whereby the desires of
the heart, expressed by the words of the mouth, might
be matter of high treason.*   On the same day, April
28, the precept was issued for the return of the petty
jury for their trial. The prisoners pleaded Not Guilty ;
and it seemed that the jury had such a reverence for
them, that they deferred their verdict. Crumwel grew
impatient, and sent to know what made them so long.
They made answer that they could not bring in such
holy persons as malefactors. Crumwel sent them word
that if they found them not guilty, they should suffer
the death of malefactors themselves. As they still
remained fixed in their former judgment, he went to
them himself, and so overawed them by threats, that

---

* The indictment sets forth the substance of the Act of Supreme Head,
26 Hen. VIII. c. i., and also the substance of so much of the Act 26 Hen.
VIII. c. xiii. (An *Act whereby divers offences be made treason*, &c.), as enacts
that maliciously to wish or attempt bodily harm to the King or Queen
and their heirs, or to deprive them of their title, shall be high treason.
"That John Houghton, Prior of the Charterhouse in the county of
Middlesex ; Augustine Webster, Prior of the Charterhouse, Axholme, in
the county of Lincoln ; Robert Lawrence, Prior of the Charterhouse of
Bevall, in the county of Nottingham ; and Richard Reynolds, Brother of
the House of Sion in the county of Middlesex, treacherously machinating
and desiring to deprive the King of his title as Supreme Head of the
Church of England, did, 26th April, 27 H. VIII., at the Tower of London, in
the county of Middlesex openly declare and say—' The King, our Sovereign Lord, is not Supreme Head in earth of the Church of England.' "
Baga de Secr. in 3rd Rep. of Dep. Keeper of Rec., App. ii. 238.

at length on the following day, April 29, they brought
in a verdict of Guilty of treason.*

The four condemned religious, Houghton, Webster,
Lawrence, Reynolds, along with Hale, were executed
at Tyburn, May 4.   A pardon was offered to each
when his turn came to step up the ladder, if he would
then obey the decree of the King and Parliament.   " I
call the Omnipotent God to witness and all good
people," answered Houghton, "and beseech you all to
attest the same for me in the terrible day of judgment,
that here being to die, I publicly profess that it is not
out of obstinate malice or a mind of rebellion that I do
disobey the King; but only for the fear of God, that
I offend not the Supreme Majesty; because our Holy
Mother the Church hath decreed and appointed otherwise than the King and Parliament hath ordained.
And I am here ready to endure this and all other
torments that can be suffered, rather than oppose the
doctrine of the Church.   Pray for me, and pity my
brethren, of whom I was the unworthy Prior."   He then
repeated a few verses of the thirty-first Psalm, and

---

* Hist. Mart.: Strype, i. 305. Mr. Froude denies that Crumwel could
have threatened the jury with death for delaying their verdict, because the
trial was begun and ended in one day. "Any doubt," he says, "which might
remain, in the absence of opposing testimony, is removed by the record of
the trial, from which it appears clearly that the jury were not returned until
the 29th of April, and *that the verdict was given in on the same day.*" —
Baga de Secretis. Appendix to the Third Report of the Deputy Keeper
of the Public Records ; Froude, ii. 357. It appears, however, that the
proceedings occupied two days, and the jury seems to have been im-
panneled on the first, though the trial may have been begun on the
second. The words are, " 28 April, 27 Hen. 8 Middlesex. The Justices'
Precept to the Sheriff for the return of the Petty Jury for the trial of
Houghton, Webster, Laurens, and Reynolds, and Panel annexed."—(App.
to Third Rep. 238.) The record then goes on to say that the four
prisoners were brought to the bar, and pleaded Not Guilty on the same
day, Wednesday, April 28 ; that a Venire was awarded, returnable next
day : and that on Thursday, April 29, " Houghton, Webster, Laurens, and
Reynolds are again brought to the bar. Verdict Guilty."—(239.)

resigned himself to the executioner. The others declared that they took their death not only patiently but cheerfully, acknowledging " that they had obtained great favour from God, that He had given them to die for the truth, and for the assertion of the evangelical and catholic doctrine, namely that the King is not Supreme Primate in Spirituals, and the Head of the Church of England."* They were executed with great, but perhaps not unusual cruelty : they were half hanged, cut down alive, embowelled and their bowels burnt, beheaded, and dismembered. The Roman Catholic writers give a horrible description of a kind of death which in itself embraced many kinds of death, and of the agility of the executioner, who sought to make every kind of death sensible to each who suffered. But we may hope that in the rest Nature's kindness outstripped the speed of skill and zeal, even if it be true that Houghton uttered a prayer after he was cut down, and was still capable of an articulate exclamation when his heart was pulled out. That they were hanged with a great rope, that they might not be quickly strangled, and endure the more pain in being cut down and ripped up, is perhaps untrue.† But the execution departed from ancient usage in one particular which has received various censure. They were hanged in their religious habits, without being degraded. To some this has seemed a studied insult to ecclesiastical law,

---

* Hist. Martyr. : Strype, i. 303. To the honour of Cranmer it must be recorded that he made an effort to save Webster and Reynolds : the former had, it seems, once promised the Archbishop never to meddle in defence of the Pope's authority : the latter the Archbishop regretted as a learned man. He begged Crumwel to allow him to use persuasion with them. " If it would please the King's Highness to send them unto me, I suppose I could do very much with them in this behalf."—*To Crumwel*, Lett. 303.

† It was, however, believed abroad that great cruelty was used. " The thing was noted here of extreme cruelty." *Harvel to Starkey, Venice,* 15 *June. Ellis,* ii. 2, 74.

in which, however, the fatuous despot who offered it overreached himself, and by not stripping them of their garb, acknowledged the innocence of his victims. To some it has seemed that in this arrangement the noblest stroke that was ever uplifted upon the proud crest of superstition fell with a crash that echoed through the world. Henceforth the world might know that no religious habit, no hypocritical pretence, should avail to screen the besotted wretches who still dared to flaunt in the light of day the farcical fragments of an effete and moribund illusion. Others see in it no more than economy, or accident, or the working of the official mind, in that being executed for a new kind of crime they were executed with an unusual circumstance.

The severed arm of Houghton was fixed as a bloody warning over the gate of his Priory, to awe the surviving brethren into submission. Two days afterwards, it fell down, or was secretly taken down.* Though their head was taken from them, the brethren were not as sheep having no shepherd. The spirit of the Prior survived in the remaining officers of the house, and was diffused through all. A few days after the executions, the house was visited by the zealous Bedyl. He brought with him books and annotations, both of his own and others, against the primacy of the Bishop of Rome and St. Peter, and declaring the equality of the Apostles. He spent an hour and a half in argument with the Vicar and the Procurator of the house, and left his books and annotations with them. The books were returned to him, to his house in Aldersgate Street, without comment in word or writing. Where-

---

* Houghton's arm was kept by one of the monks named John Fox, who afterwards fled to Louvain, leaving the relic in charge of Hickman, another brother, and of Monday, parson of St. Leonard's, in Foster Lane. They, in attempting to take it to Fox, were caught, and executed for treason, in July, 1547.—Wriothesley, 185.

T 2

upon he sent for the Procurator, Middlemore, and demanded of him whether they had perused or examined them. Middlemore made answer that he and Exmew, the Vicar, and a senior named Newdigate, had spent time over them till nine or ten at night, and that they saw nothing in them to alter their opinion. Bedyl demanded whether the rest of the brethren were of the like opinion; and the Procurator replied that he was not sure, but thought that they were all of one mind. Bedyl then informed him that the same false spirit which inspired the prophets of Ahab was in them all, and that their opinion would be the destruction of them and their house for ever. He reported to Crumwel that from what he could perceive they were obstinate, and regarded no more the death of their father than if he were living and conversant among them. He added that their pretended holiness was hypocrisy, vainglory, confederacy, obstinacy, and a desire to seem to the world more faithful and constant than any other. It was the will of God that as their religion had a simple beginning, so it should have a strange end; but procured by themselves and none others.* Bedyl, it will be perceived, was a necessitarian. Surely a necessitarian may protest against wilfulness.

Soon after this Middlemore, Exmew, and Newdigate were committed to the Tower. There, when they were examined by Crumwel and some of the Council, they kept silence under the questions that were asked of them, considering, it appears, that their judges were heretics, and not of the Church of God, and therefore not worthy to be answered.† At their trial by jury, which was under the same special commission of Oyer and Terminer under which Bishop Fisher was tried, it was charged against them that on May 25, at Stepney,

* Bedyl to Crumwel, Suppr. of Mon., 40.   † Hall.

each of them did severally say in conversation amongst one another, " I cannot nor will consent to be obedient to the King's Highness, as a true, lawful, and obedient subject, to take and repute him to be Supreme Head in earth of the Church of England under Christ."* After pleading Not Guilty, they still observed the same malicious† or superior silence, were brought in Guilty June 11, and, June 19, executed at Tyburn. They were hanged, drawn, and quartered; and their quarters set up in various places in London. These monks were all well born: and one of them, Newdigate, had been brought up at court.

Fisher and More had been in prison now above a year, from the day that they refused to subscribe the Act of Succession, and to take the Oath thereto appended. In the history of what befell these illustrious friends between their attainder and their indictment it is not always easy to separate from the substance of truth the colours, whether of enmity or of piety. At first they were allowed to write to one another in the Tower; and they used to exchange letters of comfort, and little presents of meat and drink. But this correspondence fell under suspicion, and was made to cease: all the letters that could be found were seized, and used to swell the beggarly account of evidence that was laid against them at last. They were visited and examined by members of the Council, and other emissaries, especially after the passing of the new laws in November, when they had been in prison seven months. Various efforts, and perhaps artifices, were used to bring them to submit.‡ The answers

---

* Third Rep. of Dep. Keeper of Publ. Rec., 239.

† The word malicious, which Hall applies to their silence, may have reference to the new treason Act. The Act was against speaking maliciously: the Judge soon afterwards, in More's case, interpreted it of keeping silence maliciously when the prisoner was asked questions.

‡ According to Bailie, when Crumwel and Audley, Wiltshire and Suffolk, had exhausted their efforts, the King grew angry and swore that

which they returned on these occasions were cited against them afterwards; and the man who accepted the office of witness in chief against them was the Solicitor General, Richard Rich.

The venerable bishop, who had survived a winter of cold and nakedness in the dungeon, was despatched about a month before his fellow-sufferer. What happened to him may shew both uncertainty and precipitation on the part of the King and his advisers. He was visited, perhaps about the beginning of May, by Rich, and questioned in some peculiar manner about the Act of Supreme Head :* and his answer on

both Fisher and More should take the oath—"Are there not more ways to the wood than one?" said he. Next morning the perplexed Council sent for More, kept him waiting outside for three hours, urged him for half an hour, sent him back to prison again, and gave out that he had taken the oath. Then they sent for Fisher, and told him that More had yielded, and urged him to yield also, and take the oath. He refused, but said that he would never speak against it. He was then led to a chamber near the King's lodgings, and it was given out that he had yielded, and was gone to kiss the King's hand. At this moment Margaret Roper, the beloved daughter of More, happens to come into the council-chamber with a petition that her father may have a little more liberty in the Tower. Audley tells her that Fisher has yielded, thinking that "the daughter's thimble might prick a needle into the father's conscience." She gives a spring for joy, and rushes towards her father's cell : but not being able to get admittance without a warrant, she returns to Audley, who gives her one. She rushes back and pours the glad tidings into her father's ear. "Peace, daughter," answers More, "my lord of Rochester hath not taken the oath."—"Yes, Audley said so."—"You fool, they think to take me in a puppet snatch, but they are deceived."

They then send for More, and bid him do as Fisher had done. More asks to see Fisher. "He is with the King, where you may soon be too." "Let me him see." "Yes, when the oath is taken : but it would not be so proper to see him before as after, lest it be said you pinned your judgment on another's sleeve." "Then let me see his writing." "That also is carried to the King." "I nor believe it, nor will I submit." A dramatist might have made something of this plot.

* It cannot be true, as Bailie asserts, that Rich was sent with a secret message from the King that "he would not undertake the Supremacy," if Fisher told him that it was unlawful; and offering, if it were lawful, to make Fisher his Vicar-general. (Bailie's Fisher.) But there seems to have been some private effort made by the King to conciliate him. It is said

that occasion was the principal piece of evidence brought against him on his trial.   But several singular and important events intervened between the inculpation and the condemnation of Fisher.   The new Pope, Paul the Third, celebrated his election to the chair of St. Peter by a creation of cardinals ; and, along with six other prelates chosen from the different nations, the prisoner of the Tower found himself, as the representative of England, elevated, May 21, to that lofty eminence, with the title of St. Vitale.   This act of the Pope precipitated, or perhaps determined, the fate of Fisher.   To the Supreme Head it appeared the defiance of the High Pontiff : and the witty answer of Henry, who, when he heard that the Red Hat of the Cardinal was on the way to England, is reported to have said that he should wear it on his shoulders, may have expressed a new resolution of anticipating, instead of accelerating, the tardiness of nature.*   The Pope, who justified what he had done by alleging that he sought only to honour the fame and learning of Fisher, did him the greater service of ensuring the crown of martyrdom to an old age which might have languished else in an obscure prison to the end : for while the Red Hat was stopped at Calais, the head that should have worn it rolled on the scaffold.   Scarcely could the news of his new dignity have reached the ears of Fisher, when, June 1,

that the King sent his own physician, when he was sick, to minister to him, to the charges of fifty pounds.—*Ib.*

* The English ambassador Casale sent the news from Rome to England next day, May 22. Casale remonstrated with the Pope in violent language on the elevation of Fisher. The Pope desired to excuse himself by urging that he had no intention of giving offence, and, as it was necessary to have some Englishman, he had taken Fisher, who first came into his mind, from his reputation and the fame of his writings in Italy and Germany. Casale told him that his conduct admitted of no excuse.—*State Pap.* vii. 604.

a special commission was opened at Westminster, and
a true bill was found against him, June 5. But between
the opening of the commission and the finding of the
bill, or the indictment (so strange was the course of
justice then), the prisoner was subjected to another
visitation of the Council, June 3 ; and again to another,
June 14, between the indictment and the actual trial.
On the former of these occasions the visitors were
Audley, Suffolk, Wiltshire, and others, who examined
him on the Act of Supreme Head. His answer was,
" I will not meddle with that matter ; for the statute is
like a two-edged sword, and if I should answer one
way I should offend my conscience, and if I should
answer another way I should put my life in jeopardy."*
On the latter occasion he was interrogated at greater
length by those active members of the Council, Bedyl,
Aldrich, Curwen, and Layton. First he was asked
whether he would obey the King's Highness as Supreme Head on earth under Christ of the Church of
England, according to the Statute made on that behalf.
The answer that he made has been preserved only
imperfectly : but he promised to declare his opinion
more at length in writing.† Next he was asked

---

* Third Rep. of Dep. Keeper of Pub. Rec., 241 (More's Trial).

† I cannot find that Fisher ever fulfilled this promise. There is a
curious passage in one of Bedyl's letters to Crumwel about Sion, written
July 28, six weeks after Fisher's death, in which he says that he had had
the Confessor of Sion " in very secret communication concerning certain
letters of Mr. Fisher's, of which Father Reynold made mention in his
examination, which the said Fisher promised the King's grace that he
never shewed to any other man, neither would." He adds, " The said
Confessor hath confessed to me that the said Fisher sent to him, to the
said Reynold, and to another brother of them deceased, whose name I
remember not, the copy of his said letters directed unto the King's grace,
and the copy of the King's answer also : but he hath sworn to me upon
his fidelity that the said copies tarried with them but one night, and that
none of his brethren saw these same but these three afore named : He
hath knowledged to me also that the said Fisher sent unto them with the

whether he would consent that the King's marriage with the noble Queen Anne was good and lawful, and that the other pretended marriage between the King and the Lady Katharine, Princess Dowager, was unlawful and of no effect. He answered that he would obey that and all other articles and particles contained in the Act of Succession in all points, saving only his conscience : and he was not only ready to accept and approve the succession, yea and to swear thereto, but to defend the same and condemn the other. But to answer absolutely to the interrogatory, yea or nay, he desired to be pardoned. He was then asked " wherein, and for what cause, he would not answer resolutely to the said interrogatories." He desired, he said in answer, not to be driven to answer, lest he should fall into the dangers of the statutes.*

Three days after this final attempt to bring him to an unreserved submission, Fisher was brought to trial, June 17. He rode part of the way from the Tower to Westminster on horseback, clad in a black gown, the axe being borne before him with the edge from him, as innocent : the rest of the way he went by water, being unable to remain on horseback through weakness. He was put at the bar before the Commissioners, who were Audley, Suffolk, the Earls of Wiltshire and of Cumberland, Sir John Fitz-James,

said copies a book of his made in the defence of the King's grace's first marriage, which he confessed himself to have in his keeping, which he hath willingly delivered unto me, and also 'Abel's book, and one other book made by the emperor's ambassador, as I suppose."—*Supp. of Mon.*, 45. Of course, as Reynolds was hanged May 4, these letters cannot be what Fisher promised to write June 14. But though Mr. Froude is aware of this, he seems to mix the two together, and makes a charge of breach of promise against the "unwise old man."—(ii. 365.) Bedyl's letter refers to something else, on which we can found no conclusion without more knowledge.

* State Pap. i. 431.

Lord Chief Justice, Sir John Baldwin, Chief Justice
of Common Pleas, Sir William Paulet, Sir Richard
Lyster, Chief Baron of the Exchequer, Sir John Porte,
Sir John Spelman, Sir Antony Fitzherbert, Justice of
Common Pleas.*   He was ordered, by the name of
John Fisher, late of Rochester, clerk, otherwise
called John Fisher, Bishop of Rochester, to hold up
his hand: which he did.   His indictment was then
read, which was very long, and full of words, but the
only actual charge contained in it was that on May 7
in the Tower of London he openly said in English:
"The King our Sovereign Lord is not Supreme
Head in earth of the Church of England."   He
was asked whether he were guilty of the treason:
he pleaded Not Guilty, and a jury was called to
try the issue.   The Solicitor General, Rich, deposed
that he heard the prisoner say in the Tower that
he believed in his conscience and knew by his
learning that the King neither was nor by right
could be Supreme Head of the Church of England.
Fisher answered, "Mr. Rich, I marvel that you
bear witness against me of these words, knowing
in what secret manner you came to me; but suppose
I so said unto you, yet in that saying I committed
no treason: for upon what occasion and for what
cause it might be said, yourself doth know right
well."   He then related the confidential nature of the
communication.   Rich made no direct answer, but said
that he had said no more than his Majesty commanded; and that, whatever the circumstances, they

* Bailie, who may be presumed to have given correctly those commissioners who were present.   Accordingly, the absent ones were the
Marquis of Exeter, the Earl of Rutland, Sir Walter Luke, Sir Thomas
Inglefield, Sir William Shelley, and Crumwel.   Third Rep. of Dep. Keep.
of Pub. Rec., 239.

were no discharge in law for speaking against the
statutes.   All the judges agreed that in speaking
against the statute, though at the King's own commandment or request, he committed treason by the
statute.   Fisher said that by the statute the words
should have been spoken maliciously, whereas he had
spoken them by advice and commandment.   Some of
the judges answered that the word maliciously, which
was in the statute, was superfluous : to speak against
the Supreme Head in any way was to speak maliciously.
Fisher said that this interpretation was against the
mind of those who made the statute.   He then asked
whether one witness were enough against him ; and
whether his negative might not avail against the affirmative of another.   The judges said that as it was
the King's case, it rested much in the discretion of the
jury ; and the evidence must go before them.   Audley
then summed up, or rather aggravated, the case to the
jury ; the rest of the commissioners assisted him in
threatening them : they retired, and returned with the
necessary verdict.*

When the day of execution came, June 22, the
Bishop dressed himself carefully.   It was his wedding
day, he said.   Among other adornments he put on
a fur tippet, as it was cold.   The lieutenant of the
Tower, asking why he should be careful of his health
for an hour, "I will not," he answered, "hinder my
health one minute of an hour, but prolong it all I can."
He was carried in a chair to the precincts of the liberty
of the Tower, where he was set down, and waited
while they sent to know if the sheriffs of London were
ready to receive him.   When they came, he rose in his
chair, prayed, and opened the New Testament, which

* Bailie's Fisher, 190 sq.

he carried, at the words " Hæc est vita æterna." The sheriffs took him, with many armed men around, and carried him to the scaffold erected on Tower Hill: for of the King's mercy he was to die there by the axe, instead of the gibbet at Tyburn. When he stood upon the scaffold, the south-east sun shone bright in his face; he lifted up his hands and said, " Accedite ad eum et illuminamini, et facies vestræ non confundentur." To the executioner he said, " I forgive thee with all my heart, and I trust thou shalt see me overcome this storm lustily." His gown and tippet were taken away, and his long slender body was seen as he stood in his doublet and hose. He was allowed to speak to the people; and his last words were such as these. " Christian people, I am come hither to die for the faith of Christ's holy Catholic Church. I have not, I thank God, yet feared death. I pray you all to assist me with your prayers that in the very stroke of death I may not fail in any one point of the Catholic faith. And I beseech Almighty God to save the King of this realm, and to hold His hand over it, and to send the King good counsel." Thus he died. The head was stuck on London Bridge; but as the people thronged to look at it, and paid it reverence, saying that by miracle it looked fresher every day, it was flung into the river after a time. The body was stripped naked, and left in that state on the scaffold all the day of the execution: then at night orders came to bury, and it was buried naked in the churchyard of All Hallows, Barking, hard by;* a place which a hundred years later received the headless trunk of Laud.

About this time the Supreme Head polled his hair and altered the fashion of his beard: he also prohl-bited his courtiers from wearing their hair long. Some

* Bailie's Life of Fisher.

say that this was in public token of mourning for the executions : others, on the contrary, have thought that he desired to shine forth rejuvenescent in the eyes of Anne ; others again that, having a new title, he desired to put a new face upon it.*

Sir Thomas More had now been restrained for some months from the company of his wife and children (who had been sometimes allowed to see him at first), from the services of the Church, and from the use of pen, ink, and paper.   While he possessed the latter commodities he wrote his most beautiful religious treatises, the Dialogue of Comfort against Tribulation, and the unfinished meditation upon the Passion of Christ ; but when he was deprived of them he could do no more than write with a piece of coal on casual scraps of paper a few brief letters to his family. Meantime he was visited often by the Councillors. Once Crumwel came alone, and urged him by his own friendship and the King's former favour to relent from his resolution.†   Crumwel returned again, May 7, along with Bedyl, Tregonwell, and others of the Council, and asked him formally whether he would accept the King as Supreme Head.   His answer was that " he would not meddle with any such matters, for that he was fully determined to serve God, and to think upon his Passion, and his own passage out of the world."   He was again examined, June 3, when he used words which were brought against him on his trial, comparing the Act of Supreme Head to a double-edged sword.‡   Some days after this, June 12, came the Solicitor General, Rich, accompanied by Sir Richard Southwell and one Palmer, Crumwel's man :

---

* Froude, Pole, Herbert, Sanders.
† More's Life of More, 305.
‡ More's Indictment in Rep. of Dep. Keeper of Publ. Rec., 240.

who took away More's books. While Southwell and Palmer were putting the books into bags, Rich engaged the prisoner in a conversation which was afterwards turned into a deposition against him. He urged More to be conformable to the Acts and laws. The latter replied, " Your conscience will save you, and mine will save me." Rich then, protesting that he had no authority to make any communication with More, said to him, " Suppose that it were enacted by Parliament that Richard Rich should be king, and that it should be treason to deny the same, what would be the offence if Sir Thomas More were to say that Rich was king for certain." More answered that there would be no offence in saying that Rich was king, if he were made king by Act of Parliament. " But," he added, " that is a light case, and I will put a higher one. Suppose that it were enacted by Parliament, *Quod Deus non esset Deus*, and that opposing the Act were treason : and if it were asked of you, Richard Rich, whether you would say Quod Deus non erat Deus according to the statute, and if you were to say so, would you not offend ?" Rich answered, " Certainly ; because it is impossible Quod Deus non esset Deus ; but because your case is so high I will put a medium one. You know that our lord the King is constituted chief head on earth of the Church of England : and why, Master More, can you not affirm ·to accept the same, just as you would in the preceding case, that I should be made king, in which case you say that you should be obliged to acknowledge and accept me as king ?" To which More is said to have answered that the cases were not similar. "The king can be made by Parliament, and deprived by Parliament, and to which Act every subject being in Parliament gives his consent ; but in the first case the subject cannot be obliged, because his consent cannot be given for that in Parliament; and although the King might be so accepted in England, yet many do not assent to the same in foreign parts."*

Two days afterwards, June 14, came Bedyl, Layton, Curwen, and Aldrich, the same persons who on the same day examined Fisher; and administered to More some searching interrogatories, with the view of discovering the suspected correspondence between him, Fisher, and others. They had with them a notary and two witnesses. The official answers of More to these interrogatories are important for the clearing of the character both of himself and his fellow-prisoner from the imputations cast on them after death, when the ambassadors of England were instructed by Henry and Crumwel to justify their execution by alleging that during their incarceration they had been engaged in ceaseless plots against the life and crown of their sovereign. More was asked, first, whether he had held any communication, reasoning, or consultation with any person, since he came to the Tower, touching the Acts of Succession, of Supreme Head, and of verbal Treason. He answered that he never had. He was asked whether he had received or written any letters touching the same Acts, or any other business concerning the King and the realm. He answered that he had written divers letters to Fisher, and received others from him, which for the most part contained nothing but comfortable words, declaration of the state of their bodily health, or thanks for such presents of meat and drink as they made to one another. But he

---

* Third Report of Deputy Keeper of Pub. Rec., 240. It would seem from the broken records that we have of More's trial, that he denied the accuracy of this report of his conversation with Rich, which is here given from the Indictment. Cf. More's Life of More, p. 309.

remembered that in one of them, written about three
months after he came to the Tower, he told Fisher
how he had refused to take the Oath, and had never
shewn the Council his reasons, nor intended ever to
shew them to any man.   Fisher in his answer declared
what answer he himself had made to the Council, and
how he had not refused to swear to the Succession itself.
Nothing else of that nature passed between them until
the Act of Supreme Head had been passed, and had
been tendered to them to accept in prison.   Then
Fisher had sent to know what answer More had made:
and he told him by letter that his answer had been
that he would meddle with no such things, but think
upon the passion of Christ, and his own passage out of
this world.   Then, within a while, Fisher had written
again to enquire whether, in More's opinion, the word
"maliciously" in the Act creating new treasons, would
serve to defend a man who had not spoken out of malice;
and he had answered that it would, but that it would
not be so interpreted, and that it was not good for any
man to trust in any such thing.   He added that he had
warned Fisher not to answer on the Act of Supreme
Head in the same words that he himself had used, but
to frame his answer out of his own mind, lest the
Council should think there was some confederacy
between them.*   There was another letter, which the
Solicitor General had seized, and which he produced to
him, in which he acknowledged that he had written that
it was all one not to answer at all, and to say against the
Statute what a man would; that therefore he looked
for nothing but the uttermost; and prayed Fisher to
pray for him, as he would for him again.   He had

---

* In his trial More was accused of confederacy with Fisher, but it
was because of another expression which they both used : that the Act
was like a sword with two edges.   See below.

also written twice to his daughter, Margaret Roper, to prepare her mind, and prevent her from sudden alarms, and had told her what his answers to the Council had been. And she on her part had often written, imploring him to submit to the King. Other letters he had received or written none, to his remembrance. George, the Lieutenant's servant, carried the letters. He was asked, in the third place, whether any of these letters were forthcoming; to which he answered that George always burnt them, saying that there was no better keeper than the fire. He would have had George keep them; and he had asked him to shew them to some friend who could read (for George could not), and if he saw any matter of importance in them, to carry them first to the Council, and get the thanks thereof himself. But George was afraid of his master, who had charged him highly to meddle with no such matters, and would have been extremely displeased if he had done anything against his commandment. The last interrogatory was, Whether any man of this realm, or without this realm, had sent him any letter or message, counselling or exhorting him to persist in the opinion that he was in? He answered, Nay. Some one then asked him to what intent he had sent the said letters to Fisher. He answered, that as they were both in one prison for one cause, he was glad to send to him and to hear from him again.*

A fortnight after this, July 1, a Commission, consisting of nearly the same persons who had tried Fisher, was opened in the Court of King's Bench in Westminster for the trial of More. The prisoner walked firmly into the familiar court, supported by a staff, and bearing in his looks the marks of long incarceration. An indictment, scantily furnished with facts,

* State Pap. i. 432.

but swollen to an enormous size by words, was read by
the King's Attorney. It was so long that when the
encumbered train of malicious, secret, traitorous, seditious, and diabolical epithets, augmentations, repetitions,
and explications came to an end, the Ex-chancellor
exclaimed with a touch of humour that he could
scarce remember a third part of the treasons which he
had committed. But the examinations and letters on
which it was founded seem to have given ground for no
more than the five accusations following: First, that he
had refused to answer directly to the question whether
he accepted the King as Supreme Head, saying that
he would meddle with no such matters : Second, that he
had written to Fisher to inform him that he had thus
kept silence ; and that in this letter he compared the
Act of Supreme Head to a sword with two edges:
Third, that he had written again to Fisher to warn him
not to use such words to the Council, but to frame his
answer according to his own mind, lest the Council
should suspect confederacy in making their answers ;
but Fisher nevertheless, when he was examined, had
used the same comparison of the Act with a double-
edged sword ; which was a plain proof of confederacy ;
Fourth, that on the very day, June 3, that Fisher used
these words, More used the like, and said, " The law
and statute is like a sword with two edges :" Fifth, that
he had held the conversation with Rich, of which an
account has been given.* The defence which More
made may be imagined from the answers which he had
returned to all these charges in his examinations in
prison ; and the general outline of what he said may
be gathered from the partial, but hardly extravagant
narrative of his earliest biographer. He said that he

* More's Indictment in Third Record Report, 240.

would have demurred upon the Indictment, but that he should thereby be driven to confess that he had denied the King to be Supreme Head, which he protested that he had never done: however he would plead Not Guilty, reserving for himself advantage to be taken of the body of the matter, after verdict, to avoid that Indictment. If the odious terms were taken out, he added, he could see nothing in it that amounted to a charge of treason.* He then addressed himself to the argument. So great a master of law found no difficulty in pointing out that the great accusation against him was silence, and that no law could punish any man for holding his peace. When the King's Attorney interposed that his silence was malicious; that no dutiful subject would have refused to answer, More denied the position. His silence, he said, was no sign of malice, as the King might know by many of his dealings: his conscience had procured neither slander nor sedition, for he had never revealed his thoughts and reasons to any man living. It could not be said that no good subject would have refused to answer, unless a good subject be so bad a Christian as to have no fear of offending his conscience. This was in truth the most important part of More's defence. He was not only the champion of the Church, and of the Primacy and jurisdiction of the Pope; he was the champion also of English liberty, which had been betrayed by Parliament. There are many men living in England now under laws which they mislike but obey; who if they were pressed to swear, declare, and subscribe, as More was, might feel themselves compelled in conscience to refuse to swear, declare, and subscribe, as More did. If every Act of Parliament were to be sworn to and

---

* More's More, 313.

U 2

subscribed to by all subjects, there would be intolerable
slavery. As to the alleged coincidence between Bishop
Fisher and himself in the expression of their opinion of
the Act of Supreme Head, More owned that he had used
the words, but only in a conditional sense, that if there
were danger both in allowing and disallowing, and the
statute were thus a two-edged sword, it seemed hard that
it should be offered to him. What the Bishop had answered he knew not: but if their answers were alike,
it was not from any conspiracy, but from the likeness
of their wits and learning. He then passed to the conversation which he had held with Rich, the Solicitor
General, in the Tower; and seems to have denied the
construction put upon it in the Indictment, that he
had denied that Parliament could make the King
Supreme Head of the Church. Rich was thereupon
brought forward, and deposed that the words of More
had been what they were alleged to be: upon which
More declared that he committed perjury, exposed
the profligacy of his character from youth upwards,
and asked indignantly whether it were likely that he,
who had locked his reasons for keeping silence in his
own breast from all the world, should have unbosomed
himself to a dicer and a gamester. Rich, who had at
least betrayed trust, finding his credit so deeply touched,
called in Sir Richard Southwell and Mr. Palmer, who
had been present at the conversation, to confirm his
evidence. But they both alleged that they were so
busy putting More's books into a sack at the time,
that they paid no heed to what was said. The jury
then, without asking to look over the long indictment,
proceeded to convict the prisoner of high treason:
and the Lord Chancellor Audley was proceeding
to pass sentence, when he was stopped by More, his
predecessor, and reminded that a prisoner had the

right of being heard to shew that judgment should not be passed. Audley assented to this, and the prisoner now for the first time brought forward the exception which he had reserved against the whole of the Indictment, and therewithal declared the motive on which he had acted throughout. The Indictment was founded, he said, upon an Act of Parliament which was clean contrary to the laws of God and the Church, and therefore insufficient in law among Catholic Christians; and that it was also contrary to the sacred oath taken by the King at his coronation. Audley said that it was strange in him to stick at what the bishops, the Universities, and the best learned men in the realm agreed upon; and was answered that one realm could not be set against all Christendom beside. Audley then turned to the Lord Chief Justice, Fitz-James, and asked him whether in his opinion the Indictment were sufficient. "My lords all," answered Fitz-James, "by St. Gillian, I must needs confess that if the Act of Parliament be not unlawful, then the Indictment is not in my conscience insufficient." The sentence was then pronounced in the usual form; but the punishment was declared to be changed into beheading only by the King's mercy. "God forbid," said More, with a touch of bitterness, "that the King should use any more such mercy unto any of my friends, and God help all my posterity from all such pardons." He then said that he had studied for seven years, but could find no doctor allowed by the Church who said that a layman could be head of the Church. Audley repeated his argument from the consent of the authorities of the realm; and More answered again that the realm was not to be set against all Christendom beside. The Duke of Norfolk broke out thus. "Now, Sir Thomas," said he, "you show your obstinate and malicious mind."

The condemned man replied, "Noble Sir, not any malice or obstinacy causeth me to say this, but the just necessity of the cause constraineth me." The judges then courteously offered him a favourable audience, if he had any thing else to allege; and the memorable scene closed with More's most graceful and noble farewell: "More have I not to say, my lords, but that like as the holy Apostle St. Paul, as we read in the Acts of the Apostles, was present and consenting to the death of the proto-martyr, Stephen, keeping their clothes that stoned him to death ; and yet they be now both twain holy Saints in heaven, and there shall continue friends together for ever ; so I verily trust and shall therefore heartily pray that though your lordships have been on earth my judges to condemnation, yet we may hereafter meet in heaven merrily together to our everlasting salvation : and God preserve you all, and especially my sovereign lord the King; and grant him faithful counsellors."*

The touching scenes which were enacted on the way back to prison, his parting with his beloved daughter, his son, and household, are familiar parts of history. To his daughter he sent as a last gift the hair shirt which he had worn and his whip of discipline, laying down his weapons, it was said, now that the war was over. The end, indeed, was not long delayed, though he was kept in ignorance of the near approach of it. On the morning of July 6 Sir William Pope, a personal friend, appeared, and announced that it was the will of the King and Council that he should suffer on that morning at nine o'clock. More was ready. " The King will not that you use many words at your execution," said the messenger. " I am well warned,"

* More's Life of More.

answered More, " for I meant to have said somewhat."
As he went to the Tower Hill, two women cried
against him, the one bidding him restore some books
which she had given into his hands when he was Lord
Chancellor, the other exclaiming that he had done her
great injury by his judgment in her cause. " Good
woman," said he to the one, " give me but an hour's
space, and the King will rid me of the care I have for
thy papers, and all other matters whatsoever." To
the other he said that he remembered her case very
well, and that if he were now to give sentence thereon,
he would not alter what he had already done. In this
way he reached and ascended the scaffold, which was
a weak and shaking structure. " See me safe up," said
he to the Constable, " I will shift for myself in coming
down." As he laid his head on the block, he moved
his beard aside. " It were a pity to cut that," said he,
" it never committed treason ; " and these last words of
the greatest wit of the age were redeemed from levity
by the deep irony that lay beneath them. So died the
noblest layman that the Church of England has ever
had. His head was boiled, and fixed on London Bridge,
when Fisher's head had been flung into the river.

As soon as it became known that the King of
England was slaughtering the best of his subjects, and
decorating his capital with their mangled remains, a
thrill of horror ran through Europe. In Rome the
execution of the monks, the bishop, and the chancellor
was listened to with tears by the Pope and Cardinals.
The French King expressed his disapprobation with
some freedom. The Emperor said that he would
rather have lost the two best cities in his dominions
than two such men as Fisher and More. Some of the
Protestant princes testified their dislike. The learned
vied in lamenting the irreparable loss which literature

had sustained in More. Erasmus reproached the tyrant who gave no impunity to genius, nor knew that wit and learning should be raised above the hatred of the times. Plato was not beheaded by the Æginetans when he violated their laws. Diogenes went without fear into the presence of Philip of Macedon after he had reproved him for the madness of ambition. Which of the crimes of Nero was comparable with the murder of Seneca? What weighed so heavily on the memory of Mark Antony as the death of Cicero: on the memory of Augustus as his implacable resentment against Ovid? These reproaches have been echoed in our own day. No such culprit as More, exclaims a writer of the last generation, had stood at any European bar for a thousand years: the condemnation of Socrates is the only parallel in history, nor could Socrates claim a moral superiority over More.* Even the later necessitarians, who have nothing in their treasuries but contempt for the ecclesiastic Fisher, have dropped the tear of culture over the grave of the author of Utopia. But there is little to lament in the glorious end of men who laid down their lives in the cause of the unity of the Church and the liberties of England.

So great was the outcry through Europe, that the King and Crumwel deemed it necessary to furnish the ambassadors at foreign courts with a vindication of their conduct. Crumwel instructed Gardiner, the ambassador in Paris, to repel the remonstrances of the French King, and inform him that his counsels were taken unkindly. The Bishop of Hereford, who was at the court of the Duke of Saxe, was ordered to say that Fisher and More " had been proved to be false

---

* Sir James Mackintosh, Hist. of Eng.

traitors and rebels to his Highness and his Crown,"
and that "having nevertheless the prison at their
liberties, they ceased not both to practise an insurrection within the realm, and also to use all the devices
to them possible in outward parts, as well to defame
and slander His Majesty, and his most virtuous doings
and proceedings, as also to procure the impeachment
and other destruction of his most royal person."* But
the most elaborate apology was composed by Crumwel
himself for the Court of Rome. The King, said
Crumwel, was perfectly astonished that the death of
Fisher and More had been taken ill at Rome. The
King had been meditating how, after he had got his
great cause well settled in a second marriage, he
might reform the morals of his people, with the aid
of God, when, lo! these good men under a pretended
honesty began to obstruct him. At first he regarded
them not, but they abused his lenity; and, when Parliament met, they used to enquire secretly what was
going to be done, and then held discussions in their
coteries, and put a bad construction upon everything,
with such arguments as might easily impose on the
common people. And when their conscience told
them that they must have offended the King, fearing
lest they should fail to carry out their secret designs,

---

* Froude, ii. 367, 389, from a "Rolls House MS." This is the only
distinct charge (except that the Council had some letters written by the
prisoners), which is found in these elaborate vindications. If the Council
had proof of plots to make insurrection, and to slander the King in
foreign parts, why were they not produced in the trial, to give substance
to the empty bill of indictment? I am unable to agree with Mr. Froude
that "the government" had proofs but preferred to keep them back, and
proceed on the words of the prisoners themselves. As to the alleged
letters, it all rests on what Crumwel told Casale to say at Rome (see
below). None were produced on the trials: there is only an indirect
mention of one, which seems to have fallen into the hands of Rich, and
which More explained in examination.

they chose out some bold, prompt, and zealous
adherents, whom they seduced, on the score of old
acquaintance, in familiar conversation ; and if they
found any inclined to their own evil opinion they dis-
gorged on them the gathered venom of their breasts.*
These doings went on among the vulgar everywhere ;
but the observant prince had traced them all to these
men of wondrous honesty, and had to shew against
them their handwriting, the letters which they had
sent hither and thither, and the confession of their
own lips. The case was as clear as daylight. These
and ever so many other causes had moved the most
just of princes to cast these rebellious and degenerate
subjects into chains and prisons, as ingrates to their
country, disturbers of the public peace, tumultuous,
impious, and seditious men. He would have been
wanting to his high office if he had allowed the con-
tagion to spread further. In prison they were treated
far better than they deserved. Their own chosen
servants were allowed to attend on them. The food,
the diet, and the clothing was provided for them which
those who were nearest to them by consanguinity, by
affinity, by descent, or by friendship judged best for
their constitution. And yet they persisted in opposing
laws which the public and unanimous assent and
consent of Parliament declared to be rightful, necessary,
and expedient. They gave their studies and cogita-
tions to this ; and as leaders of a very dangerous
sedition, they sought to elude, to reject, to perturb the
laws of the realm. Proofs most palpable were extant :
their own letters were extant, written with coal or
chalk (if such a thing ever happened that they had no

* Mr. Froude observes here that "many important facts are alluded to
in this letter, of which we have no other knowledge" (ii. 392). Yes, it is
even so.

ink); their letters which they sent secretly to one another; nor did they deny that they had put many letters into the fire, as the safest keeper of their wickedness : and in those letters which were burnt there was nothing but sedition.*

Such was the vindication of Henry, written by his minister. It is not often that an English monarch has found it needful to justify his rule before his sceptred compeers. Of the vindication itself the value will be weighed by the reader who compares with it the records of the trials, and who observes that it alleged the existence of a mass of evidence which was never produced, and of which no trace or incidental confirmation has ever been found; that it brought against the dead charges which were never made against the living; and that, after all, the charges which it brought were general.

But if the severities which were exercised on the upholders of the papal authority awakened animadversion abroad, the still more cruel execution of a large number of outlandish communists who had settled in England, which took place about the same time, met with general approbation at home. The Anabaptists, those terrible revolutionists who insisted too strongly on pushing the Reformation to its final tendency, began to be known in England about the year 1525, after the first decisive defeat which at the battle of Frankenhausen they sustained from the Protestant princes. But little is known concerning their doings in this country for ten years, when their increasing number and boldness drew the eyes of the Supreme Head upon them, and barbarous measures were taken

---

* Crumwel to Casale, *State Pap.*, vii. 633. There is more of it, but the residue seems only to contain that if the Pope on his part liked to kill some of the Cardinals, the King would have no objection.   Mr. Froude gives a good account of these letters of vindication.

to expel and exterminate them. Twenty-five of these sectaries, Hollanders by nation, nineteen men and six women, were carried to St. Paul's May 25, and examined there. Their opinions were that the baptism of infants was insignificant, but that sin wittingly committed after baptism (or, it may be supposed, rebaptism), was mortal; that the Sacrament of Christ's body was but bread: that children born of infidels may be saved; that Christ had not two natures, nor took flesh and blood of the Virgin Mary.* To these theological tenets they probably added the inconvenient conclusions which the disciples of Munzer and Buckhold generally drew, that there must be a visible theocratic kingdom of Christ, and that in the kingdom of Christ all must be equal, and have all things in common. Fourteen of them were condemned for heresy, of whom two were burnt in Smithfield, the other twelve were sent to other towns and burnt there. How they came to be apprehended by the ordinaries: by whom they were presented of heresy, by whom indicted, by whom accused, is unknown; but in the case of such detested sectaries there would have been no lack of willing informers; and the Hollanders may have drawn attention on themselves by some imprudent ostentation in the ceremony of rebaptism, by which they entered the visible kingdom of Christ. A royal Proclamation, issued between their condemnation and their death, assured them of the certainty of their impending sufferings; ordered those who had recanted, and all others who held like opinions, to depart out of the realm within twelve days on pain of death; and closed the ports in future against such dangerous invaders. All prelates, nobles, justices, mayors, sheriffs, bailiffs, and constables were commanded, at their uttermost peril,

* Stow, Ann. 571.

to use their good endeavours to apprehend all such offenders ; that they might from time to time suffer the pains of death.* They were put to a cruel death with the consent and applause of all men ; and their constancy in suffering excited as little compassion or admiration in the not unkindly heart of a Latimer as in the sterner bosom of a Stokesley. †

And now, the ground having been cleared by death, began the fall of the religious houses. A General Visitation, not a Visitation after the manner of those which had been held hitherto, not a Visitation to impose an oath or exact a subscription, but a General Visitation, to enquire into the morals and the money,

---

* Wilkins, iii. 779. This Proclamation says that they had "of their own presumption and authority lately rebaptised themselves." It speaks of a great number of them being then convicted, and ready to be executed. Wilkins, giving it from the Cleopatra MS. E. 5. fol. 357, puts it in 1534.

† Some years later, in the succeeding reign, Latimer alluded in one of his sermons to the persecution of the Anabaptists under Henry. "This is a deceivable argument : He went to his death boldly ; ergo, he standeth in a just quarrel. The Anabaptists that were burnt here in divers towns of England (as I heard of credible men, I saw them not myself), went to their death even intrepid, as ye will say, without any fear in the world, cheerfully. Well, let them go. There was in the old doctors' times another kind of poisoned heretics that were called Donatists ; and these heretics went to their execution as though they should have gone to some jolly recreation or banquet, to some belly-cheer, or to a play."—Park. Soc. ed. 160.

It is unfair to throw the blame of these atrocities on the bishops, as a popular historian has done. By the law of heresy, as it then stood, facilities had been given to laymen to present for heresy. Presentments might be made before sheriffs, who might then certify to the ordinaries : or two lawful witnesses might accuse a person to the ordinary at once. (See last chapter.) There is nothing to shew that the ordinaries procured the presentments, or were anxious to have the Anabaptists brought before them, though they were obliged to examine them when they were brought. In the intense abhorrence which those unhappy levellers aroused, it is at least possible that the presentments were made by laymen : and it is certain that the persecution was waged with the whole authority of the Supreme Head. In Crumwel's Memoranda we read, " First, touching the Anabaptists, and what the King will do with them."—*Ellis*, ii. 120. This was the year of the siege of Munster.

the virtues and the valuables of the religious, was
· organised under the ample powers of the Commission
of the Vicar General. When the scheme was first
propounded at a meeting of the Council, considerable
opposition was experienced. It seems to have been
resolved, however, to proceed with the undertaking, but
on the condition that no house should be surrendered
without the authority of Parliament : * a condition
which will be found to have been ill observed. There
are some traces of a design to confine the scrutiny to
such houses as were of royal foundation. It seems
also to have been resolved to defer the case of the
monasteries until a visitation should have been made
of the Universities. To suspend the ruling powers of
those little worlds, to take possession of their muniments, to abolish the study of the canon law, and to
cut down the scholastic tree in the very bed of her
growth, was a daring but prudent work, the well-planned
opening of a wider campaign. The execution was
committed in the main to two of Crumwel's most able
agents : Layton, whom we have met before in the
cloisters of Sion ; and Legh, a man who had been also
employed in the same kind of work, and who rivalled
Layton in the qualities which secured the favour of the
Vicar General. Legh indeed contrived to bring himself
under notice at this very moment.† His appropriate
province was assigned to each of these chosen instruments ; to Oxford was appointed the more sprightly
Layton, to Cambridge the more serious Legh.

---

* If the rhetorical exercises of Herbert have any foundation in fact.
See also Newcome's St. Albans, 432.

† Dr. Legh, who seems to have been on the swearing visitation at the
time, wrote to Crumwel, Sept. 3, advising him " well to consider whom
he sent to the Universities of Oxford and Cambridge, where either would
be found all virtue and goodness, or else the fountain of all vice and
mischief."—*Wright*, 66. Crumwel considered well, and sent Legh.

The turn of the more retrograde University came first, and in the beginning of September Layton was in his glory at Oxford. ¨We have set Duns in Bocardo,¨ he buoyantly wrote to Crumwel, ¨and have utterly banished him Oxford for ever, with all his blind glosses; and is now made a common servant to every man, fast nailed up upon posts at all common houses of easement: id quod oculis meis vidi. And the second time we came to New College, after we had declared your injunctions, we found all the great quadrant court full of the leaves of Duns, the wind blowing them into every corner. And there we found one Mr. Greenfield, a gentleman of Buckinghamshire, gathering up part of the said books' leaves (as he said), therewith to make him sewels or blawnsheres to keep the deer within the wood, thereby to have the better cry with his hounds.¨ He acknowledged that in several colleges he found lectures well kept and diligently frequented; but nevertheless he found some additions and alterations necessary. In place of the lecture in canon law, he and his fellows set up a civil lecture in every college, hall, and inn.* In Magdalen College they established a public lecture in Greek grammar; in New College and in All Souls two lectures, one in Greek and one in Latin; in Merton and in Queen's a public lecture in Latin. The poorer colleges they enjoined to frequent the lectures held in the richer, every student to hear one at least every day on pain of the loss of his commons. They found all men compliant; but virtue compelled them to deal more sternly with the students of the monastic colleges than with the rest. Them they forbade to come in any house within the town or suburbs,

---

* Perhaps his words mean that they added a civil lecture to the canon lecture, not that they enJoined it instead. ¨We have also in the place of the canon lecture, jonede (joined) a civil lecture.¨—*Wright*, 71. Bocardo was the name of the Oxford prison.

on pain of being sent home to the cloisters where they were professed. Greatly would this be lamented, said the chief Visitor, by the laundresses and the double honest women of the town ; without doubt those honest matrons would petition the Vicar General for redress. Such is the imperfect record of the first General Visitation ever made in Oxford by royal authority.*

The Academy of the Cam was crowded with scholars and students from every part of England, Wales, and Ireland : the confluence of nations engendered a variety and liberality of opinion : and the Vicar General himself was Chancellor of the University. In this hotbed of the early Gospellers, the foster mother of Barnes, Bilney, Latimer, and Cranmer, less strenuous measures of reform seem to have been needed than the setting of Duns in Bocardo ; and in a few days a single visitor was able to do all that was required. On the twenty-third of October, Dr. Legh issued his injunctions. The nations were admonished to cease their factions ; the heads of houses were ordered to surrender all their charters, donations, statutes, bulls, and papistical muniments, and to transmit a complete rental and inventory of all their effects to their Chancellor. But for the reformation of learning nothing more was enjoined than one public lecture to be instituted, which was to be either in Greek or in Hebrew, at the discretion of the authorities. In three days the colleges sent in their submis-

---

* Layton to Crumwel, *Supp. of Mon.*, 70, or in Strype, i. 322. Mr. Froude writes in this way : "Doubtless the visitors found Oxford a pleasant place, and cruelly they marred the enjoyments of it. Like a sudden storm of rain, they dropt down into its quiet precincts. Heedless of rights of fellows, &c., they poured new life into education. They founded fresh professorships—professorships of Polite Latin, professorships of Philosophy, Divinity, Canon Law, Natural Sciences—above all, of the dreaded Greek : confiscating funds to support them."—(ii. 421.) As to Philosophy, Divinity, and Natural Sciences, the visitors did not found a single lecture or professorship in any of them. As to canon law, their object was to discourage the study of it, not to found professorships of it.

sions; the muniments and statutes, the rentals, and inventories were collected and sent to Crumwel before Candlemas Day by the hands of the Vice-Chancellor and the Senior Proctor. In the keeping of the Vicar General they remained about a year, when they were returned unaltered to the University.*

To the genius of Doctor Legh must be ascribed the first step taken towards the dissolution of the religious houses of this country; but he must be content to share the honour with Ap Rice, another of Crumwel's more eminent instruments, who was a public notary. The first step taken was to suspend the authority of the bishops. This was suggested to Crumwel by Legh and Ap Rice.

In accordance with their recommendation, a Prohibitory Letter in the King's name was sent to the Archbishops, September 18, to forbid the bishops to visit any monastery or church, or their clergy, or to exercise any act of jurisdiction during the proposed visitation, upon pain of contempt. This Letter was sealed with the seal which the Supreme Head used for ecclesiastical causes.† In transmitting it to his episcopal brethren, Cranmer added some further monitions from his own pen. They were to be careful about their preaching and bidding of prayers, and to remember the orders which they had received of late to declare the usurped jurisdiction of the Pope; and they were to certify him of all that they had done in those behalfs. It would seem that the bishops made some sort of

---

* Fuller's *Hist. of Camb.* 109—18. He says that there had been a previous visitation by the King, in which many alterations were made, such as the establishment of lectures in the tongues, &c. : and that Legh's Injunctions were merely additional.

† "In cujus rei testimonium has præsentes litteras inde fieri, et sigitli nostri, quo ad causas ecclesiasticas utimur, appensione communiri curavimus."—*Wilkins*, iii. 797.

remonstrance; and then Legh and Ap Rice wrote
jointly to their master the singularly impudent letter
from which it appears that they had been the authors
of the suspension.   It had seemed good to them,
said they, to stop the jurisdiction of the bishops, lest
the bishops, if they enjoyed it without interruption,
should think that they held it elsewhere than from the
King.   The bishops were ingrate; it was necessary to
make them acknowledge the author, spring, and fountain of their power.   The bishops were not perhaps
impudent enough to say that their jurisdiction rested
on the law of God; but if they said so, let them bring
forth Scripture.   If they said that it rested on the
Bishop of Rome, let them exercise it, if they thought
well.   If, however, they acknowledged that it came
from the King, why were they discontent that the
King had resumed what he had given?   In truth, let
them say what they might, they referred their jurisdiction to some other source than the King's authority, or
they would not grudge.   If they claimed it as their
right, let them shew their evidence: if they took it as
a benefit from the King, let them sue for it by supplication.   Meanwhile they might exercise necessary things,
if they could shew any *

The fall of a great institution, brought about in
this petty way, would be a more memorable example
of the mutability of human things if the country in
which it took place had been a free country.   But it
was not.   England, free heretofore and free hereafter,

* Legh and Ap Rice to Crumwel, Sept. 24, Strype, ii. 216.   As
Cranmer did not send the Inhibition till October 2, the remonstrance
of the bishops must have been caused by a knowledge of what was
coming, not by the Inhibition itself.   Legh and Ap Rice wrote their
letter of Sept. 24 to fortify their master with reasons, because they
thought that "the Bishops would be in hand with him *again* touching the
inhibitions."

was passing through an interval of slavery. At the moment when the authority of the bishops was suspended, all the other institutions of the kingdom were suspended. The Parliament at that moment accepted a prorogation without a murmur. Everything was in abeyance, except the operations of Crumwel, and the creatures whom Crumwel had fostered into being. The King himself consented to become for the time the puppet of Crumwel, as completely as the seal which he used for ecclesiastical causes. There is not in history so memorable an example of the greatest interests being put in a corner and destroyed by the vilest means as the fall of the English monasteries. Crumwel remembered now that his Commission to be Vicar General allowed him to choose his deputies. He chose them. The realm was divided into districts apportioned to a set of officials whose obscure names are not all known to this day. Their commissions for their important work were not under the Great Seal, but only under the King's hand and signet. But, obscure as they may be, they wrought a greater change in English society than the greatest hero or the mightiest poet that ever fought or sung; and the names of Doctor Bedyl, Doctor Layton, Doctor Legh, Doctor London, Doctor Petre, Robert Southwell, Richard Southwell, John Gage, Elias Price, John Ap Rice, Richard Bellasis, William Hendle, and all others that can be recovered from the gulf of time, ought to be had in everlasting remembrance. As soon as they were appointed they sped ; and before the year had ended the monasteries began to fall beneath their hands.

The death of the unfortunate Pontiff who had been troubled with the divorce of the King of England, and the prudent election of a liberal and learned successor, seemed to breathe new life into the Catholic cause.

Paul the Third signalised his accession by acts which promised the pacification of Christendom. The group of illustrious scholars with whom he surrounded himself added dignity to the throne of Christendom. It had been usual hitherto, when the Conclave met for the election of a pope, that every cardinal should swear that, if he were chosen, he would indict without delay a general council. In the election of Paul this ceremonious falsehood was omitted; but he of his own will undertook the task from which his predecessors had excused or absolved themselves. His legate Vergerius traversed Germany, and appeared even in the city and presence of Luther; and a conference was held, in which was displayed, according to the various accounts, the brutal ignorance and audacity, or the intrepid humour and calm constancy, of the heresiarch. Luther accepted the proposal of a Council, to be held in Mantua, the place not unfitly fixed by the Pope.* The Catholic princes gave their consent: the Protestants in their meeting at Smalcald shewed themselves neither adverse nor intractable; and France advised Germany to admit the Primacy of the Pontiff.† But the pacification of Christendom entered not into the desires of the King of England. When the general council was proposed by the new Pope, Henry signified that he would not object, provided that the bishops and prelates who went to it were of his own way of thinking;‡ and this simple tyranny prevailed to defeat the whole project. He had his ambassadors now at Smalcald, though he had long hesitated to send them; at the head of whom

* Mantua, once a free city of the Empire, had lately been made a duchy. Sleidan, Lib. ix.

† Strype, i. 347.

‡ "Qui ad Consilium nomine Episcoporum et Prelatorum deputandi sunt, ejusmodi constituantur, qui sine ullo negotio nostris partibus favere velint," &c.—Henry to Casalis, Dec. 6, *State Pap.* vii. 636.

was Edward Fox, now Bishop of Hereford; through whom he gave advice to the Protestant League which may claim the eminence of having hindered the last chance of the reconciliation of the world. "The expedient of a council," said he, "would prove unfortunate, if the Pope were master of the dispute; since it was his interest to support his exorbitant pretences by holding princes at variance : a council would be useless unless the peace of Europe were better settled. But he had another proposition to make. Let the Protestants come to an unity of doctrine with the English Church. The difference of opinion was the cause of confusions in the state; of which the Anabaptists had been of late a lamentable instance : the present juncture called loudly for an end of differences. To bring the matter to a point, let them choose a commission of fit men to confer with him." The Germans returned at first an answer in which these overtures were treated coldly. "They were the less sensible," they replied, "of the evils of disunion, in that they were all adherents of the Augsburg Confession : as to the Anabaptists, they knew how to punish that incorrigible sect. To themselves, whose chief aim and object was to spread the Gospel, it was welcome news that the King had delivered England from the Pope." They agreed that the Pope had no privilege to proclaim or hold the proposed council without the consent of the other princes : but said that they would declare their sentence on this more fully hereafter According to this promise, the negotiations took the definite form of conditions for a treaty, which the Germans offered to the King. They required the Defender of the Faith to accept the title of Defender of their League; to assist them in their wars with a large sum of money, and to enter into an engagement for mutual defence in case of invasion; and to receive the Augsburg Confession, with the latitude of alterations to be made by common consent: as to the council, they declared their opinion that if a free and indifferent council were proposed by the Pope's Legate, it should not be refused: but, if the Pope persisted in maintaining exorbitant claims, they should reject and dissent in some public way, and the King join them in a free council: and that the common opinion of the Primacy of the Pope should be denied. On these terms they were ready to treat with the King by a select commission.*

The German conditions were sent by Crumwel to Gardiner, who held the difficult post of ambassador in France; and on this occasion the ablest of the English prelates shewed his ability. "You are asked," said he, "to receive the Augustan Confession; what would that be but to bind England to the sense of Germany, and to bring the Word of God under conditions? Of this the Bishop of Rome on his part would not fail to take advantage. You are asked to make a contract: but there is no equality between the contracting parties. On the one hand there is the King of England, who is the Head of his own Church; on the other hand are none but dukes and other subordinate personages, the head of whose Church is the Emperor. How can they pretend to stipulate on points of religion without his concurrence? They make proposals about a council, but their proposals seem very much embarrassed. They say that they would accept a council proposed by the Legate; but that implies the consent of the Emperor: but why should the King of England, who owns no dependence on the Emperor, put himself in the position of

* Sleidan, Lib. ix. s. fin., Lib. x.; Collier, i. 110; Waddington's Reformn. iii. 186.

accepting a council because the Emperor had consented to it? And if, after the consent of the Emperor had been given, they found the council not managed according to their mind, how could they hinder, and expect the King of England to hinder, an assembly that had been called by their own sovereign?"* The immediate effect of these cogent arguments is not known; but they may have had their weight in preventing at the time what has never taken place—the union of England and Germany in a common confession.

Meanwhile the English ambassadors, Fox, Hethe, and Barnes, retired to Wittemberg for the rest of the winter, and held long debates with the theologians of that celebrated city. But the ambassadors of England lacked the consummate sweetness of Germany.† They laboured in vain to bring about a concord of doctrine between England and the League, the points of irreconcilable difference being the clerical celibate, the Supper of the Lord, the Pontifical Mass, the monastic vows, and, above all, the King's Divorce. Here the English made no impression, though they set forth the variations and duplicity of the late Pope with the fullest eloquence. The utmost that the Germans would allow was that the King had great causes for what he had done. "Say rather very just causes," exclaimed the English; but the Germans shook their heads.‡ At length the King's answer to the terms of the proposed treaty

---

* Collier, Records, No. 34 ; Strype, ii. 236.

† Melanchthon seems to have had a low opinion of the English ambassadors. Hethe, he said, had some savour of religion and learning, but scarce any of them else. "Nicholas Hethe, the Archdeacon, alone excels in humanity and learning among our guests. As for the rest of them, they have no relish of our philosophy and sweetness."—*Strype*, i. 351.

‡ "Judgment of the Lutheran Divines on the Divorce," Burn. Collect., Bk. ii. No. xxxv. See also Strype, i. 354.

arrived. The conditions pleased him, if a few things could be altered. "As for invasion," he said truly, "he had none to fear. His repudiated wife was dead; and with her was buried every terror, if any terror there had been, that made him afraid: but still, for the sake of the truth, he would not refuse them the money that they asked: for the title of Patron and Defender which they offered him, he gave them thanks, nor would he decline it, provided that they could come to a harmony of doctrine, for otherwise it would not be very honorific to him. He was desirous, therefore, that the learned on both sides should meet in conference to soften certain topics in their Confession or Apology; and he again requested them to send their embassage to him, including some person of pre-eminent learning, to go through the whole controversy, and bring things to a temper." * After some deliberation the Confederation agreed to despatch an embassy into England, on the understanding that nothing should be done to the prejudice of their allegiance to the Emperor. Jacob Sturmius was chosen their ambassador; the divines associated with him were Melanchthon, Bucer, and George Draco. They set forth on their journey: but a new turn in the domestic fortunes of Henry, the disgrace and death of Anne Boleyn, retarded, or rather disconcerted, the proposed alliance.†

---

* See the Answer, Strype, ii. 239.

† Sleidan, Lib. x.; Collier, i. 116. Cf. Laurence's Bampton Lect. 195. An attempt to get Melanchthon to England had been made the year before, in 1534.

CHAPTER V.

END OF A.D. 1535 : A.D. 1536.

THE monastic institution in England was coeval and for a time coextensive with the English Church. Those who converted the English kingdoms to Christianity were monks. The first bishops, the first priests, of the Church were monks : and the missionary stations which were first planted in the midst of the Teutonic heathenism were monasteries. But, as Christianity spread, a difference arose in the condition of those who professed to teach it, which the process of time rendered greater and more ineffaceable. It became impossible for all of them to remain inmates of colleges or monasteries. The thegns and franklins, as they were converted, began to build and endow churches on their estates. For these benefices they required a resident clergy ; and the clergymen who went to reside on them, though at first no more than the chaplains of the landowners, became the parochial clergy of England, whose successors remain to the present day. Although of the monastic train, they soon became developed, by the necessity of living among the people, into a body of men not unlike to those who occupy their room. They appear to have rejected the monastic rigour, and held themselves free to marry wives. Celibacy, on the other hand, remained the glory of the cloister; and the discipline of the convent embraced the other sex. As the two systems proceeded in their development, a vast number of abbeys were founded by the various royal families of the kingdoms on the one hand; and on the other hand the churches were formed into the present constitution of rural deaneries and archdeaconries in every diocese.

The Danish invasions, which almost obliterated the monasteries, raised the differences between the secular and the regular clerks to the height of hostility. When the first fury of those terrific inroads was abated, the shattered piles which had been raised by the former piety were re-edified, after a desolation of near two hundred years, and new foundations were laid by the great princes whose arts and arms restored the shaken frame of England. But the parish churches had sprung to life again more speedily; and while the very name of monk was still almost forgotten, the secular priest was again performing his duties, were it but in edifices built with wattles and thatched with straw. The rising monasteries were therefore filled with secular canons instead of regulars; of whom many, it is believed, were married men, and many continued to hold parochial cures, while they took up their abode within the monastic precincts. But the old discipline, which seemed to be dying out, was suddenly revived by the exertions of King Eadger the Peaceful and the Archbishops Odo and Dunstan. The severe rules of foreign monasteries were adopted or imitated by those zealous reformers: the secular intruders were expelled, or compelled to put away their wives and resign their cures: and the monastic institution rose again in awful and ascetic dignity. Under the Vicar of Christ (for so the King of England called himself then) the same sweeping allegations of immorality and crime were brought against the secular canons, which under the familiar management of the Supreme Head were to be repeated in turn against the regulars.* Those charges had but a slender foundation perhaps in either case: in the former they amounted, it is probable, to little more than that the seculars were married men.

In the long struggles which followed, the regulars were displaced by the seculars, and the seculars by the regulars alternately down to the twelfth century. After the Conquest the contest was waged chiefly in the Cathedral chapters. The bishops who were appointed were usually seculars; more than half of the Cathedral chapters or convents were monkish: and it was observed that whenever a secular bishop was appointed over a Cathedral chapter of monks, great quarrels ensued. The greatest difference, however, had now disappeared, and celibacy was the universal lot of the clergy. The period of the great growth of the monasteries lay between the Conquest and the accession of the Lancastrian dynasty. The foreign orders of monks, to which every impulse of piety gave birth, arrived in succession to swell the number of the religious; and it seemed as if the invasion of Cluniacs, Cistercians, Carthusians, and the military orders of the Hospitallers and the Templars, together with the prodigious increase of the original Benedictines and Augustines, might absorb, or at least straighten and impoverish, the Church. The monks succeeded in gaining possession of a great number of benefices: in the various and indescribable mutations of property they obtained advowsons, presentations, and gifts of tithe and glebe innumerable, by charters from the Pope, with the license of the King in Chancery, and with

---

* "Vitiosiorum cuneos canonicorum a diversis nostri regiminis Cœnobiis Christi Vicarius eliminavi," are the words of King Eadger. Spelman, Conc. i. 438.

the consent of the bishop : and these changes, which were the origin of vicarages, were not advantageous to the secular clergy. The minister who served the monastic appropriations might be a secular, but he occupied a poor position. He was sometimes a mere chaplain, removable at will ; or, if he were perpetual, he was nevertheless miserably paid. When, in the reign of Richard the Second, the legislature interfered to secure that "the vicar be well and sufficiently endowed," the monasteries evaded the law by filling the vicarages with members of their own bodies ; and it was not before the accession of the Lancastrian dynasty that the scale was turned in favour of the Church by a statute forbidding vicarages to be filled by any but secular clergymen.*. When the Reformation came on it had been ordered by Convocation (as we have seen) that the abuses of monastic appropriations should be investigated and amended.

The great religious movement of the thirteenth

---

* In his Account of Iffley, the Rev. E. Marshall gives in a few sentences a clear account of the intricate subject of the monastic appropriations. There were many authorities engaged in such transferrence of property. "To make an appropriation by which the tithes of a parish were transferred to a spiritual corporation was a practice of early date. The monastic institutions were eager to obtain such a transferrence, as it was a source of considerable revenue. To effect it, they were in the habit of obtaining the patronage of such churches as they were able, as a necessary step. But in order to the appropriation of these, the permission of the Pope, as well as the license of the King and of the bishop, who both had an interest in the church in the case of lapse, was required, and who were supposed to be the best guardians of the general advantages of the parish. The consent of the patron was also implied. As an appropriation was originally made to a spiritual corporation alone, this provided the services of an officiating minister, who acted as capellane, and was removable at will. But afterwards, as there arose many abuses from such a provision, the legislature interfered by statutes of 15 R. II. 6, and 4 H. IV. 12. The former of these secured a proper maintenance for the minister, and his permanence, and the latter ensured that he should be one of the secular clergy."— P. 60.

century, from which arose the various orders of the Friars, was unfavourable to the cause which it might have been expected to aid, and less adverse than it seemed to the cause which it might have been held likely to weaken. The monks welcomed with loud lamentations the appearance of rivals who undersold them in the mart of piety : but the parish priests, even though they disliked them as interlopers, found in them auxiliaries. Instead of fixing themselves in the country like the Cistercians, the most grasping of the religious orders, the Friars built their houses in the towns : and there were few large towns which did not contain the establishments of two or three of their orders. Instead of appropriating the lands around them, the Friars demanded no more than was sufficient to furnish their own precinct. Their wandering preachers found their way into the pulpits of the churches, and gave to the parochial system an elasticity which it needed, and which it has lost since their fall. This was a benefit which may have atoned for many irritations, such as the intrusion of a religious mendicant into a parish, with pretended power of absolution beyond the curate, and his domineering presence at the country gatherings. But still it is probable that the parson had often a greater jealousy of the friar whose " limit" or begging district embraced his parish, than he had of the monk who built granges or set up tanneries on his glebe, who absorbed the best of his tithes, who diverted benefactions from him, but who never interfered with his professional duties. If it were possible to compare things so unlike as the ancient religious orders and the modern sectarians, the monks might be said to represent in some degree the Congregational principle, and the Friars the principle of centralisation on which Methodism is formed. The

several houses of the monkish orders had little more
to do with one another than one Baptist or Independent chapel has with another. Each order had, it is
true, a general chapter; but these were held at very
distant and irregular intervals, and there are instances
on record in which the summons to attend them was
resisted by particular houses. Unless a house had
cells, or smaller monasteries subordinate to it, it stood
unconnected with any other house. On the other
hand, the Friars, like the Methodists, were governed
from a common centre : the various houses of one of
their orders formed what was called a Congregation,
and were subject to the authority of a Provincial.
They possessed therefore a common government, and
had all the power of action and of motion which a
common government bestows. But however much
the various kinds of the religious societies may have
differed among themselves in their principles of association, in the position which they held towards the
Church of England they were the same. They were
free societies within the Church : they were also part
of the spiritual estate of the realm : nor could they
have been the one unless they had been the other.
As they arrived and obtained a footing in the land,
they found themselves embraced in the communion of
the Church, from which indeed there was no discrepancy of doctrine or theory to separate them. The
rivalry between them and the secular clergy was
wholly different from the contentions between con-
formists and separatists which arose afterwards.
Collectively they far outnumbered the clergy : in the
proportion perhaps of ten to one ; and several of their
orders, as the Benedictines, might have been able to
boast with probability that as many clerical men of
various grades were gathered under their single stan-

dard as served beneath all the banners of the Church. The points of intercourse and union between the two great systems were numerous. Many bishops were heads of monastic houses. Many monastic houses that were governed by their own heads were not exempt from the jurisdiction of bishops. More abbots than bishops sat in the House of Lords and in the Upper House of Convocation. As many priors sat in the Lower House of Convocation as deans, archdeacons, and proctors of the clergy. Many of the clergy had been trained in the monastic schools, or had been at one time inmates of the monastic houses. A large number of foundations existed under the names of Chantries and Collegiate Churches, which may be said to have held an intermediate position between the regular and the secular system, since they were founded, like the monasteries, for the purpose of praying for the dead, or resembled the monasteries in discipline, though consisting of secular canons. Above all, the prevalent obligation of celibacy tended to diminish the differences which existed between regulars and seculars.

Between the Conquest and the accession of the Lancastrian dynasty, during the reigns of twelve kings, nearly nine hundred houses of monks or of friars were founded,* which, along with those that were in exist-

---

* According to Tanner's Preface, there were founded, under William I., 45 monasteries; under Rufus, 25; under Henry I., 150; Stephen, 122; Henry II., 124; Richard I., 44; John, 62; under Henry III., 74 monasteries and 83 friaries; under Edward I., 16 monasteries and 61 friaries; Edward II., 5 monasteries and 20 friaries; Edward III., 7 monasteries and 24 friaries; Richard II., 4 monasteries and 4 friaries. In all 870 houses, of which 192 were friaries. Besides these there were colleges and hospitals, of which, according to the same authority, there were 78 and 192 respectively, founded within the same period: many of the colleges were monastic. In the succeeding period, from Henry IV. to Henry VIII., there were only about eight religious houses founded: of which the most

ence previously, made up a total number of about twelve hundred. But their prosperity had ceased long before the hour of their destruction arrived. From the time of Henry the Fourth the stream of benefaction was diverted from them : and while colleges and public schools were planted in numbers and magnificence, the scanty sum of six or seven foundations of monks and friars in the course of one hundred and thirty years bore witness to the change of the inclinations of the nation. Nor must it be supposed that the religious houses had been suffered to remain unmolested in the enjoyment of their possessions at any time. In their most flourishing days they were never in peace : when they acquired most, they were never free from the hand of the spoiler. One of the most constant characters assigned to good abbots in the monkish chronicles is that they were strenuous defenders of the goods of their houses : to bad abbots that they wasted or suffered the goods to be wasted. The goods needed to be strenuously defended. The people of towns, or the neighbouring landowners, often encroached. Those who held leases sometimes claimed the land which they held as their own, under the Mortmain Acts ; or sometimes absolutely refused to yield possession. In all disputes the monks shrunk from a trial by jury, and often chose to suffer loss rather than encounter the adverse feeling which was sure to be manifested against them. A bad abbot, a false treasurer or cellarer, might bring his house to beggary, or even to dissolution, by corruptly leasing or granting away

notable were the Carthusian Shene, and the Brigitite Sion, by Henry V. Henry VII. founded a few houses of Observants, which Henry VIII. began his career as a sacrilegist by plucking up. On the other hand, the same period in which monasticism declined was distinguished by the founding of about sixty colleges, hospitals and schools.

the domains. Debts were often incurred, and had to be met by alienating or selling land ; and houses were sometimes so reduced by accumulated liabilities that they were sold to private purchasers.* To private difficulties and causes of labefaction, such as these, must be added several notable measures of confiscation which took place within the same limits of time. Under King John all the priories alien, as those were called which were cells or dependencies of continental abbeys, to the number of eighty-one, were sequestrated, and their yearly revenues taken for the King's necessities. Under Edward the First the same communities, which then numbered nearly one hundred, were seized again during a war with France ; and, lest their monks should be of any assistance to his enemies, the King moved them twenty miles from the sea-board. On the pretext of every new French war the same process of sequestration was repeated by the following sovereigns, and the revenues of the sequestrated houses went to pay the army, until by Henry the Fifth they were finally suppressed, part of their possessions being bestowed on other monasteries and on schools, and part being granted or sold, though not in perpetuity, to the laity. The dissolution of the Templars, which fell in the reign of Edward the Second, was an event which in the rest of Europe was accompanied by incredible horrors. In England it seems to have been unattended with cruelty, but to have been complete. The establishments of the order, which bore the name of preceptories, to the number of twenty-three, were at first seized by the King and other lords, but afterwards, by a bull from the Pope and an Act of Parliament,

---

* Some curious instances of these difficulties are given by the author of the article in the Home and Foreign Review, Jan. 1864, to which I have already referred, and am much indebted.

transferred to the rival order of the Hospitallers. But the latter were obliged to resign the greater part of this splendid grant in order to preserve the remainder, a policy which afterwards became common enough with ecclesiastical corporations in the time of the general suppressions ; and most of the possessions of the Templars vanished into the more useful, or less useful, obscurity of private ownership. In a later instance of alteration, the well-known design of Wolsey to divert some part of the conventual revenues to education involved the suppression of twenty-four of the smaller religious houses. The diversion of property from one pious use to another was different from unchecked and aimless spoliation ; and similar schemes had been entertained before by great ecclesiastics : by William of Wickham, by Waynflete, or by Fisher. But the scheme of Wolsey, being entrusted to the management of Crumwel, was carried out with great corruption, waste, and " abomination."* Altogether, between private ruin and open confiscation, out of the twelve hundred religious houses of which record remains, not more than from six to seven hundred awaited the final catastrophe of the great suppression.

The cupidity which is the least acknowledged but most active agent of human revolutions had been inflamed by the prospect of the wealth of the religious houses, which, however, was vastly exaggerated in every recital. The more fantastic indeed the reckoning, the more boundless the credulity with which it was received. The happiest libel of the day was the famous Supplication of Beggars, written by one Simon Fish. In this diatribe it might have been supposed that the rivals of the infirm beggars, in whose person the author wrote,

---

* Such is the term applied to it in Darcy's Articles against Wolsey, see p. 48 of this work.

would have been those strong and valiant mendicants the friars and none other: but the outcries of the beggars were made to involve not only the friars but the whole spiritualty in the same condemnation; and in their bederoll, with a not unpopular confusion of speech, the spiritualty were described as "bishops, abbots, priors, deacons, archdeacons, suffragans, priests, monks, canons, friars, pardoners, and summoners." These heterogeneous personages, the writer asserts, had gotten into their hands more than a third part of the realm; a computation the value of which may be judged from this, that it rested on the astounding assertion that there were fifty-two thousand parish churches in England.* He then goes on to say that the sum total of the possessions of the spiritualty was nearer one-half than a third of the realm. In the next sentence he runs it up to one-half: and asks with natural indignation why they should have one-half and the laity no more than the other half, seeing that they were to the laity but in the numerical proportion of one to four hundred. How iniquitous that they should have half, when if they had but the four-hundredth part of half they should have too much, since they did nothing for it! But after all, his quarrel seems to be with the friars; and he computes the gains of those extortionate rivals of his clients from his own premises. There were fifty-two thousand parishes in England: each parish had on an average ten households; each household

---

* Sir T. More's comment on the fifty-two thousand parishes is good: "That is one plain lie to begin with." *Suppl. of Poor Souls.* Fox's vindication of the author is not unamusing: that perhaps in those days there were maps which set down the parishes at that number: but at any rate, whether more or less, the friars got more than they should have had: for they should have had nothing at all. More confuted Fish's fables most elaborately, step by step, paragraph after paragraph; but the Book of Beggars did its work nevertheless, and for one who read More, it is likely that a hundred read Fish.

gave a penny a quarter to the friars; the friars had five orders, each order got a penny a quarter: a penny a quarter, multiplied by quarters, orders, and households, gave a total sum of four hundred and thirty thousand three hundred and thirty-three pounds, six shillings and eightpence. The friars then, according to Simon Fish, got by begging more in a year than the whole revenue of the spiritualty, and more by half than the revenue of all the monasteries: for, according to the Valor Ecclesiasticus of Henry the Eighth, the revenue of the whole of the spiritualty was no more than three hundred and twenty thousand pounds, of which the monasteries had about half!* But the inflamed readers of the Supplication of Beggars would argue that if the unendowed friars got by beggary nearly half a million sterling a year, the endowed monks and clergy must have a great deal more, even the half of the kingdom. Such were the surmises that were in the air when the hour struck that bade the monasteries be dissolved.

The general visitation of the monasteries began with the month of October in the year 1535.† The visitors went sometimes singly, sometimes in pairs, in greater numbers at other times; commingling and disparting their mazy dance in obedience to some law not easy to be discovered. From their eagerness in soliciting the Vicar General for warrants to visit houses, it would

---

* The valuation of Henry, as we have seen already, made the whole revenue of the spiritualty 320,280*l.* 10*s.* (Speed). The share of the monasteries in this is put by Tanner (Nasmith) at 142,914*l.* 12*s.* 9¾*d.* This omits the lesser houses, of which we have no details : but they could not have made much difference. According to the writer in the Home and Foreign Review, 10,000*l.* would cover them. Tanner seems to have put the whole share of the monasteries too high. See above, p. 250.

† It must be dated from the Inhibition or suspension of the power of the bishops, October 2. But nothing was done till the end of the month.

seem that they were paid by the piece; and, so long at least as they were in the nearer counties, their zeal seems to have been tempered, their prudence encouraged, and their honesty confirmed by the presence of some servant of the household of the Vicar General. On these terms their services were great and rapid. They visited a great many houses in the four months which elapsed between their first setting out and the meeting of Parliament; and even without the authority of Parliament, or any authority whatever beyond their commission under the signet ring of the Supreme Head, they procured the surrender of seven houses at least, four of which were in the single county of Kent. Nay, more; although making the greatest allowance for their activity, they could not have visited all nor half of the monasteries in England, yet they are said to have been able to present such a report to Parliament of the abominable state of the monasteries in general, as led to the downfall of all the smaller houses throughout the realm. These are achievements which raise that first portion of the visitation which elapsed before the meeting of Parliament and the passing of the Act about the lesser monasteries to the dignity of a separate part of the drama.

The first county that was visited was Kent,* where the visitors were the now experienced Layton

---

* There is much difficulty in determining the extent and order of this momentous visitation. I suppose that it cannot have begun earlier than the last part of October, 1535, and in that case the first county visited was Kent. But there are records of a visitation in Oxford and elsewhere that was going on in August: and the letters of the visitors there, of whom one was Layton, are put by Mr. Wright (in the Suppression of Monasteries) under the year 1535. I am inclined with some hesitation to think they may belong to 1536; but at all events I think that they do not refer to the same kind of visitation as this under which the first surrenders occurred. It must be remembered that there were several visitations of different kinds going on at the same time. For instance, there

and Bedyl: and the law on which they acted seems to have been this: Layton visited a house a few days before Bedyl, and made an inventory of the goods and chattels ; Bedyl visited a house a few days after Layton, and took, or at least tendered, a surrender. The Præmonstratensian Priory of Langdon was visited October 23 by Layton, who sent to his master a ludicrous account of the skilful manner in which he caught that dangerous, desperate, and hardy knave, the abbot, in the company of his gentlewoman, or tender damozel. Layton's letters are always sprightly. He left Crumwel's servant, Bartolet, with some other men to guard the outer apertures and starting holes, of which the abbey was as full as a coney clapper ; and alone advanced he against the abbot's door. Long he knocked, and heard but the little dog that barked within ; so seizing a short poleaxe that lay there, he dashed the door in pieces and entered. The lady fled to her starting holes, but only to be captured by Bartolet. Her apparel was found in a chest. No other discovery was made. The abbot was brought on by Layton himself to Christchurch in Canterbury, and there put in prison ; the unfortunate damozel was sent to cage in Dover under the escort of Bartolet, a pretty fellow for the charge; and the visitor could only think that he had been inspired by Heaven to make that sudden search at the

is a letter from Audley to Crumwel, of Sept. 26, 1535 (State Papers, i. 450), in which it is said that Dr. Legh had been appointed " substitute to visit all the religious houses in the diocese of London." But there is no proof whatever that a single house in the diocese of London was visited as Layton and Bedyl visited Kent, until long afterwards : and the date of the letter seems too early for it to relate to the great visitation. I rather think that Legh at that time was put on the swearing visitation (that the Bishop of Rome was not Pope, &c.), not on the surrendering or smashing visitation. We have seen enough of the swearing visitation already ; but it went grinding on for some years. Legh was afterwards transferred to the smashing visitation.

beginning, because it would now appear to the country and the Commons that the visitations and deprivations were made upon substantial grounds.* A fortnight later the unlucky abbot, whose name was William Dayer, was brought back to his house, and there he and his convent in chapter assembled, alleging for the cause not moral depravity, but poverty and debt, surrendered to the King as their founder their priory, their lands, their bondmen, their advowsons and presentations, and all their other possessions. Three days later, November 16, they came together again in the presence of the Visitor Bedyl, and acknowledged their instrument of surrender.† The active Bedyl rode the same day to Folkestone and to Dover, and took the

* Wright, 75. What sort of a villain Bartolet, Bartelot, or Bartlett was may be judged from the infamous story—infamous in whatever way it be taken—which he has penned against himself.—Ib. p. 59. The glory of the surprisal at Langdon, or the disgrace of the discovery, or both, may perhaps be lessened by the consideration that there seem to have been some others of Crumwel's men, one of them named Anthony, staying in the house. They, as innocently as the rest of the inmates, wondered what fellow Layton was.

† Rym. Fœd. xiv. 555. The enumeration of their possessions in the surrender may be given ; it doubtless served as a formula in many other cases. " Dedimus et concessimus, ac per præsentes damus, concedimus, reddimus, ac deliberamus Illustrissimo Principi Domino nostro, H. 8, Dei gratia Angliæ et Franciæ Regi, Fidei Defensori, et Domino Hiberniæ, et in terris Supremo Capiti Ecclesiæ Anglicanæ, ac Fundatori et Patrono nostro et dicti Prioratus sive Monasterii ; dictum Monasterium s. Prioratum, ac omnia et singula Maneria, terras et Tenementa nostra, Prata, Pascua, Pasturas, Boscos, Redditus, Reversiones, Servitia, Molendina, Passagia, Villanos, Warda, Maritagia, Communia, Libertates, Jurisdictiones, Letos, Hundreda, Vis. Franc. Pleg. Feria, Parca, Warenna, Vivaria, Mercata, Advocationes, Nominationes, et Præsentationes Ecclesiarum, Vicariarum, Capellarum, Cantariarum, et aliorum Ecclesiasticorum Beneficiorum quorumcunque, Pensiones, Portiones, Annuitates, Decimas, Oblationes, Elimosinas, et omnia et singula Emolumenta, Prosicua, Possessiones, Hæreditamenta, et Jura nostra quæcunque infra Regnum Angliæ, et alibi infra Dominia dicti Domini Regis situata, jacentia, seu existentia : ac omnia Bona et Catalla nostra tam realia quam personalia, Debita et Jura nostra quæcunque, ac omnimoda Cartas, Evi-

surrenders of the Benedictine Priories there. The
inventories of those houses had been taken before by
the no less active Layton, on the same day that he
visited Langdon. Bedyl was accompanied by one
Polsted, and by Crumwel's servant, John Anthony; an
illustrious triumvirate, who in the joint letter which they
wrote to their master reported well of the houses of
Folkestone and Dover, which they found in good repair
and in good repute, but which nevertheless they tried
to dissolve. They gave the monks leave to depart, and
most of them, they said, desired capacities or licences
to depart to be granted to them, though some desired
to be assigned to other places of religion, and in the
meantime all remained in their houses. Their report
was concluded with a very pious wish for the preservation of their patron in good health.*

Meantime Layton, on the day following his visitation of Langdon, had proceeded to inspect Cranmer's
see, or Cathedral convent of Christchurch in Canterbury, October 23. That noble foundation, the mother
church and mother monastery of England, had always
been the centre of the opposition between regulars and
seculars; but never had that opposition risen higher
there than in the days of Cranmer. If regular chapters always quarrelled with secular bishops, much more
the Benedictines of Christchurch quarrelled with the
reforming upstart whom Crumwel and Henry had set

dentias, Scripta, et Munimenta dicto Monasterio s. Prioratui, Maneriis,
Terris et Tenementis cum cæteris præmissis pertinentia, spectantia,
sive concernentia."

* Wright, 88. It is amusing to notice the different degrees of fami-
liarity toward "their dread commander" in the subscriptions of the
visitors to their letters. Bedyl is to Crumwel "Your own;" Layton,
"Your own assured poor priest and servant;" Legh, "Your own assured."
The smaller fry are, "Your servant," or "Your bedesmen," or "Your
orator." They are fond of invoking benedictions on their benefactor.

at their head, after a smuggled consecration held in
Westminster, not in their own church; who adorned
his office neither by birth nor wealth; and who, instead
of defending them like an Arundel, a Chicheley, or
even a Warham, seemed sent among them for the very
purpose of breaking down their privileges and letting in
the spoiler on their goods. The faint murmur of many
misunderstandings alone survives; but there seems to
have been no open explosion before this visit of Layton.
The Archbishop, who introduced the visitor, took the
opportunity of preaching a sermon in the Cathedral
Church on the allotted subject of the Supreme Head
and the Bishop of Rome. The scene may be imagined:
the Archbishop in the pulpit; the dangerous guest
posted in some conspicuous place;* the fifty or sixty
Black monks, subjects of Prior Goldwell, comrades of
the late Dr. Bocking, ranged in their stalls to hear an
elaborate homily against the power, holiness, morality,
and canons of the Pope; the general congregation
dividing their eyes and ears between the dead and the
living, the old and the new Thomas of Canterbury.
Layton made his inventory, and went on his speedy
way to Faversham, to visit the abbey there; but he
left a storm behind him; nor had he the brilliant
success at Christchurch that had attended him at
Langdon. The inventory was made, but Prior Goldwell

---

* Layton was no stranger to Canterbury or to Christchurch. Exactly
a year before, 1534, he and Bartlet his scribe had been down on the
swearing commission, and swore the monks of St. Augustine's to renounce
the Pope, &c., Oct. 20. A few days before this, he and Bartlet seem to
have burnt Prior Goldwell's house. "The same time the new house of
the prior of the Church of St. Saviour's (Christchurch) was set on fire
and burnt, Doctor Layton, the visitor, and Mr. Bartlet, the scribe, being
present, the 16 day of October at midnight."—*Chron. of St. Aug.* in
Nicholl's Narratives, 282. The editor of the chronicle is, I think, wrong
in altering the date of this affair to 1535; though I observe that Strype
has done the same.—I. 318.

omitted to insert a considerable part of the costly
decorations of the most splendid house in Christendom;
jewels and plate, silver, gold and stone, to the value of
thousands of pounds, appeared not in his bill. And
now was made manifest the wisdom of Crumwel's
system of sustaining or of checking even the best of
visitors by the presence of one of his own servants.
A faithful one, Jasper Filoll by name, one who had
striven for months with the irreconcilable monks of the
London Charterhouse after the death of Houghton,
was with Layton there, and when Layton was gone,
Filoll received and carried to his master a letter from
one Christopher Levyns, in which, from the information
of certain of the monks, the concealments of the prior
were made known. There were loyal men even in
Christchurch; and the loyal men declared that though
they could not be silent, yet they fully expected to
be poisoned, or murdered in prison by the prior when
once he had discovered their loyalty. In public
the storm broke out afresh. Cranmer took an early
opportunity of repeating his objurgations against the
Pope; and the prior got a preacher to answer him in
the same pulpit. This preacher, who was the prior of
the Black Friars of Canterbury, by name Oliver,*
delivered a severe harangue against the Archbishop,
accusing him of mendacity and want of charity in what
he had said against the Pope. The Archbishop in return
convented the orator before him several times; the noise
was great in Canterbury, the quarrel went on for nearly
a year, and at last the Archbishop wrote a long letter of
complaint to the Supreme Head, requesting a commission to sit on the case, but decently, though not unnecessarily, asking to be excused from sitting among the

---

* This Oliver was an old antagonist of Cranmer's who tried to get
him displaced the year before. Cranmer's *Letters*, p. 295.

commissioners. But events seem to have moved too swiftly for this to be necessary.*

Layton, on the same day that he visited Christ-church, went on to the Abbey of Faversham, of which he reported no other evil than that the abbot was too old to be active in inspecting his domains : and some time after, March 8, a persuasive invitation was sent by Crumwel to the superannuated ruler to surrender his house. In his dignified answer the old man vindicated his own administrative sufficiency, and refused by any means to consent to the ruin of the godly and ancient foundation, in which the bones of the royal founder, Stephen, were laid in honourable sepulture.† The active Layton may perhaps have proceeded from Faversham to the neighbouring nunnery of Davington, which about that very time was made the subject of an inquisition. Davington Priory was dissolved, or rather escheated to the Crown, not because of the crimes and misdemeanours of the inmates, but for the simple reason that there were neither prioress nor nuns left therein. It seems to have been one of those cases of private dilapidation and ruin which occurred from time to time among the religious houses. What is known of the history of its fall illustrates curiously the manner in which the Vicar General exercised his sway over the ecclesiastical world. If the inquisition into a simple case of collapse was not worthy of the attention of a visitor, and Layton was not there, yet

* I have ventured to bring together, 1. Layton's letter to Crumwel (Wright, 76), in which he says that he was going to visit the " see " of Cranmer, that is Christchurch, on October 23, 1535. 2. Cranmer's letter to the King, August 26, 1536 (Jenkyns), complaining of the Black Friar ; in which he says that Layton was at the first of his two sermons, and that the quarrel began *before Christmas last.* 3. Levyns' letter to Crumwel (Wright, 90) about the false inventory made by Goldwell after an injunction given him by Layton. As to the Black Prior, see Soames, i. 490.   † Wright, 103.

at least one of Crumwel's servants, Anthony Ager by
name, failed not to be present, and to carry off the
spoils. It happened, however, that both the Archbishop of Canterbury and his brother the Archdeacon
laid claim to certain woods, lands, and tithes appropriated to the nunnery, which they thought should
escheat to them on the dissolution. The Archdeacon,
who was present at the inquest, ventured to tell Ager
that he thought that he should have the tithes : the
Archbishop made his claim for the woods and lands,
and also wrote to Crumwel to request that the property
in question might not be specified officially as belonging
to the King. Crumwel, by way of reply, charged
the Archbishop with having stayed the verdict at the
inquest, and held out a threat that he would inform
the King of his conduct ; and furthermore caused one
of his own suffragans, the new Bishop of Worcester,
Latimer, to write to his metropolitan a smart letter, and
tell him that he looked on the King's business through
his fingers. The alarmed Archbishop expostulated
piteously : " I would," he exclaimed, " you saw the
very bottom of my heart ! If I knew that it was His
Grace's pleasure to have my title in the said lands,
I would be more desirous to give it than he can be
to have it. But forasmuch as I know not but His
Grace would that I should have it, if my title be good,
I must needs make my claim and declare my title, else
I must lose it, be it never so just." As for Latimer's
letter, the Archbishop said that he marvelled not that
the Vicar General so thought of him, for he knew
not what he had done in the royal cause ; and he
then recounted his labours. The end of the matter
seems to have been reached with this answer : the
Archbishop's claim was probably pursued no further,
and the estates of the defunct nunnery were granted

afterwards to a courtier. This was not the only symptom which shewed that Cranmer's favour was hanging in the balance at that time.* How little reason he had to like the visitation may be judged in this, that as soon as the Act for suppressing the little houses passed, he was compelled to exchange the rich manors of Wimbledon and Mortlake for the poor Abbey of Bradsole, or St. Radegund's, near Dover.† The consorts who had overwandered thus the fields of Kent now parted company. Bedyl went to succeed Legh in Cambridgeshire; Layton went to join Legh in a visitation of the North.‡ Of the adventures of the former there is but a scanty record. He was at the celebrated Abbey of Ramsey, January

---

* Cranmer's Letters, 312, 313. His first letter was dated October 17, his last November 2 (1535).

† 27 H. VIII. c. 34. Bradsole was one of the houses which were considered dissolved as soon as the Act for suppressing little houses was passed, and therefore it was immediately bartered away. The annual value was under 200*l.*, so that it was liable to the Act. See below, p. 396.

‡ There is some difficulty in following the movements of the great Legh before he went to Cambridge. If the Letters of Visitors printed in the Suppression of Monasteries by Mr. Wright are arranged correctly (of which I have doubt in several instances), Legh was in Wiltshire, visiting Laycock Abbey, August 20, 1535. There he complained that Layton had been letting the heads of houses in those parts go forth from their precincts ; and said that because he would not do the same, the heads were grieved (56). Much about the same time he was in Bedfordshire, with Ap Rice (53). He, or a namesake of his, was visiting in Yorkshire, September 1 (61). On September 3 he was in Wiltshire, where he again remonstrated about the heads : and this date is certainly correct, as the letter contains his admonition to Crumwel to be careful what visitors he should send to the Universities (66). I think the two inside letters belong to the next year, 1536. I have already referred to a letter of Audley's, September 30, undoubtedly of 1535, in which he mentions that Legh had been made "substitute to visit all the religious houses in the diocese of London" (74, also in *State Pap.*, i. 450). This is the last about him before he went to Cambridge, as aforesaid. He was no doubt set to visit London at this time, but his commission slept, while he was actively engaged elsewhere, as we shall see : and it was not till the year 1538 that the London houses fell to his bow and spear.

15, of which he gave a favourable report; the abbot and convent were obedient to the King, and as upright in their lives as any religious folk, but that was to say that they were more given to ceremonies than was necessary. He found two monks only of the body who desired to leave the cloister; but he thought that he should have numerous applications for liberty as he proceeded, for Doctor Legh had given great occasion about Christmas by permitting half the neighbouring house of Sawtrey to depart. He desired to know Crumwel's mind in this behalf. And if the Vicar General would be pleased to grant him a commission to visit the unvisited houses in the diocese of Lincoln, it would be much to his commodity.*

The footsteps of the sprightly Layton are more numerous and discernible. When he had finished his work in Kent he seems to have returned to London, where, finding himself out of employment, he addressed a letter to Crumwel from his lodgings in Paternoster Row, in which he suggested that he himself, along with Legh, should be engaged to visit the diocese of York. No visitation of that diocese, he urged, had been held since the time of the late cardinal : a reformer would find much work to do there. As for himself, Crumwel would never know how serviceable he could be without some experiment; he was ready to go at a moment's notice; the Articles of Visitation, which were in the hands of Crumwel's clerk, Bartlet (apparently those already used in Kent), would do for York. He informed Crumwel further that he had been to the Dean of Arches, and laid the scheme before him; but that Cranmerian officer would fain have persuaded him to delay the motion for three or four years, till the doctrine of Supreme Head were

* Wright, 98.

better understood among the people : whereas on the contrary, in Layton's judgment, nothing would make the Supreme Head better understood than a speedy and vigorous exercise of his authority. No doubt his lordship of Canterbury and his officers would be well content if there were no visitation at all. Cranmer had resumed his metropolitical authority, and was now holding a visitation which would last till August. Let not Crumwel wait to begin until Cranmer had ended ; the Archbishop of York expected a royal visitation, and was holding his own suspended until it should take place.* If Layton and Legh were despatched thither at once, they would finish all the province by the end of. September next ensuing. And Legh might take Huntingdon and Lincolnshire, and the diocese˙ of Chester on his return, and finish them within the same. time.† The favoured petitioner obtained his requests. Legh took Huntingdon, Lincolnshire, and perhaps Chester, not indeed on his return, but in his progress northwards : a vast commission, which, however, he executed not thoroughly, but left, as it has been seen, large gleanings of commodity to the hopes of Bedyl. The modest Layton

* An inhibition had been sent to York at the same time that Legh and Ap Rice got one sent to Canterbury.— *Wilk.* iii. 797.

† Strype, i. 383, from Cleopatra E. 4. The letter is entirely dateless ; but I venture (with Strype) to assign it to this time. It was probably written immediately after Layton's campaign in Kent. Collier puts it much earlier in the year, and makes it play the important part of first suggesting the notion of a general visitation of all the religious houses in the kingdom (ii. 104, first ed.). But there is nothing in it to warrant this. Collier says that the audacious writer followed it by another letter, of June 4,'in which he again urged the scheme, and displayed the merits of himself and Legh. But the latter letter, which, after the fashion of the times, is only dated by the month, belongs not to 1535, but to a subsequent year. Mr. Wright (p. 157) assigns it to 1537. It really belongs, I think, to 1539. The fact is that Layton and Legh visited the province of York twice : in the beginning of 1536 (1535 O.S.), and in 1539. On each occasion Layton got the job by a begging letter.

himself took his way through Bedfordshire, Northamptonshire, and Leicestershire, in which counties he
visited several houses. In a Gilbertine nunnery he
found two nuns "not barren:" whose misfortunes came
of the sub-prior and a serving man. Neither the
unfortunates, nor their sisters, nor their two prioresses,
would confess this; an old beldame told the tale; and
when the visitor threatened the prioresses for their
concealment, they said that by their oath of religion
they were sworn never to divulge the secret faults
committed among them, but only to their own religious
visitor.* At Harwood, in Bedfordshire, he found four
or five nuns and a prioress: one of them had two .fair
children; another had one child, "and no more." Lord
Mordant and his eldest son had enticed the foolish
young nuns to break open the coffer in which the
convent seal was kept, and to sign a Latin writing, of
which they knew not the contents, but were told that
it was nothing but a lease of an impropriate benefice.
Lord Mordant had intimidated them to this, and
Layton thought that he ought to be called to account
by the Vicar General, unless every man were to be
allowed by power and might to use houses of religion
of the King's foundation. At St. Andrew's, in Northampton, the prior was a good husband and a great
clerk, but the house was greatly in debt, the lands sold
and mortgaged through the unthrift of the former
prior: the rents of the farms were received beforehand:
there were ten or twenty chantries to be paid out of
the lands, and great bonds of forfeitures for nonpay-
ment. It would be a good thing for the King to
promote the prior and take the house: the King

---

* This unfortunate nunnery was no doubt Chicksand in Bedfordshire
(Wright), where there was a sub-prior, six monks, and eighteen nuns
(Tanner).

might recover the lands, which the prior could never. In the city of Leicester there was a college of the King's foundation, called Newark : it was well kept, honest men were therein, and there were four hundred pounds in their treasury. But they were confederate, and though the abbot was an honest man, and did very well, yet the canons were the most obstinate and factious that Layton ever knew. They would confess nothing. However, he meant to ask some of them in the morning whether they had committed adultery and were addicted to unnatural crimes; which he had heard told against them by some : and what he should find he could not tell. The Bishop of Lincoln had commanded the preachers of Newark College not to preach but only in their own benefices. What right, Layton wanted to know, had the Bishop to prohibit any man from preaching the word of God ? He had visited his diocese in Lent last, six months before the time : and had thus contrived to do two things, to prevent the King's Visitation, and to hold his own at the time when the metropolitical Visitation was being held by the Archbishop of Canterbury. If the Archbishop, Layton had to observe, would so suffer his power, given him by the King's Highness, to be contemned, it were pity he should have his mitre.* Perhaps Layton knew an active and loyal man who would have worn it better.

The noble colleagues met at Lichfield, December 22 : and proceeded thence to certain abbeys upon Trent side and so to Southwell. They arrived at York, and visited the Archbishop, January 11 : whom they well lectured on the duties of his office in preaching and spreading the new loyalty. They visited the great abbeys of St. Mary in York, of Fountains, and of Whitby. Everywhere they found great corruption;

* Wright, 93.

as was the south, so was the north ; as was the head,
so were the members.* The abbot of Fountains was,
according to them, "a very fool, and a miserable idiot."
He dilapidated his house, cut down the woods, and
was commonly defamed for keeping six ladies ; one
day he would confess, and deny the next, thereby incurring perjury. Six days before the arrival of the
Visitors, he had committed sacrilege. At midnight
he caused his chaplain to steal the sexton's keys,
and out of the chapel he took a cross of gold with
stones. One Warren, a goldsmith of the Chepe in
London, was with him, who took the cross and some
other jewels, particularly a ruby, which he got for
nothing, persuading the abbot that it was a garnet.
The goldsmith also bought plate, which was sold to him
without weight; and how much the abbot was cheated
none could tell. This wretched creature they compelled to resign secretly, but he was still allowed to
minister in all things as before, for the avoidance of
suspicion; because if the monastery were known to be
void, the Earl of Cumberland would strive to put in the
cellarer, who was not a meet person. But they knew
a meet person, the wisest monk of that coat, who would
pay Crumwel six hundred marks for the place, immediately after the election, at one payment, and who
moreover would not fail to discharge the firstfruits to
the King, a thousand pounds in four years, and owe
no man a groat therefor. In conclusion they advised
Crumwel to send for the goldsmith of Chepe, and lay to
his charge the sins of theft and sacrilege. The Visitors,
February 9 and 23, may be traced further at the Augustinian Abbey of Merton, and the Præmonstratensian

---

* Layton gives some general accusations which can hardly be repeated
even in his Latin. Wright, 97.. But what value can be attached to
general accusations ?

Priory of Horneby; of which they took the surrenders. So far had the Visitation proceeded when the session of Parliament began, in which the smaller religious houses were presented to the King.*

The memorable assembly which was transforming England met for its final session and its greatest work, February 4. The Church Acts which it passed were numerous and important. " For the entire and hearty love which the King bore to the prelates and other incumbents," it was enacted that they should not pay tenths in the year of their promotion to any benefice, when they paid firstfruits, that being a double charge. The scheme for revising the ecclesiastical law by a commission of thirty-two persons, to be nominated by the King, was again renewed, and in being renewed again deferred. Meanwhile the ecclesiastical laws remained in suspense as before. Sanctuary persons, or girth-

---

* Rymer, xiv. 557. From the above narrative it would appear that no other visitors were employed, before Parliament, than Layton, Legh, Bedyl, and their satellites : and indeed it is remarkable that there are few traces of other visitors. But there are some traces. For instance, Richard Williams took the surrender of Tilley Abbey in Yorkshire, March 3; and, March 13, Belsington Priory surrendered to Richard Southwell. Though these two surrenders seem too late to have come before Parliament, the two worthies who took them may have done much previously. Again, is it likely that the aspiring Ap Rice, who joined with Legh to suspend the bishops, remained inactive while Legh was filling his pockets in Cambridgeshire and Yorkshire? There is, however, only one published letter from him, which has been assigned to this period (Wright, 85). According to that he was in full swing at Bury St. Edmonds. And yet there is nothing in it that might not belong to the next year, 1536; in which year that great abbey was visited beyond doubt (Wright, 144). But it may have been visited twice. There is another letter, dated September 3, from Fitzjames (*Ib.* 63), referring to a visitation of Glastonbury. The date seems too early to be of this visitation : and from the contents I think it belongs to a subsequent year. These are all the published evidences of the visitation previous to Parliament that I know. But many letters may have perished, many be still in manuscript. I conclude, 1. That the visitation before Parliament may have been wider than surviving records show ; 2. That it was much less wide than historians say.

men, as those refugees were called in the ordinary English term, were ordered to wear badges, to bear no other weapons but their meat-knives, and their meat-knives only when they ate their meat; and not to be abroad at night. On tithes the law which was passed seemed to mark the nature, while accidentally it described the limits, of the revolution which was in so rapid progress. Those customary payments had been refused or resisted of late " in more temerous and large manner than before that time had been seen," but those who pursued such detestable enormities and injuries were warned that the Supreme Head desired the spiritual rights and duties of the Church of England to be preserved and maintained ; that tithes, offerings, and other duties of Holy Church were to be paid according to custom, the offender to be convented before the ordinary, or other competent judge, " by due process of the King's ecclesiastical laws of the Church of England "—a memorable phrase which was now for the first time used on earth. If the ordinary or other competent judge found his sentence set at nought, the appeal lay to any one of the King's Council, or to two justices of the peace. The Act was but provisional and temporary ; nor was it extended to the citizens of London, who were commanded to pay their tithes for the present under the order of the Lord Chancellor, or some other councillor, or under the King's Proclamation, without reference to the Ordinary of the Church. But all these regulations were to be in force only until the King and his Thirty-two should make and establish, affirm and ratify, a body of laws " to be called the ecclesiastical laws of the Church of England." In a statute of Beggars it was ordered, for the better regulation of charity, that if any person made a common dole, or gave any money in alms but to the common boxes and gatherings in every parish, he should forfeit ten times as much as he had given.*

The bill for suppressing the little monasteries, the momentous measure which placed within the grasp of the King the prey which he had pursued so long, was preceded by a "declaration" made to Parliament by the King, of the reports of the Visitors, or a digest of them : which was made, and perhaps read, openly in both Houses ; and from the manifold abominations which it is said to have recorded obtained the name of the Black Book. This important document is not in existence : it disappeared not long, perhaps directly, after it had been used ; and the disappearance of it, due to whatever cause, may possibly demand one of the tears of history. If, according to the common opinion, the Anglo-Romanists destroyed it in the reign of Mary through indignation, they could have done nothing so fatal to the cause which they sought to defend ; † but if,

---

* 27 H. VIII. c. 8, 15, 19, 20, 21, 25.

† The common opinion began, I think, with Burnet, who says in his Preface that he met with a commission, of the fourth year of Queen Mary, issued to Bonner, Bishop of London, Cole, Dean of St. Paul's, and Martin, a Doctor of Civil Law, which ran thus : "Whereas it is come to our knowledge that in the time of the late schism, diverse Compts, Books, Scrolls, Instruments, and other writings were practised, devised, and made, concerning Professions against the Pope's Holiness, and the See Apostolic ; and also sundry infamous scrutinies taken in Abbeys and other religious houses, tending rather to subvert and overthrow all good religion and religious houses, than for any truth contained therein : which being in the custody of divers Registers, and we intending to have those writings brought to knowledge, whereby they may be considered and ordered according to our will and pleasure, thereupon these three, or any two of them, are empowered to cite any persons before them and examine them upon the premises upon oath, and to bring all such writings before them, and certify their diligence about it to Cardinal Pole, that further order might be given about them." This was a commission to examine and publish, rather than destroy. Nevertheless Burnet adds, " When I saw this, I soon knew which way so many writings had gone : and as I could not but wonder at their boldness who thus presumed to raze so many records, so their ingenuity in leaving this commission in the Rolls,

as it may be suspected with better reason, the party who used it destroyed it, they acted in a manner which did credit to their intelligence and foresight. That which remained unknown beyond one public manifestation was not diminished in report and rumour; from a source which might not have been so copious unless it had been possible to feed it by inrunning rills, a large river has issued, and acquired strength in going; and while neither the extent nor the exactness of the charges brought against the religious houses could be ascertained, their common fate itself was left to furnish the argument of their common depravity.* Of what the Declaration made before Parliament consisted, whether of the reports of the Visitors, or of the confessions of monks and nuns, or of both, or of a general narrative, or formulated statement compiled of both or of either, is unknown. It is unknown whether it referred to all the religious houses, or but to some of them; if not to all, it is unknown to how many and to what. But because the legislation which followed it was of a general scope, it has been assumed by successive writers that the Declaration referred to all the monasteries, and that all had been visited before the Declaration was made. And yet in the Act which was founded

---

by which anyone who had the curiosity to search for it might be satisfied how the other commissions were destroyed, was much to be commended." Their simplicity, if they had done any such thing, would have been much more to be wondered at. But this absurdity has got currency, and is used to account for the loss of the Black Book. Mr. Froude, for instance, says unhesitatingly that " Bonner was directed by Queen Mary to destroy all discoverable copies of it, and his work was fatally well executed" (ii. 418). I have been favoured by the high authority of Mr. Brewer with an assurance that there is no trace of wanton or designed destruction among the records.

* If I could visit the island of Glubbdubdrib, and wanted to know what became of this " Declaration," or " Black Book," I should call up the ghost of Crumwel to tell me: that is, supposing that such a document ever existed.

on the Declaration, it is not asserted that the latter referred to all the monasteries; still less that the visitation had reached them all. Now if it had been possible to make these assertions at the time, we should expect to have found them made in the Act. The little that the Act itself tells us concerning the Declaration is indeed all that we certainly know of it.

Seldom in truth has the muse of history ventured on a bolder, a more cloudy flight, than in relating the fall of the religious houses of England. The original document which assigned the causes of their ruin having disappeared, the allusions, the allegations, the vituperations of writers of a subsequent age have been collected and accepted as if they were the testimony of contemporaries; and on these secondary authorities has been formed a tertiary deposit of defamatory or disgraceful anecdotes, to which the later writers have added each his layer. Efforts at the same time have not been wanting to supply the irreparable loss itself by research, and in examining the evidence concerning the suppression of the monasteries, the first care of the enquirer will be due to the fragmentary discoveries which have been supposed to contain all that survives of the original statement of their guilt. A single manuscript which still remains has been assumed by historians to be a copy of part of the Black Book (for by that ominous name we may consent for the sake of brevity to call the Declaration made before Parliament), and to afford a sufficient specimen of the entire document.* To this manuscript must now be added a

---

* This manuscript is in the Cotton library, Cleopatra, E. IV., 147. Burnet, who was the first to notice it, terms it "an extract of a part" of the Black Book; and for such it has been accepted by the few who have occupied themselves with this difficult part of English history. Newcome, after making the dry remark that "the full report never lived long," gives his own account of the supposed extract (St. Albans, 433). Mr. Stur-

duplicate, preserved in another repository, and hitherto unnoticed or uncollated by historians, which agrees in the main with it, but in one part is different.* Both these manuscripts bear the simple title of Comperta; each of them is divided into two parts, of which the former is the same in both, and refers to one hundred and twenty monasteries, nearly all situated in the Province of York. This part appears to contain a complete set of Comperta. The second part refers, in the one manuscript, to twenty-four monasteries, which nearly all lay in the diocese of Norwich; in the other the second part is concerned with ten other monasteries of the same diocese. It would appear then that there remains one complete set of Comperta in two tran-

geon, who has kindly examined it for me, says that it is "undoubtedly a copy" of some older original, and that it is written in two hands: the bulk of it "is of an English character, scarcely old enough to be of Henry VIII. though it might be;" and there are marginal annotations in an Italian hand of about 1600. These marginal annotations, however (which play an important part in the story), belonged to the original no less than the rest of the manuscript; though they were copied later. They strongly resemble the handwriting of Sir R. Cotton himself.

* The manuscript, hitherto unnoticed, is in the Record Office. I owe the knowledge of it to Mr. Gairdner of the Record Office, and to Mr. Sturgeon. It is written on fine old paper, and is in a parchment cover which bears the title "Compendium Compertorum per Doctorem Layton et Doctorem Legh in Visitatione Regia Provinciæ Eboracencis ac Episcopatus Coven. et Lichfelden." The document itself begins with the title "Comperta" in rough English text. The body of the document and the marginalia are in the same handwriting, unlike the Cottonian, which has them in two hands. The first part is a facsimile of the Cottonian, and ends with the same entry, Combermere. Here the document seems complete; but an odd leaf of a similar document (in the same hand) has been stitched into the cover with it. This addition, or second part, is entirely different from the second part of the Cottonian. It begins in the middle of an abbey, thus shewing its fragmentary character. The second part of the Cottonian begins on the other side of the same piece of paper, shewing that all was copied together. On the Record Office manuscript is the remark: "The filthy book of calumnies invented by the Commissioners for the purpose of justifying the suppression of the religious houses and the robbery of the Church." This is in a modern hand.

scripts; of two other sets that there remain transcripts, which are perhaps incomplete. That the two manuscripts in which these three sets of Comperta are found are themselves copies of older originals, is evident on inspection.* These Comperta are very damaging to the character of the religious houses; but it is observable that they follow a very rigid and a very summary method of displaying their guilt. In them all the method is the same. The name of a house is given first, and under it follows a list of the religious persons whom it contained, ranged under several almost invariable classifications. Some are enrolled as guilty of unnatural crimes, others as incontinent, incestuous, or adulterers. Some are thieves, some appear as suspected of treason, and others are described as superstitious. Thus many persons were involved in one accusation: the character was marked entirely by a single condemnatory or defamatory epithet; and the same stroke sufficed to level a whole rank. There was no distinction made between one house and another; they varied only in the number of unnatural, incontinent or superstitious persons whom they harboured. Of the innocent there was no classification; nor was it possible to discover the proportion which they bore to the guilty, since the total number of inhabitants was never given.†

---

* The one in the Record Office is the older of the two. It ends with the attestation of the notary who copied it, and the sign that it was an attested copy of an official document. The other may be considerably later. It is known that Cotton had manuscripts copied for him, and sometimes caused the more ancient writing of originals to be imitated.

† Burnet says that the "extract," as he calls it, in the Cotton library, "contains abominations in it equal to any that were in Sodom." It contains at any rate the imputation of the abomination of Sodom. Newcome's account of it is fuller. "The general character of the house is set down in a very short and concise manner, without any notice of their general deportment and outward behaviour: thus, if any relics were found in the chapel, the monks were set down as superstitious. They were marked

By this system, if it were applied generally, it is plain that evidence of guilt could be multiplied with ease to any amount. Furnished with these heads of classification, the Visitors might in a rapid inspection put down as many members of a house as they saw fit under one or other of them, and be saved the trouble and delay of investigating the circumstances of the cases that came before them. But then arises the question whether these Comperta were the direct reports and notes of the Visitors, or (as one of their titles denotes) a compendium formed out of the fuller disclosures which the Visitors may have returned to their employer Crumwel in the first instance. It may be answered that, so far as we know directly, no such notes or reports were ever made by the Visitors. All that the Visitors wrote, of which we have knowledge, was their letters; and the letters of the Visitors are so totally different from these rigid Comperta, that they could not have been the source of them. They are vivacious or solemn, according to the temper of the writer; they abound in anecdotes and particulars; and yet they seldom mention any of the monks by name, much less give lists of them. Strange to say, those of them that remain scarcely ever traverse the Comperta. The writers of them never speak of

by another odious appellation, and Sodom was the word annexed; in nunneries the character was signified by *pepererunt*. Thus all persons were equally involved in one and the same charge, and that charge was not only never proved, but the guilt of it could never be known with certainty, and only guessed by the Visitors."—(*St. Albans*, 433.) This description is equally applicable to the manuscript in the Record Office. The marginal classifications are in both documents: and their method is the same. Each of them, after the name of the house, gives a list of inmates, one under another, bracketed to the words, "voluntar. pollutione," the same being indicated in the margin by the word "Sodom." Then follows another list of those who in the margin are termed "incontinent;" then the entry of a pilgrimage, or of images or relics, which are noted in the margin, "Superstitio." So it goes on, every house being formulated in the same way.

sending reports or notes to Crumwel, though they speak occasionally of other letters which they have sent or are going to send.

But, on the other hand, they often describe themselves as calling the monks into their chapterhouses, and holding enquiries, of which they give no particulars; so that it is probable, though no more than probable, that they kept and afterwards delivered to Crumwel the minutes which they thus collected, and these may be the original of the Comperta.

This probability brings us to another question. Those lists of names which the Comperta exhibit— whence come they? If they come from the personal admissions made by the monks and nuns in their examinations before the Visitors, are they in their original form? They cannot certainly be called confessions in the ordinary sense of the term. A confession of enormities might be made by a convent, but it would be in the form of a common paper, to which all set their names : a convent would not divide itself into various grades and kinds of crime, so many writing themselves down unnatural, so many incontinent, so many superstitious, with a residue of thieves, traitors, and apostates. There is a wide belief, however, that the monasteries made numerous confessions, subscribed by their own hands; and that it was in consequence of these confessions that they were destroyed. If such confessions could ever have been produced, they would have settled the question of depravity at once. But they have never been produced. They have been spoken of from an early period, but not before the smaller houses had been already dissolved : and they have never been seen from that day to this. In the Act for dissolving the smaller houses, when Parliament gives its reasons for what it was doing, it is not said that the confessions of houses formed part of the indictment which prompted the measure. But when the smaller houses had been destroyed, and the north of England was in arms to avenge them, the King declared for the first time that the confessions of the inmates of those houses had caused him to destroy them.* If he had published those confessions, he would have done more to justify his conduct than in all his expostulations with the rebels of the Pilgrimage of Grace. Such confessions must have been numerous and lengthy documents, and yet they have all disappeared! There are, it is true, some confessions so called, belonging to the two or three years following, which were made when some of the remaining houses surrendered themselves voluntarily, but these contain no acknowledgment of moral turpitude. One confession only, subscribed with the names of the convent, containing a general but vague acknowledgment of " voluptuous living," has been produced from first to last. This, which was made under amusingly suspicious circumstances, has been printed more than once by historians, with the insinuation that there were more of the kind, but that one specimen would be enough.† And to this day it seems to be believed, not only that such confessions were made in numbers, but that they still exist, and have been prevented by some untoward cause from being published

---

* " There be none houses suppressed where God was well served, but where most vice, mischief, and abomination of living was used : and that doth well appear by their own confessions subscribed with their own hands in the time of our visitation."—*Answer to the Rebels Articles of Doncaster.* See next chapter.

† I allude to the confession of the convent of St. Andrew's, in Northampton, which was first printed by Weaver. It fills four folio pages in his work, and is as verbose as one of Henry's statutes. It was made in the presence of Legh and Layton. Fuller has extracted the sweet kernel of it. We shall arrive at it and the other so-called confessions in due course.

to the world. Are the lists of names in these Comperta the cause of this impression? Are these names copied out of confessions which monks and nuns subscribed with their own hands, but which nobody happens ever to have seen but the King, Crumwel, and perhaps the Visitors?*

Were there ever any other Comperta in existence besides those which remain: that is to say, documents reporting the condition of other religious houses with similar rigour, or under the same classification? Accident enables us to answer this not unnecessary question in the affirmative; and to add, though but on secondary authority, that the Comperta (whencesoever derived) altogether appear to have formed a compendious register, a summary or breviary of indictments against the religious houses. The well-known and fervid Bale, in one of his Prefaces, dilates on the horror and shame which swelled his bosom because of the crimes of the religious houses, divulged in the registers in his possession: he speaks of "the houses of the hooded hypocrites to be visited by the worshipful

* Mr. Wright (Pref. to Suppression, vi.) says, " I think that even the various lists of the confessions of the monks and nuns of the several religious houses, entitled *Comperta*, and preservéd in manuscript, ought to be made public. The great cause of the Reformation has been but ill served by concealing the depravities of the system which it overthrew." Mr. Wright no doubt refers to the Cottonian Comperta which we have been examining, and which are bound in the same manuscript volume from which he took the letters which he has published. It is to be regretted that he did not make them public by including them in his book. It will be seen that he considers them to be " lists of confessions." They may possibly be so: but where are the confessions themselves? Mr. Wright had not the least thought of conveying a false impression, nor would he do so to a reader acquainted with the subject; but an ordinary reader might easily conclude from what he says that there are in manuscript a number of confessions made by monks and nuns, preserved in their original form, which completely justify the suppression, and have only been kept back by the false generosity of the advocates of the Reformation.

doctors of the law, Legh, Layton, Bedyl, and Bartlet, a notary," and adds that "the book of them is called the Breviary of things found out in abbeys, colleges, etc." He then gives a quotation, which seems to have come from a set of lost Comperta, and exhibits in part the same classification of religious persons which is found in those that we have. It concerns some of the greatest houses in England. Under Battle Abbey he gives the names of those guilty of unnatural sins, of the incontinent, of the incestuous. Christchurch in Canterbury follows, and St. Augustine's in the same city, Monkensesleye, Maiden Bradley, Bristol, Abingdon, Sulbred, Bermondsey, Windsor, and the Cathedral Church of Chichester. "These," says he, "were taken out of the aforesaid book." The classification is the same as in the manuscript Comperta, but it is not pursued into the less heinous crimes of superstition, theft, or treason ; and there are several embellishing circumstances added to some of the names. This catalogue of enormities by which the fair fame of so many of the greater monasteries has been blasted, has been repeated by more than one of our more popular historians, though the source from which it came has been forgotten, or was never known to those who have enjoyed it.*

* The literary history of this catalogue of crime is rather curious. Fuller got it out of Speed, observing at the same time that it was not to be found in Speed before the third, posthumous, edition of 1632, and that the editor of that edition had taken it from a French writer, H. Stevens, who gave it in his Apology of Herodotus. More than this Fuller knew nothing of it. It came, however, out of the Address to the Reader in Bale's Pageant of the Pope, which was translated out of Latin into English by J. S. in 1574, fourteen years after the author's death. Bale says also, in his Vocation (*Harleian Miscell.* vi. 410), "I have the Register of the Visitations of the Cloisters of England, and therefore I know it, to their confusion." Burton, in the Anatomy of Melancholy (p. 1 : 2, 1, 2), descants on it thus : " Quum enim, Anno 1538, prudentissimus Rex, Henricus Octavus, cucullatorum cœnobia, et sacrificorum collegia votariorum per venerabiles legum doctores Thomam Legh, Richaɪdum Laytonum, visitari fecerat, tanto numero reperti sunt apud

Of these Comperta, then, or disclosures concerning the religious houses, there remain to posterity four sets; of which one may be considered perfect, three fragmentary; three are unaltered copies from an original, but one has passed through the hands of an exhibitor; three are in manuscript, and one has undergone the fortunes of the press. Whether any of them were used in making the Black Book, or Declaration made openly in Parliament before the dissolution of the smaller monasteries, is the final question to be raised concerning them; a question which may be determined with absolute conviction, but not with absolute certainty. On the one hand they may all refer to the work of Legh, Layton, Bedyl, and Bartlet, who were by far the most active of the visitors employed before the session of Parliament. The longest of them begins with Lichfield, the place where Legh and Layton met by appointment to proceed on their joint expedition to the north; and it contains a pretty compact report of the Province of York, where they were actively engaged before Parliament met. It is true, however, that it contains many houses of the diocese of Durham, which they are not known from their letters to have visited on their first northern peregrination; and it contains no mention of Kent, where Layton, Bedyl, and Bartlet were busy enough before the Black Book was made. As to the two smaller sets in manuscript, they both refer to the diocese of Norwich, which may easily have engaged the attention of so active a doctor as Legh, during his sojourn at Cambridge before the meeting of Parliament.

eos scortatores, cinœdi, ganeones, pœdicones, puerarii, pœderastæ, Sodomitæ (Balei verbis utor), ganemedes, &c., ut in unoquoque eorum novam credideris Gomorram. Sed vide, si lubet, eorundem catalogum apud eundem Baleum : Puellæ, inquit, in lectis dormire non poterant ob fratres necromanticos." The date here given, 1538, confirms the later origin of the Comperta.

The see of Norwich, of which the aged incumbent was lately dead, certainly received the most particular attention of Parliament in the ensuing session. The catalogue of scandals preserved by Bale, since it condemns some of the greatest abbeys in England, would seem to be posterior to the time when the smaller monasteries alone were condemned for vicious living: or, if it formed part of the evidence read before Parliament, it afforded little warrant for the distinction made by Parliament between the greater houses and the less. But, on the other hand, all arguments that tend to make it probable that the manuscript Comperta formed part of the Black Book, vanish on the actual inspection of those curious documents. Would a declaration made before Parliament have been written in Latin? These Comperta moreover appear not to be only the result of voyages for the discovery of moral turpitude; they give the yearly revenue of the houses with which they deal; so that they look like returns made to ascertain the value of the religious houses subsequently to the Act of Suppression, by which all below a certain revenue were condemned. And they accuse not all with which they deal of moral turpitude; there are nearly thirty houses of which they record nothing worse than their yearly revenue.*

* It is now time to lay before the reader the houses contained in the manuscript Comperta. I have added the counties in most cases, and marked those of which nothing disgraceful is said by italics.

The longer series, which is the same in the Cotton Library and in the Record Office, has the following:—

Lichfield: Repton, Derbys.: Greesley, Derbys.: *Garadon*, Leicesters.: *Langley monialium*, Leicesters.: *Bredon, cella St. Oswaldi*, Leicesters.: Grace Dieu monialium, Leicesters.: *Brisol Park*, Derbys.: St. Jacobi de Derby: Domus Monial, Bte Marie de Derby: Dalle, Derbys.: Selford, Notts.: Thurgarton, Notts.: Rifford (Qy. Rufford, Cisterc. Abbey), Notts.: Welbeck, Notts.: Worsope, Notts.: Rupa, als Roche, Yorks.: Blida, Notts.: Wallingswell monialium, Notts.: *Felley*, Notts.: St. Oswaldi, Yorks.: Burton, als Monkebretton, Yorks.: Arthington monial, Yorks.:

Besides these contemporaneous fragments, there is nothing to guide the historical enquirer but the traditional reminiscences or the furious invectives of writers Hampall monial, Yorks.: Esshot (Essholt) monial, Yorks.: Birklees: Brenkborne, Northumb.: Gisburn, Yorks.: Basedale monial, Yorks.: Handall monial, Yorks.: *Middleburgh,* Yorks.: Whitby, Yorks.: *Grande Monte,* Yorks.: Yedingham (Little Mareis) monial, Yorks.: *Rosdale monial,* Yorks.: *Wickham monial,* Yorks.: Monkling monialium: Bridlington, Yorks.: *Collegium Beverley,* Yorks.: Melsa, Yorks.: Nunburnham monial, Yorks..: North Ferebye, Yorks.: Hallimprise: Warter, Yorks.: Swinkey monial, Yorks.: Nuburgh, Yorks. *:* Rivall, Yorks.: Kildham monial, Yorks.: *Mowsby monial,* Yorks.: Mons Gratie: Byland, Yorks.: Neseham monial, Dur.: Shap, Westmorel.: Mon. de Carlisle: *Armathwaite monial,* Cumberl.: Lampley monial, Northumb.: *Collegium de Kirkoswald,* Cumberl.: Wetheral, Cumberl.: Lanercost, Cumberl.: Holm Caltram, Cumberl.: St. Bees, Cumberl.: Seton monial, Cumberl.: Calder, Cumberl.: Furness, Lancash.: Cartmel, Lancash.: Conishead, Lancash.: Cockersand, Lancash.: Whalley, Lancash.: *Psalley*: *Litham,* Lancash.: Horneby, Lancash.: Penworthan, Lancash.: Holland, Lancash.: Norton: *Kersall cella,* Lancash.: St. Werburg, civit. Cestriæ: Birkenhead, Chesh.: *Stanlow,* Chesh.: Bte Marie Monial. de Chester: Madersley, Notts: Pontefract, Yorks.: Selby, Yorks.: Saningthwayte monial, Yorks.: Nunappleton monial, Yorks.: Helagh, Yorks.: Drax, Yorks.: St. Leonardi Ebor.: *Eccles. Cathedr. Ebor.*: Mon. B. Marie Ebor.: *Kirkham,* Yorks.: Nunmonkton monial, Yorks.: *Wilberforce monial,* Yorks.: Martin, Yorks.: Clementhorp monial, Yorks.: *Thickenhede,* Yorks.: St. Trinitatis Ebor.: Mons de Fontibus, Yorks.: Ripon Coll. Yorks.: Kirkstall, Yorks.: *Bolton,* Yorks.: Jerrival als Gervis, Yorks.: St. Agathe (Richmond), Yorks.: Ellerton monial, Yorks.: Coram, als Coverham, Lincolns.: St. Martini Richmond, Yorks.: Dni Cuthberti ep. Duneln: Mon. s. Prioratus de Durhem: *Feucal cella,* Durham: Gerro cella (Jarrow) Durh.: Walknoll, Northumb.: Novum monast. als Newminster, Northumb.: Alba Landa, als Blancheland, Northumb.: Hexham, als Hexeldesham, Northumb.: Tynemouth, Northumb.: Cella Bamburgh, Northumb.: Alnwick, Northumb.: Collegium Manchester: Coll. St. Johan. Baptist. in Chester: *Banbury Colleg.* Ches.: Combermere, Chest.

The shorter list which follows in the Cottonian manuscript gives twenty-four houses, all in Norfolk, except St. Olave's, in Suffolk, and Ikelinge, and Bristough.

Shuldham monialium: Shuldham Canonicorum: Blackborough: Pentney: Marham: Westacre: Castleacre: Coxford: Walsingham: Benham: Wendling: Byston (Beeston): Bromholm: St. Benedicti: Ikelinge: Ingham: Eccles. Cath. Norwicen: Aldeby: St. Fidei (Horsham): Langley: Buckingham: Wimmendesham: St. Olavi: Bristough.

The shorter list in the Record Office Comperta contains:—

Fordham, als Bigging, Cambr.: Bury St. Edmund's, Suff.: Ikesworth

of the age of Elizabeth. The most important of these
is a short account of the manner of dissolving the
religious houses, which has been edited in this century
by a modern society. In this account it is said for
the first time that all the religious houses in England
had been visited when the Black Book was made, and
that two-thirds of all the religious men in England were
no better than the inhabitants of the cities of the plain.
" This appeared in writing with the names of the parties
and their facts; this was shewed in Parliament, and
the villanies made known and abhorred."* There is
another account, perhaps of about the same date, in
which an appeal is made to the evidence of those confessions which have never been forthcoming. " Let the
horrible history of their dark, dreadful, and most
devilish doings, notified to King Henry the Eighth,
and after to the Parliament House, by the report of the
Visitors returning from their visitations of abbies, and
the monks and nuns themselves in their own confessions, subscribed with their own hands, be a proof thereof: which being registered in a Black Book, might more
justly be called Doomsday."† This is so far accurate
that it gives the manner of procedure which was
adopted. It appears from the Act under which the
smaller houses fell, that the report or reports of the
Visitors were submitted to the King before they were
presented to Parliament. But if, as it seems to be alleged here, the Black Book consisted of the confessions
of monks and nuns, as well as of the reports of the
Visitors, it must be repeated that none of those confessions, in their original form, subscribed by those who

or Ixworth, Suff.: Thetford, Suff.: St. Sepulcre's, and Thetford, Suff.
and Norf.: Colleg. Rushworth, Norf.: Thetford monial, Norf.: West
Dereham, Norf.: Crabbehouse, Norf.
  * Wright, 112, from the Cotton Titus, F. iii. f. 266.
  † Noel's Reproof, quoted by Strype, i. 387.

made them, have ever been produced, or are known on certain authority ever to have been in existence.*

On this uncertain and traditionary foundation has been built the towering structure of the defamatory stories concerning the monasteries, which have amused and satisfied the world. Some of these seem to have arisen out of a too glowing meditation of the dubious authorities which have been examined. Of course "whole convents were found with child," if in the lists of the Visitor or Visitors certain of the nuns were ranged beneath a Latin word which signified that they had brought forth children. The horrors depicted in the narratives of other writers may make us regret doubly the loss of the official documents on which they must have been founded, if they had any foundation, and admire the modest reticence of the Visitors, who excluded from their letters, which remain, and reserved for their reports, which remain not, the worst of the atrocities which met their eyes. How dreadful that "not seven, but seven hundred thousand deadly sins," were found within the walls consecrated to religion! How terrible that "in the dark and sharp prisons" should be found dead "so many of the brethren that it was a marvel;" and these despatched so cruelly—"some crucified with more torments than ever were heard of; and some famished unto death, only for breaking their superstitious silence, or some like trifles;" and that "especially to some children there was used a cruelty not to be spoken with human tongue."† It seems questionable whether were worse, the laxity or the severity of religion. But some of the merrier stories may perhaps

* We now understand by a report a formal statement after investigation. Had the word that meaning in Elizabeth's time? The word used in the Act to denote what the Visitors said is "*Account.*" This may mean nothing but their letters.

† Thomas's Pelerine, quoted by Strype, i. 385.

A a 2

be traced to other sources than the irreparable evidence
which history deplores. The story of the young man
in the nunnery one perceives to be one of Boccaccio's
daydreams transported to a northern clime.

The few who are inclined to believe that a considerable number of persons might have worn the religious habit without defiling it, have waxed indignant
over the departures from ordinary justice which, it
must be confessed, are observable in all that is certain
of the allegations on which the monasteries were destroyed. Why, they exclaim, were no witnesses produced ; why were the monks never allowed to answer
to the charges brought against them ; why was no
enquiry made into the manner in which these charges
had been concerted, the evidence on which they rested,
the character, the motives of those who made them ?
Why were those houses only condemned to destruction,
the heads of which could not be in Parliament to defend them ? And it may be further asked, Why were
not the reports (if there were any) laid at once before
Parliament, instead of going to the King first ? Why,
above all, were not the reports so published that their
truth or falsehood in each case might have been known
beyond dispute ? But perhaps there may be something
unreasonable in this indignation. Might not the Black
Book be likened to a bill of attainder ? In a bill of attainder no evidence was called, nor was the accused allowed to answer for himself : a bill of attainder was now
the process in use against those whom the King desired
to destroy, and why should monks and nuns expect
favours which were denied to prelates and nobles ? It
has sometimes been objected against the improbable
nature of the foul charges brought so freely, that no
man could ever have discovered, much less in so short
a time, all the dark and secret sins which the Visitors

are said to have reported. But those ingenuous persons who so think must not leave out of consideration
what sort of men Crumwel's Visitors were. Most of
them were clerks and doctors of law; clerical practitioners of that class who hung about the ecclesiastical
courts, and furnished them with their summoners, apparitors, and officials. These men had been accustomed
to the same sort of work on a smaller scale which the
Vicar General called them to perform on a larger: for
it must be remembered that under the old system the
vices of incontinence were punishable both in priests
and laymen; and men of this sort got their bread
by visiting suspected places, and laying informations
against transgressors. They could ask unmoved such
questions as no other human beings could have imagined, or known how to put. They could extract guilt
from a stammer, a tremble, or a blush, or even from indignant silence, as surely as from open confession. It
may therefore perhaps be too much to conclude that
there was nothing in their alleged allegations, and that
they were moved merely by interest to invent lies. They
may have been moved by zeal, and the pride of displaying skill in their vocation; and in such expert hands
the moral torture that was applied may have brought to
light things which, even if highly coloured, may not have
been the mere calumnies of venal ribaldry. The basest
part of the ancient system fledged the sharp arrows
which smote one of the highest and most venerable.

And yet, such is the sad uncertainty to which we
are reduced by the disappearance of the accusation, it
seems possible to give too much weight to the skilful
ruthlessness, even of Crumwel's Visitors. Of the religious houses which, from their own letters, they are
known to have visited before the meeting of Parliament,
they speak well or indifferently of half. They speak

of the other half in a discriminating way, specifying
the offenders among the inmates, without insinuating
against the rest, or classing them under odious appella-
tions, after the manner of the Comperta. The ardour of
modern historians, it is true, has represented these
letters in a different light: according to them there
is hardly a favourable account therein ; and the several
evil stories which they contain, instead of being the
whole, are but samples of the ordinary experience of the
Visitors.* Nevertheless if the surviving letters, which
belonged certainly to that period of the General Visitation which elapsed before the meeting of Parliament, be
taken for the test, not all, but only half of the religious
houses were in a state of moral depravity ; and in the
guilty houses not the whole community, the head and
members alike, but in some the head, in others certain
members, were accused. A great number of letters belonging to the same period may have perished ; but it is
fair to presume that the accidents of time have not falsi-
fied the proportions of good and evil which are revealed
in those that remained. This hypothesis, which is not
unlikely, might be advanced to certainty if it happened
that the letters dwelt more frequently on the minutes of
those houses which in the Comperta receive the condemnation of Sodom or Gomorrah. But unhappily, though
the letters belonging to the period under review contain

---

* Mr. Froude has given in full the stories of the houses of Langdon,
Chicksand (which he calls " Lichfield "), and Fountains, as samples of the
"more ordinary experiences of the commissioners." Whereas these are
all the bad stories that there are in their letters, written before the Black
Book, if the story of Harwood be added. It is true that Layton made
some *general* allegations against the northern houses ; but we are considering particular stories. The visitors spoke well, or at least indifferently,
of Dover, Folkestone, Faversham, and Ramsey : to which may be added
St. Andrew's, Northampton. They spoke ill of Langdon, Chicksand,
Harwood, Fountains, to which may perhaps be added St. Mary's, York,
and Whitby. They spoke suspiciously of Leicester.

the mention of several of those houses, it is only in a cursory manner, to tell that they had been visited, or that they were about to be visited. Two exceptions which occur to this general observation, appear to confirm the hypothesis. The great Cistercian abbeys of Rivaulx and Fountains, of which the ruins still adorn the vales of Yorkshire, are tabulated in the Comperta among the vilest of the abodes of vice. But in the letters of the Visitors, which are occupied with them, nothing is alleged against the body of the monks in either of them. The contumacy, the evil living, the manifold extortions and unthriftiness of the abbot of Rivaulx, and of the abbot alone, are recounted, and it is mentioned that some of the brethren were opposed to him, and had been imprisoned by him. The "very fool and miserable idiot," who presided over Fountains, receives his castigation at the hands of virtue, but his brethren are accused of nothing.* Whether these exceptions be sufficient to prove that the Visitors said one thing in their letters and another in their reports, or that the Comperta were derived from some other source, the reader must determine. It is at least certain (and this is almost the only certainty in the matter) that the damning document which is said to have been read in Parliament, however and whensoever it was composed, came not immediately from the hands of the Visitors, but from the hands of Crumwel and the King.

When the Black Book was read in Parliament, there is said to have arisen a general cry of "Down with them!"† But the cry, if general, cannot have been unanimous, if it be true that the bill, which was founded on the book, for giving the smaller monasteries

---

* Wright, 61 and 100.

† "When their enormities were first read in the Parliament house, they were so great and abominable that there was nothing but 'Down with them!'" Latimer's Serm., 123. (Park. Soc.)

to the King, stuck so long with the Commons that his Majesty sent for them and told them that if it did not pass he would have some of their heads.*   The story of attempted resistance and overbearing fury is plausible, because it was not yet proposed to share the royal spoil with the subject; and the confiscation of the monasteries would appear to many of the members the loss of their own property. Most of the houses had been founded by their forefathers : in most of them they had corrodies and other vested interests. It is not known whether the bill, in the original draft, made provision for respecting the rights of founders and their kin; but, if it did, the rights of founders and their kin might be difficult to prove and precarious to maintain. It was impossible to foresee the operation of so unprecedented a measure. Compared with such considerations it may have seemed a small thing to many of the members that their sisters, their younger brothers, the burdensome relations whom they had conveniently dedicated to poverty, chastity, and obedience, should have snatched a few of the sweets of worldly life at the cost of the violation of their vows. There remain traces of a debate in the House of Lords. The "great and fat abbots" have been taunted by the chroniclers with conniving at the destruction of their poorer brethren in order to preserve themselves : nor is it unlikely that the unexpected distinction drawn in the bill

---

* Spelman's Hist. of Sacrilege, 206. " It is true the Parliament did give them to him, but so unwillingly (as I have heard), that when the bill had stuck long in the lower house, and could get no passage, he commanded the Commons to attend him in the forenoon in his gallery, where he let them wait till late in the afternoon, and then coming out of his chamber, walking a turn or two among them, and looking angrily on them, first on the one side and then on the other, at last, I hear (saith he) that my bill will not pass ; but I will have it pass, or I will have some of your heads : and without other rhetoric or persuasion returned to his chamber. Enough was said, the bill passed, and all was given him as he desired."

between the greater and smaller monasteries may have tempted them to a silence which was as inglorious as it was fatal. It is often seen that those who stand highest in an institution are the slowest to defend it. But their compliance availed not to secure them from insult. To their faces one of the speakers compared them to putrefied old oaks, which must needs follow the lighter thorns. To which the prophetic Stokesley is said to have rejoined that "others also would follow in Christendom ere many years were passed."* At length the lords and commons, "by great deliberation," as the Act itself affirmed, proceeded to the first great measure of confiscation.

The Act gave to the King all the religious houses which had not above two hundred pounds by the year. It alleged that the houses which were under that value, and houses which contained less than twelve religious persons, were the abodes of "manifest sin, vicious, carnal, and abominable living;" that such convents spoiled their goods, lands, and tenements; and not these only, but the ornaments of their churches, to the great infamy of the King and the realm. It was therefore expedient for the King to have all their ornaments and jewels. These houses had been visited continually for the last two hundred years, but little or no amendment was made; rather their vicious living shamefully increased and augmented. But the Act, though voluminously majestic in the general allegation of guilt, seemed curiously straitened for words on the important point of evidence. The Parliament knew that all this vicious living was true, for the King had made to them "a plain declaration" of it: and the King knew it to be true "as well by the accounts of his late visitations, as by sundry credible informations."

* Grafton and Hall.

This was all that was said of the Comperta, the subscribed confessions, and all the tremendous mass of
evidence that has been believed to have been collected to support the universal condemnation of the
smaller houses.* However, it appeared that there
were "great and honourable monasteries in the realm,"
there were "divers and great solemn monasteries,
wherein religion was right well kept and observed:"
and for these the Parliament thanked God. To these
it was proposed to commit for reformation of life
those bad religious persons who had so little and
lived together in such small companies: or else to
give them capacities to live honestly abroad, some
convenient charity being disposed towards them to
help their living. The great and honourable monasteries, being destitute of their full numbers, might
well be increased by such associates. It may seem
curious that, if it were designed to send the inmates
of the little houses to replenish the great ones, the
Visitors should have ventured beforehand to take
the surrenders of houses and dismiss their inmates
into the world. It is curious also that a distinction
should have been drawn between the smaller houses
and the greater in point of morality. In the letters of
the Visitors some of the great abbeys were ill-famed,

* "The King's most royal Majesty, being Supreme Head on earth,
under God, of the Church of England, daily studying and devising the
increase, advancement, and exaltation of true doctrine and virtue in the
said Church, to the only glory and honour of God, and the total extirping
and destruction of vice and sin, having knowledge that the premises be
true, as well by the accompts of his late visitations, as by sundry credible
informations: considering also that divers great and solemn monasteries
of this realm, wherein (thanks be to God!) religion is right well kept and
observed, be destitute of such full number of religious persons as they
ought and may keep, hath thought good that a plain declaration should
be made of the premises, as well to the lords spiritual and temporal, as
to other his loving subjects the commons, in this present parliament
assembled."

and some of the small ones bore a good report. The distinction seems arbitrary, and probably arose from imitating the former suppression by Wolsey. It was well to begin at one end; the little houses were defenceless, and the monks who belonged to them were less frequently men of birth than those of the great abbeys. But the admission that there were great abbeys in which religion was observed has been so highly prized by those who can regard confiscation without admiration, that they have accepted the condemnation of the little houses, and have invented theories to shew that the little houses may have been worse ordered than the great ones. The little houses, it seems, lay in remote places, out of the way of discipline.

A retrospective clause covered and gave to the King the monasteries which had been suppressed illegally before the Act was made: just as a retrospective clause in the Act of Succession had covered the illegal imprisonment of Fisher and More : and just as a retrospective clause afterwards covered the illegal suppression of the greater monasteries, which began to fall as soon as the smaller ones were given to the King. The rights of all persons and bodies politic were saved: such as leases, pensions, portions, corrodies, annuities; but pretended founders or donors were excepted from the saving ; and fraudulent assurances, which were said to have been made by the priors and governors, in view of dissolution, were made void. The priors and heads were to have reasonable pensions and benefices given them, the more tender respect of his Majesty being promised to those who should well preserve their goods and ornaments for him. All persons to whom the King might hereafter grant or let the sites, precincts, or domains of the dissolved houses were bound under the heavy

penalty of six pounds thirteen shillings and four pence
to keep hospitality and husbandry, "an honest continual house and household in the same site or precinct,
and to occupy yearly as much of the same domains in
ploughing and tillage of husbandry" as had been kept
in tillage by the religious owners.   This piece of paper
legislation continued to the reign of James the First.
The groans, the struggles, the revolts of the poor,
deprived of the charity and hospitality of religion, bear
witness to the manner in which it was observed and
enforced.   If the King chose to decree by letters
patent that any of the houses that came within the
Act should be continued, they might be spared.   The
Act seems to bear marks of revision.*

To receive the expected prey, a court was erected,
which bore the expressive title of the "Court of the
Augmentation of the revenue of the King's Crown."
It was to be continually a court of record with a great
and a privy seal ; and was to consist of a chancellor, a
treasurer, an attorney, a solicitor, ten auditors, seventeen receivers, a clerk, an usher, and a messenger.   As
became that swearing age, a separate oath of honesty
toward the King was prescribed in full for each of
these officials ; and the salaries by which their fidelity
was to be raised above corruption were very large.
The dissolved monasteries and all their revenues were
to be in the survey of this court; and the grand
apparatus that was erected served to shew that business enough was expected.†   But the court was less
serviceable than expensive in the issue, since neither
his own avarice nor the growing cupidity of his

* 27 H. VIII. 28.   "An Act whereby all Religious Houses of Monks,
Canons and Nuns which may not dispend Manors, Lands, Tenements
and Hereditaments above the clear yearly value of two hundred pounds
are given to the King's Highness, his heirs and successors for ever."
† 27 H. VIII. 27.   Fuller, Hist. of Abb., 348.

courtiers allowed the King to wait for the slow return of an annual revenue, when many claims might be met and a large treasure immediately acquired and squandered by giving away or selling the monasteries themselves and their domains. The Court of Augmentations had less business with the greater monasteries, when the dissolution overtook them, than it had with the smaller. Three hundred and seventy-six of the smaller monasteries came under the new Act, and were dissolved, out of which thirty-one were refounded for ever in August of this year, and continued a year or two longer.*

The Universities, and the colleges of Eton and Winchester, were exonerated for ever from the ruinous imposition of firstfruits and tenths, which continued to press heavily upon all the other spiritual promotions of the realm. The excellent goodness and divine charity of his Majesty moved him to remit these dues: nor less his fervent zeal both for the advancement of the sincere and pure doctrine of God's Word and Holy Testament, and for the increase of the knowledge in the seven liberal sciences (the old trivium and quad-

---

* "By his letters patent he did anew give back in perpet. Elymosynam, for perpetual Alms, five Abbies. The first of these was the Abbey of St. Mary of Bettlesden of the Cistercian order in Bedfordshire; ten more were afterwards confirmed. Sixteen Nunneries were also confirmed, in all thirty-one Houses. The Patents (in most of which some manors are excepted that had been otherwise disposed of) are all enrolled, and yet none of our writers have taken any notice of this. It seems these houses had been more regular than the rest. . . . By these new Endowments they were obliged to pay Tenths and First-Fruits, and to obey all statutes and rules that should be sent to them from the King, as Supreme Head of the Church. But it is not unlike that some presents to the Commissioners, or to Crumwel, made these houses outlive this ruin: for I find great trading in bribes at this time, which is not to be wondered at, when there was so much to be shared."—*Burnet.* Among the new-founded houses were the Hull Charterhouse, Marrig, Nun Keeling, Byland, and Egglestone. Burton's Monast. Eboracense, 67.

rivium), and the three tongues of the Latin, Greek, and Hebrew. He would not for his own commodity or profit hinder the advancement or setting forth of the lively Word of God, and impeach the knowledge of other good letters.* In consideration of this release, each university was to maintain a public lector in any such science or tongue as the King should assign : the lecture to be called perpetually King Henry the Eighth's lecture. And as a further perpetual memorial of the inestimable goodness and bounteous gifts of his Majesty, it was ordered that in Oxford, Cambridge, Eton, and Winchester two masses should be solemnly sung, the one of the Holy Trinity, and the other of the Holy Ghost, for the preservation of the King, of Queen Anne, and their daughter Elizabeth ; and that after the decease of the King two solemn anniversaries on the same days should be yearly maintained, a Dirige overnight, and a Mass of Requiem on the morrow, in as devout form and manner as was devised for the anniversary or obit of the late King, his father.

An immense number of private Acts concerning transferrences and exchanges of lands seemed to be the beginning of the harvest of estates which was soon to be reaped. The King had bargains and exchanges with the Archbishop of Canterbury, the College of Corpus Christi in Oxford, the Abbey of Thetford in Norfolk, and the Abbey of Marten in Surrey: to which last he bartered the now dissolved Priory of Calwich in Staffordshire. To Sir Arthur Darcy, a name venerable among alieners, he sold the site and precinct, the manors and advowsons of the late houses of Sawley in Yorkshire, of Holy Trinity in York, and of Covenham in Lincolnshire. To his well-beloved

---

* 27 H. VIII. 42.   This Act is incredibly verbose.

Councillor Thomas Crumwel he granted the manor of Hackney, with all the messuages, gardens, meadows, pastures, woods, underwoods, and services thereto belonging. On the Queen he bestowed the manor of Hasellaigh, late parcel of the Abbey of Byleigh, in Essex, one of the largest houses that fell within the statute. On the other hand, the " divers abominable and detestable high treasons" of Sir Thomas More were now remembered, to the detriment of his heirs. It was discovered that the late Chancellor, with a proleptic sagacity worthy of his high renown, "a little before the said treasons were committed and done," had conveyed of "his corrupt and malicious mind" certain estates which he had purchased in Chelsea and elsewhere. He had, after thus securing something for his family, "taken boldness thereby afterwards to commit his said propensed and abominable treasons." But the conveyances were declared to be fraudulent and void, and the King took possession of the lands.*

The Bishop of Norwich being lately deceased, advantage was taken of the vacancy to give the see a thorough plundering. For this end, with that kind of phraseology which decency seems to have commanded in all such cases, his Majesty was made to declare that, minding to advance to the same see one such person which both for his knowledge in scripture and honest conversation in his living should by setting forth of the true, plain, and sincere doctrine of Christ, and good examples of life concordant to the same, much edify his loving subjects of the same see, to the only glory and honour of Almighty God, and the weal of the souls committed to his charge, he appointed William Rugg, Abbot of St. Bennet's, of Halme, in Norfolkshire, to the vacant dignity, who in return consented to

* 27 H. VIII. 33, 34, 41, 52, 53, 54, 58.

make over to his benefactor the whole of the estates of
the see, reserving only the bishop's palace and the
cathedral church. And besides the loss of the other
estates, the London house of the bishop, with seven
messuages or tenements adjoining, was given to the
Duke of Suffolk. In recompense for these sacrifices,
the new bishop was allowed to retain his abbey, and
the small Priory of Hickling was added to it. The
future dealings of the King with the Church scarcely
afforded a bolder example of sacrilege than this Her-
culean infancy. In the proof of superhuman strength
or aid, the strangling of the serpents was not exceeded
by the slaying of the hydra.*

After the smaller monasteries had been given thus
by Parliament to the King, public opinion seems to
have been somewhat moved. It was a disquieting
thing that large masses of property should thus change
owners on a bare assurance that the present occupiers
were good for nothing, an assurance given by a set of
vagabond agents of whom nobody knew anything, but
that they had been chosen for their work by Crumwel
under the scope of his commission to be Vicar General.
The claims of founders, or the representatives of
founders, were to be respected, according to the Act;
but those claims would have to be urged and proved.
This might become an expensive and uncertain process ; so that it seemed only too likely that the whole
spoil would find its way to the King. As soon as the
Act was passed, the Vicar General began to receive
letters from the nobles and gentry entreating to have
houses preserved which had been founded by their

* 27 H. VIII. 39, 45. "He also took thirty (manors) and above, as
I remember, in the 27th year, from the Bishop of Norwich, whom he left
not (that I can learn) one foot of the goodly possessions of his church,
save the palace at Norwich." Spelman's Sacrilege, 210.

ancestors, and within whose precincts the bones of their ancestors reposed : or, if they were not saved from suppression, to have them bestowed upon themselves. At the same time the priors of several of the houses which came under the statute wrote to him to deny that the accusations of disorder and vice were true of themselves; in the vain hope, it would seem, of receiving the advantage of the clause which left it in the power of the King to spare such houses as he chose. The Archbishop of York wrote to intercede for St. Oswald's and for Hexham ; the one being his own property of the see, the other being in truth out of reach of the Act, though rated below it, and holding so convenient a situation for hospitality that there would be danger of the whole country round falling desert if it should be suppressed.* Serious opposition was not aroused as yet, but there were symptoms of dissatisfaction and alarm in the nation. The Vicar General, his eye invariably fixed on the object of supplying the purse of his master, endeavoured to allay the rising murmur by a remarkable expedient, which failed of success. He continued to issue commissions for the visitation of the religious houses, but he made a change in the persons of whom they were composed. Instead of the vagrant emissaries who had been employed solely hitherto, the new commissions were mixed, consisting in part only of his private experts, and composed partly of the country gentlemen resident near the places to be visited. His more notorious instruments, Layton, Legh, and Bedyl, were withdrawn altogether from the scene for a time. But the experiment failed either to justify the accusations under which the monasteries laboured, or to calm the indignation which the hard treatment of them had excited. The mixed commis-

* Wright, 116–125.

sions sent back little else but good reports of the houses which they inspected; and from one county after another the Supreme Head and his favourite were regaled with the virtues, the piety, the strictness, the benevolence of the monks and nuns. The commissioners of Leicestershire, Warwickshire, and Rutlandshire found but two suspected brethren in one small house out of nineteen houses which they examined.* They wrote specially in favour of the Priory of Carthusians in Coventry, where there were "twelve brethren with a prior, all priests, in virtue, contemplation and religion excellent:" and more than once they interceded for the Benedictine nunnery of Polesworth in Warwickshire, where were "fourteen sisters, with the abbess and one anchress, of a very religious sort and living; and brought up others in virtue very excellent." † The commissioners of Northamptonshire wrote to the Chancellor of the new Court of Augmentations, imploring mercy for the nunnery of Catesby, the prioress of which and her nine sisters they found "as religious, devout, and obedient as they had seen, or belike should see." They wrote also in favour of the small Augustinian abbey of St. James in Northampton, where there was an abbot with eight monks. The King was furious, and charged them with having received bribes. One of them, and he one of Crumwel's private agents, George Giffard, denied the charge, and made bold to petition further in the strongest terms for the house of Woolstrope in Lincolnshire.‡ These mixed commis-

* The writer of the article in the Home and For. Rev., Jan. 1864; who says that the reports for those three counties have been discovered in the Record Office. The one house of which they reported some evil was Maxstokke, in Warwickshire, a priory of Austin Canons. "Seven members with a prior, whereof six be priests : two suspect of incontinency, and the others of good and virtuous conversation : whereof six desire capacities, if the King's pleasure be so that the house be dissolved."

† Wright, 139.   ‡ Wright, 129, 136.

sions appear to have been abandoned in haste after a short experience, and the Vicar General returned to his former method. They continued, however, it is probable, for as long a space of time as that which had sufficed for compiling the Black Book: whether they went beyond the four or five counties of which their returns are extant is uncertain: and the reader must be left to determine why it was necessary to visit so many little houses after all the little houses had been condemned; and why in some parts of the country so many of the little houses were found virtuous, while in other parts, according to the Comperta, they were all dens of infamy and treason. For the rest, it is observable that the visitation proceeded after the passing of the Act exactly as it had proceeded before: little houses and large were visited alike. But the inter-cessions of the new visitors were in vain. The little houses were already dissolved in being placed at the mercy of the King: and before the Court of Augmentations was many weeks old, collectors, appointed for the various archdeaconries, began to appear at the doors of the doomed monasteries, to take inventories of their goods, to discharge or expel those of the inmates whom they chose, and to secure the convent seal, without which the convent had no power to get in either the rents or the produce of their lands. The visit of these collectors was soon followed by the dissolution of the house.* There is no instance on record of the

* "Touching demeanour and the payment to the collectors, in the archdeaconry of Coventry, Derby, Staff., and Salop: the collectors have almost made an end in these four archdeaconries; as far I can perceive is no denying: and as for the collector of the archdeaconry of Chester, I never heard from him, so I supposed he had good speed in his gathering."—Richard Strete, priest, to Crumwel, May 12.—Wright, 128. Strete himself seems to have been a collector: he tells in this letter that he had been at Calwich before the end of April, where he took an inventory, he "discharged and put forth such persons as were not meet to be there, and

smaller convents being transferred to the great abbeys,
according to the alternative pretended by the statute.
They were turned out on capacities and pensions,
often indeed at their own request; and it has been
computed that by the dissolution of three hundred and
seventy convents, under the number of twelve apiece,
ten thousand persons were thrown upon the world.*

Their dismission into the world was not unwelcome
to many of the religious; nor can it be doubted that in
entering religion, many of them found that they had
embraced a life for which they were unfit.   Their
readiness to leave it, their groans beneath the burden
which they found to be intolerable, may excite compassion, may be a proof that an unnatural life cannot
be forced on large numbers without cruelty, but can
scarcely be alleged in evidence that the system had
fallen into laxity and corruption.   These weak brethren were quick to discover that their life was not according to Christ's law; in their artless way they hit
upon the objection which has been brought in turn
against every religious ordinance and doctrine by those
who have desired to dissent therefrom: but the experienced in religious controversies will be slow to confuse
this with a proof that their life was one of hypocritical
incontinence.   Nature was strong within them: they were
willing to say anything to be relieved of the trammels
and restraints which beset them; and they hailed the
myrmidons of Crumwel as deliverers.   When Legh
was in Cambridgeshire, before the Act about the little

left such as were husbands, he made sure the convent seal and the
evidence." I have ventured to suppose that these "collectors" were
officers of the Court of Augmentations, and that they were appointed for
more archdeaconries than those mentioned by Strete. But I have no
proof of either.

* If the computation included all who were dependent on the dissolved
houses for their living, it might not be excessive.

houses was passed, he relates that religious persons
would fall on their knees, hold up their hands, and implore of God, the King, and the Vicar General, to be
dismissed from their religion, saying that they lived in
it contrary to God's law and their conscience, trusting
that the King of his gracious goodness would set them
at liberty out of that bondage, which they were not
able longer to endure, but would fall into desperation
or else run away.*   As soon as the Act was passed,
one of the immediate consequences seems to have been
that it loosened the obedience of some of the monks in
the larger houses to their abbots and their vows.   They
beheld with envy the escape of their less important
brethren into the world; and some of them procured
by prayers, or even by money, capacities to depart
from their houses.   Of all the orders the most lax
appears to have been that of the Augustin canons;
and of the Augustin canons those who lived at
Bodmin were no better than the rest.   The prior of
Bodmin, Thomas Vivian, complained in a letter that
his convent had long been living " against the good
order of religion, to the great slander of the same, as all
the country could tell."   The bishop had lately visited
them and given certain injunctions, which the Prior
was to see observed.   These injunctions were "no
harder than their own rule and profession bound
them, and as all other religious men used and observed
where good religion was kept."   But they were so
much aggrieved by them that they intended to depart
with capacities without the Prior's consent.   One of
them had bought a capacity, but as the terms of it
required him to have the Prior's license, he had restrained him from departing, not for any great loss that
he should have of him, but for the ill example of others,

* Wright, 82.

for if he were allowed to depart in that manner, never a canon would stay in the house. These rebels were aided and abetted by some neighbouring gentlemen.* The abbot of Kenilworth, a house of the same unruly order, had sent one of his canons to have the governance of the small dependant house or cell of Brook in Rutland-shire; and the new prior, for that he was dissatisfied with his stipend, maliciously surrendered the cell to the Court óf Augmentations, thereby exposing the parent monastery to the ruinous forfeiture of one thousand marks, under the surety of which sum some-body had taken a lease of the cell.† A monk of the richly endowed Benedictine Abbey of Pershore, the superb tower of which still adorns the slopes of Worces-tershire, Richard Beerley by name, took upon him to write to the Vicar General a pathetic but somewhat sycophantic appeal for deliverance. He hailed Crum-wel as "most reverend lord in God, the second person in the realm of England, endued with all grace and goodness," to whom he submitted himself, "a sinful and poor creature, and his lowly and meek scribbling." His conscience grudged at the religion which he and his brethren observed, for it was "no rule," said he, "of St. Bennet, nor yet no commandment of God, nor of no saint, but lewd and foolish ceremonies, made some in old time and some in their own time by lewd and indiscreet fathers, which had done their duties and ful-filled their own ceremonies; and let the precepts and commandments of God go." He had been a dissem-bler long time in a religion, which was in vain, as St. James said, and brought forth no good fruits. "Better out than in the religion except it were the true religion of Christ." They nothing searched for the doctrine of Christ, but all followed their own sensuality and plea-

* Wright, 130.   † *Ib.*, 134.

sure. It was all vain glory. He had also a secret thing on his conscience which moved him to go out of the religion, were it never so perfect; the same was in other young persons as in himself, if a man might judge, for Christ said, Judge not and ye shall not be judged; and there were many other foul vices done amongst religious men, not religious men, but dissemblers with God. He would instruct his grace somewhat of religious men, and how the King's commandment was kept in putting out of books the Bishop of Rome's usurped power. Monks drank and bowled after collation till ten or twelve of the clock, and came to matins "as drunk as mice," and played "some at cards, some at dice, and at tables: some came to matins beginning at the midst, and some when it was almost done, and would not come there so only for bodily punishment, nothing for God's sake," with many other vices which they used, which he had not leisure to express. "Abbots, monks, priests, did little or nothing to put out of books the Bishop of Rome's name, for he himself knew in divers books where his name and usurped power was." "Let his most gracious lord help him out of that vain religion, and make him his servant, handmaid and bedeman, and save his soul." The writer of this curious epistle added ingenuously that he had been commanded by Crumwel's commissary thus to write his mind.*

From the beginning of the great Visitation the agents of Crumwel and the King carried with them Articles to be enquired and Injunctions, which they

---

* Wright, 132. One bit of this extraordinarily spelt document reads like an old distitch:

.   "And cum to mattens as dronck as myss,
    And sume at cardes, sume at dyyss."

It may be observed that the word ceremonies in this and all such documents is used in the extended sense of all the monastic rules and observances, the regulæ ceremoniales.

seem to have been at liberty to supplement or expand
at their own discretion. The questions which they
were instructed to put to the religious seemed to propose reformation rather than suppression; but it may
be observed that reformation demands a reformer: to
create or revive a religious institution, the inspiring
example of a saint is necessary; and the monks who
were bidden to keep their cloisters and observe their
rules by Henry and Crumwel failed to recognise in
these exhortations the voice of a Benedict or a Hilde-
brand. A reformer however may often be defined
as a man who wants to get higher action out of
another man; and the authors of this visitation
seemed very anxious to ascertain and to improve the
religious and moral state of the monks and nuns.
Their interrogations extended over everything, from
the shaving of the head to the order of the dormitories;
from occasional absence to manifest apostacy, or de-
sertion of the cloister; from prescribed fasts and
silences to the continual observance of the three great
vows; from the apparel of the brethren to the trap-
pings of their horses; from the conduct of the master
toward the convent to the conduct of the convent
toward the master. The sum of all seemed to be contained in the double question, whether they knew the
rule which they professed, and whether in their profession they observed the rule which they knew.
Intermixed with the enquiries which the love of virtue
prompted were others which might be imputed to
justice, and the desire to restore or confirm the honesty
of others. The monasteries were required to exhibit
their title deeds, the names of their founders and bene-
factors, the yearly sum of their revenues and rents,
their exemptions, if they were exempt places, and
their local statutes. They were asked whether their
houses were indebted; whether any inventory had

been made of their movables, jewels, ornaments, vestments, money, and plate; whether their plate, jewels,
and chattels were pledged, sold, or alienated; whether
their master dealt honestly with them in leases, grants,
annuities, or corrodies; or favoured his own kinsfolk
in ordering the same.

The convents indeed were encouraged or compelled to be informers concerning their masters or
superiors, and the younger part of them to make declarations concerning the conduct of the seniors in their
offices. It was asked whether the master kept hospitality; whether he admitted novices for reward or
for their willing and toward mind; whether he administered the patronage of his house purely or simo-
niacally: what benefices he kept in his own hands.
Concerning the officials it was enquired whether any
of them held more offices than one; whether the
treasurer, cellerer, and the rest gave in their accounts
regularly; whether any of the seniors were deputed to
instruct the novices in the rules according to their
profession: whether any preceptor were appointed to
teach them grammar and good learning. Such were
some of the Articles to be enquired, which, to the
number of more than eighty, might be administered
to every house of religion.*

Nor less conducive to godliness and discipline were
the Injunctions which the Visitors were empowered to
pour into the gaps which might be disclosed by their
interrogations. If, indeed, there were any error here,
it seemed to lie on the side of strictness and a desire to
promote the piety of others, rather than in a too great
indulgence of human frailty. A new Regula Henrici
seemed added to the rules which the several orders
professed, laying on the astonished monks far greater

---

* Burnet, Coll. of Rec. Bk. iii. No. 2; or Wilkins, iii. 786.

severities than those which they had bound themselves
to observe.   In every chapterhouse it was proclaimed
" that no monk or brother of this monastery by any
means go forth of the precinct of the same."   To the
captives thus immured the only entrance left for visitors
from without was by the great fore-gate, which was to be
diligently watched by a porter specially appointed for that
purpose, who was to repel all manner of women from
entering into the monastery.   Women, of what state or
degree soever they were, were utterly excluded from the
limits of the monastery, unless they first obtained license
of the King or his Visitor.   From their muniments or
books the religious orders or places were ordered to
erase all statutes which seemed to bind them to obedience or subjection to the Bishop of Rome or any other
foreign potentate; they were to observe and teach
all the contents of all the oaths and declarations lately
made about the Succession and the Supreme Head;
and diligently to instruct their juniors and scholars
" that the King's power is by the laws of God most
excellent of all under God on earth, and that we ought
to obey him afore all others by God's prescript; that the
Bishop of Rome's authority, heretofore usurped, by no
means is founded or established by Holy Scripture, but
that the same, partly by the craft and deceit of the
Bishop of Rome, and by his evil and ambitious canons
and decretals, and partly by the toleration and permission of princes, by little and little had grown up."   The
brethren were to take their refections together, on
such days as they ate flesh, in a place called the
Misericorde ; in the refectory on other days.   They
were to sit four at a mess, and to take their refection
soberly, without excess, giving thanks to God : to be
content with such victuals as were set before them, not
demanding any certain or usual portion of meat as their

due, which they had been wont to do: and at every refection some of them were to read some chapter of the New Testament or Old to the rest, keeping silence and giving audience. The abbot or master was to have a daily table for himself and his guests, not over sumptuous, but honestly furnished with common meats, at which he, or some senior in his stead, was to sit to receive and gently entertain the strangers the guests. No brother was to send any part of his meat or leavings to any person; but an almoner was to gather the leavings both of the convent and the strangers' table, and distribute them to poor people; among whom special consideration was to be had of the kinsfolk of the brethren, of the sick, and also of such persons as endeavoured to get their living, but could not fully help themselves through their chargeable household and multitude of children. But neither were these to be so cherished that they should fall to idleness, nor were alms to be given to mighty and valiant beggars and such michers as commonly resorted to such places. They were all to sleep in the dormitory in separate beds; no brother to " have any child or boy lying or privily accompanying with them, or otherwise haunting him, other than to help him to mass." In the religion of the religious, in the rules and ceremonies which they used, some alterations were made, which must have added to the first surprise of the monks, and increased the monotony to which they were condemned in future. Every day by the space of one hour a lesson of Holy Scripture was to be kept in the convent, to which all were to resort under pain of punishment; while on the other hand their long Hours, which they had been wont to sing, might be read " with a low and treatable voice." And yet singing had been, from the first institution of the monastic life, the very essence of their recurrent services. After Divine Service done, the brethren were to read or hear somewhat of Holy Scripture, or occupy themselves in some such honest and laudable exercise. Their rule, their statutes, the customs of their religion, which they had vowed to obey, were to be obeyed "so far as they did agree with Holy Scripture, and the Word of God;" the abbot or prior was to expound to them daily a certain part of the rule which they professed, and "apply the same always to the doctrine of Christ, and not contrariwise:" teaching them "that the said rule, and other their principles of religion, so far as they were laudable, came out of Holy Scripture," and shewing them the places whence they were derived. "Their other ceremonies and observances," he was directed to inform them, "were but letters, principles, or introductions to true Christianity, or to preserve an order in the Church." For such ceremonies and observances they were to look for no reward, "except they referred all such to Christ." Indeed it seemed that they were to be made to understand that their religion, so far from setting them above others, sunk them below others, and was but a means "that they might thereby the more easily keep such things as Christ had commanded as well to them as to all Christian people." "True religion," exclaimed the author of these Injunctions, "is not contained in apparel, manner of going, shaven heads, and such other marks; nor in silence, fasting, uprising in the night, singing, and such other kind of ceremonies: but in cleanness of mind, pureness of living, Christ's faith not feigned, and brotherly charity, and true honouring of God in spirit and verity; those other institutions are steps to the chief point and end of religion; let them be diligently exhorted not to stick and surcease in such ceremonies and observances, as though they had perfectly fulfilled the chief end and utmost of the whole true religion : but that when they have once passed such things, they endeavour themselves to higher things, and convert their minds from such external matters to more inward and deeper considerations, as the law of God, and Christian religion doth teach and shew."*

It is little to be wondered that the monks found it impossible to continue on such terms as these. The jurisdiction of the sanctioner of all their orders denied, their allowed liberty turned to absolute imprisonment, their religion contemned and deprived of all that was characteristic, their rules tested by Holy Scripture, their convents defamed or reproached with hideous crimes, themselves esteemed below the vilest profligate who had learned to cry " None but Christ ; " forced in some points to set aside, in others to go beyond their rules, and at the same time told that their observances were but the rudiments and introductions of true religion : they were compelled to resign at length a corporate existence so insupportable and so ignominious. The surrenders of the greater abbeys (which was the design of all) began to flow after a time into the ready reservoir of the Court of Augmentations ; but not, in many instances, until further pressure had been laid upon them ; nor has account been taken by history of the silent sufferings which must have been endured in the meantime by the imprisoned inmates.

On the moral condition of the monasteries a dissertation may be spared, if it be observed that there is not, and probably never was, evidence that would warrant a general conclusion. But the popular notion cannot be

---

* *Ib.* Mr. Froude finds the language of this passage "exceedingly beautiful," and ascribes the Injunctions to Crumwel or the King. If they must have been written by one of the two, the superior enlightenment seems to point to Crumwel ; but there are some slight grounds for believing the author to have been Bartlet.

maintained, that there was once a time when they were sublimely perfect, but that they had declined long time into corruption, sinking from bad to worse, until, amid the gathering indignation of the people, they had reached a point of degeneracy which lay beyond the sufferance of God or man. So far as their history can be traced in English antiquity, they exhibited at all times the same combination of human frailty and super-human sanctity; and the rebukes with which Arch-bishop Cuthbert in the eighth century, or in the tenth with which King Edgar denounced their shortcoming, were repeated in succeeding ages, even by their friends and wellwishers, until we come to the letters of Bishop Fox and the satires of Sir Thomas More. The wonder is, not that they were so bad as they may have been but that they were so good as they were. No human institution, it is probable, ever exhibited such diversity of conduct, or underwent so many vicissitudes. The condition of a monastery changed, from better to worse, and from worse to better, according to the character of the person who ruled it : and in the same generation, neighbouring houses might display the opposite spec-tacles of austere devotion and of profligate hypocrisy. I am inclined to believe that in the reign of Henry the Eighth the monasteries were not worse but better than they had been previously, and that they were doing fairly the work for which they had been founded. In ancient institutions it may happen that they are at their best within their own compass, when the original forces which called them into being have ceased, and they are powerless to put forth new life. The religious houses, taken altogether, may have been in a state of revived discipline, when the blast of dissolution went forth against them ; but the impulses which had called one order after another into being had spent themselves long before: the monastic tree had ceased to germinate: and an institution which is standing still may feel the touch of death in any accident. They were often found in poverty and debt: they had not kept pace with the nation in the growth of wealth; and they had great difficulty in keeping up their numbers. From such a system on so large a scale there were certain evils which were inseparable. Many who had entered religion had been forced into it by unfeeling kinsmen at an unfit age; the Visitors found some who had entered being no more than ten years old, who in their riper youth, their manhood or womanhood, cried out that they were bound with a burden too heavy for them to bear. Some of the houses were the prey of furious factions, whose hostility proceeded at least to the length of deadly menaces.

Three months after the premature delivery of a dead prince, and four months after the death of the princess whom she had supplanted, Anne Boleyn was sent to the Tower, roaring with laughter at the assurance that the poorest subject of the King would have justice. The unfortunate creature, who had borne so great a part in the revolution, was arrested by her uncle Norfolk: the same hideous crimes were laid against her which had served to destroy the monasteries: and the records of her trial have disappeared almost as completely as the Black Book. She was examined before the Council at Greenwich, May 2, when she complained that she was cruelly handled: her supposed paramours were tried by jury, May 13; she herself was condemned two days afterwards by a commission of lords, sitting in the court of her prison; two days after her condemnation she was degraded by a sentence of divorce; and her execution followed, after the same brief interval, May 19. The sound of a solitary cannon shot had announced to London that a prisoner of distinction had entered the Tower; within twenty days a second gun proclaimed that the Queen had met her doom. The King dressed himself in white on the day of her death, and married Jane Seymour the next morning.

The part played by the Primate of all England in this rapid tragedy was ignominious enough. Neglected by the King, and exposed to the insolence of Crumwel,* Archbishop Cranmer had passed his time of late in the retirement of his seats of Adlington, Otford, and Ford. Of the machinations which preceded the arrest of Anne Boleyn, he remained ignorant; nor, though one of the King's Council, was he summoned to attend her examination or trial. At length, on the day when she was before the Council at Greenwich, he received a peremptory mandate from Crumwel, in the King's name, to come to Lambeth, and hold himself in readiness there, but not to venture into the presence of His Majesty. He arrived at Lambeth in the course of the same day, and after a night of suspense and misery, relieved his mind the next morning by addressing the King in a letter, which strikingly displays the alternations of benevolence and timidity. His mind, he said, was clean amazed; he never had better opinion in woman than he had in the Queen; and this made him think that she should not be culpable. But again he thought that the King would not have

---

* Cranmer had ventured to say a word of remonstrance on the manner in which the religious houses were being handled at this time. He wrote to Crumwel, 22 April, "I was ever hitherto cold, but now I am in a heat with the cause of religion, which goeth all contrary to mine expectation, if it be as the fame goeth: wherein I would wonder fain break my mind unto you, and if you please I will come to such place as you shall appoint for the same purpose." *Letters*, 332. Religion seems used here technically: his terms for it in the now common sense are the gospel, or the truth.

gone so far if she had not been surely culpable. He was more bound to her than to any creature living except the King; God's law, nature, and kindness, bound him to pray for her, that she might declare herself innocent; but if she were found culpable, no true subject but would desire the offence to be punished without mercy. He had loved her much for her love to God and the Gospel; but if she were proved culpable, none that loved God and the Gospel but would hate her above all other, for no creature in those times had so much slandered the Gospel. He trusted that the King would bear no less favour to the Gospel than before, forasmuch as he was not led by affection for her, but by zeal for the truth. Such was the trembling voice which alone was uplifted for the unhappy Queen.

Scarcely had the Archbishop finished his letter, when he received an order from the Lord Chancellor, the Earls of Oxford and Sussex, and the King's Chamberlain, part of the Court of enquiry that had been investigating the conduct of Anne, to attend in the Star Chamber. He went: he heard what things they were empowered to tell him: and added to the letter, which he now despatched, a postscript, in which he said that he was "exceeding sorry that such faults could be proved by the Queen, as he had heard of their relation."* By this virtual resignation of the Queen's cause, Cranmer declared himself ready for whatever service might be required of him. Nothing less would satisfy the ferocious King than a nullity of marriage, a divorce, the bastardy of the daughter who had been borne him by the frail or imprudent object of his late affection; and to the sentence of the lay tribunal, which

---

* Cranmer's Lett., 323, Burnet, Froude.

gave him her life, was to be added an ecclesiastical condemnation which deprived her of rank and honour. Cranmer returned to his rest at Otford for a few days,[*] during which the Queen was in the hands of the lay judges; but repairing again to Lambeth when she was condemned, he is said to have visited her in the Tower on the day after her trial, as her confessor. She is said to have made an admission which touched the validity of her marriage; but whether this were her own præcontract with the Earl of Northumberland, or the King's previous intrigue with her sister Mary, or something else; or whether the whole story of this admission be invented, must remain uncertain.[†] It is certain, however, that Cranmer was furnished with some argument or allegation, which he professed to consider sufficient to justify him in holding a court to try the validity of the King's second marriage. In the swollen verbiage of the age his reasons appeared sufficient indeed. From all that had been "done, enacted, concluded, proposed, exhibited, alleged, proved and confessed," the prelate said that he had found reason to minister and object certain articles both to the King and Queen, "for the salvation of their souls, and the due effect of law," and he summoned them both to appear in his court to answer them.[‡] No delay was allowed; the assessors of the Archbishop were ap-

---

[*] He wrote a letter from Otford, 6 May.

[†] That Cranmer visited her in the Tower rests on a letter from Kingston to Crumwel, given in Constantine's Memoirs, Froude, ii. 501. It seems very doubtful whether, as some writers say, she was ever brought before Cranmer at Lambeth. Her Attainder says indeed that she admitted something before the Archbishop "sitting judicially," but if so, it was probably not in person but by her proctor, Sampson.

[‡] "Per acta, inactitata, deducta, proposita, exhibita, allegata, probata, et *confessata* in hoc negotio," &c. *Wilk.*, iii. 804. The last word may be the origin of the story of the Confession. It probably referred in reality to Smeeton's admissions against the Queen.

pointed, the proctors of the King and of the Queen respectively were assigned ; the time for holding the court was fixed to be the very next day.

Before the hour of four in the morning of one of the darkest days of his tormented life, the dejected Archbishop, always an early riser, and prevented now by anxiety from sleep, was walking in his garden at Lambeth. He called to remembrance the court of Dunstable, where he had pronounced the divorce of Katharine ; and sighed to reflect that now it was to be his fate to declare the nullity of the marriage of Anne, a marriage which he had examined judicially, and confirmed with the full power of his metropolitical office. For three years he had been ministering oaths, issuing monitions, bidding prayers, and preaching sermons on behalf of the validity of that marriage and the legitimacy of the offspring born of it. The whole realm had been convulsed for three years, the religious orders had been shamefully persecuted, the new-invented treasons had surrendered liberty in that behalf, the noblest heads in England had rolled on the scaffold in that question :. and now he was commanded to become the instrument of undoing his own work. He was treated with short ceremony or open contempt by men whom he truly felt to be inferior to himself in everything but force and guile : above all, he found himself the tool of the unscrupulous layman who, though a subject, held a higher office than he in the Church of which he was the Primate. What was to be the end of the degradation of the realm and of himself ? While he was thus musing, he beheld one approaching who was well known to him, and whose not altogether insignificant part in the English Reformation began at this time. Alexander Aless, an adventurous divine of Scotland, of fair repute for ability and learning, was perhaps the earliest of the long flight of foreigners which was attracted to England by the Reformation. Originally a canon of the magnificent monastic establishment of St. Andrew's, he had seen the error of his ways; and deserting the superb towers of the ecclesiastical capital of the north, whereon the golden foil, glittering afar, flashed the rare sunbeam back, he sought, after some intermediate wanderings, the truer light held forth in a milder clime by Henry, by Crumwel, and by Cranmer. It was he who persuaded Melanchthon to dedicate to the English monarch the celebrated work which defined the doctrines of the Protestants: and by his hand the Loci Theologici had been presented to the King. By the King he was rewarded with a stipend and the title or office of King's Scholar: of which the principal duty appears to have been to assist the theological learning of the King's Vicegerent. It is from him that we learn how great a concern Crumwel had in the destruction of Anne Boleyn, and how deeply he had laboured to compass it. An evil dream had prevented Aless also from repose, and by a coincidence he had directed his morning walk to Lambeth garden. His dream had taken a strangely definite shape; it was that the Queen was beheaded that day. Apologising for his intrusion, he related the circumstance to Cranmer. The Archbishop heard in silence, and then asked, " Know ye not what is to happen to-day ? " Aless answered that he had heard no public news since the Queen's imprisonment. The Archbishop solemnly raised his eyes to heaven, and said, " She who has been Queen of England on earth, will this day become a Queen in heaven ; " and he burst into tears.*

* See the remarkable letter which the stipendiary Scottish divine addressed in after years to Queen Elizabeth concerning the death of her mother. He attributes that fatal event mainly to the chagrin of the King

At the hour of nine the same morning, May 17, the barges of the assessors, proctors, and other assistants in the pageant of justice, arrived at Lambeth stairs. The assessors of Cranmer were the Lord Chancellor, Audley; the Duke of Suffolk; the Earl of Oxford; the Earl of Sussex; the Lord Sandys; Secretary and Vicegerent Crumwel; Sir William Fitzwilliams; the Comptroller of the Royal Household, Paulet; Doctor Tregonwell; Doctor Oliver of Oxford; Gwent, the Dean of Arches; Archdeacon Bonner; the active Councillor, Archdeacon and Doctor, Bedyl; the active Archdeacon and Doctor, Layton; and the active Doctor Legh. The King's proctor was Doctor Richard Sampson, Dean of the Chapel Royal, a man whose zeal in the King's business was more conspicuous about this time than his ability; and for the Queen appeared Doctors Wotton and Barbour. Witnesses and notaries were in attendance. The Archbishop led the way into the crypt of Lambeth; and in that sepulchral chamber the cause was pleaded, the witnesses were heard, the sentence was pronounced within the space of two hours.* The Archbishop declared that, having first invoked the name of Christ, having God alone before

---

at the failure of his embassy to the Protestant princes; which embassy he affirms to have been sent by the instigation of Anne. "I am persuaded that the true and chief cause of the hatred, the treachery, and the false accusations laid to the charge of that most holy Queen was this, that she persuaded the King to send an embassy into Germany to the princes who had embraced the Gospel. If other arguments of the truth of this were wanting, a single one would be sufficient, viz. that before that embassy had returned, the Queen was executed." The more common view is more probable, that the failure of the embassy was caused by the fall of the Queen. The unevangelical bishops, adds the Scot, with Gardiner at their head, were in a plot against her. *Cal. of For. Papers of Eliz.*, i. 524. See also Hook's Cranmer, i. 506. His dream about her execution was most horrid.

* "Inter horas 9 et 11 ante meridiem, in quodam basso sacello infra ædes nostras infra Lamehith." *Wilk.*, iii. 803.

his eyes, having carefully examined the whole process in that case with the help of counsel learned in the law, he found the marriage consummated between the King and the most serene Lady Anne to be and always to have been null and void, without strength or effect, of no force or moment, and to be held a thing of nought, invalid, vain and empty. Herewith the court arose; the flock of officials, great and small, dispersed, and the cell was left to darkness.*

* As this Cranmerian sentence was afterwards subscribed by Convocation, it belongs to the history of the Church of England, and may be dusted for the reader's eye.

" Nos, Thomas, archiepiscopus, primas, et metropolitanus antedictus, Christi nomine primitus invocato, ac ipsum solum Deum præ oculis nostris habentes, rimato per nos toto et integro processu, in eodem negotio habito et facto, de et cum consilio juris peritorum, cum quibus communicavimus in hac parte, præfatum matrimonium inter præfatos illustrissimum et potentissimum dominum nostrum Regem, et serenissimam dominam Annam Reginam, ut præfertur, contractum, solemnizatum et consummatum, prorsus et omnino fuisse nullum, invalidum, et inane, viribus quoque et effectu Juris semper caruisse et carere, ac nullius fuisse et esse roboris seu momenti, pronuntiamus, decernimus, et declaramus, illudque pro nullo, invalido, irrito, et inani reputamus, censemus, et adjudicamus per hanc nostram sententiam diffinitivam, quam ferimus et promulgamus in his scriptis. In quorum omnium et singulorum fidem et testimonium has literas testimoniales, sive præsens publicum instrumentum de et super prolatione dictæ sententiæ diffinitivæ inde, fieri, &c.: ac sigilli nostri majoris appensione communiri fecimus atque curavimus," &c. *Wilk.*, iii. 804.

CHAPTER VI.

A. D. 1536.

This new business of the death of Queen Anne seemed to demand a new 'Parliament with haste. To his legal sanctuary Henry flew indeed precipitately as soon as her head was fallen : the writs, the elections were expedited; and in three weeks after the execution a new Parliament, no less loyal than its predecessor, was sitting in Westminster. The King himself, fresh from slaughter, found it necessary to appear in person in the House of Lords at an early session, June 10: on which occasion the Commons presented as their Speaker Sir Richard Rich, a man whom his share in the business of Sir Thomas More had lately made scarcely less conspicuous. Rich, in an eloquent address, with the approbation of his hearers, vindicated and extolled the justice, the valour, and the beauty of the King by the comparison of Solomon, of Samson, and of Absalom.* The Act which was immediately made on the affair of the late Queen resembled a treatise more than a statute: it was so long: stupendous verbosity covered the recantation of the realm. In the way of a formal address or petition to his Majesty, the Houses rehearsed and reversed the former Acts for ratifying the marriage

---

* "Quem ut prudentem et justum Salomoni, ob corporis robur et fortitudinem Samsoni, et ob formam et pulcritudinem Absalomi, digne et merito comparuit." *Lords Journals.*

of the unfortunate Anne, for entailing the imperial crown
to her offspring, and for making it treason to slander
or speak against the premisses. "God," said they, "of
his infinite goodness, from whom no secret things can
be hid, hath caused to be brought to light, evident and
open knowledge, as well certain just, true, and lawful
impediments unknown at the making of the said Acts,
and sithen that time hath been confessed by the said
Lady Anne before the most reverend father in God
Thomas, Archbishop of Canterbury, metropolitan and
primate of all England, sitting judicially for the same :
by which plainly appeareth that the said marriage
was never good nor consonant to the laws." From
the abominable and detestable treasons of Anne and
her accomplices it appeared that there had been "most
fearful peril and danger of the destruction" of the royal
person, and the "utter loss, disherison, and desolation
of the realm." They were therefore attainted of
treason, and their goods forfeited. The offspring of
both the former marriages, the lady Mary and the lady
Elizabeth were alike declared illegitimate; and the High
Court condescended, by a special branch, to make it
high treason in anyone to say that either of them was
legitimate. The King was warmly congratulated on
the ardent love of his country, on the excellent goodness, which had led him to assay the marriage state
again : the personal charms of his new queen were
described in terms that sound a little less than delicate :
and the succession was entailed to her future offspring.
The infamous treason laws which were revoked in
Anne were renewed in Jane ; and a corporal oath to
observe the new succession was prescribed for all
subjects, as well temporal as spiritual, holding any
tenure of the King. Occasion was taken to rehearse
the inconveniences which were alleged to have arisen

from marriages within the prohibited degrees upon dispensations: and all appeals to Rome were again forbidden. By a shameful provision it was enacted that, though the Act of Succession in favour of Queen Anne was abrogated, those persons who had offended against it still remained subject to the penalties; but on the other hand, those persons who had "of no malice" spoken or done anything against the late Queen or her daughter before the repeal of the Act, and before the repeal of any other Act concerning her, should be held free of damage.* Thus, on the one hand, the London Carthusians still remained under penalty for refusing to acknowledge the validity of the marriage of Anne and the nullity of the marriage of Katharine, after Anne was divorced, beheaded, and attainted: while, on the other hand, all who had taken any part in the proceedings against the late Queen were safe, from Crumwel and Cranmer down to lieutenant Kingston and Mrs. Cosin.

The authority and jurisdiction of the Bishop of Rome had been extirpated effectually by the former Parliament: but a careful rake enabled the new assembly to scrape some remaining dregs of it out of the realm. The Bishop of Rome was pursued in a law making it a Præmunire to extol his authority: and the Renunciation of the Pope, made by the Bishops in a former year,† was followed now by an order that all ecclesiastical and lay officers should be sworn to renounce him on pain of high treason, and that all such officers should hold any oath hitherto taken in maintenance of the Pope to be invalid. By another Act all bulls, breves, dispensations and faculties that were already obtained and were in the realm were made void; and thus the privileges of many of the remaining monasteries, such as appropria-

* 28 H. VIII. 7.   † See above, p. 254.

tions and exemptions, might be supposed to have
fallen : but for the time being these were saved by a
special provision ; and the abbots and priors, the
abbesses and prioresses who were still left, along with
all other religious bodies and persons, were allowed
to retain all their customary "tokens, ensigns, and
ceremonies," understanding that they retained them
not by virtue of any faculty from the Bishop of Rome,
but by the deed of the realm now made. Their
pluralities, unions, trialties, commendams, appropriations, and exemptions were to continue for more than
a year, even to the Feast of St. Michael of the year
following, in all such uses as might be dispensed by the
Archbishop of Canterbury.* But while with apparent
justice the privileges of the greater monasteries seemed
to be preserved, the greater monasteries themselves,
reduced to an intolerable condition, ceased not to fall
rapidly in unavoidable surrender.

To prevent the confluence of idle beneficed men
at the Universities under pretence of study, it was
ordained that none under the age of forty years should
be non-resident on their benefices, unless they attended
the public lectures both in their colleges and in the
schools, and in their proper persons kept sophisms,
problems, and disputations as opponent and respon-
dent in the same. None above the age of forty should
be excused from residence on their benefices, unless
they were officials of colleges or of the Universities.

An Act about sanctuaries, and another about first-
fruits concluded the labours of the session in the reformation of the Church. In the one a brief clause took
away benefit of clergy from all persons in holy orders
offending against any of the former statutes by which

* 28 H. VIII. 10 and 16.

that privilege had been limited, and put them on the same footing as laymen. The other ordered the firstfruits to be paid to the King from the time of the first vacation of every benefice. Archbishops, bishops, and other ordinaries, it was alleged, taking advantage of an omission in the former acts, kept benefices vacant sometimes for a year, and took the firstfruits of the interval for themselves. To stop this, the fruits were ordered to belong to the next incumbent from the time of the vacancy, and he was to pay the King out of them. If any ordinary received any of the fruits, he was to forfeit three times as much, half of the fine going to the King, and the other half to the next incumbent. If an incumbent, it was added, let any part of his benefice, and then avoided it, the lease was to hold good for six years.*

A large crop of private acts concerning the exchange or grant of monastic lands, matured so soon after the ingathering of the late session, proved the fertility of the soil of the harvest of estates. Robert Warton, the defamed or infamous Abbot of Bermondsey, gave to the King the whole of the vast manor of Southwark, reserving for himself and his convent no more than a pension of twenty shillings a year out of the Rectory of St. George's. The adjoining manor of Paris Garden was bartered by Sir William Weston, the Prior of the Hospital of St. John of Jerusalem, for the dissolved Priory of Kilburn in Middlesex, with the domains thereto belonging. Southwark and Paris Garden were both bestowed on the new Queen, for the increase of her dowry. The advent to power of the Seymours, a family destined to be steeped in the spoils of religion, was marked further by the grant of the Priories of

---

* C. XIII. 1 and 11.

Furleigh and Eston, with "ground, church, precincts, steeple, and churchyard," and a vast number of manors, advowsons, and appropriations, which was made to Sir Edward Seymour, Viscount Beauchamp. To help to furnish the site of a new palace at Westminster which was designed, Covent Garden, the fair garden of St. Peter's of Westminster, with seven acres of land outside of it, was made over to the King by William Boston, the Abbot, who received for it a tract named Harley Wood, belonging lately to Harley priory in Berkshire. Nor was the King unmindful at the same time to amend the interior discipline of Westminster. The Prior of that great fraternity, holding, it seems, by some privilege the independent position of a corporation sole, was often at variance with his superior, the Abbot. Therefore the King, with that power of phraseology which ever marked his zeal for the better order of others, made void that body politic and corporation sole, seeing that it was " to the high displeasure of Almighty God, great unquietness and slander of the said monastery, let of good religion, destruction of virtue, decay of true perfection, maintenance of vice, and hindrance of divine service in the same." Lord Sandys, a nobleman who had been very active against Anne Boleyn, received his reward in the gift of Montisfont Priory in Southamptonshire, with all belonging to it, except the gold and silver ornaments of the church. Nor was Crumwel wanting to Crumwel at this season. The great manors of Wimbledon and Mortlake, which had been torn from Cranmer's patrimony of Canterbury, in the last session, in exchange for the poor abbey of Bradsole, were given to Crumwel now; and to them was added the manor of Burstow, another part of the possessions of Canterbury, Cranmer receiving in compensation for all his losses the Priory of St. Gregory without Canterbury, on which however were reserved some portions for Sir Christopher Hales, a person soon to be noted among the Visitors of the abbeys.* But while the Parliament trafficked freely in the sites, buildings and lands of the dissolved monasteries, their behaviour in regard to another species of monastic property was, though not inconsistent, of a less liberal appearance. In all ages the efforts of the Church of England had been directed to the enfranchisement of the villains, serfs, or bondmen. Notwithstanding the efforts of the Church that class of persons still remained on the soil of England in considerable numbers, especially on the estates of the religious houses, where the tenure of land was least disturbed. The servitia, or bondmen, were indeed regularly enrolled among the chattels of the houses which were surrendered. Their condition was thus brought under the notice of Parliament: a bill for their manumission was brought in, read thrice in one day, and rejected.† Why should it have been otherwise? The bondmen were among the possessions which came into the hands of those who had interest in every gift or exchange of lands. The King rewarded his loyal estates, and ended the session, by a second visit in person, July 18: and a second panegyric, pronounced by the eloquent Rich, contained another happy comparison. The sun dries up noxious vapours, and nourishes seeds and fruits with heat. So the King.‡

When the late Parliament, in its last session, had been busiest about the Church, the Convocation of Canterbury had been convened only to be prorogued;

---

* Ch. 19: 21, 38: 29, 49: 35, 50.

† "14 July: Billa concernens Manumissionem Servorum vocatorum Bondmen, semel, bis, ter lecta, et rejecta." *Lords Journals.*   ‡ *Ib.*

when the other estates were yielding the smaller monasteries to the tender mercies of the King, the clergy had met only to consult about paying the residue of the enormous fine of one hundred thousand pounds, which they still resolutely affected to call a subsidy.* But with the new Parliament a new Convocation was summoned, and the meagre interest of the clerical assembly was heightened both by the indignities to which it was subjected, and by the business which it was allowed, or which it ventured, to transact. After the Mass of the Holy Ghost had been sung by the Bishop of London in St. Paul's, June 9, the clergy moved into the Chapel of St. Mary to hear the Latin sermon.† The preacher was the Bishop of Worcester, Hugh Latimer, who was appointed by Cranmer. The choice of such a man for the office revealed the unchanged temper of the times, and must have gone far to dissipate the hopes which the Old Learning may have conceived from the fall of his patron, Anne Boleyn. Only a few years before, Latimer had knelt before those whom he now harangued, craving and receiving pardon for his acknowledged indiscretions. The Convocation which had witnessed his humiliation was dissolved ; but the present assembly consisted in great part of the same men. He took the text, " For the children of this world are in their generation wiser than the children of light." His discourse, which was divided into two parts, was a powerful invective, in which, while including himself among his brethren, he contrived to castigate those who in opinion differed from him. " Our bishops and abbots, prelates and curates," said he, " adulterate the word of God, mingling it with the dreams of men, like taverners who

* Wilkins, iii. 802.   † Strype, i. 378.

brew good and bad together in one pot. Purgatory is a fiery furnace, for it has burned away many of our pence. Images are covered with gold, and dressed in silks, and lighted with wax candles, yea, even at noon; while Christ's living images are an-hungered, a-thirst, a-cold, in darkness and all wretchedness. Such vile works are preached by some; and, blown and blasted out by the space of three hours together. Happy were the people if such preachers preached but seldom, for the devil sets them up, not God. What doth God say to us in this parable? It is as though he said, All good men in all places complain of you, accuse your avarice, your exactions, your tyranny. They have required in you a long season, and do yet require, diligence and sincerity. I commanded you that ye should feed my sheep; ye earnestly feed yourselves, from day to day, wallowing in delights and idleness. I commanded you to teach my commandments, and not your fancies: and that ye should seek my glory and advantage: you teach your own traditions, and seek your own glory and profit. You preach very seldom; and when ye do preach, do nothing but cumber them that preach truly, as much as lieth in you: that it were much better such not to preach at all than so perniciously to preach. Oh, what hear I of you? You, that ought to be my preachers, what other thing do you, than apply all your study hither, to bring all my preachers to envy, shame, contempt? Yea, more than this, ye pull them into perils, into prisons, and, as much as in you lieth, to cruel deaths. I would that Christian people should hear my doctrine: and read it also, as many as would: your care is, not that all men may read it, but that no layman do read it."

In the afternoon he let them have the rest of it. After defining the devil—and very finely—as " a

monster monstrous above all monsters, a thing wholly
made up of the hatred of God," he asked himself What
the devil he meant by going about to describe particularly the devil's nature. He would only add that
the devil was "a stinking sentine of all vices," and proceed to describe the progeny of the devil. The devil
had many descendants. Of Envy he had begotten
the World. Of Lady pride, Dame Gluttony, Mistress
Avarice, Lady Lechery, Dame Subtlety, and other
lemans, the World in turn had begotten many. There
was no corner where his children were not found : in
court, in cloisters, in cowls, in rochets, were they never
so white. But laymen were not children of the World
in being secular; nor they the children of light that
were called spiritual and of the clergy. No, no. Our
holy men said that they were dead to the world : but
none were more alive to it than some of them. They
were the children of the World by his wife, Dame
Hypocrisy : and they shewed themselves no bastards,
even though they swore that they knew not their
father by all he-saints and she-saints too. He spoke
not of all religious men, but of many, and more than
many. Grandfather Devil, father World, and mother
Hypocrisy had brought them up, and they bore their
parents' commandments, how religious, how mocking,
how monking, he would say, soever they were.* It would
be strange if there were not great sort of bishops and prelates also that were brothers-german to these: there were
bishops, abbots, priors, archdeacons, deans, and others,
in that Convocation who were called together to treat

---

* This verbal play apparently revives the dull nickname of "Master
Mock," which "Master More," i e. Sir Thomas More (Morus), bore among
the heretics. It is not kept in the Latin, "quantumvis religiosi, quantumvis monachi." The English version of this sermon was not published
until the reign of Edward VI., and bears marks of careful revision. It may
however be accepted for the substance of what was actually preached.

of nothing but what pertained to the glory of Christ
and the wealth of the people of England. Which
thing he hoped that they would do as earnestly as
they ought to do : but the end of their Convocation,
the fruit of their consultation, would shew of what
generation they were. What had they done hitherto,
the last seven years, or more ? What had been done in
the last Convocation ? "What fruit is come of your
long and great assembly ? What one thing that the
people of England hath been the better of a hair : or
you yourselves either more acceptable before God,
or better discharged toward the people committed to
your care ? For that the people is better learned and
taught now than they were in time past, to whether of
these ought we to attribute it, to your industry, or to
the providence of God, and the foreseeing of the
King's Grace ? Ought we to thank you, or the King's
Highness ? whether stirred other first, you the King
that ye might preach, or he you by his letters, that ye
should preach oftener ? Is it unknown, think you,
how both ye and your curates were, in a manner, by
violence enforced to let books be made, not by you,
but by profane and lay persons : to let them, I say,
be sold abroad, and read for the instruction of the
people ? I am bold with you, but I speak Latin and
not English ; to the clergy, not to the laity : I speak to
you being present, and not behind your backs. God
is my witness I speak whatsoever is spoken of the
goodwill I bear you."

In a strain of somewhat captious rhetoric he went
on to tell them that in the past they had only done two
things : they had burned a dead man, and they had
tried to burn a living man : the latter they hoped to
have raked in the coals "because he would not subscribe to certain articles that took away the supremacy

of the King :" a not impolitic version of the story of
his own recantation.   He proceeded, however, to
point out the things which he conceived most particularly in need of amendment : and in this, which is
the most valuable part of his discourse, we may see,
amid the turmoil of the Reformation, what were the
real abuses which an honest reformer would have had
redressed : for when Latimer descended from general
objurgations to particular recommendations, what he
had to say was sound, temperate, and sensible.   What,
he asked, of the Court of Arches ?   Was vice never
countenanced there ?. were sentences never delayed ?
were bribes never taken there ?   If all was right in
the Court of Arches, what of the Bishops' consistories ?
Were the sentences assigned by the laws often executed there, or were money redemptions used in their
stead ?   What of the ceremonies ?   Were not many of
them so defiled and depraved, that it was doubtful
whether it were better to take them away or let some
of them tarry still ?   What of holidays ?   There were
so many of them that it interfered with the sustenance
of the poor ; for none might work on them, unless they
would be cited before the officials.   They were spent
in drunkenness, gluttony, and idleness by the people ;
the devil had more service done him on one holiday
than on many working days.   What of images, pilgrimages, and relics ?   Was there not a superstitious
difference put between one image and another ? one
accounted better than another, and the further away
the higher esteemed, so that pilgrimages were multiplied, especially among women ?   As to relics, the
case was something different : when you went to an
image you knew that you were going to a mere image,
and nothing more : but in relics you might be deceived, and for the relics of a saint you might touch

with veneration the relics of a pig. What of matrimony? Was baptism always to be said in Latin? What of mass priests, and the sale of masses?

Such were the abuses which struck Latimer as the most flagrant in the standing state of things. They were great and irritating beyond all question: but they might have been removed without a revolution, if their removal had been the only thing proposed by the rulers of the times. As the preacher himself pointed out, nearly every one of them had been met by some constitution or canon of the Church of England, passed in former ages: and all that was necessary for the extirpation of abuses was that the old laws of the Church should be enforced, or new ones made.* But Latimer forgot that, at the time when he urged his hearers to reform abuses, all the ancient laws of the Church were suspended, and had been suspended from the first years of the Convocation which incurred his reproaches.

But the rebuke of a father may have seemed a light humiliation in comparison with the indignities to which the synod was now exposed. At their next session, June 16, the prelates were surprised by the appearance in their house of William Petre, one of Crumwel's doctors, who claimed the right of sitting in the place of the Most Reverend, and presiding over their assembly. He argued thus: that the King was the Supreme Head of the Church of England, and therefore that the supreme place in the synod was to

---

* For instance, he says of the last abuse which he mentioned: "Your forefathers saw somewhat, which made this constitution against the venality and sale of masses, that under pain of suspending no priest should sell his saying of triennials or annals. What saw they that made this constitution? What priests saw they? What manner of masses saw they, trow ye? And at the last, what became of so good a constitution? God have mercy upon us!" Latimer's Serm., 55, Park. Soc. The constitution referred to was by Archb. Islip, A.D. 1350.

be rightfully attributed to him : that Crumwel was the Vicegerent of the King, and that therefore the supreme place ought to be occupied by him : that Petre was the proctor or deputy of Crumwel, and therefore that the supreme place ought to be yielded to him. Which was granted accordingly. At the next session, June 21, Crumwel appeared in person, superseded the Most Reverend, and introduced an instrument for a sentence of nullity of marriage between the King and Anne Boleyn. This was "expressly approved" by both Houses of Convocation, and signed by the Most Reverend the prelates, and the Prolocutor of the clergy.* The degradation of the realm was now complete.

At the succeeding session, June 23, the new Prolocutor, Gwent, accompanied by the clergy of the Lower House, appeared before the Most Reverend and the rest of the prelates, and presented them with a long list of errors and blasphemies, which, as they complained, were taught and preached publicly. This book of *mala dogmata* has obtained the title of " The Protestation of the Clergy of the Lower House within the Province of Canterbury, with declaration of faults and abuses which heretofore hath and now be within the same worthy special reformation." It is not without importance, although it was but an impotent murmur : nor without dignity in comparison with the fulsome and unprincipled productions of other public bodies, though no more came of it than of the former petition of the lower clergy to the Fathers against the doings of the Commons. The clergy seemed able to discern nothing in the mighty movement of the age but the sordid demolition of the system which they were vowed to maintain : under the disguise of lofty enthusiasm and burning zeal their prejudiced eyes

* See above, p. 390.

beheld selfishness, covetousness, and insolence, aided by the connivance of rulers : and amid the resounding crash of the convent walls and towers, their ears attended only to the ribald songs and blasphemies to the tune of which they were falling. But they began with declaring their sincere obedience to their Supreme Head and all his laws, and their entire and unfeigned abhorrence of the usurped authority of the Bishop of Rome, "with his inventions, rites, abuses, ordinances, and fashions." They stood, or strove to stand, upon the ancient, the uncorrupted constitution of the English Church, while they protested against the errors which seemed to their eyes to endanger the Catholic faith. There were other abuses, of a different nature from the abuses of the Bishop of Rome, which they protested to be "causes of dissension" within the realm. These were the Mala Dogmata which they proceeded to enumerate.

It was "commonly preached, taught, and spoken," said the clergy, "to the slander of this noble realm, disquietness of the people, damage of Christian souls, not without fear of many other inconveniences and perils," that the Sacrament of the Altar was not to be esteemed : "for divers light and lewd persons be not ashamed or afraid to say, Why should I see the sacring of the High Mass ? is it anything else but a piece of bread, or a little pretty piece round Robin ?" Many denied Extreme Unction to be a Sacrament, and said that the hallowed oil was no more than the Bishop of Rome's grease or butter; many said that all ceremonies accustomed in the Church, which were not clearly expressed in Scripture, ought to be taken away; that priests had no more authority to minister the sacraments than laymen : that they were Antichrists who denied to laymen the Sacrament of the Altar, sub utraque specie: and that those who were present at mass, and did not receive the Sacrament with the priests, were not partakers of the mass.

Of Baptism it was said that it was as lawful to christen a child in a tub at home, or in a ditch by the way, as in a font in a church: and that the water in the font was only a thing conjured.

Of penance, auricular confession, and absolution it was commonly said that no ghostly father could enjoin penance: that it was sufficient to confess to God only, and as lawful to confess to a layman as to a priest.

Of images it was declared that they were not to be reverenced: nor should lights be put before them, nor in any place in the church in time of divine service, so long as the sun gave light. Saints were not to be invocated or honoured; and it was as much available to pray to them as to whirl a stone against the wind.

With regard to rites and ceremonies it was held that hallowed water, hallowed bread, hallowed candles, hallowed ashes, hallowed palms, and such-like ceremonies, were trifles and vanities to seduce the people. Holy water was better for sauce than other water because it was mixed with salt: for the same reason it would be good for a horse with a galled back: add an onion, and it would be a good sauce for a jigot of mutton. Holy days were not to be observed, as all days were alike: pilgrimages, fasting, or alms deeds were not to be used: the singing and saying of mass, matins, or evensong was but roaring, howling, whistling, mummying, conjuring, and juggling; and the playing at the organs a foolish vanity. It was preached against the Litany, and said that it was never merry in England since the Litany was ordained, and Sancta Maria, Sancta Katarina, sung and said.

Purgatory was denied: and the dirge, commendations, mass, suffrages, prayers, alms deeds, or oblations done for the souls of the departed, were said to be vain, and of no profit. There was no distinction of sin into venial and mortal: but all sins were venial, that is, clean forgiven, after a sinner's conversion, by the merits of Christ's passion: and that Almighty God did not require from a sinner, after his conversion from sin, any penance, but only that he amend his life.

The Church was only the congregation of good men: it was not necessary to have a church or chapel to pray in, or do any divine service in: a church was made for no other purpose than to keep the people from wind and rain, or to be the place of resort where they might have the word of God declared to them. Priests were like other men: and might marry and have wives like other men. No human constitutions or laws were binding on Christian men, except such as were in the New Testament.

It was preached that man had no free will; that all things ought to be in common; that it was as lawful to eat flesh on fast days as at other times; that our Lady was no better than another woman, and was like a bag of saffron or pepper when the spice was out; that it was sufficient to believe, though a man did no good works at all. Men were not content to speak of certain abuses found in pilgrimages, in fastings, in prayer, in invocation of saints, in reverencing of images, in alms deeds, in auricular confession; but would need have the thing itself taken away. It was even said that no divine service whatever, matins, mass, evensong, or any other, need be said, read, or sung within any church, because it was only to delude the people. Bishops and ordinaries had no authority to give sentence of excommunication, suspension, or censure. The priest's crown was the whore's mark of Babylon; the stole about his neck was the Bishop of Rome's rope. All religions and professions, whatever they were, were clean contrary to Christ's religion.

Such, said the clergy, were the errors and blasphemies set forth by seditious preachers, many of whom were apostates, infamed and abjured persons, without license of the King or the Ordinary, who would in no wise conform themselves to the Catholic Church and her canonical and approved authors, but preached their own fantasies and inventions, whereby all unity was taken away. And, besides preaching, there were many slanderous and seditious books allowed to go abroad, which were bought the more eagerly because they were published *Cum privilegio,* and so thought to have the express approbation of the King, when it was not so indeed. This bold insinuation was laid against Crumwel, whose abuse of the press was notorious.* The clergy furthermore complained that the heretical books which had formerly been condemned by Convocation, had never yet been

---

* Thomas Crumwel was "the great patron of ribaldry, and the protector of the ribalds, of the low jesters, the filthy ballad-mongers, the ale-house singers, and the 'hypocritical mockers in feasts;' in short, of all the blasphemous mocking, and scoffing which disgraced the Protestant party at the time of the Reformation."—Maitland's *Essays,* 236. So Fox (in the first edition, vol. v. 403, whom Maitland quotes) says: " This valiant soldier and captain of Christ, the aforesaid Lord Crumwel, as he was always studious of himself in a flagrant zeal to set forward the truth of the Gospel—so he always retained unto him and had about him such as could be found helpers and furtherers of the same: in the number of whom were sundry and divers fresh and quick wits pertaining to his family: by whose industry and ingenious labours divers excellent ballads and books were contrived and set abroad concerning the suppression of the pope and all popish idolatry." Among these ballads and books is one mentioned by Fox which still remains, called the Fantasy of Idolatry, which, Maitland says, is unfit for publication.

expressly condemned by the bishops, but remained still in the hands of the unlearned people.*

Many things which in their Protestation the clergy would have protected are gone; many things which they thought endangered remain. Great and little are mingled in their lamentations; the age itself is seen there. The age was as sweeping in its demands in the days of Henry as it shewed itself afterwards in the days of his son. There was as much disbelief in the doctrines and ceremonies which remained unabolished until the next generation, as there was at the time when they were abolished. And there had been as much disbelief in them in former ages as there was then. The principles of dissent were as intelligently known in the fourteenth and fifteenth century as in the sixteenth; in the sixteenth as ever they have been since. Every age kicks against the pricks. But every age thinks also that it makes progress in the discovery of principles which were never known before. This is wrong. There is no progress in principles. There may be a progress in measures, in the carrying out of principles.

But now Crumwel had other work for the Convocation than framing remonstrances to fall unheeded on the ears of terrified bishops and abbots. The abolition of the Pope, the fall of the lesser monasteries, the manifestly impending doom of the greater, the slaughter of monks on the scaffold, the generally hideous aspect which things had assumed, rendered it necessary to vindicate the realm by declaring that it still remained within the pale of Catholic Christendom. The country, heaving and murmuring under the blows which were falling upon some of its most cherished and

---

* Strype, ii. 260; or Wilkins, iii. 804; or Fuller, v. 208.

beneficent institutions, needed to be assured that there was a point beyond which these changes would not be allowed to pass; that all was for good; that no essential part of the ancient faith of England had been touched. A curb was required also for the more ardent spirits who desired to break into open dissent. It was to be proved to them that the unity of the Church of England would still be maintained; and to this extent, the designs of the King and his minister coincided with the wishes of the clergy. Crumwel came down, July 11, to the clergy house. There the Bishop of Hereford, Edward Fox, produced and read a book containing certain articles of faith and ceremonies; which was then subscribed by Crumwel, by the Most Reverend, by the prelates, and by the clergy of the lower house. This was the first English Confession of faith, the first authorised formulary of the Church of England. It bore the title of Articles to stablish Christian Quietness. It is often called the Ten Articles.

The Church of England had been well enough for a thousand years without formularies of faith. Her formularies of faith had been those of all Christendom: the Creeds, the primitive decrees. More than these she had never needed. But the age in which the ancient system was shattered was the age of confessions of faith. Germany had long been in the full blaze of confession. From the dawn of the Reformation to the recent Confessions of Augsburg and of Basle, ten or twelve symbolical books had exhibited already the harmony or the discord of the foreign reformers, their various enlightenment, the obstinacy of public dispute, or the persuasions of charity and concord. It was the turn of England now. But from the beginning to the end, the English Confessions (of which these Articles read

by Fox in the presence of Crumwel were the first) have
borne the impression of a settled intention, which was
such as caused them to be different from the curious,
definite, and longsome particularity of the Continent.
They had the design of preserving the integrity or
unity of the Church of England. This was characteristic of the nation; and exhibited an undeviating
determination which has surmounted the violence of
every age. The King, who had imbibed the notion
of having a code of doctrines during his negotiations
with the German League, sought to bring his own
realm to a concordance of which he had done his part
to deprive the whole body politic of Western Christendom : and though he enslaved and robbed the Church
of which he was the Supreme Head, he had no thought
of destroying her. It was the purpose of preserving
her unity that caused Crumwel to seek the aid of her
constitutional officers in Convocation, and to order the
first Confession to be read, and perhaps composed in
the first draft, by a bishop. Fox of Hereford, to whom
the task was assigned, was a dexterous and able man,
fresh from the difficult negotiations of Smalcald, and
acquainted with the German systems. The formulary,
however, was not the product of one mind.*

The Ten Articles, when they issued from the
hands of the Convocation, bore the character of a compromise between the Old and the New Learning.
The Catholic nation was satisfied that the Catholic
faith still remained, in spite of the innovations which
were changing the face of society. The indecencies of
the heretics were rebuked by the reasons which were

---

* I formerly brought in here the curious scene between Bishop Stokesley
and Aless : but am convinced that it belongs to the following year and the
Second English Confession, and have transferred it to the last pages of
this volume.

given for ceremonies that were retained but explained ;
and those who were waiting to applaud the King for
proceeding to destroy the Church, were convinced that
the Church was to be preserved. At the same time
that small but incessantly active party was. conciliated
by a secret infusion of Lutheranism, taken from the
King's favourite divine of the Germans, Melanchthon. But, above all, the device was found useful for
its immediate purpose, to dissipate the suspicion that
the King had brought the kingdom into a schism ; and
when the time came, to help to quell the insurrection
which the demolition of the monasteries was about to
raise against him.

This first Confession of the English Church was
divided into two parts, the one of things necessary to
Salvation, and the other concerning Ceremonies : which
division in itself signified the return of reason into the
domain of faith. In the former of these were included
the authority accepted by the Church, or the Rule of
Faith ; the Sacraments ; and justification ; and if this
enumeration exhibited the combination of two systems
of dogmatic teaching, not less strikingly might be
observed the conflict of opinions, the latitude allowed,
and the rejection of absolute definitions, in the manner
in which the several topics were treated. The Rule of
Faith was declared to be the whole body or canon of the
Bible, and the three Creeds, expounded according to the
sense or import of the words and according to the approved doctors of the Church : and all the opinions were
declared erroneous which had been condemned by the
four Councils of Nice, Constantinople, Ephesus, and Chal-
cedon, and all other Councils since that time which were
in any point consonant to the same. Of the Sacraments,
the number was neither reduced to two nor affirmed to
be seven : three only, Baptism, Penance, and the Sacra-

ment of the Altar were defined or explained; the other four, which were commonly accounted for Sacraments, had no mention. In Baptism it was said that remission of sins and the grace and favour of God were offered to all men, as well infants as those who had the use of reason : that infants or children dying in infancy should undoubtedly be saved thereby, and else not : that infants must be baptized because they are born in original sin : and that the opinions of the Anabaptists and Pelagians were detestable heresies.

In the Article on the Sacrament of Penance, which was by far the longest, it was affirmed that Penance was instituted by Christ, in the New Testament, as a thing so necessary to salvation that no man who had fallen into sin after baptism could be saved without it. The sacrament of perfect penance consisted of three parts, contrition, confession, and amendment of the former life. Contrition again consisted of two special parts, knowledge of sin with fear of God's displeasure, and a certain faith, trust, and confidence in the mercy and goodness of God. This faith is got and confirmed by applying the promises made by Christ in the Gospel, and the sacraments instituted by him in the New Testament: therefore, to attain this faith the second part of penance is necessary, that is, confession to a priest, if it may be had : for the absolution given by the priest was instituted of Christ to apply the promises of God to the penitent, and is spoken by the authority given by Christ in the Gospel. No less faith and credence was to be given to the words of absolution pronounced by the ministers of the church than would be given to the very voice and words of God himself, speaking out of heaven. Auricular confession was by no means to be condemned, but reputed as a necessary means of seeking absolution at the priest's hands. As to the third part of penance, though the death of Christ be the sufficient oblation, sacrifice, satisfaction, and recompense for sin, yet all men truly penitent, contrite, and confessed, must bring forth the fruits of penance, that is to say, prayer, fasting, alms deeds, and make restitution if they had done wrong to their neighbours.

Under the form and figure of bread and wine, it was said in the Article on the Sacrament of the Altar, is verily, substantially, and really contained and comprehended the very selfsame body and blood of our Saviour, Jesus Christ, which was born of the Virgin Mary and suffered upon the cross for our redemption : and under the same form and figure of bread and wine the very selfsame body and blood of Christ is corporally, really, and in the very substance exhibited, distributed, and received ·unto and of all who receive the said Sacrament. Therefore, every man ought first to prove and examine himself, for that whosoever eateth the body of Christ unworthily or drinketh of the blood of Christ unworthily, shall be guilty of the very body and blood of Christ : wherefore, let every man first prove himself, and so let him eat of this bread and drink of this drink. For whosoever eateth it or drinketh it unworthily, he eateth and drinketh it to his own damnation : because he putteth no difference between the very body of Christ and other kinds of meat.*

The last of the Articles on things necessary to salvation bore the title of Justification. All that needed to be said upon the method of salvation seemed to have been said already under the head of Penance : but it was here repeated without essential

---

* The reader will scarcely need to be reminded that much of the language of this article has been preserved in one of the Exhortations in the present Order of Holy Communion.

difference under the favourite watchword of the Lutherans. The definition of Justification as "remission of our sins, and our acceptation or reconciliation into the grace and favour of God," was a translation of the words of Melanchthon.* The rest of the Article turned upon Good Works.

The second part of the Confession, "concerning the laudable Ceremonies used in the Church," exhibits the same spirit of moderation and compromise : though much of it sounds like a satire on the subsequent course of the Reformation. The people were to be taught that it was right for images to stand in the church, especially the images of Christ and Our Lady, that they might be the kindlers and stirrers of men's minds. As for censing of them, and kneeling and offering to them, and such worshippings, though they entered by devotion, and fell to custom, yet the people were to be taught that it was not done to the images, but to God and for his honour, although it were done before the images.

Saints were to be honoured, but not with the honour due only to God, trusting to attain at their hands what must be had only of God: but as the elect of Christ, as examples, and as advancers, in that they may, of our prayers and demands unto Christ. It

* Melanchthon's words were, "Justificatio significat remissionem peccatorum, et reconciliationem seu acceptationem personæ ad vitam æternam."—*Loci Theol.* de Gratia et Justif. See Laurence's *Bampton Lect.*, 198. It has been denied that there was any Lutheranism in the first English confession, and certainly it must not be forgotten that at this time the doctrines of Germany were heresy in England. But, with all that is known of Henry's negotiations with the German princes, it seems impossible to explain away the plain evidence which Laurence has brought to prove that the reformed doctrines infused into the confession came from Germany. He shews that as early as March 1535 Barnes, the English ambassador then in Germany, had consulted with Melanchthon *de certis Articulis,* and that Melanchthon had given him his judgment in writing. *Ib.*

was laudable to pray to saints in heaven, everlastingly
living, whose charity was ever permanent, to be inter-
cessors and to pray for us and with us; so it were
done without superstition; as, to think that any saint
were more merciful, or would hear us sooner than
Christ: or that any saint would serve for one thing
more than another as patron of the same.   A short
model of prayer to saints was given.*   Saints' days
were to be observed, but under the restrictions lately
ordered by the King.

Of a large number of rites and ceremonies which
had been mentioned in the Protestation of the clergy
as being blasphemously insulted by false teachers,
explanations were given which would bring back their
meaning to the minds of the people.   Such were, the
wearing of such vestments in doing God's service as
be and have been most part used: sprinkling of holy
water to put us in remembrance of our baptism, and of
the blood of Christ sprinkled for our redemption upon
the cross: giving of holy bread, to put us in remembrance of the Sacrament of the Altar, that all Christian
men be one body mystical of Christ, as the bread is of
many grains, yet but one loaf: bearing of candles on
Candlemas day, in memory of Christ, the spiritual
Light: giving of ashes on Ash Wednesday, to remind
men in the beginning of Lent that they are but dust
and ashes: bearing of palms on Palm Sunday, in memory of the receiving of Christ into Jerusalem: creep-
ing to the cross; humbling ourselves to Christ on Good
Friday before the cross, offering unto Christ before the

---

* "All holy angels and saints in heaven pray for us and with us unto
the Father, that for his dear Son Jesus Christ's sake, we may have grace
of him and remission of our sins, with an earnest purpose (not wanting
ghostly strength), to observe and keep his holy commandments, and
never to decline from the same again unto our lives end." In this manner men might pray to any particular saint.

same, and kissing it in memory of our redemption: setting up the sepulture of Christ; hallowing the font, and other such exercises and benedictions. These were "not to be contemned and cast away, but to be used and continued, as things good and laudable, to put us in remembrance of those spiritual things that they do signify: not suffering them to be forgot, or to be put in oblivion, but renewing them in our memories from time to time : but none of these ceremonies have power to remit sin, but only to stir and lift up our minds unto God, by whom only our sins are forgiven." Of Purgatory it was said that the due order of Charity not less than the voice of Scripture required prayers to be said for souls departed, and alms to be given for masses and exequies, that they might be delivered from some part of their pains: but that since the place where they were, the name thereof, and the kind of pains there, were left uncertain by Scripture, these things were to be remitted to Almighty God: but that the abuses were to be put away which had been advanced under the name of Purgatory; such as the efficacy of the pardons of the Bishop of Rome to deliver souls altogether from pain, "or that masses said at Scala Cœli, or elsewhere, in any place, or before any image, might likewise deliver them from all their pain, and send them straight to heaven."

A royal greeting or declaration, which was prefixed to the Articles, discovered the solicitude of the King to promote unity. As Supreme Head on earth of the Church, the King was made to declare that it belonged to his office to preserve concord in religion, and to repress all occasions of dissent and discord. For this cause he had not only in his own person taken great pains, labour, study, and travail; but had also caused the bishops and best learned of the clergy to consult in Convocation for the full debatement and quiet determination of all diversities of opinion. They had agreed upon certain articles, which he called upon his subjects to receive with no less desire of unity and concord than he had in setting them forth.

The literary history of the first of the English attempts after unity, made at the very time when the elements of disunion were let loose, is somewhat obscure. Three manuscripts, and a single copy of a printed edition of the same year appear to be the sole relics of the originals of this momentous formulary. Two of the manuscripts alone exhibit the signatures of Thomas Crumwel and of the clergy, though with variations in the order and number of the names: the printed edition is without their subscriptions.* Thus while the authority of " the whole clergy" was claimed

* There is the transcript, made by Fuller, out of the manuscript Acts of the Convocation : this is without the subscriptions of the clergy. Fuller, Ch. Hist., v. 213. The Acts, it is well known, perished in the great fire. There is the manuscript which was or is in the State Paper Office, where Collier saw and copied it into his Eccles. Hist. This gives the subscriptions of the Upper House only (so the industrious transcriber seems to indicate), and is destitute of the royal Preface. There is also the fine vellum manuscript in the Cotton Library, Cleop. E. 5, fol. 59 : which, according to Strype, was written for the use of the King, and was sent by him towards the year's end to charm away the tumours of the north. This is complete, having the Preface, and the subscriptions of both houses in the original handwriting of the subscribers. It is observable that it gives the names of the prelates in a somewhat different order from Collier's manuscript, and that it adds the great *northern* bishops, Lee and Tunstall, to the list. Lee and Tunstall are known to have been in the Canterbury Convocation, and to have taken part in the disputations : they were no doubt requested also to sign. This Cottonian manuscript was first printed by Burnet in his Addenda, with the title " Articles about Religion, set out by the Convocation, and published by the King's Authority." The title when they were published by Berthelet, in the year of issue, 1536, was, " Articles devised by the King's Highness Majesty to stablish Christian Quietness and Unity among us, and to avoid contentious Opinions : which Articles be also approved by the Consent and Determination of the whole Clergy of this Realm."—Reprinted in *Formularies of Faith under Henry VIII.*, Oxf., 1825.

for the Articles, the names of the clergy who had signed them were not published: and the whole instrument issued in the name of the King.

The birth of modern Uniformity was not unattended with the proper portents. The day after the Articles had struggled through Convocation, the King pursued his device by addressing a letter to the Archbishop of Canterbury for the suppression of errors and the reducing of controversies to a good and Catholic conformity. He had caused, said he, the bishops and clergy, in solemn Convocation deliberately disputing and advising, to agree to certain articles most Catholic conceived: but he feared slander: he feared lest seditious persons should expound the device according to their fantastical appetite before it was fully published and divulged. He therefore ordered the pulpits to be closed for three months, to Michaelmas. No sermons were to be preached in any church, chapel, monastery, college, or other place, unless it were by the bishops themselves, or in presence of the bishops, or in their cathedral churches, where sermons were wont to be made: which cathedral sermons were to be furnished with discreet, learned, and honest preachers, at the bishop's peril.

All licenses were to be recalled: all curates and governors of religious houses were forbidden to preach or to suffer any person to preach, or to permit any manner of conventicles, of private communication, arguments or disputations of any such matters: they were "to pass over the time in a secret silence," till they were advertised otherwise. If any person presumed to intermeddle with the teaching and instruction of the people, contrary to these orders, he was to be committed to ward. The articles would be sent to the curates before the term of silence expired: and when the curates received them, they were to read them to the people without adding or diminishing, unless the bishops gave them special license under their seals to explicate them further: in which case the bishops were to answer for the success of the experiment at their peril. The curates who were thus forbidden to preach were furnished meanwhile, oddly enough, with a form of bidding prayers before sermon.*

The remaining sessions of this Convocation still exhibited the surprising spectacle of the Supreme Head consulting with his clergy, and allowing them, in appearance at least, to resume the lost liberty of free debate and final determination, according to their own constitutional forms: Though the ecclesiastical laws were under suspension, yet the presence and suggestion of the Vicar General or Viceregent of the King enabled and permitted the assembly of the clergy to pass a measure under the ancient name of ordinance : which ordinance became public law, without being confirmed by a subsequent Act of Parliament.† It was for the abrogation of superfluous holidays. The

---

* Wilkins, iii. 807. The form prescribed was as follows: "Ye shall pray for the whole congregation of Christ's Church, and specially for the Church of England: wherein I first recommend to your devout prayers the King's most excellent MaJesty, Supreme Head immediately under God of the spiritualty and temporalty of the same Church : and the most noble and virtuous Lady Queen Jane, his most lawful wife. Second, Ye shall pray for the clergy, the lords temporal, and the commons of this realm, beseeching Almighty God to give every of them in his degree grace to use themselves in such wise as may be to his contentation, the King's honour, and the weal of the realm. Thirdly, ye shall pray for the souls that be departed, abiding the mercy of Almighty God, that it may please him the rather, at the contemplation of our prayers, to grant them the fruition of his presence."

† " In sessione octava (Julii 19), concordatum erat per dominum Crumwel et utramque domum Convocationis super quibusdam Ordinationibus de festis diebus per annum celebrandis, quæ publici deinde juris fiebant." — *Wilk.*, iii. 803.

Supreme Head, with the assent and consent of the prelates and clergy, in Convocation lawfully assembled, ordered, for the avoidance of vice and idleness, that the feast of the dedication of every church should be kept on the first Sunday in October, and on no other day: that the feast of the patron of every church, called commonly the church holiday, should be observed no longer:* that neither the feasts which fell in harvest time should be kept henceforth, except the feasts of the Apostles, of our blessed Lady, and of St. George: nor those which fell in term time, saving Ascension Day, the Nativity of St. John the Baptist, Allhallen and Candlemas. The holy days were thus reduced nearly to the number now retained. Christmas, Easter, the Nativity of the Baptist, and Michaelmas, were to be taken for the four general offering days. A transcript of this Ordinance was sent to the bishops, with one of Henry's letters, commanding them to forbid the curates from indicting or speaking of the abrogated feasts in the churches, lest the people should murmur, or contemn the order and continue in their accustomed idleness. They were to "pass them over with secret silence," that they might be abrogated by disuse as they were already by the royal authority in Convocation.† From being too many, holidays became too few at the Reformation; and, the authority which ordained them at first having been shaken, not more than the fourth part of those that are left are now observed by the people.

The Roman jurisdiction in England had fallen already beneath the blows of the King, the Clergy, and the Parliament. To reject the Primacy, on which that jurisdiction depended, seemed an inevitable, though

---

* As to the "Church holiday," the reader might look at Strype, i. 212.
† Wilkins, iii. 823.

not a necessary consequence ; but the occasion had been delayed till now. The Pope had by this time indicted his long proposed Council, to be held at Mantua in the middle of the following year; and among the other Christian princes he had cited to appear there, in person or by proxy, the King of England. But Henry who two years before had appealed from the Pope to a Council, answered by denying the authority of the Pope to convoke a council, and vehemently repudiated the Primacy of the Apostolic See. The end had arrived now which had been foreseen and predicted by More and Fisher : the last labour to which the Convocation was now called by Crumwel was to declare that Christendom had no head in Rome. The libel or book in which this important declaration was made on the part of the English Church was the work of the experienced Fox : the synod, which was dissolved on the same day that it passed, was thin in number, especially among the heads of the religious orders: and of the abbots and priors no less than thirty signed it by proxy. The causes enumerated in this instrument, for which England refused to appear in the Mantuan Council, were five : but the first of them seeming sufficient, the assembly refrained from fortifying the others by authorities or arguments. Nothing, in their judgment, was ever established by their forefathers, more expedient for the extirpation of heresies and sects, and the maintenance of unity, than general councils ; provided that the assembly were lawful, the usages primitive, the matter worthy, and the place indifferent : but nothing was more pestilent and full of devilish effects than a council assembled upon private malice and ambition. All assemblies of bishops, said the English synod, were to be avoided, if that ancient father, Gregory Nazianzen, were to be believed; no good end of any synod had that father even seen, for obstinacy and glory ever conquered reason. The Bishop of Rome had no right to convoke any general council without the consent of the other princes of Christendom, and especially of such as had *imperium merum*, the whole and supreme authority over their subjects, without acknowledging any other supreme authority.*

The epithet of Henrician, which has been applied to Cranmer,† might be deserved by several of his contemporaries who stood opposed to Cranmer in the popular estimation. The period which witnessed the passage of the Church of England from the Roman unity into autonomous uniformity saw the actions of the King defended by the tongue and pen of Tunstall, of Stokesley, and of Gardiner. These celebrated prelates began that long series of vindications by which the position of the Church of England has been cleared and maintained: by which it has been shewn that in losing the obedience of England, her long faithful daughter, the mother Church of Rome but paid the penalty of her own inveterate errors and tyranny; and that by the violence of a revolution the ancient constitution was but rescued from a permitted usurpation. In these antilogies and apologies, however, a difference might be perceived: and some of the advocates of Henry appeared less anxious to attack Rome than to defend their prince. Among them was Gardiner, in his treatise on "True Obedience," who justified both the Divorce and the Supreme Head of Henry, but neither denied a certain authority and a certain

---

* Wilkins, iii. 803, 808.

† By Sanders: "Hic vir hactenus Henricianum, id est, illius Regis sectatorem in omnibus se præbuit, ne latum quidem unguem ab Henrici præscripto recedere ausus." Lib. II.

Primacy to Rome. " How ridiculous," exclaimed that
astute prelate, "to say that a man, call him John, is
subject to the prince as head of the realm; but that
the same man, call him a Christian, is not subject to
the prince! He is of the realm because he lives in
England: and, as he is a Christian, he. is of the
English Church. But what is the English Church
but the congregation of the men and women, of the
clergy and the laity, united in the profession of Christianity? To say that the prince is the head of the
realm, but not of the Church, is to make him the head
of infidels. In fact, how many of the ancient laws of
England are there concerning the Church and religion,
which were both promulgated and put in execution by
the authority of the kings! Is it pretended that the
kings made these laws only as defenders of the Church,
not with the authority of heads of the Church? · Who
then were the heads, in whom was the highest authority at the time? Not in the bishops of England,
for the king is acknowledged to be above the highest
bishop. Had then the Bishop of Rome this pre-eminence? How strange that our ancestors should have
made so many laws against him: that they should
have disapproved of the cure of the vicar of God over
them, and done all that they could to prevent him
from seeing too far out of that watch tower in which
they believed him to have been set by God! Legislation against a superior is not legitimate: inferiors
prescribe not to them that are set over them. In
ancient times the name of Rome was great: her authority was very high: but when I use that word
authority, it is in a Ciceronian sense, for the obstinate
opinion of thé multitude. Nor would I absolutely reject the word Primacy, for it is supported by great
example: but to explain that word I fly to the Gospel,

where I find it used in a double sense. Grant that
Peter had the Primacy given by Christ, what then?
Had he also dominion and pre-eminence? When he
was bidden to strengthen his brethren, was he commanded to be their lord? Let Peter have the Primacy
of zeal : let him be the foremost soldier of Christ, first
in the offices of preaching and teaching, first to defend
the Church from heresies, and to shed his blood in
persecution, as when the early Roman bishops, almost
alone, in the infancy of the Church, withstood the rage
of purple tyrants : then will the first place belong to
the first, and the Primacy to the successors of the
Prince of the Apostles. But if the Roman bishops
seek to undermine the rights of others : if they strive
to maintain their Primacy by craft and dissimulation,
they will be let down to that level which truth shall
warrant and assign. I might speak words of worse
omen, but I forbear." Thus Gardiner.*

A very different strain was chanted by Dean Sampson, of the Chapel Royal. Of all the apologies the
weakest at once and the most celebrated was Sampson's
" Oration " on the royal authority, which came forth

---

* This "Oratio de Vera Obedientia" was first published in 1535 (not
1534 as Strype), and again in 1536, with the name of Hamburg on the
title-page, and a Preface in the name of Archdeacon Bonner. It may be
seen in Fascic. Rer. Expet., ii. 800, and in Stevens' Life of Bradford.
Maitland (Essays) has exhaustively examined the literary history of this
book, and gives strong reasons to believe, 1. That the supposed Hamburg
edition was made in England ; 2. That it was put out by some nameless
heretic, and that the Preface in the name of Bonner was a forgery, by the
unknown editor, who wished to pass off a furious invective against the
Pope. Two or three other Apologies of the same time are mentioned by
Strype, i. 220, 265. One was by Fox of Hereford, " De Vera Differentia
Regiæ Potestatis et Ecclesiasticæ," in which the author is said to have
been assisted by Convocation, or at least by certain members of that
assembly. Strype, i. 263. This seems very doubtful. Gardiner's treatise
gave rise to a curious scene in his life, the disputation at Louvain in 1541 ;
see Dryander's letter, in Fox, 1st ed., p. 503.

with the highest official sanction, and was transmitted
to the courts of Europe. The proem of this extremely
poor production reads as if the writer had strung together the beginnings of several, of his sermons: he
makes so many starts, and is so long in getting to his
real subject. Nothing, said Sampson, moved him so
much to the love of God and his neighbour as the New
Commandment given by Christ in the Gospel of St.
John. It taught both by precept and example. There
were two kinds of love: the one of God to man, the
other of man to man. From this proceeded a third
kind, the love of man to God. When the cause of the
first was shewn, the cause of the last would be plain; and
it would also appear that the third kind of love (so he
confusedly has it), that of man to man, must necessarily exist. The first chapter of Genesis shewed
what the love of God to man was. He made man on
the sixth day: He gave him dominion over all his
works: He blessed him, and bade him be fruitful and
multiply. When He expelled him from Paradise, He
took not away his blessing. David said, What is
man? But, above all other benefits, God sent his Son
into the world, that man might have access to the
Father. St. Paul said, He spared not his own Son;
and Sampson described the work and the sufferings of
the Redeemer: but his benefits to the human race
were innumerable, and Sampson added that he could
not number them. Thus was love taught by example. To love God was the second kind of love.
We ought to fear none, if we were engaged in this
cause. The Psalmist said: The Lord is my defence,
of whom then shall I be afraid? Fear should not be
servile. If anyone sinned, he should not fly but seek
the Father. He who loved would keep the commandments. There were but two commandments, to love

God and thy neighbour.   If you asked, How shall I
love God? the answer was, Keep his Commandments.
So the Prophet said: Guide thou my goings in thy
paths.   Now there were many rules of civil life,
taught alike by nature and by God. He who failed to
observe these ought to be beaten with many stripes,
as the text said.   Such were, to do no harm to his
neighbour, nor take his goods wrongfully: not to steal:
not to deceive: not to bear false witness: and to obey
rulers.   Here Sampson reached his point at last; and
the rest was easy: Obey those that are in authority—
honour the King.   Whatever the King says and
commands, that believe and do.*   For his performance
he was rewarded with the next bishopric that fell
vacant: but he drew down the unsparing vengeance
of Reginald Pole, a celebrated personage who now
enters the scene of the history of the English Church,
to combat for the Papacy, but not with the arms of
More, Fisher, or Houghton.

With the years of the century, Reginald Pole, the
son of the Countess of Salisbury, boasted that he possessed the acquirements of all the learned ages.†   His
erudition, like his ambition, was extensive, but it lay
in too many fields: and though the force of his pursuit
was great, it could not overcome the disadvantages of
division.   By birth connected with the house of York,
attached by long friendship and obligation to the
reigning monarch of the house of Tudor:‡ a noble-

---

* Strype, App. xlii., or Fasciculus Rer. Expet., ii. 820.

† " I am that young man that have of long time been conversant with
old men : that have long judged the eldest that liveth at these days too
young for me to learn wisdom of, that have learned of all antiquity, of
the most ancient that ever were before me, and of my time hath had most
acquaintance and most longest conversation with those that have been
the flowers of wisdom in our time."—Pole to Henry VIII., *Strype*, ii. 305.

‡ The Poles, Reginald and his brothers, were grandsons of George,

man of the blood royal, but without a title: a theologian who was not a priest; a man of letters who was
both scholar and patron : an Englishman who had
spent half his time abroad, he united in himself more
characters than the highest talents could reduce to
harmony in life. His temper was gentle and yet
ardent: his judgment obstinate, but not exact: his
vanity was not inconspicuous; but over his whole character, as over his demeanour, there was diffused a
certain attractiveness and a certain grandeur. Men of
ability cannot always tell for what they shall be famous :
but it seemed most unlikely that the author of the
elegant life of the scholar Longolius would descend
to posterity as a controversialist, and the bitter im-
pugner of the prince whose bounty fed him. But
Pole, after finishing his education in Italy, had returned
to England at the time of the first agitation of the
Divorce : he had seen his mother regard the tearless
grief of Katharine : the daughter of Katharine, to
whose hand and the crown destiny might have exalted
him, he knew to be threatened with the infamy of a
bastard. He had resisted, as he tells, the Machiavellian advances of Crumwel : and after angering the
King by his plainness of speech on the Divorce, he
had contrived to express his opinions in writing without
offence, though not without energy and firmness. In
the silent maintenance of his opinions he had refused
the archbishopric of York : but yet, so ambiguous was
his position, he was able to leave England again and
appear in Paris at the head of a Commission to collect

Duke of Clarence, the ill-fated brother of Edward IV. Their uncle, the
young Earl of Warwick, was attainted and beheaded, as a pretender to
the crown, by Henry VII. Their mother was afterwards restored to the
title of Countess of Salisbury, which had been merged in that of Warwick,
and forfeited in the Earl's attainder. She was the celebrated Margaret
of Salisbury.

suffrages on the King's great matter:* and for four years longer, down to the very moment of his explosive rupture with Henry, he continued to receive the splendid pension with which the politic generosity of the King endowed him. The humiliating position of a reluctant dependent, of a dependent maintained lavishly, but yet deprived of higher hopes, may explain in some part the ferocity of Pole's final attack. To conciliate him, to bring him to declare himself explicitly, and, above all, to satisfy him on the title of Supreme Head, no pains indeed were spared by Henry. The agent employed for this was well chosen in one Starkey, a man of learning, one of the Henrician apologists, formerly intimate with Pole in Italy, and remarkable for the bold directness of his understanding.† This person was summoned to the King's presence, and sounded on the opinions of Pole. As became a friend, he answered that "of Pole's good will and loyalty he could not doubt: but of his opinions on the weighty matters of the King's matrimony and

---

* In his Defence of Unity (Lib. iii.), Pole explained that he was in Paris before the mandate reached him to collect suffrages for the King: that on receiving it he wrote to the King imploring to be excused, and that he only allowed his name to be used in the business until another agent should be sent. "Ad me tamen tum illic agentem literæ tuæ et mandata venerunt, ut cum Parisiensibus causam tuam agerem: quo quidem tempore memini me, ut primum potuerim per acceptam inopinatam nuncio illo dolorem, tibi rescribere, nam mihi ad aliquod tempus non vocem solum sed pene cogitationem omnem dolor eripuerat, imperitiam meam excusasse, et te rogasse, ut alterum in eo genere magis exercitatum mitteres, id quod statim fecisti, ac, ni fecisses, nullum profecto mortis genus non mihi lenius illo munere fuisset: quod nunquam plane in me recessi, personam tamen ad tempus mihi imponi passus sum, dum alter adesset."

† Starkey was one of the King's chaplains, and wrote "An Exhortation to the people, instructing them to Unity and Obedience," published by Berthelet: see Strype, i. 266. It was he who had been selected to argue with Dr. Reynolds the martyr. He had been an inmate of Pole's house at Padua: Ellis, ii. 2, 55.

authority, because Pole used a prudent silence, he could affirm nothing. Pole's judgment might be altered by study, to approve of all that the King had done through the Court of Parliament." The King, not satisfied with this uncertain account, commanded Starkey to demand Pole's opinions in writing: and Crumwel added a friendly message, inviting him to return to the service of his country, and not drown his virtue among strangers. Pole, already engaged in Spanish intrigues of a treasonable nature, of which Crumwel might have been informed by his secret agents, appears to have suspected a trap in this invitation:* he replied evasively, and sought for time. Several urgent letters were then added by Starkey, in which he laboured to prove the duty of submitting to the ruler, to distinguish between the *unity spiritual* and the *unity political,* and to show that the superiority of the Pope was a thing neither of salvation nor expediency: and the epistles of Starkey were accompanied with a copy of the Oration of Dean Sampson.† At length Pole replied in a manner which left the main questions still undecided, but enlarged on the dangers of a worldly policy. Starkey, hereupon, insisted on having his opinion expressed categorically on the main points.‡ The reply of Pole was to launch

---

* Hook, in his Life of Pole, has availed himself of the discoveries of Bergenroth in the Venetian Archives, which prove that Pole was busied in intrigues at this time: p. 71.

† Strype, i. 361. This was in 1535.

‡ He put them thus: 1. An matrimonium cum relicta fratris, ab eo cognita, sit jure divino licitum. 2. An superioritas, quam multis in seculis Romanus Pontifex sibi vindicavit, sit ex jure divino. Granting the questions, which he begs, his letter is a model of clearness. Reproving Pole for his attempt to evade these points by talking of expediency, he adds: "As touching the policy of both the matters, and of bringing them to effect (which his Grace hath now done), whether it be well done or evil, he requireth no judgment of you, as of one that in such things have no great experience as yet. As whether it be convenient that there should

an unexpected thunderbolt; to send to England a copy of the yet unpublished manuscript of his celebrated Defence of the Unity of the Church.

This once famous diatribe would ill bear to be compared with the majestic denunciations and the skilful irony with which the great masters of eloquence have assailed the enemies of their country or of their cause. It resembles more the violence of a peaceful man suddenly enraged, whose blows hurt his adversary more because they are numerous than because they are expert and well directed. Nor was Pole's performance an oration, though it was very rhetorical: it was an epistle professedly designed for the eyes of one, and not for the ears of all. He sought not to denounce but to rebuke: and though his language was very strong, it was not abusive. This sets a difference between him and the controversialists of the age, with whom to differ on any of the disputed points, from the meaning of a Greek particle to the share of free-will in justification, was to

be one Head in the Church, and that to be the Bishop of Rome. Set these aside. And in the case of matrimony, whether the policy he hath used therein be profitable to the realm or no, leave that aside. Only shew you whether, if the first matrimony were to make, you would approve that then, or no, and the cause why you would not. And thus weigh the thing in itself, as it is in his own nature, and put apart fear of all danger, hope of all good, which should succeed, and hangeth upon worldly policy." *Strype*, ii. 281. Mr. Froude, in quoting this passage, interposes the words, " Whether the *supremacy* which the Bishop of Rome has for many ages claimed to be of divine right or no ; " which seem meant for a translation of the Latin of Starkey's second main position. Starkey knew the English constitution better than to talk of the Pope's Supremacy. The Pope never had, and never claimed supremacy. Starkey's word superiority, which was carefully chosen, fairly expresses what the Pope had : primacy with a certain Jurisdiction. After permitting this superiority so long as they saw fit, "multis in seculis," the kings of England, by their inherent supremacy, rejected it, first in the one article, then in the other. This mistake Mr. Froude shares, however, with many other writers, including Dean Hook. It is curious indeed how persistently modern writers attribute to the men of Henry the very word and the very conception which they most carefully avoided.

empty the fish market. If he used strong language, it was because he professed to believe that strong language was needed to reach the heart of the schismatical monster of England, and bring him to repentance. Some of his blows fell heavily enough : but Pole often beats the air. He rebukes the King for doing what the King as constantly denied that he had done, for receding from the unity of the Church : thus the ground of his most passionate reproaches was not in the least admitted by his adversary. When he touched on the profligacy of the King, and the horrors of the revolution which the King was urging, he was happier : when he descanted on the noble qualities and the cruel death of Fisher and of More, of Houghton and of Reynolds, his indignant pathos was not unworthy of the theme : but even here he shews a want of the true rhetorical skill, and wearies the reader by repainting without heightening his scenes.

" I know not," he began, " I know not what to write, or what not to write to thee, who demandest so persistently to know my mind. Grief and indignation fire me : benefits received hold me back. How am I to address the slayer of my fellow-servants, the sick man who is ready to kill the physician who approaches him ? What a disease is thine, which fills the Christian world with rumours ! I shall better address thee as a dead man, and a dead man carried off by the judgment of God. But I will make the dead hear : the voice of the Church shall raise the dead. To the Church thou hast done the most grievous of injuries : thou takest away her Head. The Head of the Church on earth thou takest away, denying the Roman Pontiff to be her head and the Vicar of Christ. If thou makest thyself Supreme Head of the Church in thy kingdom, thou deniest that there is one head of the Church universal: the one thing follows the other. Of all Christian kings thou alone darest this: before thee none have ever dared this. So doing, thou, a king, deniest monarchy to be the best state: and thy innovations are ruining Christendom. The vilest flatterers would not have dared to give a king the title which thou hast taken, because the most impudent would never have deemed that a king would have desired it.

" I have received the book of thy champion Sampson. Sampson has a very long spear: the proem of his book is of immense length ; armed with that intolerably long weapon he is not a Sampson, but a Goliath, advancing to defy the sons of Israel, the children of the Church. Sampson is not a good man ; he wants to catch me with guile : else why should he be so long in saying that kings are to be honoured ? No one denies that : but he wants them to be honoured in a particular way: the Supreme Head is the iron tip of that long spear. Sampson is a priest who betrays his master: he is a Judas, but he had sold himself for very little : he wanted Norwich, and he has only got Chichester. Sampson is no Hercules, but he can act Cacus : he drags the sheep of Christ by their tails into the King's cave. But the sheep can bleat, and Hercules will awake. Other defenders thou hast among thy bishops: men who think one thing as private persons, another thing when they receive their pontificals. As soon as they become pontiffs, they contemn the chief pontiff. What a malicious change! Nay rather, it is malice mixed with ignorance : for they follow the blind guide of reason. Sampson and the rest of them maliciously argue, to deceive the citizens, that because the King is Supreme Head of the body politic, he is also Supreme Head of the Church. There are two Churches, the Church of Christ, and the King's Church, which is the

Church of Satan. Wouldst thou be held Vicar of Christ, and assume the person of the Son of God? Wouldst thou contend with Peter in honour?* For what then? The good Pagan Titus desired to be Pontifex Maximus that he might be free from shedding the blood of any. But thou! Thy people have suffered more in the three years that thou hast borne thy impious title than in the time of all the Popes that went before. Thou hast broken thy coronation oath. Thou sworest to preserve the privileges of Holy Church, granted by thy predecessors; and neither to diminish nor suffer them to be diminished. The whole thing began with the miserable love of a middle-aged man for a girl. Thou hast repudiated thy wife because she was thy brother's wife, though to the Emperor thou hast owned that she was never thy brother's wife but in name: and thou hast married a woman whose sister had been thy mistress. What hypocrisy could ever equal that? Thy embassies and legations have made thee the laughing-stock of Europe. Took ever man such pains and labour to prove himself below the level of the beasts: begging and praying men in every city and university only to declare that he had passed his whole youth and manhood in incest, polluted and defiled by the laws of God and man? The succession, thou sayest, was uncertain: what made it uncertain but thy divorce? Thy divorce was exploded in the English schools: thy Supreme Head was never ob-

---

* He constantly accuses the King of desiring to be the Vicar of Christ, and confound the kingly and priestly functions: he makes no distinction between the Supremacy of the King and the Primacy of the Pope. "Velis ecclesiæ, quod nullus rex ante te concupuit, Supremum Caput in regno tuo dici? velis Christi Vicarius haberi? Velis Filii Dei personam sumere?" Again, "Rex præcipit ne amplius obediamus Pontifici ut Supremo Capiti Ecclesiæ in terris: sed ut eum honorem sibi suo in regno omnes tribuant."—*Lib.* i.

tained by the consent of the English people. Dost
thou deny this? I make bold to affirm it. Their
consent has been wrung and tortured from them : not
given freely. Do men give new titles for nothing, or
worse than nothing, that they should give thee the
title of Head of the Church, who art the robber and
persecutor of the Church? Thy father was a sparing
man : but even he built a few monasteries for the good
of the poor : but who can record any good deed of
thee? What are thy public works? Houses of pleasure, built for thy lusts : ruined monasteries, churches
destroyed, and their possessions flung into thy treasury.
In twenty-six years thou hast exacted more money
from thy people and clergy than the Kings of England
who were before thee in five hundred years. I know
it : I was there, and saw the reckoning made out of
the public accounts. Thou wilt pretend that it was
to defend the nation in times of great difficulty and
danger. Thou, who never hadst an enemy whom
thou didst not make wantonly, nor a war that was
not ended in a few months! Thou hast cast thy kingdom into miserable commotions, and made it the spectacle of the world. Thy nobles thou hast slaughtered
on the least pretext, and filled thy court with the
vilest of the people, to whom thou committest everything. But what of the butcheries, the horrible executions, that have made England the slaughter-house of
innocence! The holiest, the most spotless men on
earth, have been slaughtered for new crimes in the
most ghastly and unspeakable manner. The glorious
Bishop of Rochester, the matchless More, the learned
Reynolds, and how many others, have been the victims
of thy rabid and malignant fury. In their bloody
deaths no torment was spared them ; to religion no
insult. All nations wept to hear of that fearful tragedy,

and even now, after so long a time, when I write of it, tears burst from my eyes. And thou art he that argues that the Pope cannot be the Vicar of Christ through moral depravity! Worse art thou than Korah who rebelled against Aaron, worse than the king Uzziah, who usurped the priestly office, worse than Saul, who slew the priests at Nob: Lucifer alone, who set himself against the Most High, may fitly be compared to thee."

In the mind of Pole and in the opinion of that age, the kingdom was, according to the English Constitution, not a dynasty but an office, which if the holder abused, the remedy of the people was insurrection. The English had ere now asserted the right of rebellion when the chief magistrate proved himself a tyrant or a traitor. Pole now sounded this note of alarm in the ears of Henry; and spoke as confidently as if he were but advancing a recognised principle. An insurrection was to the English, what it is to the Spaniards still, no more than an armed demonstration in defence of endangered rights. Demonstrations are made now without arms in this country; they were made formerly in arms, for all men carried arms. To this threat, Pole added the menace of foreign intervention; which came with double force from a man of his birth in his position. "Is England a Turkey," he cried, "that she is governed by the sword? The English ere now for slighter provocations have avenged the republic on the King: for profuse expenditure they have called the King to account: for violating the constitution they have deposed him. In giving the crown they reserve the right of maintaining their ancient liberties and of observing the administration. Who says that all belongs to the King? Thou, O my country, art all: the King is but thy servant and minister. Resume thy former spirit, and friends will not be wanting. The Cæsar, the greatest of monarchs, will not refuse his aid. If the Cæsar were already in arms against the Turk, if he were now crossing the Bosphorus to the attack, I myself would follow him and cry, Turn thy sails, pursue a worse enemy of the faith, a viler heretic, one who is stricken with the same plague that is devouring thy Germany. My afflicted country calls thee, Cæsar: and but that she has waited for thee would long ago have cast off the tyrant. Again, I will go, Henry, to thine ally the King of France, and say to him: Most Christian King, by the piety of France towards the Holy See, assist that man no longer; his crimes have cut him off from Christendom, even as his island is separated by the sea. To thee, Henry, in conclusion, I will address myself: I, thy friend, thy physician, thy former favourite. I say to thee, Repent, retrace thy steps: make restitution for thy enormous crimes. In penitence consists the dignity of man. I am thy Nathan, be thou my David!"

But it is not probable that Henry ever read the reproofs that were meant to edify him. He commanded the author home to explain his work, as soon as it was received; and Crumwel, vowing that he would make Pole eat his own heart,* added a letter

---

* "I heard you say, soon after you had seen that furious invective of Cardinal Pole, that you would make him eat his own heart; which you have now, I trow, brought to pass, for he must now eat his own heart, and be as heartless as he is graceless."—Latimer to Crumwel (in December), *Rem.* 411. The order of the Correspondence on Pole's book may as well be added here :—

Pole sent his unpublished book, 27 May, 1536.
The King and Crumwel wrote to Pole to come home, 14 June.
Pole got their letters, 30 June.
Pole answered King, 15 July.—Strype, ii. 295.
Starkey wrote severely to Pole about the same time.—Strype, ii. 282.
Tunstall wrote severely to Pole about the same time.
Pole answered Tunstall, 1 Aug.—Strype, ii. 306.

that was more urgent than the King's, and despatched both by a messenger who was more urgent than either. Pole replied that "he that called him would not let him come:" the King indeed called him home, but while there were such laws in operation at home as were not found in any other Christian realm, such laws as made every man a traitor who would not agree to the title of Supreme Head, he should be a traitor to his own life if he came within their danger. Meanwhile the book was committed to several persons to be examined; of whom were Starkey and Bishop Tunstall, who both expostulated with Pole very seriously.* "This is the last letter," said Starkey, "that ever I shall write to you, until your mind be altered. Once more I call upon you to consider those principal points of the whole matter, which I laid before you in my former letter. You have never considered them diligently yet; but have filled your book with lamentable complaints of false grounds conceived. I have read it from beginning to end, and more than once : and I find therein the most frantic judgment that ever I read of any learned man in my life. Herein lies the sum of your book : because we are slipped from the obedience of Rome, you judge us to be separate from the unity of the Church, and to be no members of the Catholic body. Weigh this cause yet a little, Master Pole : and despise not the consent of your country, and of all the learned men therein, with too much

---

* It is somewhat curious that Pole, anticipating that the King would never give time to his book, begged, when he sent it, that it might be submitted to Tunstall. Froude, iii. 50 ; Hooke, iii. 94 ; Burnet, Coll. But Starkey, as he himself relates, used his friendly offices to get it submitted to more than one person, and it was "committed to the examination of those who both had learning to judge and weigh the matter indifferently." *Strype,* ii. 283. He was one of this committee : he afterwards read it by himself : and again with Tunstall.

arrogance. Though we be slipt from the obedience of Rome, denying any superiority to be due thereto from the law of God, yet we be not slipt *a fide Romana nec a Petri cathedra.* We observe and keep the same faith which from the beginning hath been taught in Rome. Christian unity stands in unity of faith and of the Spirit : which may rest in all kinds of policy. The superiority of Rome sprang first of policy, as it is evident by the old story of Constantine. It began of man's wit, and it may end by the like reason. To think that the consent of the Church makes things necessary to salvation, is marvellous madness. For hereby you might confirm all the rites and ceremonies which the Church has held for a thousand years or more by common consent, to be necessary to salvation : and the alteration of any of them to be separation from the unity of the Church. You would not say that the primacy of Canterbury in England is founded in God's word, but devised among us for an order of synods and councils : so was the primacy of Rome ordered and invented by man at a time when a general council of all Christian nations was first convoked. In comparing the office of a prince and a bishop together, you deceive yourself wonderfully, for you appoint the prince to the cure of civil and worldly things alone : leaving Christian doctrine to the bishop only, as if the prince were no Christian. But the office of a Christian prince is to build his policy upon God's word, directing all his actions to the setting forth of his glory : he is a minister of God's word not less than the bishop : rather more, to say truly. For the prince can compel, and not only exhort, his subjects to the order of Christ's doctrine. Blinded they be, which judge in Christendom to be *binas quasdam politias :* wherein as bishops reign in one, so do princes in the other. This division deceives many. It may not be convenient for a prince to be a bishop or a bishop to be a prince: but there is nothing here repugnant to God's word. Much more may a Christian prince take upon him to oversee his bishops, and see that they execute their office truly: which thing only our Prince takes upon him by his new title, the which you so abhor in your folly."* The letter of the gentle Bishop of Durham was written·more in sorrow than in anger: but he was equally certain that Pole had taken a foreign view, and wholly mistaken the matter in which he accused the King.† And it must be concluded that, however

---

* It is amusing to notice that in one place in his letter, where Starkey threatens Pole that he would be known hereafter as having made as great a breach in Christian unity "as hath done *any others in our days*," he had written first "as hath done *Martin Luther*," but blotted that out. Strype, ii. 294. Such was the force of habit. The time was now passed when the English revolutionists felt it necessary always to disown Luther, and, like Crumwel, to wish that he had never been born.

† Tunstall's letter, and Pole's answer, in which he takes it sentence by sentence, form a sort of dialogue; thus: *T.* You want to bring the King by penance home to the Church: but he has never left it. *P.* You have not read my book, if you think he has not. *T.* You have fallen into the opinion of foreigners. *P.* No, I have judged the King by his manifest deeds. *T.* You make many plagues, but give no salve to heal them. *P.* Why, my book is all salve: I only discover plagues that were made already. *T.* You show yourself stirred and incensed. *P.* With very good cause. *T.* Why did you make your book so long that it had to be committed to councillors to read? *P.* If they be trusty councillors, what matter? *T.* Why did you send it so far? if it had fallen into foreign hands on the way, the realm would have been slandered. *P.* I wish that foreigners could only know of the King's deeds from my book: but he is infamous through Christendom. *T.* Oh, burn the original of your book. *P.* If the King cannot digest it, I will separate the matter from the person, but I must maintain the verity thereof: and I cannot treat a Catholic book as an heretical one. *T.* My heart grew cold when I heard that you had lost two quires of the original out of your hands. *P.* Be of good courage again: I found them afterwards in another book. *T.* You presuppose, but never prove your ground, that the King is severed from Unity. *P.* Can you prove that ground untrue? *T.* The King does not take on him the office of a priest. *P.* And how does that prove that he does not break the unity of the Church? Because he does not utterly

foolish and needless might be the title of Supreme Head which Henry took, yet as it regarded the inherent supremacy of the English crown, the bloody tyrant was right, and the eloquent purist was wrong.

The Vicegerent of the Supreme Head had, as became his office, a powerful talent for lecturing the clergy. Under the well-known name of injunctions he published this year a set of stringent regulations in which the clergy found many new duties laid upon them: and when, by the weight of royal authority, they were compelled not only to receive with submission, but to publish to their flocks the rebukes with which they were chastened, it may be acknowledged that the art of lecturing the clergy reached great excellence at an early period. Upon pain of deprivation, sequestration, or such other penalty as might seem good to the King or his Vicegerent, they were ordered to read these injunctions openly and deliberately to their parishioners once every quarter of the year: and to observe and keep them. The Injunctions were of a more intolerant tone than the King's Articles: and spoke with some opprobrium of things which were regarded and taught as part of the Catholic customs of the Church. The pulpits being now again, it would seem, unlocked from silence, the clergy were commanded to preach every Sunday for three months against the pretended power of the Pope, and after that to expound the King's Articles at least twice a quarter in their sermons: they were to discourage superstitious image-worship and pilgrimages, and superfluous holidays, in accordance with the late ordinances. They were also to see that

---

subvert the whole order of the Church, does it follow that he has not broken the unity? And how can he be the Supreme Head if he cannot exercise the highest offices, as in administering the Sacraments, and preaching? etc. *Strype*, ii. 306.

the young of their parishes were taught to say the Creed, the Pater Noster and the Ten Commandments in English, and in their sermons they were to recite the same by little and little, till the whole was learned, giving the same in writing to those who could read, or telling them where to get printed copies. All non-residents, holding benefices of above twenty pounds a year, were to dispense the fourteenth part of their living to the poor, "because the goods of the Church are called the goods of the poor, and in these days nothing is less seen than the poor to be sustained of them." This, which falls with peculiar grace from the author of the scheme for alienating nearly all the ancient charities in the country, was the prelude of another scheme, for making the clergy pay for education. Every beneficed person of one hundred pounds was to give competent exhibition to one scholar at the university or some grammar school, and for as many more hundreds of pounds as he had he was to give like exhibition to so many scholars more. The fifth part of all benefices was to be bestowed yearly in repairing decayed churches, chapels, and other buildings; and the buildings so repaired were to be kept in good state. Education is desirable: it is desirable that somebody should provide education. It is well also that somebody should keep churches and chapels in repair. In suppressing the monasteries, many schools had been destroyed already, and many more were about to be destroyed; the colleges, also, which the monasteries maintained in the universities, were about to be destroyed: and many promising youths who would have been sent by the monasteries to their colleges, would have neither monasteries to send nor colleges to receive them: and so learning might suffer. In carrying the same changes, many monastic chapels and churches which had been partly open to parish use, and many more that might have been turned to the same purpose, were destroyed, or destined to be destroyed; and many other religious edifices were about to be defaced and impaired by the taking down of images and shrines. It was really desirable that somebody should make some provision for these things.

Most of these regulations were no doubt mere paper, serving but to show the zeal of the official who issued them. Among them was one which has caused some discussion in modern times. Crumwel ordered that by the middle of the next year "every parson and proprietary of any Parish Church within the realm" should provide and place in the choir a book of the whole Bible, both in Latin and also in English.* As

---

* About these injunctions of Crumwel's there are some difficulties: I. He issued two sets of injunctions, one in 1536, the other in 1538, as Fox, who was the first to print them both, correctly gives them; but Wilkins, who reprinted them, put them both in 1536. 2. Fox rightly calls both sets by the same name: the King's Injunctions; but Wilkins calls one set the King's, and the other the Vicar General's Injunctions; whereas they were both issued by Crumwel in the King's name, and are both either the King's or the Vicar General's, but not one one, and the other the other. This is doubly cruel in Wilkins, and has misled several writers: for writers who know that Crumwel issued injunctions in 1536, turn to those which bear his name with that date in the Concilia: they find them, and they are his certainly, but belong to 1538: while those which he issued in truth in 1536 are there also, but disguised under the name of the King. 3. The true Injunctions of 1536 contain, as Fox has given them, the order to provide a Bible in Latin and English: but, as Wilkins has them, they contain no such order, and say nothing about the Bible. This is trebly cruel, for some, who are aware that there was something said about the Bible in 1536, turn to Wilkins and find that the only thing about it in that year is in the latter Injunctions which he has put there, though they belong to 1538: and as these, and these alone, bear the name of Crumwel, several writers have unhesitatingly quoted what they say about the Bible, as what he said about it in 1536. 4. Why should the important clause about the Bible be in Fox, but not in Wilkins, who took his copy from Cranmer's Register? Canon Westcott thinks that it may have been in the original draft of the Injunctions, but that it was certainly never published. (Eng. Bib., 85.) As it is not in

no English version of the whole Bible had been printed as yet, except one which had been executed abroad and published the year before by a young scholar whom Crumwel had once known and patronised, there can be no doubt that the Vicegerent meant by this order to further the literary project of a former favourite. In so doing he made a compromise between the opposite principles of authority and private enterprise in the matter of translating the Bible : and this kind of compromise was repeated afterwards in the Reformation.*

The history of the English Bible is a labyrinth in which it is easy to be lost : but a clue may perhaps be afforded in the reflection that there was from a very high antiquity a struggle between authorised, or at least not unsanctioned versions, and versions of private design : which struggle lasted until the final triumph

Cranmer's Register, it may not perhaps be found in other registers of bishops, and may never have been published. Cf. Cranmer's Rem., 346. Fox does not say where he got his copy of the Injunctions. Whether published or not, the order for the Bible remained a dead letter. But I have ventured to write as if it had official existence, because it seems to exhibit a natural phase of the process by which the English Bible came gradually to be allowed : viz., the setting of the Latin and English Bibles side by side, before the latter was allowed alone.

* This Injunction is as follows : " That every person or proprietary of any Parish Church within this realm shall on this side the Feast of St. Peter ad Vincula (Aug. 1) next ensuing, provide a book of the whole Bible both in Latin and also in English, and lay the same in the choir, for every man that will to look and read therein. And shall discourage no man from reading any part of the Bible either in Latin or English, but rather comfort, exhort, and admonish every man to read the same, as the very word of God, and the spiritual food of men's souls, whereby they may the better know their duties to God, to their sovereign lord the King, and their neighbour: ever gently and charitably exhorting them that, using a sober and modest behaviour in the reading and inquisition of the true sense of the same, they do in no wise stiffly or eagerly contend or strive one with another about the same, but refer the declaration of those places that be in controversy to the judgment of them that are better learned." As this was issued after the three months' silence imposed on the pulpits till Michaelmas in 1536, the time appointed to provide Bibles must have been 1 August, 1537.

of authority. From the earliest times the English Church or nation was possessed of the sacred writings through the labours of monks and bishops. Aldhelm and Aidan, Bede, Alcuin, and Aelfric, the most venerable names of the English Church, were among the most industrious of these translators. In those early versions, the simplicity of the times and the homogeneous state of the language alike precluded the thought that there were certain words, of the original Greek or Latin, so sacred in their meaning that it was impossible to express them in the rude dialect of barbarians, and necessary to retain them in their own form. Baptism and penance, grace and charity, the assembly of the Jewish synagogue, and the ejaculatory Amen of the worshippers therein, alike received the most ready equivalent that could be supplied from the common speech of our forefathers. But with the process of time these and many other such words which were used continually in the Latin services, acquired to themselves a venerable and mysterious character which could be transferred to no other language: it became a point in dispute whether this traditional sanctity of words should be maintained or rejected: and upon this point gradually converged a great part of the attack and defence of the standing system of faith and ceremonies. Innovation or reformation must be active; and the multiplication of new versions by Wickliffe and his school, in the fourteenth century, was disliked by ecclesiastics who had nothing to object against the earlier versions. The earlier versions, indeed, had grown partly obsolete, and so may have shared the venerable character of the originals. The surprising industry of the Wickliffites in translating and multiplying copies of their versions by the pen, has given rise to the common mistake (which it was necessary even for More to correct, less than two hundred years later)* that the Bible was first made English in the fourteenth century. A large number of their manuscripts still remains: most of which are very sumptuous, as if made for the use of rich and liberal persons. But in the same age there were not wanting efforts on the part of calmer spirits to supply the wants of the times : and the works of Rolle and Shorham are remembered yet. At length, however, at the beginning of the fifteenth century, the resolute prelate Arundel passed his famous Constitution to forbid any man from making new translations on his own authority, or reading those that had been made in or since the time of the lately deceased Wickliffe.† He thus proclaimed the war of authority against private versions ; though certainly he neither forbad the ancient versions to be used, nor denied that an authorised version might be made.‡ The effect of this edict, however, was to stop both friends and foes : and for a hundred years, during the most retrograde century of English history, not a single version of any part of the sacred text is known to have been executed. The long stagnation may account for some of the violence with which the ques-

---

* " The whole Bible was long before Wickliffe's days, by virtuous and well learned men, translated into the English tongue, and by good and godly people with devotion and soberness well and reverently read."— More's *Dial.* So Cranmer and Fox: see Blunt's Plain Account, 27.

† " Statuimus et ordinamus, ut nemo deinceps aliquem textum Sacræ Scripturæ auctoritate sua in linguam Anglicanam vel aliam transferat per viam libri, libelli aut tractatus, nec legatur aliquis hujusmodi liber, libellus, aut tractatus jam noviter tempore dicti Johannis Wickliff, sive citra, compositus aut imposterum componendus, in parte vel in toto, publice vel occulte, sub maJoris excommunicationis pœna ; quousque per loci diocesanum, seu, si res exegerit, per concilium provinciale, ipsa translatio fuerit approbata : qui contra fecerit, ut fautor hæresis et erroris, similiter punietur."—*Wilkins,* iii. 317.

‡ So his Constitution was interpreted twenty years later by Lyndwood.—*Provinc.* cited in Lewes' Bible Hist.

tion was agitated, when, with the invention of printing
and the dawn of the sixteenth century, it was revived
again.

There is nothing for which the gestures of indignation and contempt have been so freely used against the
clergy of the Reformation, by the graphical writers ·
who have adorned this part of history with the graces
of a modern style, than for their alleged unwillingness
to allow the Scriptures to the people in their own
tongue.   A narrow and prejudiced caste stood in the
way of general enlightenment: the hypocrites who had
taken away the key of knowledge would have hindered
all from entering in : a herd of corrupt and time-serving
officials, callous in heart and besotted in brain, would
fain have prevented the proclamation of the everlasting charters of spiritual freedom.   The Scriptures
would never have been allowed by the bishops : they
were won by the blood of Tyndale and Roye, by the
zeal of Coverdale, by the stern resolution of Crümwel
and the King.   And certainly it must be admitted
that the Levites hastened not the work.   But, before
joining in the shout of condemnation, it seems rational
to enquire whether the delay which they were able to
interpose was great, whether they stood alone in their
opposition to the Scriptures, whether their opposition
was to the Scriptures alone, and whether their motives
were altogether base.

It was Tyndale and his fellow-labourers who awoke
the question of translating the Scriptures, after the
slumber of a century.   The admirers and the guests
of Germany, these voluntary exiles poured from their
foreign refuges, upon their native land, an inexhaustible
succession of printed versions of the various books of
the Bible.   These, it may be thought, should have
been welcome to the clergy in place of the old manu-

script translations, which must have become rarer and more obsolete than ever. Instead of that, they were condemned by Convocation among the books of *mala dogmata*: they were seized or bought up by the bishops, and committed to the flames. If the clergy had acted thus simply because they would have kept the people ignorant of the Word of God, they would have been without excuse. But it was not so. Every one of the little volumes containing portions of the sacred text, that was issued by Tyndale, contained also a Prologue and Notes written with such hot fury of vituperation against the prelates and clergy, the monks and friars, the rites and ceremonies of the Church, as, though an extensive circulation was secured to the work thereby, was hardly likely to commend it to the favour of those who were attacked. Moreover, the versions themselves were held to be hostile to the Catholic faith, as it was then understood, and to convey the sense unfaithfully or maliciously. The venerable words were ignored in them: and every variation that indicated opposition to the standing system was introduced. One of the bishops declared that he had found more than two thousand heresies in Tyndale's versions. A great layman, Sir Thomas More himself, found it necessary to write a formal treatise against him, in which he exhibited a considerable number of venerable words, for which Tyndale had found unauthorised and dangerous substitutes. There were in particular three such words, which seemed the cardinal points of the Catholic system: they were, Priests, Church, and Charity. The first of them Tyndale constantly turned into Seniors: he rendered the second by Congregation: the third he gave as Love.* It is

---

* More, Dial. concerning Heresies, Bk. iii. ch. viii. (Works, 220.) Tyndale afterwards changed *senior* into *elder*. (Ans. to More, p. 16.)

difficult to see how a body of men, vowed to maintain a system, could have acted otherwise than the clergy did in this case. Nearly three centuries later a more powerful body than the clergy ever were, the Commons of England themselves, found themselves exposed to assaults which were not altogether unlike the ferocious invectives of Tyndale and his fellows. Their debates were published by the newspapers, severe comments being added by anonymous writers : and the Commons sought their remedy in imposing restraints upon the printers from whose presses the offensive strictures flowed.

For ten years the private versions of Tyndale continued to issue. For ten years the opposition of authority was maintained against them. The King assisted the clergy : and for every condemnation pronounced by Convocation, two royal proclamations at least might be produced in which the activity of justices and bailiffs was evoked against all who read or concealed the obnoxious volumes. Meanwhile a movement was made amongst the clergy themselves for an authorised version : fit, Catholic and learned persons were to be selected for the work, instead of the private heretics who had presumed to undertake it : and the head of the realm was petitioned (as we have seen) more than once to name those to whom he would have it committed. If Henry had been in earnest in the matter, it cannot be doubted that he could have nominated the translators and had the work done, as certainly as he was obeyed when he ordered the bishops to preach the Supreme Head at Paul's Cross. The theory that the thing nearest his heart was a noble and unfeigned desire to give his people the Bible in their own language is too absurd to be confuted. But though an authorised version was not undertaken by the com-

mandment of the King, an authorised version was
actually begun by the metropolitical authority of the
Primate. Taking one of the early English versions of
the New Testament, Cranmer divided it into nine or
ten portions, one of which he committed to each of his
bishops, and to some other learned men, to be carefully corrected and returned to him. The work was
performed by all but Stokesley, who refused to have
anything to do with it, alleging in excuse that liberty
to read the Scriptures would do nothing but infect the
people with heresy.* Cranmer designed undoubtedly
to have extended this work to the Old Testament, so
as to have had a version of the whole Bible executed
by persons of competent authority. But whether he
ever went beyond designing it may well be doubted.
There is no proof that he ever took with the Old Testament the same measures as he had taken with the

---

* This is thus related by Cranmer's secretary, Ralph Maurice. "My
lord Cranmer, minding to have the New Testament thoroughly corrected,
divided the same into 9 or 10 parts, and caused it to be written at large
in paper books, and sent unto the best learned Bishops and other learned
men, to the intent that they should make a perfect correction thereof, and
when they had done, to send them unto him to Lambeth by a day limited
for that purpose. It chanced that the Acts of the Apostles were sent to
Bp. Stokesley to oversee and correct, then Bishop of London. When
the day came, every man had sent to Lambeth their parts correct, only
Stokesley's portion wanted," &c. Nicholl's Narratives, 277. This movement of Cranmer's may have arisen out of the petition of Convocation to
the King to have the Bible translated, December, 1534; since by 10 June
1535, Gardiner informed Crumwel in a letter that he had finished the
translation of St. Luke and St. John, wherein he had "spent a great
labour." *Stat. Pap.*, i. 430. It is a curious illustration of the want of
knowledge of the state of parties which is found in some writers, that
Anderson, in his Annals of the English Bible, should say that the old
English translation which Cranmer used was "Tyndale's of course:" and
that for the remarkable reason that "as yet there was no other" (i. 453).
Strype believes that Cranmer took the same course with the Old Testament. Cran., Bk. i. c. 8. He most likely designed it: but there is no
proof that the undertaking went farther than the New Testament. ' It is
to be regretted that no fragment remains of what was done.

New, dividing it among the bishops, and setting a day for their work to be ready. So far as he is known to have proceeded, he had little cause to complain of the backwardness of those whom he engaged : * but the work was superseded by Crumwel's Injunction to have the Bible both in English and in Latin forthwith provided in every church.

This injunction bears the marks of compromise. The English Bible thus ordered was a private version : but if errors were found in it, they might be corrected by the Latin Bible that lay beside it. Of the whole Bible the first printed version had been finished some months before, and published in foreign parts, by Miles Coverdale, some time an Austin friar of Cambridge, but long converted to the Reformation, and resident abroad. He had been known to Crumwel in former years, when he was still under the gentle government of his prior, Barnes : but he had been out of the country for the last six years. In his voluntary exile he had put together "out of Dutch and Latin" a complete version of the Bible, which now, in the year of the death of his precursor Tyndale, was imposed upon the realm of England by the Vicar General. It was an inferior and patched performance : and though the outrageous language in which Tyndale had indulged was avoided, yet the author shewed his mind in a dedication to the King, in which he told him that his title of Defender of the Faith had been given him by the blind Balaam and the crafty Caiaphas of

---

* And yet, two years later, Cranmer could so far slander his own order as to tell Crumwel that " we the bishops " would never send forth a translation "till a day after doomsday." Lett., 344. This was said after the work of the bishops had been stopped by Crumwel's patronage of Coverdale's Bible : and it was said to justify Cranmer's patronage of another private version, that of Matthew, in the following year. See next chapter.

Rome, for no other reason than that he allowed his bishops to burn the Bible.* Crumwel's Injunction to have it in the churches probably remained a dead letter, since it was renewed two years after concerning another edition. The delay in getting a complete version of the Scriptures (by whomsoever caused) was not at all events so great as it might have been thought from the strong language that has been used. It was but fifty years since the first book had been printed in this country. Twenty years are not too much to allow for the invention of printing to have got into general use : and in thirty years more, in a single generation, a translation of the whole Bible was prepared and allowed.

Meanwhile the suppression of the smaller monasteries had been going on, amid the sullen indignation of the nation. Every order of society was incommoded, none seemed benefited, by this enormous scheme for filling the royal purse. The daily scenes of ejection, the spectacle of monks and nuns, whose bounty had fed the beggar, reduced to beggary, or at best to the humble subsistence of a pension, touched a not ungenerous people with anger and pity : and the opposition which the King and those around him had challenged so long seemed to be aroused at last. Of the numerous sparks that he and Crumwel were flinging about, one suddenly kindled a conflagration which was considerable, and might have been universal but for the address used to extinguish it. At the end of September a party of commissioners were suppressing the

---

* It seems disputed among the authorities on Coverdale whether the story of Fox be true or not, that he lived with Tyndale and helped him, and to what extent he embodied Tyndale's labours in his own. His Bible was finished at the press 4 October, 1535 : as on the last page of it we are told. The first copies that were struck off made mention of the King's "dearest Just wife Anne :" for which the author speedily substituted "Jane." Lewes.

small nunnery of Legbourne in Lincolnshire, where there resided ten nuns of the Cistercian order. The prioress of this little community had lately invited the scrutiny and invoked the pity of Crumwel in a letter which only the more surely drew on her the doom that she dreaded.* Her house was entered, her convent summoned and dissolved, and two of Crumwel's servants left in possession. The next day when the commissioners, one of whom named Heneage was afterwards rewarded with a grant of this priory, entered the neighbouring town of Louth in pursuit of their business, they found the people in tumult, and were compelled to join them or fly for their lives. Crumwel's servants were brought from the priory and set in the stocks. The rising spread from one town to another: a shoemaker who received the name of Captain Cobbler put himself at the head of the movement: the gentlemen and the clergy joined the people in considerable numbers, and among the rest, Doctor Mackerel, the Abbot of Barling, a great house of Præmonstratensian canons, appeared in full armour with all his fraternity. The blood of one of the commissioners, the hated Chancellor of Lincoln, who incautiously arrived on the scene and was killed at the instigation of the clergy, cemented the alliance; and the demands of the insurgents of Lincolnshire were carried from the field of the assembly

---

* "And whereas we do hear that a great number of abbies shall be punished, suppressed, and put down, because of their misliving, and that all abbies and priories under the value of two hundred pounds be at our most noble Prince's pleasure to suppress and put down, yet if it may please your goodness we trust in God ye shall have no complaints against us neither in our living nor hospitality keeping. In consideration whereof may it please your goodness in our great necessity to be a mean and suitor for your own poor priory, that it may be preserved and stand, ye shall be a more higher founder to us than he that first founded our house. We have none other comfort nor refuge but only unto your goodness," &c. *The prioress and sisters of Legbourne to Crumwel, Wright,* 116.

to the court of the King.* Declaring themselves the faithful subjects of the King, and acknowledging him to be by inheritance the Supreme Head of the Church of England,† the commons of Lincolnshire nevertheless alleged themselves aggrieved by the suppression of so many religious houses, whereby the service of God was diminished, the poor left unrelieved, and many persons put out of their livings. The statute of uses, which two years before had begun a revolution in land by transferring uses into possession, they required to be repealed, because it restrained their liberty in disposing of their land.‡ The subsidy of the fifteenth lately granted to the King, they asked him to remit, considering the scarcity of sheep and cattle. They complained that the King had in his council men of low birth and small reputation, who had procured these incommodities for their own lucre and advantage : and among them they named Crumwel and Rich. The payment of tenths and firstfruits to the crown by the clergy they held to be a great exaction. They remonstrated

---

* The history of "The Great Insurrection" has been written graphically by Mr. Froude. It was throughout more of a demonstration than a civil war, and with the exception of the murder of the Chancellor and of a serving man, the behaviour of the so-called rebels was wonderfully temperate and orderly. On the other hand, the bloody perfidy of the strangely chosen hero of Mr. Froude comes out more conspicuously in his excited narrative than in any of the histories.

† "Whereby we shall not only accept your Grace to be the Head and Sovereign of us your subjects, but also accept and take your Grace to be Supreme Head of the Church of England, which we do knowledge your Grace's true inheritance and right." *Lincolnshire Articles, Speed,* 1017.

‡ The Statute of Uses, 27 H. VIII. 10, for making persons, who before had only the use of their lands, the true owners or possessors, struck a heavy blow at the rights of the feoffees, and the old feudal system. The gentlemen of Lincolnshire thus described the inconveniences of it : "By the said Act we be clearly restrained of our liberties, in the declaration of our wills, concerning our lands, as well for the payment of our debts, for doing of your Grace service, as for helping and relieving of our children," &c. *Ib.*

against the promotion of the bishops of Canterbury, Rochester, Salisbury, St. David's, and Dublin.* And in especial they concluded that the whole beginning of the trouble had been through the behaviour of the Bishop of Lincoln, and the other servants of Crumwel, through whom a great rumour had arisen that the jewels, plate, and ornaments of the Parish Churches would be taken away and spoiled as the religious houses had been.

The messengers who took these demands were accompanied by Heneage, the commissioner.† They were detained in London a few days by the King, while the forces which had been collected under the Duke of Suffolk marched to attack the rebels.‡ But the disordered tumult broke in pieces almost before the royal troops advanced : Suffolk entered Lincoln unopposed. The leaders of the movement, Captain Cobbler, Abbot Mackerel, and the rest, were surrendered by the various towns to which they fled : and in a fortnight the formidable demonstration was at an end. It fell more before the words than the weapons of the King: whose answer to the petitions of the rebels was as the roaring of the lion. " Rude commons of a most brute and beastly shire," so, with some condensation ran the royal reply, "how should ye presume to find fault with your Prince for the election of his councillors

---

* "There be divers bishops of England, of your Grace's late promotion, that have subverted the faith of Christ, as we think : which is the Archbishop of Canterbury," &c. *Lincolnshire Articles, Speed,* 1017.

† " Perhaps to save him from being murdered by the priests."—Froude, iii. 109. Perhaps not.

‡ Henry got some of his levies from the clergy. Amongst others he required the Bishop of Exeter to furnish four hundred men, six score of them to be bowmen. Speed, 1017. He desired Crumwel to " tax the fat priests thereabout : " naming some whom he thought the richest : and some of them sent him heavy contributions of their own will. State Pap., i. 472.

and prelates? Ye call yourselves true subjects, but ye are foul traitors. Ye speak of the suppression of the religious houses: but the religious houses were given to us by Act of Parliament: none are suppressed where God was well served, but those where most vice, mischief, and abomination of living were used: and that doth well appear by their own confessions, subscribed with their own hands, in the time of our visitation.* We have more to answer for in suffering many to stand than for all that we have suppressed. Are ye not ashamed to affirm that they kept hospitality to the relief of the people, when many, or most of them, had·but four or five religious persons in them, and divers but one, who spent the goods of the house in vice and abominable living? And yet ye would rather that they should enjoy their possessions than we, who spend of our own six times as much in your defence! Ye complain of the Act of Uses: but the Act of Uses was made by Parliament, oh base commons; and on good grounds, for your Uses never stood upon any law. Ye murmur at the fifteenth, and yet was not that granted lovingly at first? And think ye that we be so faint-hearted that ye can compel us to remit it? No: ye are but of one shire, and the rest of the realm is with us. The fifteenth is not the tenth penny of the charges which we have in your defence. Never was there a king more dedicate to the welfare of his people. But ye are ungrateful and unnatural, with your insurrections and such rebellious demeanour. Beware, lest we resolve not to study your tuition and safeguard so much as we have hitherto done. Ye complain of the firstfruits: but the firstfruits were granted us by Act of Parliament,

---

* This is the first mention made, so far as I know, of the confessions subscribed by the convents. See above, p. 348.

and for the further supportation of the great and excessive charges which we bear for your welfare.   Before
this time ye were always complaining that most of the
lands were in spiritual hands : and now ye cannot find
in your hearts that your Prince and Sovereign Lord
should have a part thereof."*   When the legality of
the King's actions, his virtues and his sacrifices to the
good of his people were thus laid before the men of
Lincolnshire, they expressed their remorse; and a
gentler letter from the King assured them of his pardon.†   The leaders only of the rebellion, including the
unfortunate Abbot of Barling, were reserved in prison
to be tried as traitors.

But at the very moment that Lincolnshire subsided,
a more formidable insurrection, which arose in Yorkshire and the northern counties, demanded the tongue
of Henry.   A wide confederation of gentry, clergy and
commons was formed under the name of an Assembly,
or Pilgrimage : an obscure gentleman of Yorkshire,
who had been a barrister of Westminster, was suddenly
raised by the popular instinct to the head of this gathering : and in the name of Robert Aske, chief captain
of the commonalty, a Proclamation was issued, setting
forth the reasons which called the loyal subjects of the
King to arms.   " Simple and evil-disposed persons," it
was declared," being of the King's council, have incensed
his Grace with many new inventions, contrary to the
faith of God, the honour of the King, and the weal of
the realm : they intend to destroy the Church of
England and her ministers : they have robbed and
spoiled, and further intend utterly to rob and spoil,
the whole body of this realm.   We have now taken
this pilgrimage for the preservation of Christ's Church,
of the realm, and of the King : to the intent of making

* State Pap., i. 463.   † *Ib.* 468.

petition to the King for the reformation of that which
is amiss, and for the punishment of heretics and subverters of the laws : and neither for money, malice,
nor displeasure of any persons but such as be unworthy to remain about the King.   Come with us,
lords, knights, masters, kinsmen, and friends!   If ye
fight against us and defeat us, ye will but put both us
and you into bondage for ever : if we overcome you,
ye shall be at our will.   We will fight and die against
all who shall be about to stop us in this pilgrimage :
and God shall judge between us."*   Appended to this
Proclamation were the same six Articles which composed the petition of Lincolnshire : in every parish a
summons was posted, bidding the inhabitants appear
in their best array on the day appointed to each : and
all who joined the Pilgrimage were bound by a solemn
oath.†   At the head of a formidable force, Aske, the

---

* See it at large in Speed, p. 1018.

† Speed, 1019, has preserved these curious documents.   The summons
to one of the parishes, that of Hawkeside, was as follows : " Well beloved,
we greet you well : and whereas our brother Poverty and our brother
Rogers goeth forward, (it) is openly for the aid and assistance of your
faith and Holy Church, and for the reformation of such abbeys and monasteries now dissolved and suppressed without any just cause.   Wherefore, good brothers, forasmuch as our said brethren hath sued to us for
aid and help, we do not only effectually desire you, but also under the
pain of deadly sin, we command you and every of you to be at the stoke
green beside Hawkesdale Kirk the Saturday next, being the 28th day of
October, by eleven of the clock, in your best array ; as ye will make
answer before the high Judge at the dreadful day of Doom, and in the
pain of pulling down your houses, and leasing of your goods, and your
bodies to be at the Captain's will : For at the place aforesaid, then and
there, you and we shall take further direction concerning our faith so far
decayed, and for good and laudable customs of the country.   And such
naughty inventions and strange articles now accepted and admitted, so
that our said brother be subdued, they are like to go forwards to utter
undoing of the Commonwealth."   Brother Poverty was a poor fisherman
in command under Aske.   Aske was styled " the Earl of Poverty."
The oath was "to enter the Pilgrimage of Grace—only for the love
that they bore unto Almighty God, his faith, and to holy Church militant,

Captain-general, a man of haughty demeanour and considerable ability, entered the city of York, where he fixed a Proclamation on the doors of the Minster, inviting the ejected monks and friars to report themselves to him, and return to their domiciles. He was eagerly obeyed : and it was observed that, however late at night the religious persons arrived, they celebrated their restoration by a solemn service in the chapel before they sought the dormitory.* The pilgrims maintained a strict discipline : they allowed no pillage : everything was bought at a fixed price. Within a few days they moved from York to Pomfret, where Lord Darcy, the Archbishop, and many nobles and gentlemen held for the King : and before the walls of that celebrated stronghold, in the hearing of those high spiritual and temporal dignities, Aske proclaimed the grievances of the commonalty. " The lords spiritual," he cried, " have not done their duty, in that they have not been plain with the King for the speedy remedy and punishment of heresy, and the preachers thereof, for the taking the ornaments of the churches and abbies suppressed, and the violating of relics by the suppressors ; the irreverent demeanour of the doers thereof ; the abuse of the vestments taken, extraordinary and other their negligences in doing their duty, as well to their sovereign as to the commons. The lords temporal have misused themselves in not declaring to the King the poverty of his realm : the property of abbies suppressed, tenths, and firstfruits, go out of these parts : in a little while there will be no money left either to tenant or lord : and the country

---

to the preservation of the King's person, his issue, to the purifying of nobility, and to expulse all villain blood, and evil counsellors against the Commonwealth," &c.

* Froude, iii. 133.

will perish with scaith, or of very poverty make commotion or rebellion. The lords know this to be true,
and have not done their duty in that they have not
declared it."* The next morning Pomfret surrendered,
and Darcy, the Archbishop, and all within the walls,
by compulsion or by compact, took the oath of the
Pilgrimage of Grace. At the same time a division of
the rebel army succeeded without bloodshed in the
capture of Hull. The strong castles of Skipton and
Scarborough alone in Yorkshire remained faithful to
the King, when the insurgents, to the number of thirty
thousand, displaying their banner of the Five Wounds
of Christ, the chalice, and the host, and bearing em-
broidered on their sleeves the name of the Lord, moved
southward to the attack of Doncaster. The Earl of
Shrewsbury, who had played an important part in the
reduction of Lincolnshire, threw himself into the town
at the head of his tenantry, whom without a commission he had ventured to arm : and there he was joined
by the Duke of Norfolk, the King's lieutenant, with five
thousand men. Over this small force the victory of
the host of the pilgrims seemed certain, if the battle
had been given. But a swollen river and a fortified
bridge held the armies asunder : on the one side the
pilgrims were unwilling to shed the blood of their
countrymen, on the other the cautious King had instructed his general "never to give stroke but upon
great and notable advantage,"† and in case of necessity to retreat on Nottingham and Newark. A pause
ensued : and in the interval recourse was had to the
weapon in which the King had no superior. "Unhappy
men," exclaimed his lieutenants to the insurgents, "what

---

* Froude, iii. 136 : Aske's Narrative addressed to the King, printed in
the Engl. Hist. Rev., vol. v. p. 330 : April, 1890.
† State Pap., i. 494.

frenzy hath seized you! Ye rebel against a prince who is worthy for his innumerable graces, noble virtues, and gentle conditions to be governor not only of England but of all Christendom. Complain ye that he hath had much of your goods, who spends infinite sums of his own to keep you in peace against all enemies? Fie! for shame! Ye grieve not only your natural sovereign lord, but us too, who love you, and have often won victories at your side. Fie! for shame! We can say no more. Go home, or else we will give you battle: go home, and we will be suitors to the King for you: go home, or take and do the worst. How honest and charitable we are to give you this warning!"*

When defeat or retreat would be fatal to either party, hesitation should not mark the conduct of the stronger. But the pilgrims agreed to prolong the parley into an armistice, to draw up their demands into articles to be submitted to the King, and to await his reply. In the complex code which they produced, the working of many minds may be discerned: the acuteness of the theologian, or the rage of the religious partisan, are balanced by the intelligence of the statesman and the sense of the farmer. To their former demands for the restoration of abbeys and the revival of uses, for the discharge of firstfruits, tenths, and of the fifteenth, they now added that the order of Friars Observants should be restored, that the common law in general should be respected, and that a remedy should be provided in general against extortionate fee-taking and escheating. The Lady Mary they required to be made legitimate by Parliament: the Act for declaring the succession of the Crown by will, and the Statutes of treasons for words and such like, to be repealed: and a parliament to be held

* See at large State Pap., i. 495.

in Nottingham or York. With regard to the faith and the Church their demands were extensive and severe. The heresies of Wickliffe, Huss, Luther, Melanchthon, Bucer, Barnes, Tyndale, Marshall, and others, were to be extirpated. The power of the Supreme Head, "touching *cura animarum*" and the consecration of bishops, was to be reserved to the See of Rome. The heretics, both "bishops and temporals, and their sect," were to have condign punishment by fire, or otherwise ; or to try the quarrel by battle. The Lord Crumwel, Lord Chancellor Audley, and Sir Richard Rich were to receive condign punishment as innovators, fosterers of heretics, and subverters of the laws. Condign punishment was to be dealt to Doctor Legh and to Doctor Layton for their extortions, bribery, and other abominable acts in the time of the visitations.* The privileges and rights of the Church were to be confirmed by Act of Parliament : benefit of clergy and right of sanctuary were to be renewed.

Even in a war of proclamations it might be difficult to believe that the general should leave his army in the presence of the enemy, and proceed in person to the capital with the conditions which the enemy proposed. The Duke of Norfolk, however, himself, in company with the deputies of the rebels, carried these Articles to the royal hand, and was absent from the seat of war a whole month. His confidence was shared by the

---

* "That Dr. Legh and Dr. Layton may have condign punishment for their extortions in the time of visitation, as bribes of nuns, religious houses, forty pounds, twenty pounds, and so to —— leases under one common seal, bribes by them taken, and other their abominable acts by them committed and done." See the Articles, printed in full by Mr. Froude, iii. 157. That on the Supreme Head, touching cure of souls, is curious : and seems to shew that the King's explanation of his title, which he made to the northern clergy when he took it, had not wrought conviction. See above, p. 66.

other lieutenants of the King: who the day after his departure dissolved the royal army, and sent the great ordnance to Nottingham.* Delay and negotiation had already dispersed the army of the pilgrims; the heart of their enterprise ceased to beat at the fatal moment when they consented to a conference: and when the King's forces withdrew, the greater part of them were gone or were going home, while the leaders retired to Pomfret. Henceforth it was an affair of notes and messages. Henry, while he detained their deputies in London, strove by private letters to detach the insurgent nobles from their meaner captain Aske: meanwhile two dangerous, though futile, plots to take off Aske by assassination were contrived or fostered by Henry's two dukes, Suffolk and Norfolk.† Into some of the towns of the disturbed parts heralds were sent, who, with the royal coat upon their backs, expostulated with the people on the innocence, the integrity, the truth and justice of the King.‡ While the King tried persuasion, Crumwel used threats, warning the commons by his letters that, unless they submitted speedily, there should be such vengeance taken that the whole world would hear thereof.§ It was not before the end of two weeks at least that the rebel envoys returned: who came alone, the Duke of Norfolk remaining still at the court. They brought with them nothing definite, nothing beyond general expressions of conciliation.

Meanwhile the King's musters in the south were rapidly proceeding: Shrewsbury had again advanced, and occupied the line of the Don. On their part the pilgrims had recalled some of their dispersed followers to the banner of the Five Wounds: but they lacked

---

* Shrewsbury to the King, 29 Oct., State Pap., i. 497.
† Froude, iii. 167.   ‡ *Ib.* 163: State Pap., i. 473.
§ Froude, iii. 170.

the strength or the inclination to move from York and Pomfret. At the end of the month the Duke of Norfolk returned from the King; and dilatory negotiation took once more the place of action in the field. Not unmindful of his most recent theological weapon, the King had furnished Norfolk with many copies of the "Articles to stablish Christian Quietness," to be dispersed among the rebels: while, to convince those who might doubt the authenticity of the first English Confession, the original itself, that ark of Henry's safety, with the names of the clergy appended, was transported to the camp.* These credentials of his orthodoxy were accompanied by a letter to his Bishops, written in the strain familiar to those unfortunate functionaries. "We," said the Supreme Head, "have advanced you to the room and office of a bishop within this realm, and endowed you with great dignities and possessions, judging you a virtuous and learned person, that would set forth the word of God plainly and purely, and instruct our people therein, after a simple and plain sort: we have admonished and commanded you to preach sincerely, to declare abuses plainly, to

* So Strype, "In the Rebellion in the North, which happened this year, 1536, chiefly raised by Priests and Friars, many copies of these Articles (for the Book was printed by Barthelet) did Crumwel send by the King's order to the Duke of Norfolk, the King's lieutenant there, to disperse in those parts together with the Original Copy itself, as it was assigned by the hands of the Convocation, amounting to the number of 116 Bishops, Abbots, Priors, Archdeacons, and Proctors of the Clergy: Which the said Duke had order to shew unto the clergy and others, as occasion served: that they might understand it was a proper act of the Church, and no innovation of the King and a few of his Councillors, as they gave out. And after he had made his use of the original, he was required to reserve it safe for the King. This choice treasure which the King himself required such care to be taken of, Sir Robert Cotton afterwards procured, at his no small expense, no doubt. It is very fairly written on vellum: and at the bottom of the first page is written *Robertus Cotton Bruceus*, in Sir Robert's own hand, signifying his value of this monument."—Strype's Cranm. Bk. ii. ch. 11. So Speed.

treat of matters indifferent, in no wise contentiously. But by some so little regard was paid to our advertisement, that we were constrained to put our own pen to the book, and to conceive certain Articles, which were agreed on by the whole clergy in Convocation as Catholic and necessary to bring our subjects to unity and concord.* But our labours are defeated : general and contemptuous words are spoken by light and seditious persons : there is a want of plain and direct declaration of our Articles : and the people, instead of becoming quiet, are risen against us in insurrection! We therefore warn you peremptorily to demean yourself for the redubbing of these things, upon pain of deprivation and punishment for contempt. Read and declare our Articles every holiday plainly and distinctly : and never add any word of your own that may make them doubtful to the people. Travel from place to place, as you commodiously can, and every holiday make a collation to the people, declaring the obedience which they owe to their prince, whose commandment they ought not to resist, though it were unjust, and also commending and explaining the honest ceremonies of the Church. In your private communications use no words that may sound to the contrary of this commandment : if you have any person about you, or if you hear of any stranger that speaks contentiously or contemptuously of these matters, send him to us and our Council. Give the same strait commandment to all parsons, vicars, curates, and governors of religious

---

* On this passage Henry has been pronounced by his admirers the author of the first English Confession. It is a phrase of studied ambiguity, but it probably gives the truth, in reverse order. Henry "conceived" certain articles : others delivered him of them by writing them for him : and then "he put his pen to the book" in the way of correcting them. Henry went as near as he could to say that he was the author : but he was writing to the very men who had written them for him.

houses within your diocese. Finally, whereas we hear that some priests have married themselves, contrary to the custom of our Church of England, make secret enquiry after such, and if ye find any that have so presumed, and have since notwithstanding exercised the office of priesthood, send them up to us."*   In the midst of the tyranny which this document reveals, and along with the characteristic fear of opinion in which it is steeped, may be heard at once the sound of the doctrine of the right divine of kings, into which the new loyalty was developing itself, and the first notes of the so-called Catholic reaction, or repentance after pillage, which marked the later years of Henry.

The Duke was armed besides with particular Instructions of great length, which still remain.†   He was to invite the insurgent chieftains to a conference, and exhibit to them an answer to their demands or Articles, which had been laboriously penned by the King himself.‡   He was also furnished with a " proclamation implying a pardon," which he was to shew secretly to some of them.   But Norfolk from the day that he had set out on his journey had shewn himself dissatisfied with his orders.   He knew that the answer which he was to exhibit reserved some of the rebels for the punishment of traitors, without naming them : an exception which would cause every one to tremble for himself.   He knew that the proclamation, which he was to shew secretly to some but not to all, contained the names of the excepted persons ; his instructions told him with what design he was to shew it :§   and

---

* Wilkins, iii. 825.   The date is Nov. 19.   The letter would arrive in the north about the same time that Norfolk did.

† State Pap., i. 498.   ‡ Froude, iii. 169.

§ " That they (to whom it was shewn) may the better endeavour themselves to the apprehension of those vile persons that be excepted in the same."—*State Pap.*, i. 504.

he may have shrunk from inviting some of the rebel leaders to betray the rest. On his way down he wrote more than once to his master in a desponding tone: and at length despatched Sir John Russell from Nottingham to represent to him his fears more strongly by word of mouth. Meanwhile he invited the rebels to a conference, according to his instructions.

The King's Answer to the Articles of the rebels is too characteristic a production to be passed over in silence.* In this effusion, which was a sort of apology for himself, the royal author proceeded on the not unknown device of ignoring some of the representations of his adversaries, and affecting not to understand what was meant by others. " They spoke," said he, " of the maintenance of the Faith : but the terms were so general that it was hard to understand them. If they meant the Faith of Christ, to which all Christian men were obliged, then he protested that he meant to live and die in the same : and he marvelled not a little that ignorant people should take upon them to instruct a prince something noted for learning what the right faith should be. They spoke of the maintenance of the Church and her liberties : but here again they made so general a proposition that no man could answer it either by God's laws or the laws of the realm. What Church did they mean ? Were the liberties of which they spoke lawful or unlawful ? If they meant the Church of which he was Supreme Head, he protested that he had never done so much prejudice to that as many of his predecessors upon much less grounds : and what he had done pertained to none of them. They spoke of the laws, the commonwealth, and the directors of the laws under him. Never, he protested, had there been made so many wholesome,

* State Pap., i. 506: Speed. Herbert gives a good account of it.

commodious, and beneficial laws in the days of any of his predecessors as in the twenty-eight years of his reign ; never had any king kept his subjects so long in wealth and peace : ministered justice so indifferently to all : so well defended all from outward enemies : so carefully fortified the frontiers, though at his own enormous cost : no king had ever dispensed pardons so freely, none had shewn mercy more willingly. As to his councillors, of whom they complained, it appertained nothing to them to appoint him his council : but he remembered well that in the beginning of his reign he had but two worthy of calling noble : now he had many who were nobles indeed, both of birth and condition.* They named certain of the Council to be subverters of the laws ; in his opinion, however, these persons were just administrators of the laws, so far as their commission went. If the contrary could be proved, he said that he would punish them ; but if on examination this were shewn to be a false report, as he believed it to be, then they who wrongfully brought it must be prepared to suffer the same punishment which those whom they accused would have had if they had deserved it. The offer of a free pardon to all except certain ringleaders unnamed, whom the King required to be rendered to him, concluded this royal apology.

Pomfret, the last acquisition, had remained the head-quarters of the Pilgrims of Grace. Here, November 27, they held an assembly which in a manner

---

* The King illustrated his argument by the names, among the temporal men, of Norfolk, Suffolk, Shrewsbury, Exeter, Sussex, Sands, Fitzwilliams, and Paulet. Of his spiritual advisers he considered the most noble to be Fox of Hereford, Sampson of Chichester, and Gardiner of Winchester. Burnet, in his account, zealously supplies the name of the Archbishop of Canterbury : which the King was careful to omit. So Herbert.

imitated the meetings of the estates of the realm. Thirty-four peers, knights, and gentlemen gathered themselves together in the castle hall, and drew up certain resolutions which were read and passed with shouts of " Fiat, fiat." Simultaneously the clergy who were in Pomfret, with the Archbishop of York as president, met in the church in convocation. Their deliberations were guarded, or menaced, by armed men. The long suspected primate opened this convention with a sermon, in which he boldly and unexpectedly told them that their proceedings were unlawful and traitorous. He was dragged out of the pulpit by the soldiers, thrown on the ground, and with difficulty rescued by his friends. The convocation then proceeded, in a set of brief Articles, to protest against almost everything that had been done since Crumwel had come into power. Preaching against purgatory, saints, pilgrimages, and images ought, they declared, to be condemned by Convocation: all books written against the same ought to be condemned : the pain that was decreed against the doers of such things ought to be executed ; and process made against heresy, as was in the days of King Henry the Fourth. Holidays, bidding of bedes, and preaching were to be observed according to the laudable customs of the Church. No temporal man might be Supreme Head of the Church, or exercise any jurisdiction or power spiritual therein : no temporal man had authority by the laws of God to claim the tenths or firstfruits of any spiritual promotion. No clerk was to be put to death without degradation by the laws of the Church: no man ought to be drawn out of sanctuary, except in certain cases allowed by the laws of the Church. Lands given to God, to the Church or religion, might not be taken away and put to profane uses. The Pope of Rome ought to be taken for the Head of the Church and the

Vicar of Christ. The examination and correction of deadly sin belonged to the ministers of the Church. Clerks now in prison or fled the country, for withstanding the King's superiority in the Church, might be set at liberty and restored; apostates from religion, who were without dispensation from the Pope, should be compelled to return to their houses. All Acts of Parliament made of late years to the contrary of these things were to be repealed.* Such were the resolutions or ordinances of Pomfret. They might have been admirable after a victory : as it was, they were only the preliminary declarations by which the pilgrims fortified themselves for the impending conference with 'the King's lieutenant.

Two days after this, Aske, Darcy Constable, and three hundred of their followers, rode over the bridge of Doncaster, wearing their pilgrim badges of the Five Wounds crossed on their breasts. They did obeisance before the Duke and the Earls of Shrewsbury and Exeter, and presented the resolutions at which they had arrived. On his part the Duke, it is probable, exhibited the partial Pardon which he had with him, and the King's answer to the first Articles of the rebels. The difficulties which Norfolk had foreseen arose; three days were spent in fruitless negotiations; but at length the timely arrival of Sir John Russell from the King with fresh instructions led the way to an amicable settlement. A free general pardon, and the promise of a parliament to be held in some place appointed by the King within the year, were the concessions on which

---

* Froude, iii. 173 : Strype, ii. 266, or Wilkins, iii. 812 : "The opinion of the clergy of the north parts in Convocation upon ten Articles sent to them" (from Cleop. E. v.). What the ten Articles sent to them were, seems unknown : they were certainly not the Articles to stablish Christian quietness, which are sometimes cited as the Ten Articles.

the pilgrims were invited to lay down their arms.* Believing that they had obtained the objects for which they had taken them, or falsely persuaded by Norfolk that all their resolutions of Pomfret† were granted by the King, the Pilgrims of Grace, headed by their leader Aske, pulled off their badges, with the words, "We will wear no badge nor figure but the badge of our Sovereign Lord." The coalition which had promised or threatened so much appeared to be suddenly dissolved; and for a moment all was joy and confidence. The rebel leaders and others of the northern gentlemen in large numbers received invitations to go and see the King: and a policy of graciousness seemed to recognise and reward the maintenance of loyalty in the bloodless demonstration of force. Aske himself, among the rest, received a flattering letter conveyed by a gentleman of the Privy Chamber;‡ in obedience to which he travelled south, saw the King in private, and wrote to him, at his

---

* The King's new instructions to his general were very characteristic of their author. He sent him the general free pardon and the promise of a parliament, but ordered him to keep them close : if the rebels would treat on no other terms than these, then Norfolk was to say that he would do his utmost with the King to obtain them, and gain a delay of six or seven days by pretending to send to the King for that purpose. "And when that time shall be expired, at the day to be prefixed, declare unto them that with great suit you have obtained their petitions ; and so present unto them the general pardon, which, at this time, we send unto you by our servant Sir John Russell." If they added any other conditions he was to get a further delay of twenty days to acquaint the King: and in the meantime secretly bring up the forces of Chester, Lancashire, and Lincolnshire. *State Pap.*, i. 515. Norfolk, however, preferred to conclude the whole business at once, and proclaimed the pardon as soon as he got it.

† According to Aske, they were led to believe that all the Articles of Pomfret were granted. (Froude, iii. 176.) Mr. Froude says that, if so, Norfolk exceeded his instructions. Nothing more likely. Norfolk would have no scruple in that. He had expressly declared that he would regard no promise made to the rebels, "nor think his honour touched in the breach and violation of the same." State Pap., i. 519.

‡ State Pap., i. 523.

request, a letter which contained a plain and honest narrative of the late events and his own share in them.* But in no long time the northern people began to ask themselves whether they had not been deluded. They saw the great author of evils, Crumwel, in as high favour with the King as ever he had been. The deportation of the gentlemen to the south on the pretence of paying their court to their sovereign seemed dangerous, both to those who went, and to the country which they left. Large bodies of troops continued to hover round the disaffected region ; there was a rumour that a strong garrison was to be thrown into Hull. Was the north to be treated like a conquered province, and held down by a chain of strong posts ? † On his return home, Aske wrote a second letter to the King, in which he seriously represented the prevailing dissatisfaction. The people, he said, were in doubt both as to the pardon and as to the parliament which had been promised ; to their great disquietude the severe answer of the King to their first Articles had been put in print : and now the tenths were being demanded, which looked very little like the granting of their reasonable petitions. There was so much indignation and commotion everywhere, that he feared that the end could only be by battle. Such were the forebodings of the most honest of rebels.‡

* Froude, iii. 182.

† This was in fact the policy advocated by Crumwel, and afterwards carried out. See his "Scheme for the Government of the North," Froude, iii. 177.

‡ See his Letter, Froude, 182.

CHAPTER VII.

A. D. 1537.

THE predictions of Aske were soon fulfilled, and at the beginning of the next year the discontents of the North gave rise to new disturbances. The promises of the King appeared more and more delusive : when the late insurgents sued for the advantage of his general pardon, they found it clogged with oaths and conditions which had not been propounded before: without having fought, they were treated as conquered. Their strongest towns were occupied by garrisons: detachments of the royal army made their way into the remoter districts ; and a permanent council, with the King's general at the head, was to be established for the government of the whole country. But if their irritation was great, the insecurity in which they were involved was greater. The policy of separating the gentlemen from the commons had not been tried in vain : with the commons the cry was that they were betrayed by the gentlemen. Darcy, Stapleton, and Aske, the late leaders, were known either to have made their peace with the King, or at least to have retired into the quietude of private life. A bloodless commotion, to be followed by a tame submission, was not sufficient to satisfy the swelling thoughts of men : and now that it was too late, it seemed as if protestations and demonstrations were to be converted into the activity of war. But if in the Pilgrimage of Grace itself there had been exhibited something of the forbearance of superior strength, the spasmodic movements by which it was succeeded shewed only the rage of weakness. A commotion began in Cleveland, and other parts of the bishopric. Bills and scrolls were set on the church doors by night, exhorting the commons to "stick to one another" though the gentlemen had betrayed them, and promising them that they should lack no captains.* Sir Francis Bigod, a gentleman of Yorkshire who was as familiar with the pen as with the sword,† Mr. Hallam, a retainer of Sir Robert Constable, and George, eldest son of Lord Lumley, made, in the beginning of January, a simultaneous attempt to seize Hull and Beverley. They were captured in the unsuccessful enterprise: the design was disavowed by the leaders of the former insurrection, and the country was appeased by the exertions of Aske and Constable.‡ Relying on the King's favour, however, Aske committed the imprudence of pleading for the lives of Bigod's followers, and even put a stop to the trial of Hallam, when it had been begun by the royal commissioners at Hull. The country continued to be disturbed by rumours after this; but no further outbreak occurred for a month. An ambassador of the King, who passed through the North on his way to Scotland at that moment, heard everywhere the rumours of risings, but found every town that he visited tranquil. Every town between London and York this emissary

---

* State Papers, i. 526.

† Bigod, who was a zealous Churchman, left a work on the abuse of the Impropriation of Benefices, and also some translations from the Latin, which were published after his death.   Church Hist. of England, i. 192.

‡ For his services on this occasion Aske received a letter of thanks from the King.   State Pap., i. 529.

reported to be in good quiet: and though he heard that the people throughout the bishopric were very wild, yet, when he went from York to Newcastle, he met with no disturbance, except a slight tumult which occurred in the streets of one town. The whole cause of the agitation of the country he found to be the uncertainty in which it was held concerning the designs of the Duke of Norfolk. It was certain that the Duke was coming with an army to hold the country: some said that if he came to do them good they would receive him, but if he came to do them evil they were enough to resist him. Others believed that he was coming "to do execution, and to hang and draw, from Doncaster to Berwick, in all places northward, notwithstanding the King's pardon." Others said that they would take the part of him that came first: "if the King's army came first, they would take that part, but if there were a new insurrection, and the commons came first, they would go with them, lest they should be spoiled of all they had."* Meanwhile, Norfolk advanced to Pomfret, where he had been little more than a week when a new commotion invited him to penetrate farther. At Kirkby Stephen, in Westmoreland, under Nichol Musgrave, Thomas Tylbie, and others, a body of men assembled from various parts, and marched, numbering eight thousand, upon Carlisle. The place was as stoutly as easily defended by Sir Thomas Clifford and Sir William Dacre, who, with the forces that were within, repulsed and pursued the disorderly assailants: but Norfolk

---

* See Sadler's two letters to Crumwel, State Pap., i. 526, 529. [Cf. an original printed in the *Engl. Hist. Rev.*, *vol.* v. 343, *April*, 1890, a " Breve shewing whereby his Grace may obtain the hearts of his subjects in the north, and that before the coming down of the Duke of Norfolk." It is very reasonable.]

again advanced : and, with the applause of the King, proclaimed martial law by spreading the royal banner. While the dreadful ensign floated in the air, those terrible executions were done which for three months turned both London and the North of England into a slaughter-house.* These last commotions, wild and ill-advised as they were, afforded the King and his minister a pretext for departing from the former convention, and fixing upon the quiescent leaders of the first insurrection the penalties of treasons in which they were nowise concerned. Aske and Constable, notwithstanding their exertions to pacify the country, Lord Darcy, in spite of his advanced age, were suddenly arrested in their houses. In London Sir John and Lady Bulmer, who had been tempted to trust the dangerous hospitality of Henry, were seized, and added to the Lincolnshire prisoners who were awaiting the stroke of fate.

These futile attempts to renew the insurrection had not been made without some foreign encouragement. In the Catholic kingdom of Scotland the course of the English Revolution had been regarded with fear and horror : the Pilgrimage of Grace, before the inglorious termination of it was known, seemed to offer the means for the reconciliation of the ancient animosity of the two kingdoms : and the visit which the Scottish monarch paid to France at this time, appeared to afford the opportunity of enlisting his active services in the cause of the unity of the Church. James the Fifth accepted from Paul the Third the

---

* " Our pleasure is that before ye shall close up our banner again, ye shall cause such dreadful execution to be done upon a good number of every town, village, and hamlet, that have offended, that they may be a fearful spectacle to all others hereafter." The King to Norfolk. *State Pap.*, i. 538.

present of a sword and cap, the emblems of attack and protection, which had been consecrated on the altar of St. Peter's, on Christmas Eve, at the midnight Mass. On january 1st, he married Magdalen, the sister of the French King: an alliance which Henry, as he informed Francis, liked as little as a perfect lover would like to find his mistress entertaining his mortal enemy. The King of England despatched immediately into Scotland one of the most dexterous of his agents, the astute Sir Ralph Sadler, who had been Crumwel's serving-man: by whom he was kept informed of all that happened there in the absence of his Scottish brother.* Returning into Scotland with his bride, the unfortunate James was denied a passage through England unless he would come as homager of the English King.† Preferring a dangerous passage by sea, he touched at Scarborough, where some of the commons of the country, twelve in number, came on board his ship, and falling on their knees before him declared their sufferings under martial law, and besought him to come into

---

* Sadler's letters, written on his journey through the North into Scotland, have been referred to above. They give the best picture of the real state of things. Two other active agents of the King, Hutton and Wallop, wrote from France a lively account of the adventures of the King of Scots in quest of his bride. He arrived at Dieppe with "the slenderest fleet of ships that ever any king did willingly adventure his body with." There was but one that was fit for a king, and she was a ship of England. As soon as he landed, he rode post to Rouen, accompanied but by three persons; and when he got there he kept himself so secret that few knew of his being there. At Paris, however, his entry and marriage were very triumphant: there was a grand banquet, and the French princesses were so richly dressed that cloth of gold was little set by, by reason of broideries, pearls, and precious stones. "The King of Scots never saw no such sight." He had with him an honourable company of his own countrymen, "right well apparelled *now* after the French fashion," and they were "goodly gentlemen, and very proper men." The king of Scots, Wallop found, was "very firm in opinion: the French king, the Grand Master, my lord of Winchester, and I, could by no means persuade him to such things as we spoke to him of."—*State Pap.*, vii. 667–9.

† State Pap., i. 535.

England, and take the kingdom.* But the intervention
of Scotland, even with the aid of France, was little
to be dreaded; the death of the bride within a few
months could scarcely be said to dissolve an alliance
which had scarcely been formed: and the cloudlet
which had arisen again in foreign parts to overshadow
the sunshine of Henry was melted once more into
thin air.

At Rome a creation of eleven cardinals, December
22, had crowned the former year: and in the group,
which included Sadolet, Carpi, and Cajetan, not the
least conspicuous or renowned personage was Reginald
Pole. Soon after despatching his famous though unpublished treatise to the King of England, Pole had
received a Papal breve inviting him to Rome, where
he might be one of a small company of the most
learned men of every nation, with whom the Pontiff
desired to deliberate concerning the reformation of the
church, before holding the general council.† Hesitating to take a step so decided, he sent a copy of the
breve to Crumwel: and from Crumwel he received in
answer an official mandate ordering him to return to

---

* "Certain of the commons of the country thereabout, to the number
of twelve persons, Englishmen, your Highness's servants, did come on
board the King's ship, and being on their knees before him, thanked God
of his healthful and sound repair; shewing how they had long looked for
him, and how they were oppressed, slain, and murdered: desiring him,
for God's sake, to come in, and all should be his." Sir Thos. Clifford to
Henry VIII.—*State Pap.*, v. 80: *Froude*, iii. 186.

† "Quoniam generale concilium ad Reipublicæ Christianæ beneficium
nuper indiximus, et in animo Nobis est ex omni Fidelium natione doctos
congregare, qui in tam laudibili opere Nobis assistant, te, de cujus nobi-
litate, doctrina, ac probitate, sinceraque in religionem et Dei Ecclesiam
mente, cum ex operibus tuis, tum fide dignorum testimonio, plurima acce-
pimus, pro natione Anglica deputandum censuimus."—Paul III. to Pole:
Epist., vol. i. 466. Cf. the important letter of Cranmer to the King, as
to the high esteem of Pole amid the selected band, *Rem.* p. 330, or
Ellis, ii. 1, 66.

England instantly, without visiting the abode of the spiritual enemy of his sovereign. To the commandment of the minister were added the strong remonstrances of Tunstall, of Stokesley, and of Starkey : and the private or dictated entreaties of his mother, the Countess of Salisbury, and of his brother the Lord Montague.* But the prohibitions which reached him from England found Pole already on the road to Rome. He arrived there, and became a member of the not unimportant conclave whose recommendations formed the final effort before the Council of Trent to carry out a Catholic reformation of the church. His obedience was rewarded by the highest dignity that the Pontiff could bestow : and the layman, submitting to the tonsure, and entering deacon's orders, was invested with the scarlet of a cardinal. At the moment when he underwent the ceremony, he received from England a missive that was intended to prevent it. A memorial subscribed by Crumwel, and by the hands of such members of the Council and of the Parliament as Crumwel could reach, set before him that to accept the purple would be an act of hostility to the King and realm of England : urged him not to make Rome his abode, and offered to depute some learned persons

---

* Among the government papers in the Record Office is still preserved the original draft of these *private* letters. "There can but be one inference deduced from this fact—namely, that the letters received by Pole were a mere transcript on the part of his relatives of letters composed by order of the government : and when we consult the documents themselves, this natural suspicion is fully confirmed by internal evidence."—Hook's Pole, 102. Pole himself relates the alarm of the King of England, who sent back his Italian messenger by relays of flying horses, to be in time to prevent the dread catastrophe of his journey to Rome : the fearful threats which that messenger brought from Crumwel : the prolixity of Tunstall's arguments : the anguish with which he perused the appeal of his mother and brother : and his own resolution in persisting in his journey.—Epist., vol. i. 483. For Pole's mother's letter see Gairdner's *Lett. and Pap.* xi. p. 44.

on the part of the King, to confer with him on the points in controversy, if he would go as a private person into Flanders.* Pole replied by his elaborate "Apology to the Parliament of England." The title of that long epistle magnified both the importance of the writer and the position of those who had expostulated with him; for the Parliament of England had never condescended to remonstrate with a single subject.† The proposed conference, to be held in Flanders with such persons as the King might appoint, he accepted: and to Flanders he presently repaired: but not as a private person but a Cardinal, not as a cardinal only, but in the character of a Legate of the Holy See. His retinue was splendid; his expenses compelled him to draw upon the purse and credit of the Pope: but the austerities which he observed during his unfortunate mission and the season of Lent, were calculated to strike a deeper impression than the magnificence that surrounded him.‡ Blinded, like all Rome, by false rumours of the magnitude and success of the Pilgrimage of Grace, he came prepared, when all was ruined, to form the combinations which should lead the imagined victory of the insurgents to the triumphant end of the restoration of the kingdom to the Apostolic See. He was armed with letters from the Pope addressed to the various potentates whom, in accordance with his avowed principles, he sought to band together in a holy league against the heretic of

---

* Cf. Froude, iii. 188, *note.*

† [But Mr. Gairdner says that the title "Ad Parliamentum" in Poli Epp. i. 179, is inaccurate, and that the letter was to the Council.—*Lett. and Pap.* xii, Pt. i. 214.]

‡ "I hear that thou art obstinately endangering thy health," wrote Contareni, "by eating fish, and the rest of thy spare diet. Contumacious man! Obey the bishop where thou art, and our dear Priuli."—*Epist.* vol. ii. 20.

England—to the Regent of the Netherlands, to the
French King, and the King of Scots: and in the
curious affair of the first Legation of Cardinal Pole, it
may be questioned which was the greater delusion, the
belief that the Pilgrimage had succeeded, or that, if it
had succeeded, England would have endured it to be
followed by foreign intervention : whether the reigning
faction in England were more deceived in their
estimate of Pole's influence in foreign courts, or those
who sent him on his journey in their opinion of his
weight in England.   But all were soon undeceived.
At Lyons Pole heard of the failure of the insurrection.
At Paris, though he was received with honours by the
clergy, he found that the French King feared to see
or receive him, and advised him to quit his dominions.
The King of England had proclaimed him a rebel,
and set a price upon his head ; the King's ambassador
Gardiner had received instructions to demand him
to be delivered as a prisoner.   The forlorn legate
withdrew himself to the neutral territory of Cambray :
where the trembling bishop warned him that it would
be impossible for him to remain with safety.*   He

---

* From Cambray he sent, May 2, a long expostulation to Crumwel,
protesting the innocence of his intentions, and the unworthiness of the
treatment that he received.   The rights of nations were violated in him,
his office was insulted, his life in danger : the king dishonourably required another king to betray him, though an ambassador.   Worse than
all, he was now outlawed, and therefore ignored.   No messenger from
him was now admitted to the King.   And yet he had done nothing amiss :
he loved the King, and before leaving Rome he had stopped the Pope
from censuring him publicly, and had sent his servant purposely to
offer him his services, and had exhorted his kindred in England to be
constant to him.—*Strype*, ii. 327.   Mr. Froude (iii. 203) has contrasted
this with a letter which Pole wrote soon afterwards to the Pope : from
which he holds Pole to have been dishonest in his professions to the
King.   Both letters are full of the long explanations which are the relief
of weak men : but they shew no dishonesty, allowing for a natural difference of tone.   To the Pope Pole gives the whole story of his Legation :

attempted to penetrate to Brussels : but the English
monarch had required, through his ambassador,
Hutton, that he should not be admitted into the
Netherlands; the Emperor was making overtures of
amity to England: and the Queen Regent of the
Netherlands informed him that his presence would be
unwelcome and dangerous. At length he was compelled to throw himself on the hospitality of the
Bishop of Liege, where he remained to the end of his
Legation. Wherever he went, he was pursued by the
spies of Crumwel, who seem, however, to have been
unable to discover any attempt made by him to communicate with the disaffected in England. At length,
in August, he took his departure from Liege with
public solemnity, giving his benediction to the people
as he rode through the city, a cross and "two other
ceremonies" being borne before him.* He made his
way back to Rome, protesting to the last that his
legitimate commission was but to dispute against the
errors of England.† When he found himself in safety,
he published his long threatened book on the Unity of
the Church.‡

and then lays before him the reasons (1) why he should be recalled, viz.,
the failure of the English commotions, and the fearful perils in which he
stood: (2) why he should remain ; viz., that if the commotions were renewed, it might be an encouragement to the malcontents to have so
eminent a countryman within call. He was *mediis in periculis*, but
dauntless : and he left the decision with the Pope (*Epist.* ii. 50). The
Pope sounded the recall. Pole's principles were never concealed. He
loved the man, but would have coerced the heretic. A man less fit to
apply coercion could not have been found. In this letter to the Pope he
says that he felt himself half a traitor to his own cause through his tender
dealing with the King.

 * Hutton to the King. *State Pap.*, vii. 707.
 † So he declared before the Queen Regent. *Ib.*, 700. He seems to
have forgotten that he had been asked to come as a private person only.
 ‡ Pole's Epistles, vols. i, ii, the *State Papers*, vol. vii, and *Lett. and Pap.*
vol. xii, are the chief authorities on Pole's unfortunate Legation. Of

While the Friend of the Kingdom was hovering thus fruitlessly about the opposite coast, a bloody retribution was being enacted within the realm. The new treason acts were a weapon which smote alike those who had taken arms in defence of the ancient liberties of the Church, and those who had whispered an audible word of goodwill to their cause. While the northern men were still in the field, a butcher near Windsor, where the King was, exclaimed, as he sold his meat to a customer, who offered him less than he had asked, " Now, by God's soul, I had rather the good fellows of the North had it among them, and a score more of the best I have ! " The words were reported : it was remembered that the same imprudent tradesman had abetted a priest in preaching that to take part with God's people, the Yorkshiremen, was to

Crumwel's correspondents, the most observant was Hutton, the ambassador in the Netherlands, who kept up a complete system of espial on Pole, but seems to have been unable to detect any very dangerous matters. He employed, among others, one Vaughan, an escaped murderer, who had got into Pole's household. This man told him that Michael Throgmorton, one of Pole's gentlemen, was to be sent into England with letters to divers of Pole's friends : the letters were to be baked in a loaf ; and Vaughan, Throgmorton, and one Philips were to take them. (*State Pap.*, vii. 697.) But Throgmorton never reached England. *Ib.*, 703, *note.* At another time Vaughan showed Hutton a letter from Friar Peto to Throgmorton ; but there was nothing in it, but that Peto recommended Vaughan to Pole's service, a great mistake in Peto. Vaughan also captured a letter from Throgmorton to Peto, which he gave to Hutton, who sent it to Crumwel, June 17. *Ib.* As to Throgmorton, he is believed by Mr. Froude to have entered Pole's service as a spy, and to have remained in it as a friend. A letter, which he wrote to Crumwel the day after Pole began his retreat back to Rome, spoke very favourably of him, and gave many particulars of his Legation. *Strype*, i. 478. Amongst other things he said that Pole had been importuned to leave his unpublished book behind him in the hands of the Pope, and that it would have been published forthwith, if he had left it. It was this favourable report perhaps which moved Crumwel to write to Throgmorton the furious letter which Mr. Froude has printed (iii. 228–233): but which the delinquent seems not to have received. *State Pap.*, vii. 710. [The Pope's Bull appointing Pole legate directly incited to the rebellion, *Lett. and Pap.*, xii. 338.]

fight and defend God's quarrel. Both the butcher and
the priest were arrested, examined, condemned, and
hanged in a single day.* When the last struggles of
the insurrection had ceased, the doings of Norfolk and
of Sussex continued to be unsparingly severe. Seventy-
four persons who had been taken in the attempt upon
Carlisle were hanged by the former upon the walls of
that city.† But a single case, of which the record
remains, illustrated still more forcibly the politic
rigour which animated the counsels of the victors. An
old man, who was tried by martial law, made so much
lamentation at the bar, alleging his former services
in war against the Scots and elsewhere, that Sussex
gave him a respite, and wrote to enquire the royal
pleasure in the case. The answer of the King was
that his former merits made him but the more worthy
an example to suffer : and he was remitted to the
executioner.‡ At the same time the trial of those
who had been prominent in the various movements
from the first was proceeding by the more regular
forms of law. The trial of the Lincolnshire prisoners
was begun in March. Of more than a hundred, who
had been taken at first, half had been released. Thirty
of the rest, along with the Abbot of Kirkstead, were
tried at Lincoln : and, in spite of the eloquent defence
made by one of them, a gentleman named Thomas
Moigne, " the diligence of the King's sergeant " procured their condemnation : three of them, the Abbot,
Moigne, and another, were hanged at Lincoln on the
following day : four others at Louth and Horncastle :
the rest were pardoned.§ Twelve others, among them

---

* The butcher was hanged on a new gallows before the Castle gate,
and the priest on a tree at the foot of Windsor Bridge.—Hall, 823.
　† Hall, 824.　　　　　　　　　‡ State Pap., i. 541.
　§ Froude, iii. 211.

the Abbot of Barling, were brought for trial at the Guildhall of London : and hanged in the various towns of their own county.* Lord Hussey of Sleford, who had been included in the same indictment, put himself upon his peers, was found guilty, and executed at Tyburn.†

In Yorkshire, by means of intimidation which was openly applied by the King and Norfolk, true bills were returned against all the leaders of the insurrection, from Aske, Darcy, and Constable to Bigod and Lumley. They were charged not only with the first insurrection, but with having conspired again, after the King's pardon, to deprive the King of his Supreme Head, "his royal power, liberty, state, and dignity," to compel him to hold a parliament and convocation, and to amend or annul divers good laws made for the common weal. Among those indicted were Sir John and Lady Bulmer, otherwise Margaret Cheyne, Sir Thomas Percy, Sir Stephen Hamerton, Nicolas Tempest, Esquire, James Cockerel, rector of Lythe, and formerly Prior of Gisborough, William Wood, Prior of Bridlington, a man in infirm health,‡ John Pickering, clerk of Lythe, John Pickering, a brother of the Order of Preaching Friars, Adam Sedlar, Abbot of Jervaulx, and

---

* Their names were, Nic. Leche of Belcheforth, clerk; Thos. Relforth of Sneland, clerk; Barnard Fletcher of Fullerby, yeoman; Rb. Sotheby of Horncastle, draper; Rt. Leche of Fullerby, husbandman; Ph. Trotter of Horncastle, mercer; Roger Neve of Horncastle, saddler; Brian Stone of Menningsby, labourer; Thos. Kendal, Vicar of Louth; Wm. Burreby, monk of Louth Park; Matt. Mackerel, Abbot of Barling; Geo. Huddeswell of Horstowe, gentleman.—*3rd Rep. of Dep. Keeper of Rec.,* 246.

† *Ib.,* 249.

‡ Crumwel had long had his eye on Bridlington. There is a letter, probably of the October of 1535, extant, from this Prior Wood to him, from which it appears that Crumwel had advised him to acknowledge the King for founder: and that the Prior refused so to do, and excused himself from attending on Crumwel in person by reason of his infirmities. Wright, 80.

William Thrisk, Abbot of Fountains. The fate of these prisoners was various. The aged Darcy put himself upon his peers, and was executed on Tower Hill. When he came before the Privy Council, one of those scenes occurred which illustrate an age by a single flash of passion. Turning to the Lord Privy Seal, who sat at the board, " Thou, Crumwel," exclaimed the prisoner fiercely, "art the very special and chief causer of all this rebellion and mischief: thou art the causer of the apprehension of us, and dost daily travail to bring us to our ends, and to strike off our heads : but though thou shouldest procure all the noblemen's heads within the realm to be stricken off, yet I trust that there shall one head remain that shall strike off thy head." The hand of the Lord Privy Seal himself has recorded and preserved the incident : and that good-natured functionary, always the better for the correction of a nobleman, undertook the vain task of interceding for the life of his indignant enemy.* Percy, Bigod, Bulmer, Hamerton, Lumley, Tempest, and the two abbots were hanged at Tyburn. Lady Bulmer was burned alive in Smithfield. Aske and Constable were sent down to Yorkshire, to receive their punishment on the scene of their exploits : and were exhibited as traitors in the towns of the counties through which they passed. Constable was hanged in chains at Hull, confessing the offences which he had committed, but denying that he had added to them since the Pardon. Of the fate of the brave but simple Aske some interesting particulars have been preserved. That such a man was chosen to lead the Pilgrimage of Grace was the strange accident which preserved the throne of Henry. If he had crushed the small army of the King at Doncaster, and then marched on London, the

* Froude, iii. 215.

history of England might have been other than it
is : but the ambition appears to have been wanting to
Aske which might have been found in many a breast
less candid and in many a head less capable. After
the failure of the movement, he seems to have acted
with good faith towards the monarch whom he believed
to have pardoned him. The charges brought against
him concerning his conduct after the Pardon seem, so
far as they are known, to have been flimsy enough.
He and Darcy had not delivered up some cannon which
they took during the insurrection : he had interfered
to stop the trial of Hallam, at Hull : and in a letter
to Darcy he had used some words which might by
possibility be construed into a treasonable meaning.*
It argues an attractive and gentle nature in him, that
his serving-man died of grief when he was arrested.
When he was condemned, he, like Darcy, petitioned
Crumwel for his family, for his life, or for an easy
death : that he might " be full dead ere he were dismembered, that he might piously give his spirit to God
without more pain."† From Crumwel he seems to
have received a promise of life : which promise the
Privy Seal was unable to keep. At York, when he
was laid on the hurdle, he made open confession that
he had grievously offended God, the King, and the
world ; adding a confident declaration that the King
was so gracious that he would trouble no man for any
offence committed within the compass of the Pardon.
As he was being drawn through the city he constantly
desired the people to pray for him. When he was
taken off the hurdle at the place of execution, he was
made to ascend into the dungeon, to await the coming

---

* Froude, iii. 209. His words were that "he had played his part,
and all England should perceive it." This might indicate treason, or the
opposite of treason.   † Froude, iii. 218.

of the Duke of Norfolk, who had not arrived: and there he told his confessor that he remembered with some offence the sore words of Crumwel, who had called all the northern men traitors: that he had received from Crumwel at divers times the promise of his life; and that from the King he had a token of pardon, for confessing the truth. These two things he said that he had kept secret: not perhaps without hope that they might be redeemed at the last. When Norfolk arrived, he ascended into the tower where the gallows was prepared: and after asking pardon of the King, the Lord Chancellor, the Lord Privy Seal, and all others, he commended his soul to God.* To these victims or martyrs of the Pilgrimage of Grace may be added a royal partisan, the Lancaster herald: who having been sent to the head-quarters of the rebels in the first days of the insurrection, had disgraced the King's coat, which he had upon his back, by kneeling before Aske in Pomfret Castle, while the rebel leader, stretching himself, "with an inestimable proud countenance," received from his hand the royal despatches. For this misdemeanour the delinquent received the sentence and the punishment of death.

For the rest, the King evaded for the time the parliament which he had promised to hold in the north: for reasons which he saw good to lay before Norfolk at length. He had, he said, to entertain an important embassage which was expected from the Emperor, and so he must stay in London: his marriage prevented him from coming: the French King had many men near Calais, and though Calais was well fortified, yet the nature of men of war was such that if they should know that the King of England were in the remoter parts of his realm, they might attempt some exploit:

* Coren, Aske's confessor, to Crumwel. State Pap., i. 558.

the year was so late, it being June 12, when he wrote, that, if he went now, he could neither get far nor stay long, and the people of the north would not have any fruition of his presence: his legs were so bad that he could not travel.*

The King was content with the heads of his lay subjects: nor were their families molested or their estates confiscated after the end of the rebellion. But with the religious, as might be expected, another course was pursued. The execution of the abbots and priors who had been concerned in the commotions was followed sooner or later by the dissolution of their houses: and the enquiries or suspicions of the victorious faction succeeded moreover in securing the suppression of several other important monasteries, the heads of which had taken no open part in the rebellion. But it must be observed that no new visitation was ordered at this time:† and that of the houses which were suppressed on account of the insurrection, the greater part fell not immediately, but in a gradual manner, as it best suited the convenience of the King. The King claimed those houses as having been already confiscated for treason,‡ and there was no need of a

---

* State Pap., i. 551.

† Burnet says that there was; but he must be mistaken.

‡ Burnet argues well upon the injustice of this. "How justly soever these abbots were attainted, the seizing on their abbey lands, pursuant to those attainders, was thought a great stretch of law, since the offence of an ecclesiastical incumbent is a personal thing, and cannot prejudice the church: no more than a secular man, being in office, does by being attainted bring any diminution of the rights of the office on his successors." He goes on to say that the case seemed covered by some words in 26 H. VIII. 13, that whatsoever lands any traitor had, "of any estate of inheritance in use or possession, by any right, title, or means," should be forfeited to the Crown. But, as he argues, this only applied to estates of *inheritance*, among which church benefices and abbey lands could not be included without a great stretch of law. The word *successors*, in the statute, could not be held to favour those seizures, since if the whole

new visitation. Of the surrenders which fell within the year, the greater part were caused merely by the old machinery of dissolution.

At the beginning of February the Duke of Norfolk made the observation that the religious persons who had been replaced in their houses seemed likely to remain, because the King's farmers dared not take possession of those houses which were liable to suppression.* About the same time the King ordered his general to cause all the faulty or suspected monks of Sawley, Hexham, Newminster, Lanercost, St. Agatha in Richmond, and every other place that had resisted, conspired, or kept any force, "to be tied up without further delay or ceremony."† Soon after this the hand of Henry's generals began to fall upon the Cistercians of Yorkshire and Lancashire. The Abbot and the Prior of Sawley were hanged, and one of their monks, Richard Eastgate, was taken to London for examination at the King's command.‡ The Abbot of the large house of Whalley, John Pastow, and two of his monks, John Eastgate and William Haydock, were hanged by the Earl of Sussex in March :§ and the

---

Abbey were suppressed, the Abbot could have no successors. The whole passage is well worth reading.—Bk. iii.

* State Pap., i. 534.

† "Forasmuch as all these troubles have ensued by the solicitation and traitorous conspiracies of the monks and canons of these parts, We desire and pray you, at your repair to Sawley, Hexham, Newminster, Lanercost, St. Agatha, and all such other places as have made any manner of resistance, or in any wise conspired, or kept their houses with any force, since the appointment at Doncaster, you shall, without pity or circumstance, now that our banner is displayed, cause all the monks and canons that be in any wise faulty, to be tied up without further delay or ceremony, to the terrible example of others : wherein we think you shall do unto us high service."—*Ib.*, 539.

‡ Speed, 1025 : State Pap., i. 543. What became of Richard Eastgate I know not.

§ Speed, 1025 ; Stow : Whittaker's Hist. of Whalley. From the last

King thereon laid claim to the house, declaring that by the attainder of the abbot he was justly entitled to it, but promising to establish it anew. The monks he ordered for that end to be moved into other houses of their coat, or else to take capacities and receive secular habits;* and to the house thus swept and empty, was conveyed Roger Pyle, the Abbot of the magnificent monastery of Furness, of the same order and county; on whom the scrutinies and severities of Henry and his generals had been directed of late. Him and some of his monks the King had already ordered to be committed to ward, and others to be dispersed in

author (p. 123) it appears that the two abbots of Sawley and Whalley, and the two monks of Whalley, John Eastgate and Wm. Haydock, were all tried together at Lancaster : that the abbot of Sawley, whose name was Trafford, was hanged there, March 10, but that the others were taken back to Whalley, where Pastow and Eastgate were hanged, March 12 : and Haydock on the following day. Eastgate (Speed's Castlegate) was particularly obnoxious. On the dispersion of the rest of the fraternity of Whalley, he had desired leave to go to the abbey of Methe (Meux?) : but the sagacious king ordered him to be detained till he explained why he preferred that place to any other (*State Pap.*, i. 542). He was not only hanged, but drawn and quartered, and his quarters set up in several places. Haydock was hanged in a field five miles from Whalley, and left hanging a long time there.

* "As it appeareth that the house of Whalley hath been so sore corrupt, amongst others, that it should seem there remaineth very few therein that were meet to remain, and continue in such an incorporation, We think it meet that some order be taken for the remotion of the monks, now being in the same, and that we should take the whole house into our own hands : as by our laws we be justly, by the attainder of the said abbot, entitled unto it : and so devise for such a new establishment thereof as shall be thought meet for the honour of God, our surety, and the benefit of the country. Wherefore our pleasure is that ye shall with good dexterity lay unto the charges of all the monks there, their grievous offences towards us and our common wealth ; and therewith assay their minds, whether they will conform themselves gladly, for the redubbing of their former trespasses, to go to other houses of their coat, where they shall be well received ; or else whether they will take capacities and so receive secular habits. Also we require you so to move them to enter into other houses, that they may choose the same : for it cannot be wholesome to permit them to wander abroad."—Henry to Sussex, *State Pap.*, i. 540.

other monasteries, although in lengthened and repeated examinations held by Sussex nothing had been discovered to criminate them.* From his new prison or refuge of Whalley the abbot wrote the formal surrender of his own house, "knowing the misorder and evil life, both unto God and the prince," of his brethren : his deed, said he, came freely, of his own self, and without enforcement, in consideration of the evil disposition of his brethren, and in the presence of the King's general and commissioners.† The officers

---

* As to Furness, I. "All the members of the community," says Lingard, "with the tenants and servants, were successively examined in private : and the result of a protracted enquiry was that, though two monks were committed to Lancaster castle, nothing could be discovered to criminate either the abbot or the brotherhood" (vi. 339). 2. The King grew impatient, and urged Sussex to use dexterity. "Forasmuch," wrote he, "as by such examinations as ye have sent unto us it appeareth that the Abbot of Furness and divers of his monks have not been of that truth towards us, that to their duties appertained, we desire and pray you, with all the dexterity you can, to devise and excogitate to use all the means to you possible, to ensearch and try out the very truth of their proceedings, and with whom they, or any of them, have had any intelligence : for we think verily that you shall find thereby such matter as shall shew the light of many things yet unknown. And our pleasure is that you shall, upon a further examination, commit the said abbot and such of his monks as you shall suspect to be offenders to ward ; there to remain, till you shall upon the signification unto us of such other things as by your wisdom you shall try out, know further of our pleasure."—*State Pap.,* i. 541. 3. Thus urged, Sussex hit upon the plan of separating the abbot from the monks, and singly proposing a surrender ; and he was soon able to give the King a better account of the abbot at least. "Devising with myself," he wrote to his master, "if one way would not serve, how, and by what means the said monks might be rid from the said abbey, and consequently how the same might be at your gracious pleasure, I determined to assay him as of myself, whether he would be content to surrender, give, and present unto (you), your heirs and assignates the said monastery : which thing so opened to the abbot fairly, we found him of a very facile and ready mind to follow my advice in that behalf." (West's *Hist. of Furness,* App. x. [from Cleop. E. iv. 111], &c., also ap. Lingard.) It was probably on this understanding that the abbot was taken to Whalley, to execute the deed of surrender there.

† The *unenforced* surrender was made in the presence of the Earl of

were despatched to take possession: in a few days came the commissioners, with the abbot in their company: and the brethren, assembled in their stately chapterhouse, heard and ratified the deed of their superior. The vast and magnificent edifice of Furness was forsaken: the lamp of the altar of St. Mary went out for ever: and in the deserted cloisters no sound was heard but the axe and hammer of those who came to cut away the lead, dash down the bells, hew away the rafters, and break in pieces the arches and pillars. Thus dismantled, the ruin was left as a common quarry, for the convenience of every countryman who could cart away the sculptured stones for building a pigsty or a byre. Nor was the fate of the next great abbey that fell in consequence of the insurrection long delayed: and in November the commissary Belassis was able to report that he had taken down the lead of Jervaulx, of which there was no less than eighteen score fathoms when it was cut into lengths: a load too heavy for the roads of winter. The bells, he said, were ready to be sold: but on the spot they would fetch less than in London, though the carriage might balance the profit. As for the demolition of the house, a formidable undertaking, the thrifty agent of Crumwel counselled that it might stand to the spring of the year, when, the days being longer, more work might be got out of the workmen.* Bridlington Priory, a rich house of Austin canons, which Crumwel had long been eyeing, the same prudent commissioner announced that he hoped to be able to despatch in the ensuing March,

Sussex, Sir Thos. Butler, Sir Wm. Leyland, Mr. John Claydon, clerk, Sir John Beron, and Sir Anthony Fitzherbert.—Wright, 153.

* Wright, 164. Jervaulx had incurred the suspicions of the King, who wrote in March to Sussex, "The house of Jervaulx is in some danger of suppression by like offence as hath been committed at Whalley."—*State Pap.*, i. 542.

after such fashion that his master should find no fault.*

Besides these, . which were the firstfruits of the Pilgrimage of Grace, there were some others of the greater houses, or those whose revenue exceeded the limit prescribed in the Act to poverty and wickedness, which sunk this year under the intolerable conditions imposed on them by Crumwel and Henry. The process of confining the monks within their walls, starving them slowly, visiting them incessantly, taking away their ceremonies, and insulting their darkness by the new light, was not without a sure though slow effect. In the south, and in the midlands, may be noted at this time the successful activity of the visitor William Petre, a chancery clerk who has been already seen high in official eminence. Beginning, like some other great men, in Kent, where he was appointed by Crumwel, in 1536, to visit all the clergy, Petre invaded the venerable Benedictine abbey of St. Augustine in Canterbury: which was suppressed about a year afterwards.† The great Benedictine abbey of Chertsey, the Cluniac priories of Castleacre in Norfolk, and of Lewes in Suffolk, were dissolved this year by him: and, in conjunction with Layton, whose activity or success was less conspicuous just now, he smote in Bedfordshire the Cistercian abbey of Wardon.‡ To these, the spoils of the Crown and the toils of Petre, must be added Leicester Abbey, a rich Augustinian foundation,

---

* Wright, 164.

† "The same year (1536) the 20 and 21 day of September, Doctor Petre being sent of the Lord Crumwel to visit all the clergy throughout all Kent, did visit this Abbey of St. Augustine, making enquiry of the observing of the InJunctions which we in the first visitation received by Doctor Layton."—*Chronicle of St. Aug. in Nichol's Narr.*, p. 284. The suppression, according to Dugdale and Burnet, of this famous abbey, fell in December, 1537, when the abbey was surrendered by John Sturvey, alias Essex, the last abbot.　　　　　　　　　　　‡ Wright, 53.

Halywell in London, a Benedictine nunnery,* and the Præmonstratensian abbey of Tichfield, which fell to Cave, to Pekyns, and to Crayford.†

Of the fall of these great establishments but few particulars are preserved : nor is it probable that much could have occurred to break the monotony of a common ruin. The weary monks were assembled in their chapterhouse : they acknowledged and signed a prescribed deed of surrender : they generally, but not always, received pensions in compensation for the vested interests which they resigned : and took their way into the world. The suppression, however, of Chertsey, and the destruction of Lewes, illustrate the art which sometimes affected to mitigate, and the violence which always attended the ruin of the abbeys. The mitred abbey of Chertsey, in Surrey, was surrendered on July 6, by John Cordrey the abbot, and fourteen monks. Instead of being dispersed into the

---

* Halywell Nunnery, to which, a year or two before, the reformer of monasteries came dressed like a Turk, with some of his courtiers : and had a dance with the ladies.—Wriothesley's *Chron.*, 50.

† Rym., xiv. 590–593. A great many excusable mistakes have been made by Rymer, Willis, Cayley, and many of the local and country historians as to the year-date of the surrenders of houses. The surrenders were generally dated by the year of the King's reign, which began April 22. Hence some houses fell, for instance, in 1537 A.D., and some in 1538, which are alike described in their surrenders as having fallen in the 29th year of the King. For instance, Chertsey Abbey, mentioned in the text, was surrendered July 6 "anno Regni Dom. Regis vicesimo nono ; " and, as Henry's 29th year ended April 22, 1538, the July in which Chertsey surrendered must have been that of the previous year, 1537. On the other hand, Abingdon surrendered February 9, "anno Regni Dom. Regis vicesimo nono," and therefore in 1538. But both Chertsey and Abingdon are put down by Rymer as having surrendered in 1538. This mistake, running through the three or four years of the Suppression, has confused the general tenor of the history, muddled the details, and made the activity of Crumwel's visitors preternatural. The same man was in two places in distant parts of the kingdom, sometimes on the same day, often within a few days.

world, they and the possessions of their house were
translated to the abbey of Bisham in Berkshire, which
had been surrendered the year before by the com-
mendator, the notorious William Barlow, Bishop of
St. David's, and refounded by the King. This new
royal foundation was for an abbot, and thirteen monks
of St. Benedict, the order most venerable in England:
to form the ample patrimony, the King generously
added to the lands of Chertsey those of the little priories
of Cardigan, Bethkelert, Ankerwike, Little Marlow,
and Medmenham (which had fallen to him under the
Act about little houses), to the annual value of near
seven hundred pounds: the translated abbot, Cordrey,
retained the privilege of the mitre: and the whole
establishment lasted—nearly a year.* Of the abbey
of Lewes the complete demolition has left not a trace:
but the record of the process of ruin remains as an
enduring monument of the zeal and ingenuity of the
destroyers. Four months after it had been visited
by Petre, Lewes was approached by the appointed
ministers of destruction: who presently advertised
Crumwel of the formidable strength and greatness of
the church, which they were engaged in pulling down
to the ground. A vault beside the high altar, upborne
by four great pillars, surrounded by five chapels which
were compassed by walls more than two hundred feet
in length, was down, they said, already. Another
vault of still vaster dimensions, raised on four pillars
that were forty-five feet each in circumference, they
promised to destroy. They had brought down from
London a company of seventeen workmen more skilful
than those who were to be found in the country: three
carpenters, two smiths, two plumbers, and one that

* Willis's Hist. of Abbeys, ii. 6: Tanner, s. v. Bisham was surrendered
June 19, 30 Henry VIII. (1538), by Cordrey, the abbot.

kept the furnace. To each of these his own office was assigned : there were ten who hewed the walls about, and broke and cut them : the three carpenters underset with props what the others cut away. And yet, so great was the labour, more workmen of the like skill were wanted. The walls were five feet thick, and in some places ten : the steeple was eighty feet high : in the church there were thirty-two pillars standing equally from the walls, and of these some were more than forty feet in height, the others nearly twenty feet. The height of the church was over sixty feet: in the part above the high altar it was twenty feet higher. They had begun to cast the lead : and would do it with all diligence and saving. What more could Crumwel require ? Might God maintain Crumwel's health, Crumwel's honour, Crumwel's ease of heart.*

Of the state to which the greater monasteries were reduced, one of the effects appears to have been to divide the unfortunate inmates into factions, which strove the one to shorten, the other to prolong, the pangs of dissolution, by granting or denying the wishes of the King. An intrepid superior here and there, whether supported or opposed by the fraternity, struggled to defy the miseries of his position, and to preserve his house to religion and posterity. Such was the case at one of the places called Stratford : of which the abbot excommunicated his brethren for betraying the secrets of the convent to the visitors; declaring that they ought to obey the superior of their order abroad, and with a rare impunity, defying the new Acts of Parliament.† At Woburn, the abbot, whose name was Robert Hobbes, was less fortunate.

---

* Portinari to Crumwel.—Wright, 180.

† Froude, iii. 241. This was probably the Cistercian Abbey of that name in Essex.

He, like every abbot in England, had subscribed to the Act of Supreme Head and Succession in the year 1534 : but in secret he lamented his compliance; and when the execution of Fisher, More, and the Carthusians occurred, he testified his horror and remorse openly before the convent, on whom he imposed the weekly repetition of a penitential Psalm. The convent meanwhile was distracted between the old and new opinions : sallies of raillery or fierce altercations took place among the brethren when they met together; while the talk of the shaving house, or the incidents of the chapel were diligently reported to the Vicar General by the traitors among them. The abbot, these informers observed, neglected to preach on the topics commanded in the Order for Preaching : nor in the bidding of prayers would he make use of the prescribed form, which spoke of the King as Supreme Head, and of his beloved Queen Anne. The erasure of the Pope's name from the Mass Book he forbad, contenting himself with striking it out with a pen, that it might be made legible again whenever the Pope was restored. When the Act for dissolving the smaller monasteries was passed, he again called his convent together, and, in spite of their reluctant murmurs, caused them to sing daily chants and versicles of lamentation for the wasted inheritance of Sion. Surrounded by monks who grew daily more impatient and turbulent, his troubles at length brought on a sickness, which was increased by the rigorous fasts of Lent. Believing his end nigh at hand, he called his brethren to his bedside, and sought to infuse into them the spirit of repentant martyrdom which animated his own bosom. " Be in charity one with another," said he, " never consent to go out of your monastery : or, if you should chance to be put from it, yet in no wise forsake your habit. I would to God it would please Him to take me out of this wretched world: I would I had died with the good men that have suffered death heretofore, for they were quickly out of their pain." This exhortation, which failed to arouse in the hearers the contempt of suffering and death, procured to the speaker the fate which he had envied so long. He recovered from his sickness, but only to be carried before the Council: his words and actions were there deposed against him: and his name is to be added to the list of those who perished on the gibbet at the end of the Pilgrimage of Grace.*

The silence of a year hangs over the history of the Charterhouse of London after the execution of Houghton, Middlemore, Exmew, and Newdigate. The dreadful scenes of the scaffold were left perhaps to work their effect upon the minds of the surviving monks: and no further severity is known to have been exercised upon them than the appointing of two of Crumwel's servants, Filoll and Whalley, to preside over their house, the vacant offices of prior, vicar, and procurator remaining unfilled. The interval is filled only by the record of the singular vision of one of the brotherhood, John Darley: to whom, in that abode of religious imagination, an apparition was presented, whose shadowy being and boding words might image forth the thoughts of many hearts. Standing in the nightly exercise of contemplation beside the entry of the common hall or chapel, the awe-struck monk suddenly beheld the form of an aged brother of the religion, by name Raby, who had died in the house some time before the beginning of the troubles. He

---

* Froude, iii. 242. Mr. Froude, in his Short Studies on Great Subjects, vol. ii, has given a full and interesting account of Abbot Hobbes and the monks of Woburn.

remembered now that, at the time of his departure, he had remained with the dying senior to the last, even after he had taken the Sacrament in the presence of the rest of the brethren ; and that he had received from him the promise that " if the dead came to the quick," he would visit him from the grave. The dead man appeared in his habit, with a white staff uplifted in his hand : he lamented that he had not lived long enough to be among the martyrs of the house ; he demanded why the living brethren followed not their late head and father to the crown of martyrdom. " He," said the vision, " he and my lord of Rochester are next to the angels in heaven : the other fathers who died are well, but not so well as he : and I am well, but not so well as if I had died a martyr."* As this spirit continued to animate the brethren, four of the most obstinate of them were carried on Quinquagesima Sunday, in 1536, to St. Paul's Cross : to hear one of the sermons which the bishops had been ordered to preach against the authority of the Bishop of Rome. On that day the preacher was the gentle and learned Tunstall, to whom, if to any, they were likely to give ear. The monks were placed in front of the preacher, where also sat Archbishop Cranmer and eight bishops : in the pulpit, behind Tunstall, stood the Lord Chancellor Audley, the two dukes, Norfolk and Suffolk, and several other lords.† But neither the array of authority, nor the spectacle of consent, nor the arguments of the orator, wrought any conviction upon them. Nor in a private .conference, which he tried four months afterwards, could the benevolent Cranmer boast of more than a partial success. Sending for two of the monks, whose names were Rochester and Rawlins, he endeavoured to prevail by persuasion : but, though he induced the

---

* Wright, 34. † Wriothesley's Chronicle, 34.

latter of them to break his rule by eating flesh, and to become a secular priest, he returned the former to his monastery.* Shortly afterwards, a Scottish friar, Madewell by name, was sent to the convent: who exhorted and admonished them with fervour, but without effect. When Filoll, the overseer of the house, requested them to allow this person to preach the sermon in their chapel, their answer was that they would not hear a blasphemer of sanctity, who preached against the honouring of images and of saints.† Up to this time their liberty had not been taken away. Crumwel had directed that the ancient order of the house should not be broken by his servants: the monks still retained their keys to the cloister and the buttery, so that they could converse with one another. But Filoll now represented to his master that it would be expedient to take away their keys; to diminish either their number or their dainty fare, and the delivery of alms to strangers and vagabonds; and to replace the lay brethren by temporal persons.‡ The representation was effectual: the time of clemency and persuasion was past: and strict order was taken for the government of the Charterhouse. Six governors, who were temporal men, were appointed; some of whom were to be there day and

---

* Wright, 68.

† This Madewell was somewhat famous it would appear from the curious examination of Roland Philips before Cranmer in July this year. Among the interrogatories administered by the Archbishop there was this: "Item, whom he knoweth that do damn all singing, and reading, and organ-playing. Respondet, specially the Scottish friar Madewell."— Cranmer's *Lett.*, 339.

‡ Filoll to Crumwel, Wright, 67. Of course the revenue of the house was diminishing under the hands of Crumwel's servants: and yet, as Crumwel's servants complained, the monks unreasonably insisted that there should be "that same fare continual that was then (in better days) used; and like plenty of bread and ale and fish given to strangers in the buttery and at the buttery door, and as large livery of bread and ale to all their servants, and to vagabonds at the gate!"

night: the monks were to be called together, and warned that, as their past heresies and treasons were forgiven, and their pardon purchased under the Great Seal, so they should die without mercy, if they offended again. Their keys were to be taken away, and all rents and payments were to be received by the governors. By the governors the monks were to be examined after dinner severally on their opinions; and invited to leave religion on the promise of a convenient stipend for a year or two until they had got livings. In the meantime they were shut in the cloister, and no man was permitted to speak to them but by license of the governors: they were starved, while Filoll and Whalley pampered themselves: even the aqueduct which supplied the house with water was cut off.* Their books were taken away, but they were supplied with Bibles: their ceremonies that were nought they were ordered to forsake: they were to hear discreet sermons three or four times a week, the discreet preachers to have board and lodging in their house: the obstinate were to go to prison, but the yielding were to be gently handled, and separated from the company of the rest.† Crumwel, who probably had no desire to go to the utmost extremity, appears to have spoken confidently to the King of the anticipated effect of this treatment. But the King was so thoroughly enraged by the long resistance of the Charterhouse, that he instructed Sir Ralph Sadler to inform his minister that they had been so long obstinate, that he would not now admit their obedience.‡ A new and more con-

* Strype, i. 307.

† Order for the Charterhouse of London. Strype, *Ib.*, from Cleop. E. iv. 6.

‡ " I commanded," said Henry to Sadler, " my lord Privy Seal a great while ago to put the monks out of the house, and now he wrote to you that they be reconciled : but seeing that they have been so long obsti-

formable prior, vicar, and procurator, were appointed in William Trafford, Edmond Sterne, and William Wayte, to give the house the power of surrendering in form :* and after some months of the severe discipline inculcated in the orders of Crumwel, the Visitors Bedyl and Gwent appeared in the chapterhouse, summoned the monks, and propounded the Oaths against the Pope and for the Supreme Head. The officials, headed by the Prior and followed by seventeen of the monks, swore and subscribed : the rest of the house, to the number of ten, absolutely refused.† Their names were Johnson, Bere, Green, who were professed monks : Davy, who was called "referendarius :" Salt, Greenwood, Redyng, Shryne, Pierson, Horne, who were "conversi," or lay brethren. All these had sworn formerly to the succession, except Green and Shryne.‡ There had been enough, however, of the scaffold already for the Charterhouse : and for the ten recusants were reserved the more horrible but less conspicuous torments of the dungeon. They were committed to Newgate, May 29 : and were subjected there to such frightful treatment that in the space of a fortnight five of them were dead, and of the other five four were dying. In a standing attitude they were chained to posts, so that they could not move day or night : and in that posture they were deliberately and slowly starved to death. Their sufferings were rather prolonged than mitigated by the piety of a woman named Margaret Clement, who, bribing the gaoler,

nate, I will not now admit their obedience ; and so write to my lord Privy Seal."—*State Pap.*, i. 460.

* The two latter had subscribed formerly.—Rym., xiv. 492.

† Rym., xiv. 588-9 ; May 18, 1537.

‡ If the Shryne of Bedyl's list of them in Ellis's Lett. (i. 2, 78) be the same name as the Schryven of the list in Rymer, xiv. 491, they had all sworn but Green.

entered the prison in the disguise of a milkmaid, bearing a pail filled with meat, not milk : with which she
fed them, putting the food into their mouths, because
they were not able to feed themselves, and afterwards
removing from them their natural filth. This she
continued to do until the gaoler, alarmed by a message
from the King, who sent to enquire whether the culprits were not dead yet, refused to admit her any
longer. She then, however, with his connivance, got
upon the roof of the prison, and let down her meat in
a basket, approaching it as near as she could to the
mouths of the Carthusians, as they stood chained to
their posts.* This horrible story, which might be
doubted if it rested only on the narratives of the
Anglo-Roman party, is confirmed in the main by the
unimpeachable testimony of Bedyl himself. The
zealous Archdeacon had taken up his quarters in the
Charterhouse, perhaps in the capacity of one of the
discreet preachers who were to preach three or four
sermons a week there : and while the unfortunate
malignants were rotting thus in Newgate, he brought
the new prior and the more compliant residue of the
brotherhood, June 10, to execute a surrender of the
house.† Two days after this he was able to report to
Crumwel that of the ten, five were dead, two at the
point of death, two sick, and one whole : " for which,"
added he, " I am not sorry, considering their behaviour
and the whole matter : and I would that all such as
love not the King's Highness and his worldly honour,
were in like case."‡ It seems probable that out of ten
men there would have been more than one who could
have borne a fortnight's incarceration without death

---

* Morris's Troubles of our Catholic Forefathers.—*First Series*, p. 27,
Life of Mother Margaret Clement.

† Rym., xiv. 591.   ‡ Ellis, i. 2, 76. Morris's Troubles.

or deadly sickness, unless extraordinary severity had been used: and the general result may be taken to confirm the only particular narrative that remains. Bedyl saw here his former advice carried out to the letter; to kill off the best of the monks, and disperse the others. For the rest, in the same letter in which he announced the success of the treatment, he recommended the obedient prior, Trafford, for promotion: and advised that the house should be put to some better use, seeing that it stood in the face of the world. So fell the Charterhouse of London.

The declaration which the clergy of England had made in their last Convocation against the Primacy of the Apostolic See, though decisive, was incomplete. After a year of fruitless negotiations between the Pope, the Augustan princes, the Emperor, and the King of France, after several prorogations of the Mantuan Council proposed by the Pope, the citations were issued at length by the Holy Father for the month of May: and it seemed not impossible that an assembly might meet for the pacification of Christendom. But the dispute of the place where it might be held indifferently had never ceased: the time seemed unfavourable through the unabated war raging between the Empire and France: and against the authority which pretended to convoke such an assembly the formidable voice of Luther was raised in age with not less than the vehemence of his youth. The Smalcaldic League met again, February 7; and declined alike the citation and the primacy of the Pontiff, setting forth their reasons in an elaborate manifest. The King of England had his share in securing this result: two of his agents, William Paget and Christopher Mount, passed in disguise through France to Smalcald, with instructions to dehort the German princes from according with the indicted council, or joining with the Emperor. On their way they saw Gardiner and the French King ; and acquainted them with all : and by skilful management at the critical moment the design of the Pope for the reunion of Christendom was defeated.* Henry received the declaration of the Augustans against the Council : and hastened to reinforce his allies, and publish his own determinations, in as strange a document as was ever issued in diplomacy. A furious diatribe, which would have better graced the Wittemberg pulpit, or Paul's Cross, was transmitted in the name of the King, the Council, and the Clergy of England to the various cabinets of Europe : it conveyed to them the fury, apprehension, and disdain which agitated the bosom of the King : and ignobly terminated the long connection of the English kingdom with the Holy See. " The Bishop of Rome," said the Defender of the Faith in this protestation,† " is calling learned men together, and making Cardinals of those whom he thinks most meet to defend frauds and deceits : men sworn to think all his lusts to be laws. But we better know Romish subtleties and Popish

---

* Herbert.

† I suppose that this queer production must be of the importance which I have ventured to assign to it. It is preserved in Fox's Acts. where it bears the title of " A Protestation in the name of the King, and the whole Council and Clergy of England why they refuse to come to the Pope's Council at his call." From the style of this Protestation the author should be Latimer. The abrupt questions piled on one another : the points raised, talked, left, and taken up again : the scolding, the screaming, and abuse, all point to him. Crumwel, who was a statesman, seems to have disliked this effusion : and ordered Moryson, his secretary, to mend it before printing, and to make it more like the declaration of the Germans. But when Crumwel gave this order the thing had been already sent abroad : and Moryson thought that as it had been sent abroad so it should be printed : and he only altered one clause. Strype, i. 379 ; ii. 258. In Sleidan's version or epitome it has a more dignified appearance : Lib. xi. See also Herbert.

deceits. Paul of Rome has called a Council, to which
he well knew that few or none of the Christian princes
would come. The time and place appointed might
assure him of this. But whither wander not these
Popish bulls? Whither go they not astray? What
king is not cited by a proud minister and servant of
kings to come and bolster up errors, frauds, deceits, and untruths? Does Paul desire a General
Council, now that he pretends one? No! who can
less desire it than they who despair of their cause
unless they can be judges themselves, and give sentence against their adversaries? We need neither
come ourselves or send procurators, nor make excuse
for either of both. Who can accuse us if we come
not at his call who hath no authority to call us?" The
King proceeded to allow that there were a sort of
blindlings who said that the Pope had authority.
"Grant this for a moment, what would it avail to
come to this council, but to oppress truth and establish error? Who would venture his life to go to
Mantua, and speak for trodden truth? It was a
device for setting up again the falling authority of
Rome. The Roman bishops ought, like their fellows,
to be pastors in their own dioceses : not to make
laws not only to other bishops, but also to kings and
emperors. But England had taken her leave of
Popish crafts for ever: Roman bishops had nothing
to do with English people."—"At the same time,"
declared the Supreme Head, "we protest before God and
all men that we embrace, profess, and ever will so do,
the right and holy doctrine of Christ. All the articles of
His Faith, no jot omitted, be so dear unto us, that we
should much sooner stand in jeopardy of our realm
than to see any point of Christ's religion in jeopardy
with us. We protest that we never went from the

unity of His Faith, neither that we will depart an inch from it. No. We will much sooner lose our lives than any article of our belief shall decay in England." As to a council, the King of England affirmed that there was nothing that he so much desired, provided that it were general, and that it were holy : but if it were general and holy, neither the Pope nor his Cardinals would be in it. What impudent arrogancy was this, which Paul took upon him! The time chosen, when the Emperor and the French King were at war, shewed the malicious design. " Go to, go to, Bishop of Rome : occasion long wished for offereth herself unto you : take her : she openeth a window for your frauds to creep in at : call your Cardinals, your own creatures : show them that this is a jolly time to deceive princes in. O fools, O wicked men !" In such an assembly reason would promote pride, virtue would serve vice, holiness be the slave to hypocrisy, prudence to subtlety, justice to tyranny. " Paul," exclaimed his Majesty, " how can any of ours not refuse to come to Mantua, through so many perils, a city so far from England, so nigh your friends, kinsmen, and adherents ? It might cost any person his life. Popes are false : Popes keep no promises with God or man : but, contrary to their oath, imbrue their hands in honest men's blood. The Pope hates me," cried the monarch, " he is burning with hatred, and cannot keep the flame in : he hates our nobility and our bishops, and all Englishmen. We have pulled down his usurped power and proud primacy. The good Vicar of Christ is an open enemy now : for three years he has laboured nothing so much as to stir up the commons of England, and to corrupt some with money, others with dignities. God send them that immortally hate us a better mind! But yet, if it were not that we have learned to owe good will even to

them, what could we wish them so evil, but they have
deserved much worse ?   Good were it to go to Mantua,
and leave their whelps among our lambs!   They see
their merchandise stopped : they see that we will no
longer buy chalk for cheese.   They see they have lost
a fair fleece : vengeable sorry that they can despatch
no more pardons, dispensations, totquots, with the rest
of their baggage and trumpery.   No man here but
knows that it is foolish to give gold for lead, though
Peter and Paul's faces be graven on the lead, to make
fools fain.   No : we be sorry that they should abuse
holy saints' visages, to the beguiling of the world.
Surely, except God take away our right wits, not only
his authority shall be driven out for ever, but his name
also shall shortly be forgotten in England." Such was
England's farewell to Rome.

The force with which the Vicar General could
smite a bishop was displayed, but to less advantage
than usual, in an altercation which arose about this time
between him and Shaxton, the lately appointed Bishop
of Salisbury.   Shaxton, who had received his see at
the same time with Latimer, appears to have been
urged by the difficult ambition of distinguishing himself equally with his contemporary in the cause of the
Reformation.   A man of learning and benevolence, of
strong but inconstant opinions, his zeal was obscured
at this time by some irritability of temper, his use by
some now futile notions of the dignity of his office.
From the beginning of his episcopate he had found
himself checked and corrected by Crumwel in a manner
that was little to his liking.   For his own part, he was
" continually preaching and setting forth the truth," as
he complained : and yet Crumwel grieved him by
telling the Residentiaries of Salisbury that the King
was likely to take his doings in ill part.   In some

controversy that arose between him and the city of Salisbury, he was bold enough to say that the Mayor of Salisbury was the Bishop's Mayor, and the citizens of Salisbury were the Bishop's citizens, alleging an old writ of a former King. Crumwel hereupon informed him that he had committed a great error, in that he had made no mention of the confirmation of this writ by the present King, adding that if he had not had the confirmation, he dared not have written such a word for his head. These sneaps and reproofs weighed so much on the mind of the Bishop, that, as he declared, he watered them many times with salt tears. But his zeal soon exposed him to a new and more severe collision. A lecture in divinity, to be regularly held and attended diligently in the monasteries, was among the Injunctions given by the royal reformer to the religious houses : but such an institution, unless it were carefully managed, might contribute but little to the progress of the Reformation : and Shaxton conceived that it belonged to him to prevent error and protect the truth by his own exertions : to examine, and even to inhibit a reader in divinity who might be suspected or convicted of teaching evil doctrine. In the defamed Abbey of Reading, the reader, Roger London by name, was accused of heresy before him by three of the monks, Bennet, Sutton, and Ludlow. He was alleged to have taught that Holy Scripture was not sufficient of itself for a Christian man to live by : that preaching constituted no cure of souls without confession : that faith without works justified none : and that grace, justification, and a higher place in heaven were to be gained by works.* For these novel and unheard-of heresies

---

* "The matters were no trifles. The first, The Holy Scripture is not absolutely sufficient of itself for a Christian man to live by. Item. If any good man can preach the word of God sincerely and truly, both in word

the reader was inhibited by the zealous bishop, and
another appointed, who was a priest degraded for
having married : but the Abbot of Reading, the ill-
famed, unfortunate, and learned Farringdon,* disregarded the inhibition, and ordered the monk to continue his lectures. Both parties appealed to Crumwel:
and then the bishop discovered how mistaken he had
been in supposing the Vicar General to be concerned
one jot with the fluctuating shades of theological
opinion, or anxious to push the question of faith further
than it might be necessary for the purpose of a gainful
revolution. He was smartly reproved by Crumwel for
meddling beyond his province : his reader, the degraded
priest, was rejected : and the abbot and the monk
were maintained in their cause. On this he poured
out his griefs in a long and heated letter : which,
with the prompt and severe reply which Crumwel
sent by his secretary Moryson, may be digested into
a curious and not uninstructive dialogue between the
Vicar General and not the most unworthy of his prelates.† " Are you using your office to edification or to
destruction ? " cried Shaxton : " God will judge such
using of authority ! The judge standeth, as St. James
saith, before the door : and, St. Peter saith, the day of
the Lord cometh as a thief. Is this the assistance
that I shall look for from you against proud contemners

and example, yet is he not sufficient to keep a cure, unless he have somewhat more ; that is to say, he must have the cases of conscience. Item.
The evangelical faith justifieth no man before God, without his own
works. Item. A man may deserve grace, justification, and a higher
place in heaven by his own works."—Shaxton to Crumwel. Strype, ii.
222. Times were supposed to have changed indeed when a bishop could
boast of his clemency in not compelling the *heretic*, who held these doctrines, to bear a faggot. Shaxton was sadly before his age.

* Willis, in his Hist. of Abbeys, i. 101, gives some particulars of the
learning of Farringdon, the last Abbot of Reading.

† Strype, ii. 222 : Burnet, Coll. Bk. iii. No. 8.

of God and the King?"—"For your plain monition," answered Crumwel, "I would thank you: but that you are fuller of suspicion than it becometh a prelate of your sort to be, and worse persuaded of me than I thought a man of your learning and judgment could have been. If you be offended with my sharp letters, how can your testy words please me? I took a matter out of your hands to mine: but who quarrels with a man for using his office? If I had done it upon affection, or intending prejudice to you, you might have expostulated, but yet after a gentler sort. You say that I abuse my power. God, I say, will judge such judges as you are: and charge such thoughts as you abuse."—"I examined the monkish reader as favourably as I could," proceeded the bishop, "I found him a man of small learning and worse judgment: but I put him to no open penance or recantation. The reader whom I chose is rejected, but I value that not a farthing, so that a good reader be provided. It is not true that I wanted to put my man into the office, that I might be rid of him: he is right dear to me, being an honest layman now, whatever he was being a priest."— "As to that," answered Crumwel, "it was I who required you to use no extremity against the reader: but might I not gather that you proceeded the sorer against him, when I perceived how much you desired your servant to have that revenue?"—"You misconstrue all my doings," exclaimed the bishop, "full ungodly and uncharitably: but *nemo læditur nisi a seipso.* Our Lord have pity on you, and turn your heart to amendment! Your displeasure may undo me in the world, as your favour has advanced me without my desire. If so it come to pass, I hope to have in mind Job's sentence: The Lord hath given, and the Lord hath taken away; blessed be the name of the Lord.

As Paul saith, He will make with the temptation a way to bear it : for I know that Thou couldst have no power against me at all, unless it were given thee from on high. Though all the men on earth, and all the devils in hell incite and stir you against me, not a hair of my head shall perish without the goodwill of my Father in heaven. If you hate me without a cause, then let God alone, on whom I wholly depend."—" To what purpose are your texts?" answered Crumwel, " the end of one of them, Blessed be the name of the Lord, is always in place; or else I would say that it is misplaced here, so great a divine as you be. You would shew more patience, and perhaps more prudence, if you sought not to overwork me by shrewd words and sharp threaps of Scripture. I know who it is that worketh all that is well wrought by me: and I cease not to give thanks that he hath chosen me for an instrument. My prayer is that God give me no longer life than I shall be glad to use my office to edification, and not to destruction. As for your Nemo læditur, I pass it over : for your prayer, I join in the first part, the Lord have pity upon me : the other part, that He would change my heart, is not in my prayers : for though I may err for want of knowledge, I willingly bear no overdoers, I willingly hurt none whom honesty and the King's laws do not refuse. Undo not your own self. I intend nothing less than to shew you any displeasure. If I have shewed you any pleasure, I am glad of it. I shewed it to your qualities, not to you. If they tarry with you, my goodwill cannot depart from you, except your prayer be heard, that my heart may be turned." Then the Bishop, " Mine own dear good lord, hate not them that love you : be not grieved with them that from the bottom of their heart pray for you. Be displeased with your flatterers rather, who care not whether you float or sink. Aid them who serve God and the King: among whom I reckon myself. I will not give place therein, for my talent, to the best bishop in England, except Canterbury and Worcester." But Crumwel: "Teach patience better in your deeds, or else speak as little of it as you can. Another in my place would have had less patience with you. But I can as well take the heat of your stomach, as I can beware of flatterers."— "Last year," expostulated Shaxton, "you said openly among all the bishops that we should suffer no minishment of authority, but rather have more than ever we had. But now it appeareth, *quod verba sunt hæc.*" —"You charge me with a crime which I cannot and ought not to bear," responded Crumwel, "you say that I inhibited your just doings. I did not intend to inhibit your just doings, but to require you to do justly. You must use your privileges as things lent unto you, so long as you shall use them well: that is, according to the mind of them that gave you them." Said Shaxton, "Forgive me, Sir, if I have grieved you through my rudeness in this or any of my letters." Said Crumwel, "I love evil readers as little as you do. Would God that all of your sort were as diligent to see good done in all their dioceses, as I am glad to remove evil things when I see them. If you had sent up at first what you now send against the reader, there would have been no occasion for you to divine of my good or evil will towards you, nor for me to be cumbered with answering you. As for the abbot and monk, I will deal with them as I shall find them."—"Become again my good lord," said Shaxton. "I will not become your good lord," said Crumwel, "for I am more, I am your friend, and I take you to be mine."—"If you still continue sore against me, I could wish I were no bishop," Shaxton said. Said Crumwel, "Whilst I am your friend, take me to be so: if I were not, I should not fear to tell you what had alienated me, nor would my displeasure last longer than the cause."—"Little good shall I do in mine office without your assistance," sighed Shaxton, "before I was a bishop I lived in much more ease." And Crumwel, "Cast out vain suspicion: wilfulness becomes all men better than a bishop. I will do what shall be in me to aid you in your office, and maintain your reputation among your flock. I am your friend, and take you to be mine." Thus both. But to Shaxton alone of bishops, belongs the praise of a lance fairly broken with the formidable favourite of fortune and the King.

Of Coverdale's Bible a second was succeeded by a third edition this year: but in the same space of time the patronage of Crumwel and Cranmer was divided by a new publication of the whole Scriptures, in which the labours of Coverdale were partly embodied. By two London publishers an imperfect conglomerate of Tyndale and Coverdale, which had been commenced in the usual way abroad, was taken up, finished, and published, with a dedication to the King, in the name of Thomas Matthew, the real or pretended editor.*

* Matthew's Bible is made up of Tyndale as far as 2 Chronicles: the rest of the Old Testament comes from Coverdale, with occasional modifications. In the New Testament Tyndale is reproduced entirely. The printing seems to have been begun abroad, and carried to the end of Isaiah: in which place a new pagination begins, and the names of the London printers, Grafton and Whitechurch, appear. See Plumptre's Article on Authorised Version in Smith's Dict. of the Bible. On the identity of Thomas Matthew with John Rogers, the martyr who died in Mary's reign, modern authorities are divided. Canon Westcott says, "Nothing can be more unlikely." Professor Plumptre thinks it all but indisputable that they were the same. The arguments he gives for the identity are these: 1. Fox says that John Rogers went abroad: where "it chanced him to fall in company with that worthy servant and martyr of God, William Tyndale, and with Miles Coverdale," and that he "joined him-

The spirit of Tyndale's furious prologues and free interpretations was retained in the prologue, preface, and notes which adorned this Bible when it first appeared: but the publisher Grafton, who had embarked his capital in it, hesitated not to send it to the Primate, in order to secure his recommendation. Cranmer read and admired what appeared to him to be a new Bible, a Bible "both of a new translation and of a new print" dedicated to the King: and he liked it so well, that he sent it to Crumwel with the request that he would get it licensed to be read and sold, until such time as a better translation should be set forth by the bishops: "which," said he, "I think will not be till a day after doomsday,"*

self with these two in that painful and most profitable labour of translating the Bible into the English tongue, which is entitled, *The Translation of Thomas Matthew.*" 2. The sentence against Rogers, which was drawn up by Gardiner in Mary's time, calls him, "John Rogers, Priest, alias called Matthew." 3. The initials, J. R., occur in the Preface to Matthew's Bible, at the end of a short exhortation to the study of the Scriptures. 4. Matthew's Dedication speaks as if the writer had been "with the godly men in strange countries," as Rogers had been, or then was. 5. No person of the name of Thomas Matthew figures elsewhere in the religious history of Henry VIII. 6. To these arguments Mr. Blunt adds that Queen Mary's Council Register, printed in Hayne's State Papers, bears an entry ordering "John Rogers, alias Matthew," to keep his house at Paul's, being a seditious preacher (*Plain Account,* p. 44). The argument from the *alias* seems to me to be weakened by the Christian names being different. It was very usual at that time for ecclesiastical persons to go by two surnames, but I have not found that they had also generally two Christian names. "John Rogers alias Matthew" may have been John Rogers alias *John* Matthew: and therefore not the same as *Thomas* Matthew. In this case, however, a Christian name, as well as a surname, may have been assumed, in order to conceal the identity more entirely. The opponents of the identity may argue that John Rogers was concerned with Thomas Matthew and others in translating the Bible abroad, and the work appeared with the name of the latter. What Fox says may bear this meaning. It may be added that it was Bale, not Fox, who first said, in 1548, that John Rogers wrote under the name of Thomas Matthew. "Opus ad Henricum Anglorum regem sub nomine Thomæ Matthew epistola prefixa dedicabat." *Centur. sub nom.*

* "You shall receive by the bringer a bible in English, both of a new translation and of a new print, dedicated unto the King's majesty,

His request he obtained, and he expressed his gratitude : " You have shewed me more pleasure than if you had given me a thousand pound."* Thus was Cranmer led to approve of versions, published collectively and pseudonymously, which, when they appeared severally, had been condemned by Convocation : thus the King gave his license to works which by his former Proclamations he had condemned. But this was not enough to satisfy the printer Grafton, who feared to be undersold by smaller and cheaper editions of the same work. He made bold to sue to Crumwel for a license under the Privy Seal :† and when he was answered that this would be unnecessary, he wrote again, to ask either that he might have the privilege that no other person should print the book for three years, or that the King would command every curate to have one copy, and every abbey six : though, he considerately added, it was the papistical sort alone that he would have compelled to buy them. In the diocese of London alone, said he, there would be found

as further appeareth by a pistle unto his grace in the beginning of the book, which in mine opinion is very well done, and therefore I pray your lordship to read the same. And as for the translation, so far as I have read thereof, I like it better than any other translation heretofore made : yet not doubting but that there may and will be found some fault therein, as you know no man ever did or can do so well, but it may be from time to time amended. And forasmuch as the book is dedicated unto the king's grace, and also great pains and labour taken in setting forth of the same, I pray you, my lord, that you will exhibit the book unto the king's highness, and to obtain of his grace, if you can, a license that the same may be sold and read of every person, without danger of any act, proclamation, or ordinance heretofore granted to the contrary, until such time that we the bishops shall set forth a better translation, which I think will not be till a day after doomsday," &c.—Cran. to Crumw., Aug. 4, *Lett.*, p. 344.

* Letters, Aug. 13, p. 345 : he wrote again a few days later, Aug. 28, to the same effect.

† See his Letter, Aug. 28, Strype's *Cranmer*, i. 84, or Cranmer's Lett., 346.

enough of the papistical sort to dispose of a great part
of the stock of fifteen hundred : and a commission from
Crumwel would cause the zealous bishops of Canterbury, Worcester, and Salisbury to have it throughout
their dioceses.   Then would cease the whole schism
and contention between the Old and the New Learning; for all would then follow one God, one Book, and
one Learning.*   These petitions bore fruit in the
Injunctions of the following year.

The King's Articles to stablish Christian Quietness had been a remedy prepared to heal a pressing
distemper ; which, however, was subdued more by
worldly policy than by the balm of spiritual persuasion.
They were not complete enough to remain the standard of faith : and the design of promoting uniformity
in religion was now resumed in the form of a sum of
theology.   At Lambeth, under the presidency of the
urgent Primate, in the summer, sat a commission of
bishops and divines, who were employed in the composition of the second English Confession.   Besides
Stokesley and Tunstall, besides Latimer, Shaxton, and
Fox, there sat on this commission some other prelates
of the sort now cast up by the fortunes of the times,
and destined to have some share in shaping the course
of the future.   William Barlow, who has been seen
already as the Prior of the Austin Canons of Bisham,
had now received successively in two years the bishoprics of St. Asaph and St. David.   His employment
in Scotland, for which he had been lately selected
along with the astute Sadler, was a sufficient testi-
monial of his general ability.   In conduct somewhat

---

* Strype's *Cranmer*, App., No. 20.   Grafton's letter is a rare specimen
of eloquent zeal for religion.   The " poor young man," as he calls himself,
might well be importunate, for he had invested five hundred pounds in
the speculation, part of it borrowed.

rapacious, in his writings scurrilous, he was so enlightened in his views as to maintain that the true
Church of God might consist of two elected cobblers
in company, and that any layman, being learned, if he
were chosen by the King, would be as good a bishop
as himself or the best in England, without mention made
of any orders. By some less enlightened persons of his
diocese he was indeed subjected to some persecution
about this time, because of these opinions.* Voysey,
or Harman of Exeter, and Salcot, or Capon, of Bangor,
both became remarkable for spoiling their bishoprics
by selling away lordships and manors from them, and
for a rapid compliance with the changes of the times.
Hilsey, a learned Black Friar, recently promoted to
Rochester, who bore afterwards a conspicuous part in
the reformation of the service books of the Church,
appears to have been a reformer of the better sort.
William Rugge, *alias* Reppe, another promoted regular, who had lately entered on the pillaged see of
Norwich, was less accordant with the spirit of the
age. He appointed, it was observed, none to be
preachers in his diocese who were of the right judgment : and he had a chaplain who was worse than
himself. There seemed danger lest his diocese, after
being so thoroughly awakened, should fall back again
into the old ways.† But the most notable of the new
prelates was Goodrich of Ely, a man whose character
seems to have been as versatile as it has been variously
represented by different writers. To the eyes of the

---

* Articles against Barlow, Strype, ii. 273.

† Cranmer interfered in the diocese of Norwich to correct the bishop
and his chaplain, whose name was Dale. He asked Crumwel to give the
King's license to three or four preachers in that diocese, whom he could
recommend. "For it were great pity that the diocese of Norwich should
not be continued in the right knowledge of God, which is begun among
them."—*Lett.*, p. 336, May, 1537.

fervid Bale this bishop appeared to be one of those who hated the Harlot of Revelation, even though they were before the horns of the Beast. And yet he sat on his see immovable through twenty changeful years. The historian Hayward saw in him a man of but slender capacity, though he was employed in many great commissions, though he received his preferment as the reward of his dexterity, and though it was his fate to be one of the last ecclesiastics who held the office of Lord Chancellor of England. He was, it may be concluded, more of a statesman than a zealot: and he bore the rare praise of being an impartial judge, a lenient enemy, and a severe friend.

This Commission, which has been described, perhaps erroneously, as a national synod,* consisted of the bishops of both Provinces, eight archdeacons, and seventeen doctors, who were called together by the King's express commandment, not by writ. The opening of it was marked by the presence of Crumwel; distinguished by a warm encounter between the Old and New Learning; and diversified by the interposition of the Scottish divine Aless, the theological assistant of the Vicegerent. Taking his place at the head of the table along which the bishops sat, the doctors standing about them, Crumwel thanked the right reverend fathers for obeying the King's commandment without excuse: that the King desired to determine certain controversies which were now moved throughout the world, in order to set a quietness in the Church: that, though by his excellent knowledge the King understood these controversies well enough, yet he would not make alteration without the full determination of them and of the Parliament: that they were to conclude all things by the Word of God. The disputation which ensued

* As by Joyce, Sacred Synods, p. 387.

turned chiefly upon the Sacraments, which had been doubtfully treated in the former English Confession, the Articles of the previous year.* The Bishop of London maintained the received number of seven Sacraments : in which he was supported by York, Lincoln, Bath, Chichester, and Norwich : while on the other hand stood the champions of the New Learning, Canterbury, Worcester, Salisbury, Hereford, and even Ely. When the discussion had proceeded to some length of acrimony, Cranmer arose, and delivered an exhortation to avoid needless variance, and remember the greatness of the work in which they were engaged. "Be not sophisters," said the Most Reverend, "to make much babbling and brawling about bare words. You are to treat of weighty things. You are to determine the true difference between the law and the gospel : the manner and way in which sins be forgiven : the true use of the Sacraments, the number of them : whether the outward work of them do justify, or we receive our Justification by faith. You are to agree first of all what a Sacrament doth signify in Holy Scripture; what we mean

* [Burnet, Collier, and the Parker editors of Cranmer (*Remains*, p. 79) have referred this debate to the year 1536. In former editions of this volume I have followed them, and connected this debate with the Articles to stablish Christian Quietness of that year. But Fox, who in that part of his work which is devoted to the life of Crumwel, has preserved the whole account of this debate, and is the authority for it, puts it in 1537. And Fox is now confirmed by Mr. Gairdner, who, though without mention of Fox, has given an abstract of Fox's original, a black-letter book published by Aless, " Of the authority of the Word of God," &c.; which he assigns to 1537. *Lett. and Pap.*, vol. 12, p. 346. As to the place where it was held, Fox says the Convocation House, Aless says the Parliament House. I cannot but think it was at Lambeth, and that Aless mistook Lambeth for Westminster. There was no parliament or convocation going on in 1537. The great point of dispute was the number of the Sacraments, four of which had been lost or omitted in the Articles to stablish Quietness. The day after the conferences were ended, Archbishop Lee was able to say triumphantly to Dr. Dakyn, " Those four Sacraments that were omitted be found again now." Gairdner's *Lett. and Pap.*, ib.]

by calling Baptism and the Supper of the Lord sacraments of the Gospel : and whether such ceremonies as
Confirmation, Orders, or Annealing, which cannot be
proved to be institute of Christ, nor to certify us of
remission of sins, ought to be called sacraments. So
they are indeed called. And St. Ambrose calls the
washing of the disciples' feet a sacrament; which I am
sure you yourselves would not suffer to be numbered
among the received sacraments. With you it rests to
determine which be the good works that please God
and make a perfect Christian man : whether the vows
of monks and priests, the choice of meats, the difference
of garments be such : or whether these be a vain service, and false honouring of God, not confirmed by His
word, but resting upon man's tradition." When Cranmer
had finished, Crumwel invited his assistant Aless to
declare his opinion : and the learned Scot delivered an
unpremeditated harangue, in which he defended and
illustrated Cranmer's definition of a sacrament, as
a ceremony instituted by Christ, and signifying some
special virtue or grace of the Gospel. " It is false, and
not to be allowed," exclaimed the Bishop of London,
" that all sacraments ought either to have a manifest
ground in Scripture, or shew forth some signification
of the remission of sins." Aless replied by offering to
prove his position not only by Scripture, but by the
doctors and schoolmen. But the wary Fox of Hereford, perceiving that the zeal of his friend was leading
him on to dangerous ground, breathed a caution in his
ear. " Cease," said he, " to contend with the bishop
in such a manner : the doctors do not all agree with
themselves or with one another in this matter : nothing
can be established by them : and the King's commandment is that we keep to the Scriptures." He then
made his oration to the assembly. " Make not your-

selves the laughing stock of the world," cried he, "light is sprung up, and is scattering all the clouds. The lay people know the Scriptures better than many of us. The Germans have made the text of the Bible so plain and easy, that many things may be better understood now without glosses than by all the commentaries of the doctors. Think not that the Pope's power can quench all heresy. Ye must turn your opinion: for nothing that is true is weak. Truth is the daughter of Time: and Time is the mother of Truth." This open exaltation of the Germans before men who five years previously had condemned the Augsburg Confession, must not pass unnoticed: when Henry's former ambassador spoke thus, the Lutheran opinions were still liable to repression within the realm. The eager Aless then assailed the Bishop of London again. "Sacraments," said he, "are seals ascertaining us of God's good will: without the Word there is no certainty of God's good will: therefore without the Word there be no sacraments." "And is there none other word of God," fiercely answered Stokesley, "but that which every sutor and cobbler read in their mother tongue? If ye think that nothing pertaineth to the Christian faith but that only that is written in the Bible, ye err with the Lutherans." On this hot contact of the mutually impregnable positions of the Old and New Learning, the Vicegerent and the Most Reverend smiled upon one another: and the Scot was about to answer the bishop, when he was stopped by Crumwel on account of the lateness of the hour. He therefore ended the curious scene by a formal challenge to the bishop to renew the contest on the following day. "Right reverend Master Bishop," said he, "you deny that our Christian faith and religion doth lean only upon the word of God which is written in the Bible:

which thing if I can prove and declare, then you will grant me that there be no sacraments but those that have the manifest word of God to confirm them?" The challenge was instantly accepted by the bishop: and the assembly dispersed with the expectation of a hot combat on the morrow. But though the champions were ready, this encounter was prevented by the prudence or propriety of Cranmer. The intrusion of a forward stranger among the English divines, his temerity in attacking so high a prelate as Stokesley, and the indignant fierceness with which he was met, aroused the pride or woke the alarm of the Archbishop, who sent his Archdeacon to command Aless to abstain from disputation. The latter was fain to content himself by declaring his mind in writing: his protestation he delivered to Crumwel, who afterwards presented it to the bishops.

The work composed by these commissioners was described by themselves as "a plain and sincere doctrine concerning the whole sum of all those things which appertain unto the profession of a Christian man."* It was wanting in condensation and coherence; and in tone it was pious rather than theological. The Articles of the former year were embodied in it, with some variation of order, but with no other important alteration: and the three parts into which it was divided answered to the three things which in his Injunctions the King had lately commanded the clergy to teach; the Creed, the Lord's Prayer, and the Ten Commandments. Quotations of Scripture, which in the Articles were made in Latin, were made in English;

---

* "'The Institution of a Christian Man:' containing the Exposition or Interpretation of the Common Creed, of the Seven Sacraments, of the Ten Commandments, and of the Pater Noster, and the Ave Maria, Justification, and Purgatory."—Reprinted in Lloyd's *Formularies.*

or, if in Latin, yet with an English translation. The
desire for uniformity was shewn by a more comprehensive spirit than could be perceived in the Articles:
and so evenly balanced were the additions or alterations made, that it was a disputed question whether of
the two great religious parties gained or maintained
the advantage. On the one hand the New Learning
were gratified by seeing Faith put before Sacraments,
by the immense length at which the question of
Faith was treated, by the large allowance given to
Original Sin, and by the scrupulous care with which
the several elements of Justification were weighed
against one another.* On the other hand, the Old
Learning perceived with hope and pleasure that the
four doubtful Sacraments of Confirmation, Matrimony,
Orders and Extreme Unction, which had been omitted
in the former Articles, were restored to their place,
and completed the received number of seven. They
had not been restored without a struggle: but the
Primate, warned perhaps by the opening passage between Stokesley and Aless, seems to have controlled
or suspended verbal debate by written questions.
Upon each of the disputed Sacraments he propounded
to the theologians the three interrogatories: Whether
it were a Sacrament of the New Testament: What
were the outward signs ordained, what the invisible
grace therein conveyed: and What were the promises
on which it was to be believed that the grace should
be received. The written answers which were received from the divines were various: but most of
them were supported by a shew of argument and
proof, which was not unworthy of a learned assembly.

---

* Laurence (Bampton Lectures) observes that in this treatise the
Augustinian position is maintained, which Melanchthon afterwards
abandoned, that the Freewill of man has no share in his Justification.

Those concerning the first of the four, Confirmation (which alone have been printed),* must suffice for a specimen of the rest. " Confirmation is a Sacrament," said Archbishop Lee, "if it had not been instituted by Christ, the Apostles would not have taken upon themselves to institute it : this is the opinion of St. Clement, of St. Dionysius, of St. Augustin."—"There is no place in Scripture," answered Archbishop Cranmer, " that declares this Sacrament to be instituted of Christ : the acts and deeds of the Apostles, done by a special gift at the time, are not to be confounded with their institutions." —" Confirmation," said Longland, " is a Sacrament of the New Testament, instituted by Christ : the external signs are Imposition of hands, the Sign of the Cross in the forehead, and the Chrysm, or anointing with oil : which latter ceremonies Fabian and Dionysius declare that they received from the Apostles."—" Chrysm is used by the Church for the external sign," proceeded Cranmer, " but the Scripture makes no mention of Chrysm : as for the efficacy of the Sacrament, the bishop who administers prays in the name of the Church ; and the Sacrament is of such efficacy as the prayer of the bishop in the name of the Church."† The brave Stokesley, who was now near his end, in his answer declared the gifts received in Confirmation to be more especially " fortitude to speak, shew, and defend the truth, and to suffer for the same, if need were :" adding a solemn declaration that he relied on the authority of ancient and learned fathers, and of the Catholic

* The answers of some of the divines, under each of the four disputed Sacraments, still remain in the Cotton MS., Cleopatra E. 5 : and as a specimen Strype has printed those under Confirmation (ii. 340).

† Cranmer added to his answers the saving clause, " Hæc respondeo, salvo semper eruditorum et ecclesiæ orthodoxæ judicio." This he wrote with his own hand, the answers themselves being written by his secretary. —Strype.

Church ; to which authority regard ought to be paid even in things not expressed in Holy Scripture : as, for example, the Baptism of Infants, or the perpetual Virginity of the Blessed Virgin, which could not be rejected without denying the faith. " I affirm that it is so," exclaimed Doctor Richard Smith, Professor of Divinity at Oxford, a man who met with much trouble long afterwards, "many things were left to the Church by the word of Christ ; which word was not always written on parchment, but in the hearts of the Apostles :" and to the examples adduced by Stokesley he added Transubstantiation, the doctrine of the Trinity, the release of the converted Jews from the law of Moses, the Sacrifice of the Mass, the validity of heretical baptism, and some others, well or ill chosen. To these determined testimonies on the one side or the other may be added the less certain voices of the new prelates, Goodrich and Salcot : of whom the one replied: "There is no express mention of the institution of this Sacrament by Christ: but the holy and ancient fathers have taken it for a Sacrament of the New Testament :" while the other said : " It is a Sacrament of the New Testament : by which is meant instituted since the time of the New Testament preached, not of Christ, so far as we can know from Scripture, but of the fathers of the Church." So keenly was disputed, so variantly was defined, by the chief of her ministers, the authority of the Church.

In the composition of the important treatise, which resulted from these debates, the main share appears to have fallen to Cranmer and Bishop Fox of Hereford.* To Latimer there was in the contest of opinions a tediousness which moved him to impatience ; and he

* See their letters, Cranmer to Crumwel, *Remains and Lett.*, 337 : Fox to Crumwel, State Pap., i. 556.

sighed for obscurity and retirement.* Neither the Vicegerent is known to have appeared again, nor the ablest of the Old Learning, Gardiner, was present at the deliberations.† Stokesley and Tunstall, the two other eminent leaders of the same party, who were present, were observed to be much together, conferring with one another in the Archbishop's gallery, or conning old books of doctrine, as they crossed to Lambeth in the same barge. The plague was raging in Lambeth, and men were dying at the Archbishop's gate, while the commissioners debated within. By the end of July their work was finished: by Cranmer or by Fox it was brought to Crumwel, by Crumwel to the King.‡ It was accompanied by a petition from the bishops that the King would oversee and correct it according to his excellent wisdom, and suffer it to be printed, set forth, and commanded to be taught. But their diligence and assiduity met with a scanty recognition from the royal courtesy. The King kept the book for six months: he then sent them an answer, in which he told them that he had not had time to overlook their work: but that he trusted to them that it was according to Scripture, and commanded all who had cure of souls to read a portion of it every Sunday

* For his part he declared that it was " so troublous a thing to agree upon a doctrine in things of such controversy, with judgments of such diversity, every man meaning well (he trusted) but not all meaning one way," that he had rather be poor parson of poor Kynton again, " than continue bishop of Worcester. He prayed God that when it was done it might be well and sufficiently done, that there might be no need of any more such doings."—*State Pap.*, i. 563.

† Fox laments Crumwel's absence in his letter to him, State Pap., as above. That Gardiner was not there is expressly asserted in a letter of Sampson's, Strype, ii. 381. Gardiner was in France, though he signed the book, as well as all the other bishops. Strype was therefore misled (by Fox) when he said that Gardiner was present, and offered all opposition to the book.—Strype's *Cranm.*, Bk. i., ch. 13.

‡ Fox and Latimer to Crumwel.—State Pap., i. 556, 562, 563.

for three years, and to preach conformably.* It may, therefore, be observed that the book was only meant to have a temporary use : and indeed at the end of the period assigned by the King it was superseded by another. Nor would the King allow his answer to the bishops to be published, so as to give authority to the publication of the book : the unanswered petition of the prelates was made to stand, both absurdly and adroitly, for the Preface to their own work.† It was published with the signatures of the two archbishops, of all the diocesan bishops, and of twenty-five doctors, who wrote in the name of "all other the bishops, prelates, and archdeacons of the realm." But, as it was neither passed by Convocation nor by Parliament, it had no other authority than could be given by the names of those who had signed it, and by being printed at the King's press. Such was the history of the second English Confession : which bore the

* There are some difficulties connected with the publication of this book. Bishop Fox of Hereford, who saw it through the press, writing to Crumwel on August 25, promised to bring him it "on Monday or Tuesday next perfectly printed." *State Pap.*, i. 562. If this promise was fulfilled how could the bishops afterwards petition the King to allow it to be printed ?

† In this so-called preface, the prelates said of their book, "We most humbly submit it to the most excellent wisdom and exact judgment of your majesty, to be recognised, overseen, and corrected, if your grace shall find any word or sentence in it meet to be changed, qualified, or further expounded, for the plain setting forth of your highness's most virtuous desire and purpose in that behalf." *Formularies of H. VIII.*, 26. It is well known that in a printed copy of the book Henry wrote a large number of corrections which he proposed to have inserted in it, and Cranmer wrote on these royal emendations a great many bold annotations, in which he shewed most of them to be superfluous, illogical, or ungrammatical. *Rem.*, 83. It has been disputed among Cranmer's editors at what time these labours of the Supreme Head took place, whether when the Bishops' Book was in process or afterwards. It may perhaps be concluded that it was afterwards, and that the Supreme Head was moved thereto by this Preface, in which he was requested to revise the book : and which he would see whenever he opened the book.

title of the Institution of a Christian Man, and became popularly, but properly, known by the name of the Bishops' Book.

The birth of a prince, and the death of a queen, happening in the autumn of this year, the one raised to the extravagancy of joy the hopes of the favourers of the New Learning, the other awoke within the bosom of a king the pious sadness of a husband. "God," exclaimed Latimer, "is not only the God of England. He is an English God: if the Devil of all Devils be not in us, we are now compelled to serve Him, and promote His word." Twelve hundred masses, ordered for the soul of Jane, expressed the sorrow of the mind of Henry.*

* State Papers, i. 571, 574.

NOTE:

To be added to the footnote on page 217.

AMONG the "Miscellaneous Books of the Chapter House" in the Record Office there is one, A $\frac{3}{11}$, that contains a list of the Observant Friars in England. I owe the knowledge of this to Dr. Jessopp. It is probably of the year 1535. Anything that adds to our knowledge of that obscure but deeply interesting Order is of value. The list is as follows:

THE NAMES OF THE FRYARS OBSERVANTS IN THIS REALM.

Nomina Fratrum Observantium permanentium in Regno.

Frater Willielmus Robynson est Londoniis
Frater Johannes Game est ibidem
Frater Jacobus Kello est ibidem
Frater Jacobus Laycus est ibidem
Frater Antonius Laycus est ibidem
Frater Johannes Foreste est ibidem in carcere
Frater Johannes Varton et Frater Willielmus Crafurth sunt in Cancia (Kent) ad voluntatem Episcopi Cantuariensis
Frater Johannes Gorge est Norwyci
Frater Benedictus Dewo est ibidem
Frater Thomas Peresone est Lynniæ
Frater Willielmus Marewhate est Babwelliæ
Frater Gabriel Pecocke est Lincolniæ
Frater Antonius Hoode est ibidem
Frater Thomas Sydman est in Cancia cum domino Willielmo Hawt milite
Frater Willielmus Perith est Eboraci
Frater Robertus Hychon est Lyncolniæ
Frater Bonaventura Jonson est frater Augustinensis
Frater Robertus Neseweke est apud Ware
Frater Henricus Sotyll est ibidem
Frater Walterus Freman est ibidem
Frater Johannes Elstony est ibidem

Frater Johannes Hore est apud Ware
Frater Johannes Hemmysley est Scarburgiæ
Frater Johannes Babare est Rychemundiæ
Frater Willielmus Penrith est ibidem
Frater Thomas Pack est ibidem
Frater Willielmus Curson est Bedfordiæ
Frater Willielmus Stupeley est ibidem
Frater David Jones est in Cancia
Frater Willielmus Lee est Cardiniæ
Frater Johannes Kebyll est Gloucestriæ
Frater Johannes Lye est Brystolyæ
Frater Elyas Moody est in Cancia cum Abbate de Feversham
Frater Franciscus Luberte est in Cancia cum Magistro Crayforth
Frater Robertus Rufford est Bedfordiæ
Frater Willielmus Ele est Carmardiniæ
Frater Bernardinus Blackborne est Eboraci
Frater Rogerus Harltone est Scarburgiæ
Frater Johannes Brymstone est frater Augustiniensis
Frater Thomas Robynsone est Cardiniæ cum Domino Castelli ibidem
Frater Christopher Burrell est Cantuariæ, et demens
Frater Willielmus Brivellus est Bedfordiæ
Frater Hugo Norrysse est Stamfordiæ
Frater Radolphus Creswell est Redingiæ

Nomina Eorundem Observantium defunctorum.

Frater Johannes Spens obiit Londoniis
Frater Thomas Artte obiit ibidem
Frater Thomas Rellam obiit ibidem
Frater Jerominus Manson obiit ibidem
Frater Johannes Kinge obiit ibidem
Frater Johannes Kyxe obiit ibidem
Frater Nicholaus Harpforthe obiit ibidem
Frater Indocus Asterdam obiit Cantuariæ
Frater Andreas Danolde obiit Grenewyziæ
Frater Johannes Scryvner obiit apud Redynge
Frater Antonius Lewes obiit ibidem
Frater Alexander Hill obiit in patria
Frater Theodoricus Backham obiit apud Grenewych
Frater Jacobus Wyllyamson obiit Colcestriæ
Frater Cornelius Symondys obiit in patria
Frater Edwardus Pope obiit ibidem
Frater Johannes Biltone obiit ibidem
Frater Willielmus Mill obiit Lancasciæ
Frater Gerardus Lyryson obiit in patria
Frater Johannes Martyne obiit apud Newcastell
Frater Robertus Binks obiit apud Redynge
Frater Franciscus Caro obiit apud Bristowe

Frater Henricus Heltryne obiit in patria
Frater Adrianus Delphe obiit in patria
Frater Thomas Danyell obiit ibidem
Frater Franciscus Carre obiit ibidem
Frater Ludovicus Wylkyson obiit Cantuariæ
Frater Brianus Fishborne obiit apud Yarmouthe
Frater Willielmus Hasarde obiit apud Dunwiche ·
Frater Johannes Welles obiit apud Yppyswych
Frater Robertus Bukare obiit apud Doncaster

Nomina eorundem Exemptorum.

Frater Barnardinus Conertt exemptus
Frater Antonius Browne Heremita
Frater Johannes Lawrence exemptus
Frater Robertus Lanham exemptus
Frater Thomas Tyngyll laicus ad mundum reversus
Frater Thomas Martyne exemptus
Frater Alexander Holdene exemptus
Frater Johannes Lordinge exemptus
Frater Franciscus Dente exemptus
Frater Radolphus Massy exemptus
Frater Thomas Packe exemptus
Frater Thomas Rocke exemptus
Frater Thomas Quyntuns exemptus
Frater Thomas Butlere exemptus
Frater Michael Knyffton exemptus
Frater Willielmus Fullmer exemptus
Frater Franciscus Backnall exemptus
Frater Willielmus Petitt laicus et exemptus
Frater Henricus Becher exemptus
Frater Willielmus Attperrture exemptus
Frater Thomas Myllenge laicus ad mundum reversus
Frater Ricardus Daniell laicus ad mundum reversus
Frater Franciscus Eanewe exemptus
Frater Robertus Latomer exemptus
Frater Thomas Tyngyll exemptus
Frater Willielmus Peter laicus ad mundum reversus
Frater Petrus Jacson laicus ad mundum reversus
Frater Johannes Jonson laicus ad mundum reversus
Frater Johannes Tyndale exemptus
Frater Johannes Sawere exemptus
Frater Franciscus Landye exemptus
Frater Robertus Corbete exemptus
Frater Thomas Sayer exemptus
Frater Johannes Cutlearte laicus exemptus
Frater Hugo Payne exemptus
Frater Nicholaus Bullyn exemptus

Nomina eorundem qui fugam petierunt.

Frater Sebastianus Begone fugit trans mare
Frater Ricardus Eloyn fugit trans mare
Frater Robertus Sharte fugit in Scotiam
Frater Joannes Jobbe fugit in Scotiam
Frater Cornelius Simons fugit trans mare
Frater Johannes Wolls fugit trans mare
Frater Johannes Lambert fugit in Scotiam
Frater Abraham Wharton fugit in Scotiam
Frater Willielmus Symson fugit in Scotiam
Frater Robertus Hunte fugit trans mare
Frater Philippus Wylkynson fugit in Scotiam
Frater Thomas Adam fugit trans mare
Frater Cornelius Brylys fugit trans mare
Frater Ricardus Hadley fugit trans mare
Frater Willielmus Gumluy fugit in Scotiam
Frater Willielmus Bartram fugit in Scotiam
Frater Willielmus Smyth fugit in Scotiam
Frater Thomas Cony fugit in Scotiam
Frater Petrus de Muguntia fugit in Scotiam
Frater Thomas Huntio fugit trans mare
Frater Thomas Packe fugit in Scotiam
Frater Henricus Halter fugit trans mare
Frater Johannes Byllinge fugit in Scotiam
Frater Johannes Rycket fugit in Scotiam
Frater Ricardus Wallrode fugit in Scotiam
Frater Georgius Webstere fugit in Scotiam
Frater Thomas Curtney fugit in Scotiam
Frater Thomas Elkyn fugit in Scotiam
Frater Arnoldus Forgate fugit trans mare
Frater Jacobus Lansy fugit trans mare

Summa Omnium vii *Score* i.

INDEX TO VOLUME I.

OXFORD: HORACE HART, PRINTER TO THE UNIVERSITY

HISTORY OF THE CHURCH OF ENGLAND.

OPINIONS OF THE PRESS.

" It is seldom, indeed, that a book contains so much evidence alike of independent thought and of conscientious labour."—*Athenæum*, Feb. 9th, 1878.

" The author has come to the study of history with the dispassionate endeavour to discover the truth of facts which are alleged ; and has come to his conclusions for himself by consulting the original documents of the period. We do not hesitate to· say that it is the best history of the Reformation yet written from the Anglican standpoint."—*Mr. Pocock (the Editor of Burnet) in the Academy*, Feb. 16th, 1878.

" It is likely to be the most considerable contribution to the history of the Church of England made in our time : it is written in an interesting style, and is founded on careful and extensive research."—*Contemporary Review*, Oct. 1878.

" We wish to repeat our sincere appreciation of the merits of the present work. Apart from principles and theories, a consecutive history of the English Church on this scale will be an invaluable boon to literature. The learning and laborious accuracy of the author leave nothing to be desired."—*London Quarterly Review*, Oct. 1878.

" We look with hopeful interest to the completion of this work, which bids fair to be the first full, true, and adequate history of the English Reformation ever published."—*Church Times*, Oct. 25th, 1878.

" The Rev. R. W. Dixon offers us the opening volume of a *History of the Church of England from the Abolition of the Roman Jurisdiction*, which, for vigour of style, width of view, careful, conscientious research and impartiality, deserves high praise among the very best books of its class. No reader of history, and no theological student, can walk through Canon Dixon's gallery of great statesmen and ecclesiastics, and bestow on every portrait and every summary of events the attention it deserves, without being convinced that the work is that of a master's hand, and that the artist's desire from first to last has been to get at the truth, and the whole truth, and to bring that into living expression at all cost."—*Standard*.

" The work maintains the high character of the first instalment, and we cordially recommend it to our readers, as the most thoughtful and accurate history of the English Reformation which we at present possess."—*Athenæum*.

" Every page of this volume contains fresh materials for the history of the critical era of which it treats, and enhances our respect for the writer's industry and sound judgment. He is well furnished with the most essential qualities—diligence, love of truth, habits of patient research, knowledge of human nature, and deep sympathy with it in its higher aspects."—*Saturday Review*.

" The second volume of this noble history is, if possible, even more satisfactory than the first."—*American Literary Churchman*.

Opinions of the Press.

"A lasting monument of research, historical sagacity, and literary skill, almost unique in the present generation."—*Carlisle Patriot.*

"Mr. Dixon's previous volumes have already established his character for scholarly research and patient investigation. They have also done much to recover for English literature a style of prose writing which is admirably adapted for historical purposes. This last characteristic has met with little recognition. Historical students are rarely heedful of literary merits. Those who are interested in literature seldom look into long histories, unless they have the popularity accorded to the pages of Lord Macaulay. It is indeed a difficult task to write history and preserve any distinctive features of style. Mr. Dixon retains throughout his pages a clearly marked individuality, which is never obtruded, but which speaks in hints. He is serious, sober, even massive: but flashes of dry humour meet us at every turn. Moreover, he has in a way identified himself with the times of which he writes. His extracts from contemporary papers do not strike the reader as remote or foreign to the narrative; rather the narrative itself bears the impress of the source from which it came. Mr. Dixon's account of theological controversies is not a dry summary, but rather an echo of original voices. All this is done without affectation, or traces of conscious effort. Sometimes, it must be admitted, Latinized words of unfamiliar form and doubtful advantage seem to show that Mr. Dixon was thinking too entirely about the past, and had forgotten the present. But his pages have all the charm that comes from a feeling of dainty workmanship—so dainty that we fear it is but slightly perceived by the hasty reader. His diligence and thoroughness of workmanship is admirable. He is fair-minded and impartial."—Bishop Creighton, in the *Academy*, Feb. 27th, 1886.

"The best and most accurate history of the great religious movement of the sixteenth century in England as yet given to the world. It is based entirely on the original sources and authorities, with which the author has a remarkably minute firsthand acquaintance (often hidden away in the footnotes, and therefore easily missed): and it counts the events which are commonly grouped together under the single head of 'the Reformation' as incidents—incidents indeed of great importance, but still only incidents—in the long history of the Church of England. In reality the former of these merits implies the latter: but generally previous writers have contented themselves in mentioning those facts only which tell in favour of their own particular views: and even when this is not the case, not one of them has planned or carried out his work on the large scale which has approved itself to Canon Dixon. It has been reserved for our author to show, documents in hand, what the true meaning, character, and extent of 'the Reformation' was in England."—*The Guardian*, April 7th, 1886.

"So far as our information extends, Mr. Dixon is writing—from an Anglican standpoint, of course—far the fullest and most impartial history which has yet appeared of the English Reformation: and the manner, as a rule, is not unworthy of the matter."—*Saturday Review*, July 3rd, 1886.

Lightning Source UK Ltd.
Milton Keynes UK
UKHW010136310119
336487UK00010B/741/P